International Enterprise Education

T0384426

The important debate on the growing graduate skills gaps, the value of universities to their business communities, and their role (or lack of) in building entrepreneurial attributes among graduates is growing internationally.

Using case studies from universities across the globe, this edited book seeks to bring together leading authors with knowledge, and/or experience, of the challenges of embedding enterprise education in university and college programmes. The text identifies and presents the current debates around the future role of universities and colleges in providing 'fit for workplace' graduates, as well as offering insights into the challenges and practices involved in delivering innovative enterprise education. The approach collates examples of 'best practices' from global institutions enabling educators to develop 'blueprints' for implementing in their own institutions.

This innovative and comprehensive text is designed to be a 'seminal resource' for academic stakeholders on enterprise education collating diverse international contributions from enterprising universities and colleges. Drawing on both theory and best practice, it provides invaluable guidance to researchers, educators and practitioners considering embedding or expanding enterprising activities into their learning strategy.

Jason J. Turner is Head of Department in Postgraduate Business at Taylor's University, Malaysia. For over 16 years he has published, edited and reviewed international journals and written for practitioner publications in the area of enterprise education, preparing learners for the employment market through experiential learning and enterprise activities.

Gary Mulholland is Associate Director Innovation and Enterprise at Dundee Business School, UK. His research interests include teaching roles in enterprise education, leading and managing innovation, UK leadership models and the influence of American management literature, and the implications of social relationships (Guan Xi) on leadership in Chinese SMEs.

Routledge Studies in Entrepreneurship
Edited by Susan Marlow
and
Janine Swail
University of Nottingham, UK

This series extends the meaning and scope of entrepreneurship by capturing new research and enquiry on economic, social, cultural and personal value creation. Entrepreneurship as value creation represents the endeavours of innovative people and organisations in creative environments that open up opportunities for developing new products, new services, new firms and new forms of policy making in different environments seeking sustainable economic growth and social development. In setting this objective the series includes books which cover a diverse range of conceptual, empirical and scholarly topics that both inform the field and push the boundaries of entrepreneurship.

International Enterprise Education

Perspectives on Theory and Practice

**Jason J. Turner and
Gary Mulholland**

Routledge
Taylor & Francis Group

LONDON AND NEW YORK

First published 2018 by Routledge

2 Park Square, Milton Park, Abingdon, Oxon, OX14 4RN
605 Third Avenue, New York, NY 10017

Routledge is an imprint of the Taylor & Francis Group, an informa business

First issued in paperback 2020

British Library Cataloguing in Publication Data
A catalogue record for this book is available from the British Library

Library of Congress Cataloging in Publication Data
A catalog record for this book has been requested

ISBN: 978-1-138-69875-8 (hbk)
ISBN: 978-0-367-73529-6 (pbk)

Typeset in Times New Roman
by Wearset Ltd, Boldon, Tyne and Wear

Contents

Figures

Tables

Contributors

Katja Lahikainen, MSc (Economics and Business Administration), works as Project Manager at the Lappeenranta University of Technology (LUT), Finland, coordinating various projects related to university–industry collaboration and commercialisation of research outcomes. Since 2015, she has been a PhD student at the LUT School of Business and Management.

Timo Pihkala, PhD, is a Professor of Management and Organisations, specialising in entrepreneurship and small business management. He received his doctorate from the University of Vaasa, Finland. Since 2001 he has been working at the Lappeenranta University of Technology (LUT), and he is the academic leader of the entrepreneurship master's programme at LUT.

Elena Ruskovaara, DSc (Economics and Business Administration), is working as a Postdoctoral Researcher and Director of Entrepreneurship Education at Lappeenranta University of Technology, Finland. Since the early 2000s, she has worked in the field of further education for teachers and has been involved in many national and international entrepreneurship education projects.

George Solomon is currently Professor of Management and co-founder and Director for the Center for Entrepreneurial Excellence (CFEE) at the George Washington University School of Business. Since 2010 he has served as Editor-in-Chief of the *Journal of Small Business Management*. He is the past president of the United States Association for Small Business and Entrepreneurship (USASBE) and the International Council for Small Business (ICSB) and since 1996 has served as chair for the Wilford L. White Fellows. He has published and edited over 130 articles, books of readings, book chapters, reference materials and proceedings articles in both the areas of entrepreneurship/small business management and organisational behaviour and dynamics. He is the founder and principal investigator of the Global Survey of Entrepreneurship Education, which is an expansion of the US Survey of Entrepreneurial Education which he developed in 1979.

Nawaf Alabduljader is a PhD student at the George Washington University (GWU), School of Business. He received his BA from the University of

Southern California and his masters in management from IE Business School (Spain). Prior to joining GWU, he worked at Wafra Investment Advisory Group, as well as being a teacher's assistant in Kuwait University. During his time at GWU, his work has been published in the Academy of Management Annals. He has also taught an undergraduate course in entrepreneurship, helped create a one week program to teach Kuwaiti students about entrepreneurship in GWU, and presented at several conferences on the topic of entrepreneurship education, entrepreneurship cognitions and new venture teams.

Ravi S. Ramani is a doctoral candidate in the Department of Management at George Washington University School of Business (GWSB). His research interests include organisational research methods, employees' emotional experiences of work and meaningful scholarship. His work has been published in outlets such as the *Academy of Management Annals*, the *Journal of International Business Studies*, and *Industrial and Organizational Psychology: Perspectives on Science and Practice*. His work received the Best Paper award from the Academy of Management Entrepreneurship Division, and has been presented at several conferences. Previously, he worked in Human Resources for Hilton Worldwide in New York City. His business experience includes roles in organisational learning, executive coaching, talent development, recruitment, labour negotiations, benefit administration and revenue management.

Weili Teng, PhD, is a Professor of International Management and Innovation at Nottingham Business School, Nottingham Trent University in the UK.

Jason J. Turner, PhD, is Head of Department, Postgraduate Business at Taylor's University, Malaysia.

Joseph Tixier is a PhD student at EM-Lyon Business School and a consultant for the OECD and UNIDO on entrepreneurship education.

Michela Loi, PhD and Assistant Professor in Organisation Studies – Department of Economic and Business Science (University of Cagliari, Italy).

Sandrine Le Pontois is a PhD candidate at Grenoble Alpes University (CERAG), research fellow at Entrepreneurship Research Centre EM-Lyon Business School and full-time teacher at the University of Lyon, France.

Mohsen Tavakoli is a PhD candidate at Grenoble-Alpes University, (CERAG), research fellow at Entrepreneurship Research Centre and lecturer at EM-Lyon Business School, France.

Alain Fayolle, PhD, is Professor of Entrepreneurship and Director of the Entrepreneurship Research Centre at EM-Lyon Business School.

David Devins, PhD, is Professor of Enterprise at Leeds Business School, Leeds Beckett University. For more than 20 years he has been undertaking applied policy research on leadership, management development and labour markets. Most recently he has been leading transnational projects, seeking to develop university curriculum for small and medium sized enterprises.

Martin Reynolds is Professor of Management Practice at Leeds Business School, Leeds Beckett University. He has worked in UK higher education for nearly 40 years and has championed approaches to practice based management education in business schools and has led numerous initiatives in the area of work based learning and specifically in-company degrees.

Rickard Enström, PhD, is Chair, Department of Decision Sciences at MacEwan University, Canada.

Peter Daly, PhD, is Professor of Management Communication, Head of Business Communication and Language Studies and Director of the MSc in Management Studies at EDHEC Business School, Roubaix, France.

Isabelle Sequeira is Professor of Culture, Head of Culture and Society and Director of the MSc in Creative Business and Social Innovation at EDHEC Business School, Roubaix, France.

Bernhard Herold, PhD, Professor and Head of Department, Business Administration – Management in Commerce, Baden-Wuerttemberg Cooperative State University Karlsruhe, Germany.

Luísa Cagica Carvalho is Assistant Professor at the Department of Social Sciences and Management, Open University of Portugal. She is a researcher at the Center for Advanced Studies in Management and Economics (CEFAGE), University of Évora (Portugal). She received her PhD in Management from the University of Évora (Portugal).

Iara Yamamoto, PhD Student, University of São Paulo, São Paulo, Brazil, Department of Administration; member of the research group: NETS – Center for Studies in Technology, Modelling and Systems on Organisations.

Adriana Backx Noronha Viana is Associate Professor of the Faculty of Economics, Administration and Accounting at the University of São Paulo, São Paulo, Brazil. She is a member of the research group: NETS – Center for Studies in Technology, Modelling and Systems on Organisations.

Nicholas Lancaster, PhD, as Director of Innovation and Enterprise at the University of Bedfordshire, develops opportunities for businesses to work with the university, through funded programmes, to access skills and expertise and help promote regional economic growth and innovation.

Mary Malcolm is Professor and Deputy Vice-Chancellor (Academic) at the University of Bedfordshire, where her portfolio includes strategic responsibility for teaching and research.

Charles Beraza is originally from France. He has been studying in Russia for three years. He writes about the future of work and the incoming fourth industrial revolution. Now he is working in business consulting in Paris at Magellan Partners.

Jessica Lichy, MBA, PhD (digital user behaviour in a cross-cultural context), is currently employed as *enseignant-chercheur* at IDRAC Business School.

Bénédicte Favre, MBA, Director for International Development, France International Graduate School (FIGS).

1 European approaches to enterprise education

Katja Lahikainen, Timo Pihkala and Elena Ruskovaara

Introduction

For the past 10–15 years, European universities have faced growing expectations for their role in promoting enterprise, innovation and small business development. As a response, European universities are rapidly developing new approaches to incorporate enterprise promotion in the university structure.

The increasing pressure on the universities' enterprise activities comes from different sources. First, the growing interaction between universities and businesses has stemmed from the need to increase non-governmental funding, due partly to decreasing governmental funding. Second, university students' growing interest in enterprising is transforming the universities from the inside. The objectives and intentions of university students are changing to include entrepreneurial careers, and as a consequence, students expect university education to provide extensive opportunities for entrepreneurial learning. Therefore, a dynamic, effective and holistic entrepreneurial profile has become a competitive advantage for universities.

Enterprise education has been reviewed in European universities since 2000. Hytti (2002) provides a state-of-the-art description of European enterprise education. She suggests that enterprise education is seen in terms of three partly converging aims: learning to understand entrepreneurship, learning to become entrepreneurial and learning to become an entrepreneur. European universities have become important partners in regional and national development together with administration and business. This development has been supported by the rise of the third generation university (cf. Wissema, 2009) and the triple helix model (e.g. Etzkowitz and Leydesdorff, 2000). Close industry relationships are expected to accelerate the commercialisation of innovations, employment of young people and updating of skills and competences. Wright *et al.* (2007) focus on academic entrepreneurship in Europe, analysing especially the commercialisation of university research. They suggest that besides the traditional licensing of innovations, a new approach to creating new business is emerging: spin-off businesses based on technologies and knowledge generated in universities.

Wilson (2008) assesses enterprise education in European higher educational institutes and compares it with the US. She considers enterprise education to be the first and most important step in developing an innovative culture in Europe. Furthermore, most enterprise courses are offered within business and economic studies (European Commission, 2008).[1] So, the real challenge is to make enterprise education systematically accessible to all students in every institution. Zahra and Welter (2008) examine the role of enterprise education in the former Soviet Bloc. They point out that in many respects, the central, eastern and south-eastern countries in Europe differ largely in their valuing of enterprise and entrepreneurs. This has important implications for the promotion of enterprise education in Europe.

The purpose of this chapter is to provide comprehensive insights into European approaches to enterprise education. Even if universities are facing the entrepreneurial turn (Goldstein, 2010), the development in European higher education seems to have taken varying routes. To analyse this, we introduce different approaches and identify examples of national and academic enterprise education in Europe. The research question we address is: **How is enterprise education guided, encouraged and implemented in European universities?**

This chapter is organised as follows: First, we review the literature relating to enterprise education in Europe and universities. Second, we present the methodology and describe the cases and examples. Finally, we conclude by discussing the findings and limitations of the study.

Positioning enterprise education in universities

Enterprise education within European universities varies vastly (European Commission, 2008). To catch the variance, we present a framework to position enterprise education in universities (Figure 1.1). The framework emphasises two important aspects related to entrepreneurial activity: the unit of activity (single vs multiple) and the mode of activity (facilitation vs enterprising). We

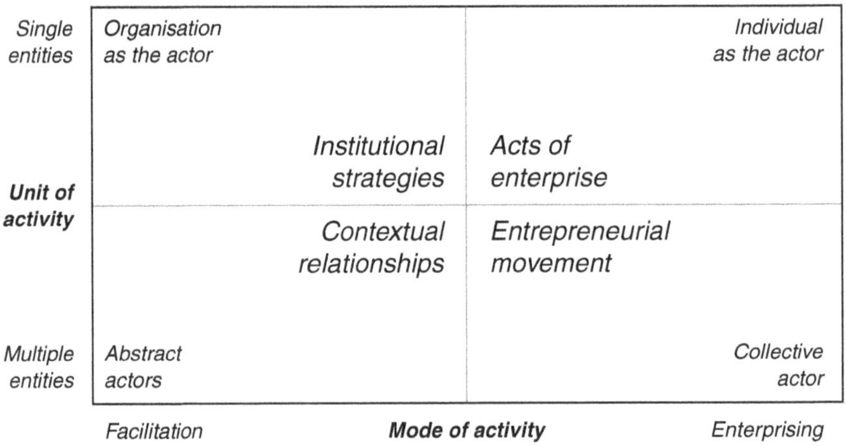

Figure 1.1 Typology of entrepreneurial activities in universities.

stress that entrepreneurial activity in this context may refer simultaneously to different numbers of actors. While the university could be considered a single decision-maker, it also comprises multiple individual and collective actors that operate both jointly and independently. However, while most activities related to enterprising in universities involve facilitation and the creation of an infrastructure, also the actual concept of being enterprising can be recognised in the university setting.

First quadrant: institutional strategies

In the first quadrant, the central actor is the university as an institution. Universities have been identified as distinct actors promoting and supporting enterprise and even acting entrepreneurially. A university with an entrepreneurial mission based on technology or knowledge transfer (third generation university, cf. Wissema, 2009) supports economic growth by fostering academic enterprise. (Kolhinen, 2015) Academic enterprise refers to the efforts and activities that universities and their industry partners undertake in commercialising research outcomes (Wood, 2011). Hence, entrepreneurship is an intentional choice for the organisation. To operate entrepreneurially, educational institutions adopt different strategic, structural and administrative solutions (Pittaway and Hannon, 2008). Besides the commercialisation process, academic enterprise also includes promoting an entrepreneurial mind-set and skills for entrepreneurs, resource providers, suppliers, customers and policy makers (Rice, Fetters and Greene, 2010). The concept of an entrepreneurial university is based on this holistic view that enterprise is embedded in all activities of the university, starting from its strategy. The entrepreneurial turn of a university requires new governance, management and institutional capacities; for example, teaching, rewards and incentives, strategic alliances, and teams and intermediate functions, e.g. technology transfer offices (TTOs) and business incubators (Goldstein, 2010).

Second quadrant: contextual relationships

The second quadrant refers to the involvement and support of the university in local entrepreneurial ecosystems, regional innovation systems (RIS) and other contextual platforms (Foss and Gibson, 2015; Stam, 2015). From this perspective, the various actors operating in the context or infrastructure – such as possible customers, networking partners and competitors – form an abstract group necessary for new entrepreneurial ventures. The individual actors are seldom recognised separately because in this perspective the main interest is in the functioning of the innovation system as a whole (Kallio, Harmaakorpi and Pihkala, 2010). Instead, the focus is on the relationship between universities and their operational context from the perspective of enterprise development. These relationships can be studied through the triple helix model, which consists of trilateral networks and hybrid organisations between academic entities, governmental organisations, and business (Etzkowitz and Leydesdorff, 2000). The concepts of entrepreneurial and innovation ecosystems have emerged to describe the enterprise and interactions of independent actors in a given context (Stam, 2015). Universities contribute to local and regional eco-systems by promoting an entrepreneurial culture, generating and attracting talent, conducting basic and applied research, and providing formal and informal technical support for companies. Moreover, universities act as catalysts for start-ups and spin-offs and offer links to international academic networks. (Bramwell and Wolfe, 2008; Cohen, 2006; Isenberg, 2010; World Economic Forum, 2013)

Third quadrant: entrepreneurial movement

The third quadrant concerns the social aspect of enterprise. Academic entrepreneurs tend to collaborate with their peers, their own social network and actors beyond the university (Hayter, 2016; Rasmussen, Mosey and Wright, 2011). In addition to single entrepreneurial teams, enterprise has become interesting also for wider audiences and attracted people to join in. Altogether, the widespread activities are characterised by the emergence of new social groupings (Gibb, 2005). These entrepreneurial teams, networks and student societies create a platform or 'the entrepreneurial movement'. They also promote an entrepreneurial culture, spirit, learning and ventures in universities and their entrepreneurial eco-systems. The enterprising activities of different collective actors are important in universities. (Morris, Shirakova and Tsukanova, 2017; Pihkala, Ruskovaara and Hytti, 2016) Meanwhile, being emergent, independent and separate from the university organisation, they seem to be difficult to manage with traditional mechanisms. Therefore, the contributions of universities depend on the existence and interrelationships of loosely coordinated knowledge intermediates, and spin-off success relies upon these academic and non-academic networks connected by the intermediates (Hayter, 2016).

Fourth quadrant: acts of enterprise

The different individual actors – students and academics – compose an important group. While the distinct measures to promote enterprise seek to facilitate the entrepreneurial behaviour of single actors, the actual academic enterprise and student enterprise depend on the entrepreneurial spirit, intentions, risk-taking propensity and entrepreneurial competences of the individuals (Mwasalwiba, 2010; Liñán and Fayolle, 2015; Piperopoulos and Dimov, 2015). This quadrant is central in the sense that without the actual enterprising of individual people, the abstract, collective and organisational efforts to support enterprise may be a waste of time and resources. The promotion of entrepreneurial action, however, bears some challenges. Most academics see themselves as teachers and research-ers, not entrepreneurs (Kolhinen, 2015; Lundqvist and Williams Middleton, 2013). Furthermore, it has been argued that faculty members do not necessarily see or understand their role as an enterprise promoter (Kothari and Handscombe, 2007; Mwasalwiba, 2010). Fostering academic enterprise would require overcoming these barriers and conflicting norms.

Methodology

In this chapter, we present small illustrative cases (Patton, 2002) to analyse the state-of-the-art of the approaches of the European enterprise education in universities. Cases allow us to focus on distinctive characteristics and achieve a deep understanding of the dynamics within individual settings (Eisenhardt, 1989). In this chapter, we focus on three national or international cases and four university-level cases.

The national cases were selected based on the following criteria (Patton, 2002): (1) they represent different parts of Europe; (2) they represent different organisations; and (3) they are demonstrably able to promote enterprise. As a result, we selected the South East European Centre for Entrepreneurial Learning (SEECEL), Portugal and Finland as the cases. The following criteria were applied to the university cases (Patton, 2002): (1) they operate in different countries; (2) they successfully promote enterprise; and (3) their approaches to enterprise differ. Consequently, we selected the Norwegian University of Science and Technology (Norway), Swansea University (UK), Lappeenranta University of Technology (Finland) and the University of Wuppertal (Germany).[2]

We collected data from multiple sources, such as email correspondence and written or electronic documents, between September 2016 and February 2017. The case informants were invited to describe the current state-of-the-art of enterprise education briefly at their respective levels, depending on the informant's national (decision-maker, researcher) or academic position. Furthermore, they were asked to describe the objectives and needs of future development, and measures and incentives that guide and support enterprise education.

Manual content analysis was applied to the data. The material was read repeatedly with care to understand it fully. The data was used to illustrate the entrepreneurial practices of the case institution. From the theory, the analytical perspectives of the enterprise activities were identified, and the characteristics of these elements were drawn from the data. Finally, we applied comparative analysis to determine the similarities or differences of the cases.

As with any methodological tool, the qualitative content analysis of small illustrative cases has its limitations. Our cases enable no statistical generalisations on the issues studied and therefore suit exploratory or pilot studies best. Hence, we emphasise that the cases were selected to showcase good performance in enterprise education and to provide variety. Furthermore, the in-depth case study strongly reflects the researchers' personal preferences, which is likely to cause researcher-based bias in the data collection, analysis and interpretation. To minimise this bias, the research group continually discussed the enterprise education, the participants, and the data and its analysis.

Enterprise education in Europe – cases and examples

National guiding frameworks and country-specific approaches to enterprise education

Portugal

INSTITUTIONAL FOCUS ON EMPLOYABILITY, COLLABORATION AND
LOCAL DEVELOPMENT

In Portugal, the present higher education policies linked to *employability*, economic growth, science and technology promote *the local knowledge economy*. Significant investments and support have strengthened the *collaboration between higher education institutions and the business sector*, bringing innovation to companies, aiding technological research centres, and developing incubators. The Portuguese enterprise education policy mainly aims to stimulate the development of higher education institutions and their specific characteristics in their territorial, economic and social contexts. There is an emphasis on developing academic areas that have meaning and stimulating the exchange of activities linked to research and enterprise within a regional framework (Heitor and Horta, 2014).

PROGRESS IN PORTUGUESE UNIVERSITIES

In Portugal, the first enterprise courses were offered in the 1990s, but the more systematic promotion of enterprise education in Portuguese higher education institutions (HEIs) started in the early 2000s (Redford and Trigo, 2007). Later, from 2006 onwards *enterprise was included in the curricula in most Portuguese universities* (Saraiva and Paiva, 2014). Since the late 2010s, universities continued to develop their *enterprise programmes*. The enterprise courses offered at the time were mainly postgraduate courses of doctoral programmes. Portuguese HEIs focus on both *business creation* and, more recently, *enterprise as a transferal of competence* within the curriculum and *through extra-curricular clubs and activities* (Saraiva and Paiva, 2014).

GROWING OUTREACH FOR ENTREPRENEURIAL CAPACITY

Portuguese universities have acknowledged that they should be connected and work in partnership with other institutions that offer the conditions and support for enhancing the potential of new entrepreneurs. Some incubator and start-up programmes *have emerged beyond the university system*, and these national partners *have increased entrepreneurial support and the needed follow-up to enterprise within the education system* (e.g. Global Startup Program; The MIT Portugal Program; BETA-I Accelerator). Many universities benefit from connecting to these outside programmes, as they do not have their own accelerators, incubators or co-work spaces.

FUTURE CHALLENGES

Portugal has achieved much since the early 2000s in enterprise education, but some challenges still need to be addressed through education policy development and a culture shift. The culture in Portugal is not favourable to enterprising, especially risk-taking and graduate entrepreneurs (Silva, Gomes and Correira, 2009). Efforts are needed to *change the mind-set* and embrace competitiveness, innovation and enterprise as keys to future growth. A way to move forward would be to raise awareness of entrepreneurial role models, entrepreneurial opportunities related to university studies and entrepreneurial career prospects for university graduates. Promoting innovation in universities *should mainly be understood as a learning process* and not just an inventory of definitions and priorities.

Finland

GOVERNMENTAL GUIDANCE FOR UNIVERSITIES TO PROVIDE CITIZENS
WITH ENTREPRENEURIAL SKILLS

The promotion of enterprise has been one of the aims of the Finnish higher education policy since the early 2000s. In 2006, the Ministry of Education and the Ministry of Trade and Industry established a working group for promoting enterprise in higher education. The most important document for the Finnish enterprise education policy has been the national guidelines for entrepreneurship education (Ministry of Education, 2009). The guidelines underlined that *enterprise education is part of lifelong learning*; in it, *entrepreneurial skills* are developed and supplemented at different points in life. Furthermore, the Government Programme (2011) specified that efforts will be made to *increase interest in, and preparedness for, enterprise* by means of training at all levels of education and to *highlight the links between education and the working world.*

BUILDING INCENTIVES FOR ENTERPRISE EDUCATION

Based on the Finnish Universities Act, Finnish universities have extensive freedom of research, art and teaching. Consequently, the Ministry of Education and Culture can only promote enterprise policies through non-binding incentives and steering. A recent survey by the Ministry of Education and Culture (2016) shows the extensive variation between universities in terms of how they implement enterprise policies. For example, some universities have developed a full range of enterprise activities, while others co-operate with businesses and support entrepreneurship rather limitedly. In this regard, technical universities seem to excel in connecting with businesses and the other external stakeholders. (Ministry of Education and Culture, 2016) Furthermore, the Ministry of Education and Culture is including enterprise in the yearly objectives of and negotiations with the universities for the period 2017–2020.

Additionally, the ministry has set up a new governmental project and guidance group for enterprise education. The guidance group defines the objectives for the whole education system based on good practices identified.[3] The unique approach of the Finnish Ministry of Education and Culture effectively engages educational institutions. Furthermore, it indicates the importance of enterprise education for Finland.

ENTREPRENEURIAL COMMUNITY BUILT ON STUDENTS' AND RESEARCHERS' ACTIVITIES

The Finnish entrepreneurial scene is largely built on students' activities. Student entrepreneurial societies have become popular, and currently nearly all universities have them. This has impacted regional and national enterprise policies. Student initiatives also have international importance – Europe's leading start-up event Slush[4] is closely related to the Aalto University Entrepreneurship Society. Furthermore, to foster the generation and leverage of entrepreneurial knowledge, the Scientific Association for Entrepreneurship Education was established in 2011. It brings together Finnish enterprise researchers and teachers in annual meetings.

FUTURE CHALLENGES

Finland's approach to enterprise education can be attributed to the collective efforts of government, institutions, teaching staff, researchers and students. However, only some Finnish universities have a clear strategy for promoting entrepreneurship. In addition, the universities co-operate with businesses in very different ways, and raising the level of industry co-operation may be one of the key tasks for the Finnish universities in the future. (Suomen yliopistot ry, 2016).

South East European Centre for Entrepreneurial Learning (SEECEL)

INSTITUTIONAL MISSION

The South East European Centre for Entrepreneurial Learning (SEECEL) was founded in 2009 in Zagreb, Croatia, by the joint initiative of eight countries.[5] SEECEL develops policies at the regional (South-East Europe) and EU levels and frameworks for implementing enterprise education, and coordinates regional initiatives. SEECEL's mission is the systematic development of life-long entrepreneurial learning in the context of the Small Business Act for Europe[6] through structured regional co-operation. SEECEL applies evidence-based policy making, and its operations are either integral or complementary to various key EU policy documents, such as the Europe 2020 Strategy, the Entrepreneurship 2020 Action Plan, the South East Europe 2020 Strategy, the EU Strategy for the Danube Region, and the EU Strategy for the Adriatic and Ionian Region.

INTRODUCING ENTERPRISE IN UNIVERSITIES

The piloting activities of SEECEL were developed within a regional pilot project framework, on which SEECEL based its 2013–2016 work programme. The project concerned 16 higher education institutions in South-East Europe and Turkey. The specific objective of the project was *to incorporate entrepreneurial learning* into existing study programmes and *develop awareness of and aspirations for enterprise among students*. This was done, for instance, by developing and embedding curricula for enterprise (e.g. pedagogical support and assessment practices) and by engaging students in enterprise learning (e.g. extracurricular events and societies and business idea competitions). Entrepreneurial learning was considered an integral part of the learning outcomes and of all study programmes and courses. Another crucial aspect of the framework programme was that it focused on universities' programmes beyond the academic disciplines of business or engineering, such as natural sciences, education, humanities and social sciences.

ENTREPRENEURIAL LEARNING IN FOCUS

The framework project approached *entrepreneurial learning holistically*, including changes not only in the curriculum, teaching, learning and assessment practices, but also in teacher training and educational institution management. The project regarded entrepreneurial learning as a gradual process, *in a region in which entrepreneurial learning was not yet included in the higher education policy* Moreover, SEECEL avoided using a 'top-down' or 'one size fits all' approach; instead, it provided pilot institutions with helpful tools to define *their own needs, activities and methods*. Each pilot institution established Entrepreneurial Learning Teams, which began their interaction with other stakeholders within the university and implemented selected activities in five key areas: (1) developing and embedding curricula for enterprise; (2) engaging students in enterprise learning; (3) partnering with external stakeholders; (4) engaging senior managers; and (5) generating third stream projects such as business incubation and knowledge transfer. The piloting actions between the institutions varied. For example, the University Entrepreneurship Centre at the University of Banja Luka (Bosnia and Herzegovina) provided 30 hours of training for 13 students from different faculties of the university. The main aim was to introduce and involve students in the world of entrepreneurship, to teach them to analyse themselves and their personal skills, to recognise new opportunities and to develop their own business ideas.

PROMISING RESULTS FOR FURTHER PROMOTION OF ENTERPRISE EDUCATION

The project results exceeded SEECEL's expectations. The project showed that there is *fertile ground for entrepreneurial learning* in all participating institutions. Both management and teaching staff felt that *entrepreneurial learning should be incorporated* in their study programmes. The participation of non-business students showed that entrepreneurship is relevant beyond business studies. Students of technology, humanities and other fields recognised that entrepreneurship was more largely about turning ideas into action (whether in a business or non-profit context). However, students were not highly motivated to take part in extracurricular entrepreneurship events. In institutions where the management staff played a leading role by enhancing the *development of new modules and courses*, the project paved the way for real changes and sustainable results.

FUTURE CHALLENGES

The project showed that in addition to carrying out administrative work, leadership is necessary in engaging academic staff and students in entrepreneurial learning and in addressing potential obstacles, such as the lack of time or implementing changes to existing study programmes or extracurricular activities.

Cases from universities

Norwegian University of Science and Technology (NTNU), Norway

The history of the Norwegian University of Science and Technology (NTNU) dates back to 1910. After several mergers, NTNU is currently the largest university in Norway and offers education in humanities, social sciences, economics, health sciences, education science and aesthetic disciplines. However, about half of the 39,000 students study technology and natural sciences, which is the focus of NTNU.

INSTITUTIONAL FACILITATION CREATED THE MOMENTUM

The university has a 30-year history of research and education in the field of innovation and technology-based enterprise. Enterprise education started out as a combination of technology students requiring more knowledge about how to start a company and a dedicated professor who wanted to test out new ways of teaching enterprise and small business management.

ENTERPRISE PROGRAMME CREATING BUSINESSES AND
ENTREPRENEURIAL SKILLS

The NTNU School of Entrepreneurship (NSE), founded in 2003, is a *two-year masters programme* with a focus on business development and technology-based entrepreneurship. The programme combines academic insight with hands-on experience. The students are working in interdisciplinary teams of three to five. Through three semesters, they have to develop a business idea of their choice to ensure its commercial success. A deeply rooted culture of contributing, engagement and mutual support enables *student-to-student learning in a community* of both current and previous students. NSE strives to be *a resource for the university and the whole of Norway*, and seeks to spread enterprise competence (e.g. marshalling resources, seeking opportunities and risk tolerance) across study programmes and regions. At the university, NSE spreads *enterprise competence* through a course for 1200 masters students annually.

ENTREPRENEURIAL MOVEMENT

The NSE students are an important part of Spark NTNU, which the local energy company TrønderEnergi and NTNU established as a joint venture in 2013. Spark NTNU, *run by students and supported by faculty members and industry partners*, facilitates idea development and venture creation with students from all programmes of study. It has guided approximately 230 start-up teams between 2014 and 2016. Currently, *about 70 start-up teams* with students from 36 different study programmes receive guidance from 17 student mentors drawn primarily from the senior class of NSE. Moreover, the NSE students together with the Spark NTNU students compose the core of FRAM, *the students' innovation centre*, where students interested in enterprise from all study programmes meet and learn from each other. *The growing community of students interested in enterprise* is in line with the strategies of NTNU. University actors focusing on seed funding, incubator services and technology transfer therefore support the development.

MAKING A DIFFERENCE IN THE ECOSYSTEM

In Norway, NSE has created the Centre for Engaged Education through Entrepreneurship (ENgage). In 2016, ENgage was appointed as a Centre for Excellence in Education by the Norwegian Agency for Quality Assurance in Education. The vision of ENgage is *to increase the number of students in Norway and around the world with entrepreneurial skills and the mind-set* to become change agents in all contexts. ENgage consists of NSE, Spark, Nord University and Troll Labs (experimental living labs of NTNU). It provides action-based, challenge-based and experience-based learning models for interdisciplinary interactions and complementary skills and approaches. *Students and student organisations are an important part* of ENgage in its endeavour to combine, develop and disseminate action-based learning, student-to-student learning, collaborative skills, rapid prototyping and student engagement. ENgage provides train-the-trainer (student-to-student learning) courses and activities for students in all disciplines to increase the number of higher education students with entrepreneurial skills. ENgage's interpretation of entrepreneurial learning seems to be comprehensive, wide and successful, and focuses primarily on student engagement. Furthermore, students' role in the learning process is crucial. However, the example does not explicitly show elements of intentional 'learning from the failure' kind of an approach (e.g. Cope, 2011).

University of Wuppertal, Germany

The University of Wuppertal (Bergische Universität Wuppertal, BUW) was established in 1972. BUW offers education in multiple disciplines covering engineering, art and design, economics and humanities. The university has around 20,000 students.

INSTITUTIONAL STRATEGY DRIVEN BY GOVERNMENTAL POLICY

The efforts to establish enterprise education at BUW began in the late 1990s with a policy initiative of the German Government for improving enterprise at German higher education and research institutions. This resulted in the programme EXIST – Start-ups from universities, which aimed to increase the number of technology and knowledge-based business start-ups and supported university graduates, scientists and students in establishing technology and knowledge-based start-ups. This early-stage institutionalisation of enterprise is still important for the *structure and 'policy thinking' of enterprise* at BUW today. The initial project contributed to *the establishment of two chairs* in entrepreneurship education, which still represent *the main infrastructure of staff and resources* for teaching enterprise at Wuppertal. Aside from the curriculum, there is a hands-on seminar series for students and external parties on start-up building offered through the Bizeps network which was established as a regional venture support network during the EXIST project.

CONTEXTUAL RELATIONSHIPS

Through *the regional network approach* of EXIST, entrepreneurship education has long been integrated in the regional entrepreneurial ecosystem of the 'Bergische' region around Wuppertal (e.g. university start-ups coached and domiciled in the city's technology park, venture funding through local investors, and external staff from the region teaching entrepreneurship courses). Additional resources for enterprise education and research are provided by two university institutes: the Jackstädt Centre of Entrepreneurship and Innovation Research and the Institute for Entrepreneurship and Innovation Research.

BUILDING INCENTIVES FOR ENTERPRISE

The university leadership employs different measures and incentives to define its strategic focus in research and education. Typically, incentives are set indirectly by allocating university resources to individual themes and *supporting efforts of faculty members to attain external third-party funding* for novel projects (e.g. hands-on, design-thinking courses and extra-curricular, project-based entrepreneurial learning) and to increase the visibility and reputation of faculty members through the university's communication and public relations efforts. At the faculty level, enterprise is at the heart of the Schumpeter School of Business and

Economics, a whole department dedicated to enterprising and innovation. At the chair level, the concept is based on three core pillars: (1) a portfolio of entrepreneurship teaching modules; (2) extra-curricular activities; and (3) social responsibility and entrepreneurship related to the chair's UNESCO activities. One example of BUW's new initiatives is to increase the organisation's visible engagement in civil society projects within its third mission. The UNESCO chair's extra-curricular 'Enactus Student Team' has been advocating this initiative since 2004. Enactus is an international organisation where students collaborate with corporate and organisational partners to propel societal development through entrepreneurship.

GROWING ENTREPRENEURIAL CAPACITIES

Enterprise education modules are integrated into further curricular and extra-curricular courses and targeted also for non-business students. Overall, extra-curricular initiatives constitute a flexible and fast means to engage in action and project based forms and new themes of teaching enterprise, recently in particular with regard to ecosystems as well as sustainable and socio-cultural enterprise. The most salient single aim of enterprise education is to support and broaden not only business and technological enterprise but also social, sustainable and cultural enterprise. This is also reflected in encouraging students to think and act entrepreneurially, for example the 'Enactus Student Team' addressing social or ecological problems in civil projects. Correspondingly, BUW strives further to increase its education in social, cultural and sustainable enterprise. This has led to the expansion of the *portfolio of regional partners in enterprise education*, e.g. with the Wuppertal Institute for Climate, Environment and Energy and the 'Neue Effizienz' initiative, connecting the university, which provides basic and applied research, with the private sector and the local community in order to find practical solutions to social challenges.

Lappeenranta University of Technology, Finland

Lappeenranta University of Technology (LUT) is located in South-East Finland and established in 1969. LUT operates in the fields of technology, science and business and has roughly 6000 students. Clean energy and water, the circular economy and sustainable business are the key focus areas to which LUT seeks solutions through technology and business.

INSTITUTIONAL STRATEGY

LUT's latest strategy, Trailblazer 2020, was prepared in 2014. Entrepreneurship formed its core, setting a competitive target: 'We will be the first Finnish entrepreneurial university'. To fulfil this strategic target, LUT has action plans for entrepreneurship and education. The *action plan for entrepreneurship* takes a holistic approach to entrepreneurship and the entrepreneurial university, as it emphasises LUT's strategic management, commercialisation of research results, entrepreneurial culture, collaboration with businesses, and promotion of entrepreneurial competencies of students and staff. Furthermore, the development is followed and guided by HEInnovate, a self-evaluation tool prepared by the OECD and the EU. The *action plan for education* aims at incorporating entrepreneurial learning into all degree programme contents and methods. This means that from introductory courses onwards, students' active role in learning processes is emphasised, degree programmes are cultivated to further the development of transferable skills, and teachers are trained to adopt entrepreneurial teaching methods.

ACTIVITIES AND INCENTIVES FOR ENTERPRISE

The *action plan for entrepreneurship* includes activating enterprise-related communication, expanding the range of enterprise support services, and creating guidance and incentives for entrepreneurship. For example, LUT rewards its researchers for inventions and patents. Its intellectual property rights (IPR) portfolio, generated through research results, is larger than that of any other Finnish university. LUT aims for the rapid *commercialisation of research results and start-up acceleration*. LUT builds on active collaboration with businesses and interaction in entrepreneurial ecosystems. In 2015, it received the THE ranking[7] award for business interaction. Moreover, the university has organised a special seed fund company to support the fast development of spin-offs and start-ups, and it is initiating new activities to develop the university's role as a business accelerator. For example, the seed fund company plays a key role in building a new clean-tech ecosystem that brings together large corporations, small to medium sized enterprises (SMEs), internationally networked clean-tech intermediate organisations, and universities. Universities provide the ecosystem with state-of-the-art research knowledge and new ideas for further development according to open innovation practices.

LUT has committed to using the EU Commission's and OECD's HEInnovate[8] self-evaluation tool to follow its development as an entrepreneurial university. LUT seeks to improve its entrepreneurial culture through wide-ranging trials and learning environments and promotes the entrepreneurial competencies and entrepreneurial activity of both students and staff. Furthermore, LUT is expanding its range of enterprise-related courses. For example, LUT has developed a new entrepreneurship course for all doctoral students in the university.

BUILDING ENTREPRENEURIAL CAPACITY

In a recent report by NORDTEK (Gulieva 2015), LUT was recognised for building entrepreneurial capacity. Furthermore, according to the Ministry of Education and Culture (2016), LUT is one of the entrepreneurial universities in Finland. Since the early 2000s, LUT has offered the Masters programme in Technological Entrepreneurship and a Masters programme focusing on innovation, and as of 2016, all LUT students have been able to minor in enterprise. Additionally, LUT offers its undergraduate and postgraduate students venture creation programmes, course modules, and individual enterprise courses. In continuing education, its co-operation with industry is long-standing, and it trains teachers of all levels in enterprise education.

ENTREPRENEURIAL COMMUNITY

As in most Finnish universities, LUT has a very active *student-driven entrepreneurship society* (LUTES) that organises different entrepreneurial student networking events, such as business boot camps, hackathons and guest lectures, and helps students create and develop business ideas. The events organised by LUTES are free of charge and open to everyone. The most important event organised annually by LUTES is the Summer Launchpad. During the ten-week programme, the participating teams are given the opportunity to develop their business ideas together with business professionals. The goal is for the teams to set up a company after the programme and realise their business ideas. The Summer Launchpad has also attracted student teams from other HEIs in Southern Finland.

Additionally, *regional enterprise developers are co-operating with LUT* e.g. in the Willi idea[9] (wild idea) business competition, which annually attracts more than *100 competitive business ideas*. In 2016, the winning team of the competition was a start-up established by a group of LUT students who are currently developing a hearing aid application for mobile phones. During the years some of the business ideas have proved successful.

Swansea University, United Kingdom

Swansea University, founded in 1920 and located in Wales, the United Kingdom, is a full-scale university with 16,000 students. In 2015, it opened a new campus focusing on science and innovation.

INSTITUTIONAL STRATEGY

Swansea University recognises the benefits of enterprise education to students regardless of their faculty or discipline. The need for enterprise education has been acknowledged for several years. Swansea University now has a defined, high-level strategy designed to give all students enterprise skills and entrepreneurial support for those who desire it. The aim is to develop entrepreneurial graduates as well as graduate entrepreneurs, but the main goal is to increase the employability of all students regardless of their subject. Furthermore, different staff training sessions have been organised to progress entrepreneurial teaching and related curriculum work. The university has excellent relationships with industry and the regional Welsh Government departments, which support the university financially and operationally.

TOOLS AND METHODS FOR PROMOTING ENTERPRISE EDUCATION

Swansea has two dedicated institutions – the Institute for Entrepreneurial Leadership (IFEL) and the Swansea Employability Academy (SEA) – which have developed cross-campus enterprise modules, events and awards. In 2016, 3400 students participated in events developing enterprise thinking and entrepreneurial or intrapreneurial capacity. Furthermore, Swansea University participates in the Global Enterprise Week initiative,[10] which showcases the entrepreneurial activities for students and staff throughout the year. The Global Enterprise Week includes various events, activities and competitions for students who are looking to build their entrepreneurial skills, e.g. a business idea competition, pitching competitions, networking events, role model entrepreneurial talks and employability information.

OBJECTIVES AND NEEDS OF ENTERPRISE EDUCATION DEVELOPMENT

At present, the institution provides enterprise education widely. The university aims to integrate entrepreneurial modules into different disciplines and offer enterprise modules to students to increase employability. The ultimate target is awareness at an academic level and educating practitioners to understand that enterprise education is not solely about teaching people to start businesses, but helping them adopt tools, skills and a mindset that make them well-rounded and employable graduates. Moreover, the university provides continuous professional development opportunities for staff to cultivate their entrepreneurial teaching and embed enterprise skills into existing curricula or new programmes. The primary focus of the latest institutional strategic plan is to develop entrepreneurial graduates and graduate entrepreneurs.

MEASURES AND INCENTIVES TO GUIDE AND SUPPORT
ENTREPRENEURSHIP

Swansea University is committed to increasing the perception of itself as an entrepreneurial institution, providing enterprise education to all students and support to those interested in venture creation. Respectively, Swansea has received recognition for the quality of teaching and student satisfaction. Furthermore, the overarching aim of the university is to be recognised as the THE Entrepreneurial University of the Year.[11] Swansea's active work in organising different events and activities for students and staff has been recognised: for many years, the university has won the High Impact Host Award during the Global Entrepreneurship Week, but has also been recognised for having the second most events of any institution globally.

HEInnovate[12] is one of Swansea's strategic support mechanisms for assessing and benchmarking its progression as an entrepreneurial university. Additionally, Swansea University has close relationships with industry and regional Welsh Government departments, which support the university both financially and operationally.

Discussion and conclusions

The cases display three distinct motives driving European enterprise education policies:

1   Enterprise education is a vehicle to transform the business culture of the nation.
2   Enterprise education is a reaction to competitiveness problems and unemployment.
3   Enterprise education is a way to promote the knowledge-based society and increase the value added of the nation.

The promotion of enterprise education in Europe has faced the challenge of taking the national circumstances into account. Our cases show vividly that differences in national circumstances largely determine the national policies and targets of enterprise education. That is, in some European countries entrepreneurship education may concern the introduction and acceptability of the market economy and liberalism to the population. In that sense, SEECEL has an important societal mission. Meanwhile, other countries have progressed with their enterprise policy and are fine-tuning their educational targets regarding employment and competitiveness. Portugal prioritises the development of the knowledge society, and enterprise education is a way to promote that. It seems, however, that none of the countries systematically measure their progress in enterprise education, although both LUT and Swansea mention using the HEInnovate tool for self-reviewing their progress. As a holistic, multi-dimensional phenomenon with several intertwining levels, entrepreneurship has proved to be difficult to measure and evaluate.

The university cases highlight three main points:

1   University level strategic impetus is decisive in enterprising education.
2   The entrepreneurial movement has extensive implications for universities, regions and the national enterprising policy.
3   The scope of enterprising activities in the universities seems twofold: some universities follow a holistic approach and pursue a rich variety of enterprising activities, some aim at a focused target and can thereby direct specialised resources for those efforts.

The university cases demonstrate the importance of a top-level strategy. This is somewhat surprising even though we intentionally chose prime European examples, presenting holistic and strategy-oriented approaches. All case universities seem to have strategies encompassing enterprise education. Especially Swansea University and LUT seem to emphasise the top-level enterprising strategy guiding their action plans and enterprising activities. Surprisingly, none of the universities give examples of how the faculty members or other internal stakeholders are encouraged to implement enterprise education. Yet, universities organise training for teachers to improve their knowledge and develop their entrepreneurial learning practices. For universities, the personnel's own entre-preneurial activity remains a difficult issue, and incentives for enterprising or entrepreneurship education remain low. From our perspective, however, university staff are in a key position to promote entrepreneurship, and new approaches to exploit this opportunity are sorely needed.

The variation in enterprising activities between universities is significant. All case universities highlight enterprise-related courses and programmes. In Wuppertal University, the enterprise programmes and courses are the main vehicle for promoting entrepreneurship. Wuppertal also shows serious interest in local and regional development through enterprise promotion. In contrast, Swansea employs multiple ways of promoting enterprise: start-ups, programmes and courses. Likewise, LUT invests in enterprising education but also stresses the role of patents, start-ups and the community. NTNU emphasises the students' role in creating new ventures and supporting the community.

As enterprise courses and programmes were deemed important in enterprise education, it is no wonder that extra-curricular activities were mentioned infre-quently. All informants in this study represented the staff, and as such, their per-spective is naturally restricted. However, we think that universities need to learn more about extra-curricular activities and integrate them into entrepreneurial learning. LUT reports about the students' entrepreneurship society and Wupper-tal about active students in enterprising courses, and Swansea continuously keeps the student movement vibrant and creative. Finally, NTNU's enterprising activities revolve around the enterprising movement stemming from the enter-prise programme and student activity. NTNU's approach is strongly student-led, and therefore, the students' entrepreneurial movement has even modified univer-sity practices. Furthermore, NTNU is pursuing a stronger national role in Norway. As emergent models, all the cases show very different approaches to student-led processes – each model is specific to a country, region or university, and it would be difficult to determine the best one. At the moment, the best approach to evaluate the models would be to examine their ability to generate entrepreneurial outcomes: that is, student start-ups, entrepreneurial learning activities, entrepreneurial networks, etc.

Finally, the cases highlight the introduction of enterprise education through different projects. We cannot currently estimate whether project-based prac-tices will be embedded into universities. New activities started through short-lived project funding have a tendency to cease after the funding stops. Moreover, it was somewhat surprising that universities did not mention utilis-ing their alumni in enterprise education. Especially successful entrepreneurs could bring novel approaches to entrepreneurial learning and courses. The alumni could contribute knowledge and even funding, thus helping the univer-sity in its resource challenges. European universities may currently have no real incentives to approach their alumni, but we think they are very likely to develop contacts with alumni in the future to exploit opportunities related to both funding and learning. Furthermore, entrepreneurial learning in universities seems to occur in classrooms, whereas companies might have seemed a more logical setting. In that sense, universities still have a great deal to learn about 'the world out there' – co-operation with outsiders is a fast track to entrepreneurial learning.

The results of our study underline the need for further research. It seems evident that there are no single solutions for universities to undertake the enterprise education in their activities. However, we still know relatively little of successful models of entrepreneurial universities. For example, it would be interesting to study the pathways universities take to promote their enterprise education. In that sense, universities start from the very different standing points and they set their targets regarding enterprising in very different ways. Furthermore, more comprehensive studies are needed to understand universities' technology transfer and entrepreneurial university processes and their combinations. Besides the policy-guided HEInnovate self-evaluation tool, there may be need for development of research-based evaluation tools to help universities measure and develop their enterprise education practices. It is our conviction that universities' development of enterprising activities should be based on evidence and systematic planning. Combining science, education and enterprising is a complicated task that should not be underestimated.

Notes

1 See European survey on Higher Education Institutions at: https://ec.europa.eu/growth/smes/promoting-entrepreneurship/support/education/projects-studies_en.
2 We express our gratitude to Mr Simone Baldassarri of the European Commission (DG GROW), Ms Johanna Moisio of the Finnish Ministry of Education and Culture, Associate Prof. Lise Aaboen of the Norwegian University of Science and Technology, Ms Ana Mateus of the Ministry of Higher Education, Science and Technology in Portugal, Prof. Teresa Paiva of the Polytechnic Institute of Guarda in Portugal, Prof. Dana Redford of the Portugal Entrepreneurship Education Platform, Mr Thomas Farnell of the South East European Centre for Entrepreneurial Learning, Mr David Bolton and Prof. Paul Hannon of Swansea University, and Prof. Christine Volkmann of the University of Wuppertal. Their role as inside informants was decisive in forming a comprehensive case description of each organisation.
3 www.minedu.fi/export/sites/default/OPM/Julkaisut/2009/liitteet/opm07.pdf_1924203 533.pdf).
4 See www.slush.org/about/what-is-slush/.
5 The eight SEECEL member states are Albania, Bosnia and Herzegovina, Croatia, Kosovo, the former Yugoslavia Republic of Macedonia, Montenegro, Serbia and Turkey.
6 http://eur-lex.europa.eu/legal-content/EN/TXT/?uri=CELEX:52008DC0394.
7 Times Higher Education World University Rankings is one of the world's most highly regarded university ranking systems. The areas assessed are research, teaching, international outlook and funding.
8 See www.heinnovate.eu.
9 See www.startupmill.fi/en/willi-idea-competition.
10 See http://gew.co/.
11 See http://ncee.org.uk/leadership-and-management/the-entrepreneurial-university/.
12 See www.heinnovate.eu.

References

Bramwell, A. and Wolfe, D.A. (2008). Universities and regional economic development: The entrepreneurial University of Waterloo. *Research Policy*, 37(8), 1175–1187.

Cohen, B. (2006). Sustainable valley entrepreneurial ecosystems. *Business Strategy and the Environment*, 15, 1–14.

Cope, J. (2011). Entrepreneurial learning from failure: An interpretative phenomenological analysis. *Journal of Business Venturing, Volume*, [e-journal] 26(6), 604–623. ISSN 0883–9026, http://dx.doi.org/10.1016/j.jbusvent.2010.06.002.

Eisenhardt, K.M. (1989). Building theories from case study research. *Academy of Management Review*, 14(4), 532–550.

Etzkowitz, H. and Leydesdorff, L. (2000). The dynamics of innovation: from national systems and "Mode 2" to a Triple Helix of university-industry-government relations. *Research Policy*, 29, 109–123.

European Commission. (2008). *Entrepreneurship in higher education, especially within non-business studies*. Final Report of the Expert Group. European Commission, Directorate-General for Enterprise and Industry.

Foss, L. and Gibson, D.V. (2015). The entrepreneurial university: context and institutional change. In: L. Foss and D. Gibson, eds. *The entrepreneurial university: Context and institutional change*. London and New York: Routledge.

Gibb, A. (2005). Towards the entrepreneurial university: Entrepreneurship education as a lever for change. *Policy Paper #003*, National Council for Graduate Entrepreneurship.

Goldstein, H.A. (2010). The "entrepreneurial turn" and regional economic development mission of universities. *Annals of Regional Science*, 44(1), 83–109.

Government Programme. (2011). Programme of Prime Minister Jyrki Katainen's Government 22 June 2011 [online]. Available at: http://valtioneuvosto.fi/documents/10184/367809/Programme+of+Prime+Minister+Katainen%E2%80%99s+Government/64238eca-58cd-43bb-81dc-963a364a422e [accessed 10 February 2017].

Gulieva, V. (2015). Mapping of entrepreneurship activities at NORDTEK Universities [online]. Available at: http://nordtek.net/wp-content/uploads/2015/05/Nordtek_entrepreneurship_mapping_22.06.pdf [accessed 10 February 2017].

Hayter, C.S. (2016). A trajectory of early-stage spinoff success: The role of knowledge intermediaries within an entrepreneurial university ecosystem. *Small Business Economics*, [e-journal] 47, 633–656. http://dx.doi.org/10.1007/s11187-016-9756-3.

Heitor, M. and Horta, H. (2014). Democratizing higher education and access to science: The Portuguese reform 2006–2010. *Higher Education Policy*, 27, 239–257.

Hytti, U. (2002). *State-of-art of enterprise education in Europe – Results from the Entredu project*. Small Business Institute, Turku School of Economics and Business Administration, Finland.

Isenberg, D.J. (2010). The big idea: How to start an entrepreneurial revolution. *Harvard Business Review*, 88(6), 40–50.

Kallio, A., Harmaakorpi, V. and Pihkala, T. (2010). Absorptive capacity and social capital in regional innovation systems: The case of the Lahti region in Finland. *Urban Studies*, 47(2), 303–319.

Kolhinen, J. (2015). *Yliopiston yrittäjämäisyyden sosiaalinen rakentuminen: Case Aalto-yliopisto*. Acta Universitatis Lappeenrantaensis, 659. Lappeenranta: Lappeenrannan teknillisen yliopiston yliopistopaino.

Kothari, S. and Handscombe, R.D. (2007). Sweep or seep? Structure, culture, enterprise and universities. *Management Decision*, 45(1), 43–61.

Liñán, F. and Fayolle, A. (2015). A systematic literature review on entrepreneurial intentions: Citation, thematic analyses, and research agenda. *International Entrepreneurship and Management Journal*, [e-journal] 11, 907–933. http://dx.doi.org/10.1007/s11365-015-0356-5.

Lundqvist, M.A. and Williams Middleton, K.L. (2013). Academic entrepreneurship revisited – University scientists and venture creation. *Journal of Small Business and Enterprise Development*, 20(3), 603–617.

Ministry of Education. (2009). *Guidelines for entrepreneurship education*. Publication of the Ministry of Education, Finland, 2009: 9. Helsinki: University Print.

Ministry of Education and Culture. (2016). *Yrittäjyyden tukemisen hyvät käytänteet korkeakouluissa 2016*. Opetus- ja kulttuuriministeriön julkaisuja, 2016: 4.

Morris, M.H., Shirakova, G. and Tsukanova, T. (2017). Student entrepreneurship and the university ecosystem: A multi-country empirical exploration. *European Journal of International Management*, 11(1), 65–85.

Mwasalwiba, E.S. (2010). Entrepreneurship education: A review of its objectives, teaching methods, and impact indicators. *Education + Training*, [online] 52 (1), 20–47. Available at: http://dx.doi.org/10.1108/00400911011017663 [accessed 6 February 2017].

Patton, M.Q. (2002). *Qualitative research and evaluation methods*. Thousand Oaks: Sage.

Pihkala, T., Ruskovaara, E. and Hytti, U. (2016). *Global university entrepreneurial spirit students' survey*. National Report 2016, Finland, 69, 1–25.

Piperopoulos, P. and Dimov, D. (2015). Burst bubbles or build steam? Entrepreneurship education, entrepreneurial self-efficacy, and entrepreneurial intentions. *Journal of Small Business Management*, [e-journal] 53(4), 970–985. http://dx.doi.org/10.1111/jsbm.12116.

Pittaway, L. and Hannon, P. (2008). Institutional strategies for developing enterprise education: A review of some concepts and models. *Journal of Small Business and Enterprise Development*, 15(1), 202–226.

Rasmussen, E., Mosey, S. and Wright, M. (2011). The evolution of entrepreneurial competencies: A longitudinal study of university spin-off venture Emergence. *Journal of Management Studies*, 48(6), 1314–1345.

Redford, D.T. and Trigo, V. (2007). Entrepreneurship education in Portugal and the United States: A comparative study. In: M. Cannice, R. Chen and Z. Li., eds. *Silicon Valley Review of Global Entrepreneurship Research*, 3(1).

Rice, M.P., Fetters, M.L. and Greene, P.G. (2010). University-based entrepreneurship ecosystems: Key success factors and recommendations. In: M. Fetters, P. Greene, M. Rice and J. Butler, eds. *The Development of University-Based Entrepreneurship Ecosystems: Global Practices.* Cheltenham UK: Edward Elgar Publishing, pp. 177–197.

Saraiva, H. and Paiva, T. (2014) Entrepreneurship education in Portugal – considerations on the topic and its development environment. *HOLOS* [e-journal], 30(6), 3–15. http://dx.doi.org/10.15628/holos.2014.2587.

Silva, M.A.O.M., Gomes, L.F.A.M. and Correia, M.F. (2009). Entrepreneurial culture: A comparative study of entrepreneurs in Brazil and Portugal. *RAC, Curitiba*, [online], 13(1, 4), 57–61. Available at: www.anpad.org.br/rac [accessed 12 February 2017].

Stam, E. (2015). Entrepreneurial ecosystems and regional policy: A sympathetic critique. *European Planning Studies*, 23(9), 1759–1769.

Suomen yliopistot ry (UNIFI). (2016). *Yliopistojen yrittäjyyssuositukset*. [pdf] Available at: www.unifi.fi/wpcontent/uploads/2015/11/Yliopistojen_Yrittäjyyssuositukset_final_syyskuu2016.pdf [accessed 11 April 2017].

Wilson, K. (2008). Entrepreneurship education in Europe. In: *Entrepreneurship and higher education*, OECD. [online], Chapter 5, pp. 1–20. Available at: http://ssrn.com/abstract=1392369 [accessed 13 February 2017].

Wissema, J.G. (2009). *Towards the third generation university: Managing the university in transition*. Cheltenham, UK and Northampton, MA, USA: Edward Elgar Publishing.

Wood, M.S. (2011). A process model of academic entrepreneurship. *Business horizons*, 54(2), 153–161.

World Economic Forum. (2013). *Entrepreneurial ecosystems around the globe and company growth dynamics.* Davos: World Economic Forum.

Wright, M., Clarysse, B., Mustar, P. and Lockett, A. (2007). *Academic entrepreneurship in Europe*. Cheltenham, UK and Northampton, MA, USA: Edward Elgar Publishing.

Zahra, S. and Welter, F. (2008). *Entrepreneurship education for Central, Eastern and Southeastern Europe*. Entrepreneurship and higher education, OECD.

2 U.S. approaches to entrepreneurship education

George Solomon, Nawaf Alabduljader and Ravi S. Ramani

Introduction

Entrepreneurship and new venture starts are key drivers of economic growth (Amezcua, Grimes, Bradley and Wiklund, 2013; Raffie and Feng, 2014). According to the Small Business Administration in the U.S. alone, small businesses make up 99.7 per cent of firms and 64 per cent of net new private-sector jobs. Thus, entrepreneurship is essential for social and economic wellbeing because new ventures are the primary source of job creation and economic development in many economies (Aldrich, 1999). Entrepreneurship is also seen as a solution for the fast-changing markets, and as a competitive advantage that can be used by companies to outperform their competitors. Schumpeter coined the term 'creative destruction' to describe entrepreneurship and its essential role in capitalism (1942). Furthermore, the success of companies like Dropbox, Snapchat and Facebook means that colleges are actively looking to collaborate, and sometimes invest in, businesses and ideas that might have potential. Resources such as entrepreneurship clubs,[1] hatcheries/incubators and campus-based business offices[2] encourage students to apply their classroom learning to their own businesses, with the college playing a supporting role. Accordingly, there has been growing demand for entrepreneurship education from students, existing companies, and policy makers.

To examine the current landscape in entrepreneurship education in the United States this chapter reports results of the National Survey of Entrepreneurship Education (NSEE). The first NSEE started collecting data in 1979, and has ever since collected data in different time periods, with the most recent being in 2014. Using these data, the goal was to gauge best practices and trends within the field of entrepreneurship education while providing a foundation on which to develop entrepreneurship education programmes across the United States.

The first section of this chapter offers some important conceptual and theoretical background information regarding entrepreneurship education. The focus of this background section is to provide a definition of entrepreneurship education and a historical context of the growth of entrepreneurship education. Next, the second section: (1) explains how entrepreneurship education differs from traditional business education; (2) distinguishes between two major types of entrepreneurship education courses – small business management courses and new venture courses; (3) provides an overview of learning theories relevant to entrepreneurship; and (4) presents a brief discussion about the impact of entrepreneurship education. The third section reports findings on the state of the art in U.S. entrepreneurship education and best practices based on the 2014 NSEE. Finally, this chapter concludes with a view of future directions and areas of improvement in entrepreneurship education.

Background information

Definition of entrepreneurship education

Entrepreneurship education can be defined as "any pedagogical or process of education for entrepreneurial attitudes and skills" (Fayolle, Gailly and Lassas-Clerc, 2006: 702). Entrepreneurship education crosses several disciplines to help entrepreneurs envisage and start a new business venture by combining information from functional disciplines and from the external environment, and having the ability to operate in the context of uncertainty and ambiguity which faces a new business venture (Shepherd and Douglas, 1997; Solomon, 2014). Entrepreneurship is essentially linked with the exploitation of opportunities to create value (Shane and Venkataraman, 2000). Entrepreneurship manifests itself in unique thinking to develop an awareness of trends, market changes to create or discover opportunities, and acting on these opportunities to create value through adopting creative strategies, innovative tactics and leadership despite the uncertainty that exists. What institutions teach in their respective entrepreneurship classes should serve to instil and enhance the abilities of learners to act on opportunities to create value.

Historical perspective

Entrepreneurship education in the United States at both the two- and four-year college and university levels has grown in both the number and diversity of course offerings from 1971 to 2016. This expansion of educational offerings has been fuelled in part by dissatisfaction with the traditional Fortune 500 focus of business education voiced by students and accreditation bodies (Solomon and Fernald, 1991).

The dilemma is not that demand is high, but that the pedagogy selected meet the needs of the next generation of innovative and creative students and practising entrepreneurs. As the diffusion of technology continues to speed up the rate of change in the world, both students and established businesses demand increased focus on entrepreneurship principles to help them be creative and innovative to keep up with the continuous changes, as well as to allow students to start their own businesses within the fast-changing environment they find themselves in (Rideout and Gray, 2013; Solomon, 2014; Valerio, Parton and Robb, 2014).

Entrepreneurship education has experienced remarkable growth since the 1960s, moving from a single course offering to a diverse range of educational opportunities available at more than 1500 colleges and universities around the world (Charney and Libecap, 2000). Myles Mace at Harvard Business School taught the first entrepreneurship class in the United States in 1947 with a course about 'new enterprise' for veterans returning from the Second World War. The first major push towards entrepreneurship education, however, began in 1971 when the University of Southern California offered the first Masters in Business Administration, with a concentration in entrepreneurship (Katz, 2003). Since then, entrepreneurship education has become one of the fastest growing areas of study.

Compared with 16 colleges and universities teaching entrepreneurship in 1971, a recent estimate suggests that today, entrepreneurship and small business education may now be offered in as many as 2,400 post-secondary institutions in the United States alone (Solomon, Duffy and Tarabishy, 2002) with educational experiences ranging from traditional course work to integrative curricula that includes marketing, finance, new product development and technology (Charney and Libecap, 2000). What is more fascinating is that the growth of entrepreneurship education does not seem to be slowing down.

In 1985, 253 colleges or universities responding to the National Survey of Entrepreneurship Education offered courses in small business management or entrepreneurship, and in 1993, 441 responded that they in fact offered entrepreneurship courses to interested students (Gartner and Vesper, 1994). Fourteen years later, Foote (1999) reported student enrolment in entrepreneurship classes at five top American business schools increased 92 per cent from 1996 to 1999 (from a total of 3078 to 5913), and the number of entrepreneurship classes offered increased 74 per cent. The number of structured entrepreneurship programme offerings by U.S. colleges and universities increased fourfold in the last quarter of the twentieth century alone, which was further accelerated by both government interest and economic conditions (e.g. the dot-com boom and the economic downturns of the late 2000s). Clearly, entrepreneurship programmes have become an integral part of most educational institutions. Such extraordinary proliferation of entrepreneurship education programmes and courses is further reflected in the growing number of studies focusing on the 'revolution' or as Schumpeter (1934) observed 'creative destruction' that entrepreneurship education has introduced in academic institutions.

Nonetheless, the evolution from negligible to massive interest in entrepreneurship presents significant curricular and pedagogical challenges for administrators, professors and other instructors in high education institutions. In its purest form, 'entrepreneurship' is the art and science of creating a new venture and value for multiple stakeholders (e.g. customers, employees and communities). At the core of entrepreneurship is the identification and exploitation of opportunities (Shane and Venkataraman, 2000). Entrepreneurship is an ongoing process that requires a myriad of talents, skills and knowledge leading to unique pedagogies capable of stimulating and imparting knowledge simultaneously. If entrepreneurship education is to produce entrepreneurial founders capable of generating real enterprise growth and wealth, the challenge to educators will be to craft courses, programmes and major fields of study that meet the rigours of academia while keeping an action-oriented approach, integrated with a reality-based focus and entrepreneurial climate in the learning experience environment (Jones and English, 2004; Rideout and Gray, 2013; Solomon, 2007; Valerio, Parton and Robb, 2014).

The entrepreneurial experience can be characterised as being chaotic and ill-defined, and our entrepreneurship education pedagogies should reflect this characterisation. In addition, we often assume that it is relatively easy for entrepreneurship students to develop new ideas for their business start-ups. Many researchers have written about entrepreneurial competencies (e.g. Frese and Gielnik, 2014; Martin, McNally and Kay, 2013; Unger, Rauch and Rosenbusch, 2011). However, the competencies that are required for new business start-ups are often addressed by educators in an ad-hoc manner. There is little consensus on just what exactly entrepreneurship students should be taught. For entrepreneurship educators, the challenge is to provide the subject matter, resources and experiences that will prepare entrepreneurship students to cope with the myriad of expectations and demands they will face as they start their new ventures.

Next, we describe the way entrepreneurship education is being taught and the challenges the field faces. We begin by differentiating entrepreneurship education from business education, as well as making a distinction between small business courses and entrepreneurship courses, a distinction that is often overlooked.

Entrepreneurship education

Differentiating entrepreneurship education from business education

Despite the remarkable growth in entrepreneurship education since the 1970s, the field continues to evolve. As the field evolves, discussion continues regarding course content, the use of technology-driven pedagogy and outcome measures. Early discussions focused on the need for entrepreneurship education and questioned whether entrepreneurship courses were not simply traditional management courses with a new label (King, 2001). While there is general agreement that the core management courses offered in traditional business programmes are essential for success in any business career (Block and Stumpf, 1992), there are fundamental differences between business principles applied to new ventures and those applied to large corporations (Davis, Hills and LaForge, 1985).

First, unlike the functional 'specialist' focus of traditional business programmes such as accounting, finance or marketing, entrepreneurship education requires a 'generalist' approach that integrates and combines a variety of functional skills and knowledge (Block and Stumf, 1992; Hills, 1998). Second, entrepreneurship education is also differentiated by stage of development of the business. Compared with large firms, most new ventures fail within five years. Therefore, new ventures are differentiated in that they are temporary entities that aim to become established firms. In other words, start-ups, which as Steve Blank (2012) described are 'temporary organizations' looking for a scalable business model is a unique focus of entrepreneurship. Traditional business management education presents skills, knowledge and functional information that is required in large firms and assumes it is applicable to all stages of the venture development (McMullan and Long, 1987). Accordingly, entrepreneurship programmes and courses focus on the early lifecycle development challenges, particularly those related to new start-ups, such as opportunity recognition, business model canvas, market entry, protecting intellectual property, the legal requirements to set up a new entity and how to manage resource constraints (Solomon, Duffy and Tarabishy, 2002). It is no surprise then, that the majority of entrepreneurship courses are structured around these new venture developmental challenges (Edelman, Manolova and Brush, 2008; Solomon, 2007; Solomon *et al.*, 2002). Although new ventures are a unique area of study for entrepreneurship, entrepreneurship education is not constrained to new ventures and early stages, rather, different programmes, courses and topics can focus on different stages of development (Bae Qian, Miao and Fiet, 2014).

Based on these differences, a core objective of entrepreneurship education that differentiates it from typical business education is the challenge "to generate more quickly a greater variety of different ideas and approaches for how to exploit a business opportunity, and the ability to project a more extensive sequence of actions for entering business" (Vesper and McMullan, 1988, p. 9).

Business entry is a fundamentally different activity than managing a business (Gartner and Vesper, 1994); entrepreneurial education must address the equivocal nature of business entry (Gartner, Bird and Starr, 1992; Solomon, 2007). To this end, entrepreneurial education must include skill-building courses in negotiation, leadership, new product development, creative thinking and exposure to technological innovation (McMullan and Long, 1987; Vesper and McMullan, 1988). Other areas identified as important for entrepreneurial education include awareness of entrepreneurial career options (Hills, 1988; Donckels, 1991); sources of venture capital (Vesper and McMullan, 1988; Zeithaml and Rice, 1987); idea protection (Vesper and McMullan, 1988); ambiguity tolerance (Ronstadt, 1987); the characteristics that define the entrepreneurial personality (Hills, 1988; Hood and Young, 1993; Scott and Twomey, 1998) and the challenges associated with each stage of venture development (McMullan and Long, 1987; Plaschka and Welsch, 1990).

The integrated nature, specific skills and business life cycle issues inherent in new ventures differentiate entrepreneurship and therefore entrepreneurial education from a traditional business education. An additional comparison, within the context of entrepreneurial education, can be made between small business management courses and entrepreneurship courses – a distinction, as we mentioned earlier, which is often overlooked. We discuss this distinction, and then we discuss entrepreneurship education learning approaches, methodologies and impact.

Distinction between small business management courses from entrepreneurship courses

As mentioned earlier, both entrepreneurship and small business management focus on the total firm, rather than a specialised business course emphasising functional skills. Both courses provide a breadth of creative managerial skills and knowledge, and aim at providing students with the knowledge, skills and resources to: (1) generate a business concept; (2) determine its feasibility; (3) launch and operate a business; and (4) develop exit strategies (Solomon *et al.*, 2002). Nonetheless, there are also important conceptual differences between the two education types (Rideout and Gray, 2013 Solomon and Fernald, 1993; Winslow, Solomon and Tarabishy, 1999). Specifically, small business management focuses on achieving normal sales, profits and growth within an *existing*, yet young and small organisation. The traditional objective of small business management courses, then, is to provide students with the management knowledge related to managing and operating small, post-start-up companies including setting goals and objectives, leading, planning, organising and controlling a small business (Solomon, 2007; Solomon and Fernald, 1993). In contrast, entrepreneurship courses focus on originating (generating) an idea and developing a new growth venture with an emphasis on high profitability and rapid growth. In essence, entrepreneurship courses focus on generating the business concept, determining feasibility, launching a business, and having an exit strategy, while small business management focuses on continued development of an existing business concept, continued efforts to determine the feasibility of an existing business given changing market environments, how to operate a business and evolving the exit strategies (Solomon, 2007; Solomon and Fernald, 1993).

Entrepreneurship education learning approaches

Although entrepreneurship education courses have been a fixture of business school curricula for over 40 years, early educators in the field were often confronted with a thorny question: Can entrepreneurship be taught? The pertinence of this question was amplified even more given that the constructs studied by early entrepreneurship researchers were relatively stable, that is, a trait-based approach. However, Gartner's (1988) seminal article that defined entrepreneurship in terms of what entrepreneurs do, that is a behavioural approach, gave educators the ammunition needed to answer the question. Today, there is widespread consensus amongst educators that entrepreneurship can be taught (Kuratko, 2005). While entrepreneurship skills are difficult to train (Hills, 1988), just like leadership, people can learn entrepreneurship (Drucker, 1985).

In this upcoming section, we briefly review the theories of learning that underlie the development and course content of many entrepreneurship courses. As a relatively young field, many learning approaches used in entrepreneurship are drawn from more established fields such as psychology, organisational behaviour and adult education. Additionally, entrepreneurship courses often feature learning approaches seldom found in the more established academic disciplines. In entrepreneurship education, instructors address learning as a cognitive and a practical process, and seek to impact both implicit and explicit knowledge (Fayolle and Gailly, 2008).

The desire to impact implicit (cognitive) and explicit (practical) knowledge necessitates the use of a two-pronged approach, whereby instructors seek to educate students about what entrepreneurship is, and to provide students with the tools to become successful entrepreneurs (Mwasalwiba, 2010). An overview of the differences between these two aims is provided in Table 2.1. The first of these aims, focused on education and the imparting of knowledge, is met using the skills-based approach followed in many college courses and relies on traditional pedagogy. This aim, sometimes referred to as the 'Know What' (Williams Middleton and Donnellon, 2014), is best served by structured courses that utilise resources such as books, articles, lectures, case studies and assignments to develop the student's knowledge of entrepreneurship (Powell, 2013; Robinson and Josien, 2014). The second aim, focused on providing tangible experiences with the actions and day-to-day lives of entrepreneurs, is anchored in an attitude-based approach more specific to entrepreneurship that relies on andragogy. This need encompasses entrepreneurial 'Know How' and 'Know Why' (Williams Middleton and Donnellon, 2014), and is best served by incorporating uncertainty and real-life experiences into the course, and utilising resources such as business plan competitions, self-assessments, internships and field consulting projects to develop the student's skills as related to entrepreneurship (Powell, 2013; Robinson and Josien, 2014). The rest of this section delves deeper into this second, entrepreneurship-oriented need, as it is more closely related to the specific focus of this chapter (Haase and Lautenschläger, 2011).

Perhaps the most influential theory guiding the development and delivery of entrepreneurship-specific course content is experiential learning. According to this theory, learning is a "process whereby knowledge is created through the transformation of experience. Knowledge results from the combination of grasping and transforming experience" (Kolb, 1984, p. 41). Experiential learning

Table 2.1 Needs of entrepreneurship education

Need	Question addressed	Approach used to educate students	Resources used
Know What	What is entrepreneurship?	Primarily skills and knowledge-based	Books, articles, lectures, case studies and assignments
	What do entrepreneurs need to do?	Primarily attitude and experiential-based	Business plan competitions, self-assessments, internships and field consulting projects
Know How and Know Why	What is best way to accomplish these tasks?		

is especially powerful for entrepreneurship education because it brings together universal theories of human learning and andragogy. This approach to learning emphasises active learning that draws upon a student's own life experiences to tackle problems of interest to the student by exposing them to real-world problems and challenges. In a traditional learning approach, students receive knowledge from the instructor, that is, a unidirectional flow of information. In experiential learning, students discover knowledge by working on real-world problems, and learn by doing (Kozlinska, 2011). The role of the instructor in experiential learning is more akin to that of a coach or facilitator (Beard and Wilson, 2006; Maritz and Brown, 2013) – helping students critically examine, develop and expand their understanding of entrepreneurship (Robinson and Josien, 2014). Experiential learning helps educators address issues of 'Know-How' and 'Know-Why' that are harder to teach, but which have greater value for entrepreneurs, and is therefore highly suited for entrepreneurship education (Beard and Wilson, 2013; Haase and Lautenschläger, 2011).

Three inter-related methods that can be used to facilitate experiential learning are the lean start-up model, the business model canvas and the reverse or flipped classroom. The lean start-up model is based on research that shows that the knowledge, assumptions and context that characterise the start-up phases for most new companies differ dramatically from those they will encounter as the venture matures (Ries, 2011). Thus, traditional learning tools such as business plans are relatively less useful for entrepreneurship than a lean start-up model that emphasises the need for students to go out into the market and test the critical assumptions underlying their thinking about a business (Neck, Greene and Brush, 2014). Instead, under the lean start-up model, students are encouraged to use the business model canvas, which advocates that future entrepreneurs develop a minimum viable product and continually iterate their ideas and pivot as needed based on customer feedback (Leschke, 2013; Neck *et al.*, 2014). By de-emphasising the elaborate planning and detailed projections in favour of first-hand experience, the lean start-up and business model canvas give students the chance to gain first-hand knowledge of the entrepreneurial experience, which contribute to learning and the development of entrepreneurial self-efficacy. Last, in the reverse or flipped classroom model students review the course curriculum independently before they come to class by watching pre-recorded videos and/or reading cases and articles containing important information. The instructor then uses the classroom time to clarify and build upon core concepts, and to help students put into practice what they have already learned (Bergmann and Sams, 2012). Again, this model emphasises experience and 'learning by doing' to help students develop the requisite 'know-how' and 'know-why', rather than listen to a lecture from the instructor, and helps entrepreneurship education move from being teacher-centred to becoming student-centred (Robinson, Neergaard, Tanggaard and Krueger, 2016).

Besides experiential learning, entrepreneurship education is also characterised by a focus on competency development. Entrepreneurship competencies are the knowledge, skills, attitudes and values that influence an individual's desire and ability to work in entrepreneurship (Brophy and Kiely 2002; Rankin 2004). As illustrated in Table 2.2, these competencies fall into three broad categories: (1) Venture creation and management; (2) Skills such as persuasion, risk-taking, and networking; and (3) Development of entrepreneurial intentions and convictions (Haase and Lautenschläger, 2011). The first competency addresses issues related to starting and managing entrepreneurial ventures such as financing, legislation, staffing, etc. The second competency addresses topics not typically covered in business courses, but which have been shown to be important for entrepreneurial success (Gibb, 1996; Ronstadt, 1990). The last competency is more self-directed and aimed at motivating entrepreneurs to critically self-examine their own values and beliefs to foster entrepreneurial intent, which has been shown to be a significant predictor of future entrepreneurial action (Fayolle and Liñán, 2014).

Although experiential learning and competency-based learning approaches dominate most entrepreneurship education efforts, some newer approaches are also being explored. These include approaches derived from sensemaking theories, emotional and affective regulation theories, appreciative enquiry and equilibration (Cooperrider and Srivastava, 1987; Robinson and Josien, 2014; Williams Middleton and Donnellon, 2014), amongst others. Driven, in part, by the changing demographics of the workforce and the economic turbulence prevalent in the U.S. since the early 2000s, these approaches advocate a more holistic view of both entrepreneurship and entrepreneurs. Here, the emphasis is on developing self-learning, self-awareness, and the ability to learn from mistakes and experiences. By emphasising reflexive learning, these approaches are beginning to expand the scope of entrepreneurship education. Currently, these approaches are most prominent in the field of social entrepreneurship, but their visibility within the broader field of entrepreneurship education is growing (Robinson *et al.*, 2016; Williams Middleton and Donnellon, 2014).

Educational methodologies

To examine the current state of entrepreneurship education in the U.S., and answer the question of how entrepreneurship is being taught, we first need to identify and explain two key educational methodologies: course content and pedagogy, as well as explain our position of what we believe should be the impact of entrepreneurship education.

Table 2.2 Three competencies addressed in entrepreneurship education

Competency	Educator focus
Venture creation and management	Issues related to starting and managing entrepreneurial ventures such as financing, legislation and staffing
Entrepreneurial skills	Soft-skills such as persuasion, risk-taking and networking
Developing entrepreneurial intent	Influencing student cognitive style and human capital resources

Course content and pedagogy

Across the U.S. two- and four-year colleges and universities present many courses aimed at providing entrepreneurial skills and encouraging entrepreneurial behaviour. There is however little uniformity within these groups. This may be a function of an emerging field with a limited, but growing, body of knowledge. As researchers and scholars develop frameworks and sets of hypotheses for the study of emerging business successes and failures, the content of courses will evolve based on what is needed and can be taught for successful development (Block and Stumpf, 1992).

Per Ronstadt (1990), the programme focus of 'the old school' was on action, the business plan and exposure to experienced visitors who inspired students through stories and practical advice. This era of entrepreneurship education was 'one venture' centred and was essentially based on the premise that entrepreneurial success was a function of the 'right human traits and characteristics'. The new school, while still action oriented, builds, and relies on some level of personal, technical or industry experience. It requires critical thinking and ethical assessment and is based on the premise that successful entrepreneurial activities are a function of human, venture and environmental conditions. This newer form of entrepreneurship education also focuses on entrepreneurship as a career process composed of multiple new ventures and the essential skills of networking or 'entrepreneurial know-who' (Ronstadt, 1990).

Another view from McMullan, Long and Wilson (1985) calls for courses to be structured around a series of strategic development challenges including opportunity identification and feasibility analysis; new venture planning, financing and operating; new market development and expansion strategies; and institutionalising innovation. Real-time entrepreneurial activities include "projecting new technological developments, strategically planning, assisting in attracting necessary resources and arranging for joint ventures" (Vesper and McMullan, 1988: 10). Ideally, students should create multiple venture plans, practice identification of opportunities and have extensive exposure to entrepreneur role models. Student interaction with these role models may occur in several important ways including having entrepreneurs serve as coaches and mentors (Hills and Welsch, 1986; Mitchell and Chesteen, 1995); classroom speakers (Hills, 1988); and interview subjects (Hills, 1988; Solomon, Weaver and Fernald, 1994; Truell, Webster and Davidson, 1998). Effective entrepreneurial education requires students to have substantial hands-on experience working with community ventures so that they can learn to add value to real ventures and thus be prepared to add value to their own ventures (McMullan and Long, 1987).

In addition to course content, educators are challenged with designing effective learning opportunities for entrepreneurship students. Sexton and Bowman (1984) suggested that programmes for entrepreneurship students should emphasise individual activities over group activities, be relatively unstructured and present problems that require a "novel solution under conditions of ambiguity and risk" (p. 12). Students must be prepared to thrive in the "unstructured and uncertain nature of entrepreneurial environments" (Ronstadt, 1990, p. 72). Offering students opportunities to "experience" entrepreneurship and small business management is a theme among many entrepreneurial education programmes.

To determine how entrepreneurship programmes are commonly designed to ensure student's entrepreneurial success and identify the various resources and materials that faculty members provide to students, we examine the learning opportunities provided to students both outside and inside the class room.

The impact of entrepreneurship education

The goal of entrepreneurship education should be to improve the quality of entrepreneurs. That is, entrepreneurship education does not only aim to increase interest among students in entrepreneurship (e.g. Bae *et al.*, 2014; Matlay, 2008), but rather aims to provide students with the resources (skills, knowledge, abilities, experience, personalities) that increase their likelihood of succeeding when engaging in entrepreneurship (Martin *et al.*, 2013). In other words, the three core objectives of entrepreneurship should be to: (1) increase the awareness about the possibility of choosing entrepreneurship (i.e. starting a new venture) as a career choice (Bae *et al.*, 2014; Fayolle and Gailly, 2006); (2) promote the skills and qualities (e.g. risk-taking, creativity, proactivity) needed to succeed at entrepreneurship (Martin *et al.*, 2013; Oosterbeek, Van Praaq and Ijsselstein, 2010); (3) provide students with the technical and management skills needed to start, run and grow a new venture. As the field of entrepreneurship has expanded so has the education of entrepreneurship to provide other supplementary objectives such as new venture financing and legal issues related to new ventures.

As entrepreneurship education continues to develop it has become an effective mechanism to create more and better entrepreneurs. In general, studies (e.g. Bae *et al.*, 2014; Martin *et al.*, 2013) that have evaluated the outcomes of entrepreneurship education report that entrepreneurship education: (1) increases student's intentions to start a business, (2) is effective in providing students with the knowledge and skills that are relevant for success in entrepreneurship (e.g. knowledge of entrepreneurship process, competency in identifying opportunities and making decisions despite ambiguity), and (3) leads to higher entrepreneurship performance (actually starting a business, how long the business survives, financial performance and personal income gained from the business), compared with general education. Despite the effectiveness of entrepreneurship education in achieving its goals, the relationship between entrepreneurship education and outcomes is generally weak, indicating that there is substantial room for improvement.

Current state of U.S. entrepreneurship education and best practices

In this section, we review the state of entrepreneurship education in the U.S. by analysing the trends in the data as reported in the 2012 National Survey of Entrepreneurship Education (NSEE) conducted by George T. Solomon of George

Washington University. NSEE began in 1979 and is the oldest and one of the most frequently cited source of entrepreneurship education trends within the U.S. The 2012 survey was conducted in partnership with the United States Association for Small Business and Entrepreneurship (USASBE), which is the "largest independent, professional, academic organization in the world dedicated to advancing the discipline of entrepreneurship" (USASBE, 2017). The wide reach of USASBE's membership (currently over 1000 members) and its dedicated focus on entrepreneurship made it the ideal partner for this iteration of the survey. An invitation to participate in the 2012 NSEE was electronically distributed via the USASBE listserv to all its academic members at four-year colleges and universities across the U.S. The results presented in this chapter thus represent an educator's view of the state of entrepreneurship education in the U.S. today. We received 206 unique completed surveys from schools located in 41 different states. We examine the data and highlight key findings from the survey in five key areas: (1) course content; (2) pedagogy; (3) use of technology; (4) resources and offerings; and (5) how educational institutions measure the success of their entrepreneurship education. Table 2.3 summarises results of the most popular course content and pedagogy in entrepreneurship education based on the NSEE results.

Course content

Programme types

Entrepreneurship programmes at the college-level are primarily housed within business schools. Therefore, it is not surprising that the most popular choice of entrepreneurship programme amongst students continues to be a minor in entrepreneurship, often combined with a business major. However, two trends that are rapidly gaining momentum are entrepreneurship concentrations and majors. Due to the growing acceptance of entrepreneurship as a viable career option around the world, many more students are coming to the U.S. to study and learn from U.S. expertise, fuelling the demand for entrepreneurship majors. Additionally, the inclusion of entrepreneurship into the curricula of non-traditional sources such as schools of engineering, medicine and technology means more students are undertaking entrepreneurship concentrations within their field of study.

Courses offered

Within entrepreneurship education programmes, it is no surprise that the most popular course is simply titled 'Entrepreneurship'. The widespread use of this label has both good and not-so-good implications for entrepreneurship education. On the positive side, use of this broad label means that taking classes in entrepreneurship is quickly becoming – if it hasn't already – as ubiquitous for college students as taking classes in finance or marketing. This is a positive development, and further proof can be found in the variety of entrepreneurship-related courses offered by universities. The three most popular courses (after

Table 2.3 Results based on National Survey of Entrepreneurship Education (2012)

	Most popular	Second most popular	Third most popular	Fourth post popular	Fifth most popular
Programme types	Minor	Major/concentration	MBA with entrepreneurship certificate	Entrepreneurship MBA	Graduate entrepreneurship certificate
Student enrolment in programmes	Undergraduate major	Undergraduate minor	MBA	Master of Science	Undergraduate certification
Courses offered	Entrepreneurship	Business planning	Entrepreneurial finance	New venture creation	Innovation
Student enrolment in courses	Technology	Entrepreneurship	Venture capital	Business planning	Creativity
Courses in small business management	Management	Marketing	Legality	Strategy and growth	Financing
Courses in entrepreneurship	Psychological traits and start-up characteristics	Financing	Management	Marketing	Strategy and growth
Teaching pedagogies used inside classrooms	Discussions	Creation of business plans	In-class exercises	Lectures from small business owners and guest speakers	Case studies
Programmes used outside the classroom	Business plan competitions	Entrepreneurship clubs	Distinguished speaker series (lectures by guest speakers)	Elevator pitch competitions	Incubators
Teaching pedagogies used inside classroom	Discussions	In-class exercise	Creation of business plans	Lecture by small business owners	Case studies

entrepreneurship) are: business planning; entrepreneurial financing; and new venture creation. Perhaps less positive is that the use of a broad label such as entrepreneurship often obscures the fact that many of these courses either address issues more central to small business management than entrepreneurship, or broad business issues that are just as likely to reflect the concerns of managers as they are of entrepreneurs. This is evident as in addition to the top-five data presented in Table 2.3, the rest of the top-ten most popular courses (excluding 'Other') are: innovation, creativity, small business consulting and small business management.

Another trend we want to highlight is the growth in social entrepreneurship related courses. In the early 2000s, the concept of 'social' entrepreneurship did not even feature in Solomon *et al.*'s (2002) survey of U.S. entrepreneurship education. A watershed moment for this category of courses might be the worldwide recession that began in the U.S. in 2008. In fact, although social entrepreneurship courses have been around since 1978, a major growth in the number of programmes offering courses on this topic only began in 2009. Today, based on results of surveys collected from the National Survey of Entrepreneurship Education since 1971, social entrepreneurship related courses and topics represent the fastest growing category of educational offerings to students of entrepreneurship, and the interest in this topic has led to a rapid increase in the number of programmes offering social entrepreneurship as a separate programme.

Topics covered

To delve deeper into the curriculum of entrepreneurship education across the country, respondents were asked to provide information regarding the various subjects covered in their curriculum. The most popular topics in small business management courses (in order) were: management, marketing, legality (tied on third with), strategy and growth. In contrast, the most popular topics covered in entrepreneurship courses (in order) were: entrepreneur's psychological traits and start-up characteristics, financing, management. One positive sign is that there does not seem to be much overlap between the courses, suggesting that students can benefit by taking both courses. Surprisingly though, we find that sustainability is the least covered topic in both courses. Given the findings that most businesses fail after five years, a greater focus on the topic of sustainability is needed.

Student enrolment

Enrolment in entrepreneurship courses has steadily increased (Rideout and Gray, 2013; Solomon *et al.*, 2005). Regarding courses and topics, the largest enrolments, not surprisingly, were found in general entrepreneurship courses. As noted earlier, these courses are often introductory-level seminars offered to or required of all students (similar to an introductory finance course). Thus, it is not surprising that the average enrolment in these courses is high, and is accompanied by a lower number of sections being offered each semester. Besides this broad topic, most other courses averaged between 20 and 30 students, per section. The fact that courses as varied as business planning, entrepreneurial financing, franchising, entrepreneurial marketing and new product development are attracting robust numbers of students speaks to entrepreneurship's growing popularity.

Pedagogical approaches

Most popular pedagogical methods used inside the classroom

In terms of the frequency in which faculty use various teaching pedagogies inside their entrepreneurship courses, the five most frequently used in-class pedagogies include: discussions, creation of business plans, in-class exercise, lectures from small business owners and guest speakers, and case studies. In comparison, Twitter, blogging, computer simulations, counselling programmes, and small business institutes were cited as the least frequently used in-class pedagogies. Our results thus complement the conclusions of other researchers (Haase and Lautenschlager, 2011; Sirelkhatim and Gangi, 2015; Solomon and Matthews, 2014) who concluded that the use of technological advancements and innovative pedagogies represent an important way in which to enhance entrepreneurship education in the future.

Project based, experiential learning is widespread in entrepreneurial education and may take myriad forms such as the development of business plans (Gartner and Vesper, 1994; Gorman, Hanlon and King, 1997; Hills, 1988; Vesper and McMullan, 1988); student business start-ups (Hills, 1988; Truell *et al.*,1998); consultation with practising entrepreneurs (Klatt, 1988; Solomon *et al.*, 1994); computer simulations (Brawer, 1997); and behavioural simulations (Stumpf, Dunbar and Mullen, 1991). Other popular activities include interviews with entrepreneurs (Solomon *et al.*, 1994), environmental scans (Solomon *et al.*, 1994), 'live' cases (Gartner and Vesper, 1994), field trips and the use of video and films (Klatt, 1988). Nonetheless, out of these experiential learning methods, the creation of business plans and behaviour simulations seem to be more popular than other forms such as consulting projects, computer simulations, 'live cases' and the use of videos and film. Therefore, the use of more 'live' and actual experiences such as working with actual small business owners and entrepreneurs represent an important area of future growth for entrepreneurship education. Overall, while the use of experiential learning seems to be increasing, there is still much room for improvement.

Most popular academic journals and periodicals used inside the classroom

In addition, we examined the survey results with regard to the most popular academic and periodicals used in the classroom to help shed light on where faculty and educators get information that they present to students. Based on our survey results, the most popular teaching methods include textbooks (64 per cent), websites (26 per cent), reading books (20 per cent), and assigning sets of readings and text materials (19 per cent). Specifically, the most frequently used periodicals include *Entrepreneur, Inc.*, and *Fast Company*. This highlights that the growth of specialised periodicals is effectively being used to supplement traditional teaching methods such as textbooks. Additionally, in terms of the most frequently used academic journals, educators cited *Entrepreneurship Theory & Practice, Journal of Small Business Management* and *Journal of Business Venturing* as the most widely used. Overall, however, periodicals were used more frequently compared with academic journals. The findings suggest that educators may use periodicals as an effective method to keep up with the latest evolutions in terms of new companies and new ideas.

Most popular pedagogical methods used outside the classroom

The most common programmes outside the classroom include business plan competitions, entrepreneurship clubs, distinguished speaker series (lectures by guest speakers) and elevator pitch competitions. Given the importance of business plan competitions, it is important to measure how many schools participated in competitions versus those who hosted. From a sample of 206, 53 per cent of respondents indicated that they participated in other business plan competition, compared with only 38 per cent indicating that they hosted a competition at their school. Additionally, the majority of institutions offered internship opportunities, yet relatively few offered executive development courses, continuing education or online learning. Given the growth and success of these pedagogical methods within business schools in general (Friga, Bettis and Sullivan, 2003), this suggests that these are potential areas growth for entrepreneurship education in the future.

Technology

Many entrepreneurship educators indicated that they used web-based assignments and posting information regarding entrepreneurship and new venture creation online. Surprisingly though, out of 206 academic educators, only 33 per cent indicated that they use online resources to provide students with management and technical assistance, and only 27 per cent indicated that they offered entrepreneurship courses online. Given the conflux of growing global demand for entrepreneurship education, rapidly evolving technology, increases in online education within business schools, and the comparative lack of the use of such advances in entrepreneurship education (Arbaugh, Desai, Rau and Sridhar, 2010; Friga *et al.*, 2003; Haase and Lautenschlager, 2011; Lima, Lopes, Nassif and da Silva, 2015), it seems inevitable that we will see greater and greater adoption of technology and online resources in entrepreneurship education.

Additionally, in terms of technology we highlight a rather significant mismatch between student demand and course offerings in technology. Specifically, as shown in Table 2.3, technology had the highest student demand in terms of student enrolment, yet it ranked in the bottom five least offered courses in entrepreneurship education. As we elaborate in the discussion section of this chapter, entrepreneurship education should evolve to incorporate more learning on technology in the classroom, including how students can start a technology based company as well as how students can leverage technology to start their business in any other field.

Resources

To teach entrepreneurship effectively, institutions need to have resources that help support entrepreneurship education. Accordingly, we examine the state of resources entrepreneurship education institutions in the U.S. have in terms of three metrics: the average number of entrepreneurship professors per institutions, the additional activities and resources available to students that support entrepreneurship education, and the most common source of funding (e.g. endowment/chairs) to support entrepreneurship education.

On average, out of the 206 academic institutions surveyed, there are five full-time faculty teaching entrepreneurship per entrepreneurship programme and three part-time faculty. Additionally, entrepreneurship programmes seem to make great use of others such as community partners, contract positions, co-op teachers, doctoral students, entrepreneurs-in residence and faculty from other departments to teach entrepreneurship. In fact, compared with full and part-time faculty, the average institution uses six 'Other' faculty members to teach entrepreneurship. In other words, entrepreneurship education is certainly not confined to those with doctoral degrees focusing on entrepreneurship. The use of different faculty helps broaden the perspectives and topics that could be taught, and helps bring both theoretical and practical insights into the classroom.

The use of additional programmes within the entrepreneurship programme is also a key resource to help support teaching entrepreneurship. Specifically, the most common programmes within entrepreneurship include, based on the responses from 206 educators working in 206 unique institutions: entrepreneurship centres/institutions (57 per cent of academic institutions), entrepreneurs-in-residence positions (30 per cent), endowed chairs of entrepreneurship (26 per cent), and small business development centres (26 per cent). These programmes help support entrepreneurship education in several ways. For example, entrepreneurs in residence can help provide mentorship to students, serve as guest speakers, as well as teach some courses in entrepreneurship. Similarly, entrepreneurship centres help expand the university budget by serving as a revenue stream through which donations, endowments, grants and the commercialisation of technology flow (Finkle, Kuratko and Goldsby, 2006). Other initiatives being adapted throughout colleges and universities include incubators, family business centres and fellows programmes. Most of these programmes are housed within existing departments (management, followed by business), and they are least likely to be housed within the department of small business or entrepreneurship.

These data show the growing trend towards integrating entrepreneurship across various disciplines within a university, and lend support to the conclusion that such multi-disciplinary programmes will continue to grow in the future (Duval-Couetil, 2013; Rideout and Gray, 2013; Solomon and Matthews, 2014).

To fund courses, programmes, and research initiatives, entrepreneurship programmes (like other programmes) need to have the money to do so. Survey respondents indicated that entrepreneurship funding comes from alumni (29%), followed by non-alumni entrepreneurs (20%), the federal government (14%), the Coleman and Kauffman foundations for entrepreneurship (9% and 3% respectively), and the rest from private donors or foundations, public agencies, other university divisions or individuals and grants. The fact that non-alumni entrepreneurs are the second most common source of entrepreneurship education funding suggests that entrepreneurship programmes have a wide pool to tap into for support. Although entrepreneurs are often busy managing their own businesses, greater collaboration between entrepreneurship programmes and real-life entrepreneurs (in terms of guest lectures, mentoring, or funding) is a great resource available for entrepreneurship education programmes to help support their education goals.

Impact of entrepreneurship education

To assess the overall entrepreneurship education industry, we also asked survey respondents to provide insight on how they viewed the future of entrepreneurship education (predicted trends in entrepreneurship education) and where they believed their school fit into this ecosystem (distinguishing programme features). We received 88 responses from educators regarding how they felt their programme distinguished them from other entrepreneurship programmes. The three most common categories that educators felt distinguished their entrepreneurship programmes from other schools were: experiential learning (32%, or 28 out of 88 respondents), interdisciplinary programmes (15% of respondents), and providing students with a network of mentors and programme partners as a resource to help them (13%). The fact that entrepreneurship education programmes view networks as a valuable resource further confirms the idea that maintaining connections with alumni is essential for effective entrepreneurship programmes as they offer funding, expertise, and other resources to students. Unfortunately, data suggests that the majority of institutions do not put a focus on maintaining connections with alumni, with only 43% of respondents indicating that they keep in touch with alumni who have started their own business.

We also asked educators to identify if their institution employed or used any metrics to measure the success of their entrepreneurship education programmes. We received 89 responses. The most popular metrics reported were: number of businesses started during and after the programme (21 respondents, 24%), student course evaluations (13 respondents, 15%), number of participants in programmes and events held within the school (11 respondents, 12%), and number of students enrolled in the course or programme (10 respondents, 11%).

Future directions

Based on survey results from 176 educators the top expected future trends within entrepreneurship education, are: (1) Social entrepreneurship (20% of 176 respondents), (2) Experiential learning (13%), (3) Interdisciplinary programmes (10%), and (4) International considerations (6%). We comment on these issues below. The use of business model canvas and lean-start up methodology was also cited as a future trend, but we refrain from commenting further on these issues as others have extensively covered these topics.

Social entrepreneurship

Social entrepreneurship is playing a bigger role in venture success, with many millennials giving increased attention and value to the social causes behind businesses (Godfrey, 2015). Michael Porter called for a radical transformation in which business schools teach shared value creation across the value chain of a business (Driver, 2012). Strategies such as integrating social entrepreneurship topics across curricula, teaching cases in different courses that emphasise social entrepreneurship, and making greater use of social entrepreneurs as guest speakers can help universities meet these demands (Driver, 2012; Tracey and Phillips, 2007). Accordingly, Porter suggests that in the future, social entrepreneurship will be a broad foundation in business education rather than a specialised field (Driver, 2012).

Moreover, while social entrepreneurship share many similarities with traditional entrepreneurship focused on new venture creation and growth, it differs in its greater purpose of providing benefits to society (Blenker, Korsgaard, Neergaard and Thrane, 2011; Tracey and Phillips, 2007). Specifically, social entrepreneurship is concerned with generating income in the pursuit of social outcomes (Tracey and Phillips, 2007). Thus, the tools (e.g. donations, grants, volunteers), resources, and motivations of social entrepreneurs are different (Blenker *et al.*, 2011). For example, social entrepreneurs require a stronger emphasis on networking to develop relationships with the societies it seeks to influence (Blenker *et al.*, 2011; Tracey and Phillips, 2007). Similarly, social entrepreneurs have the challenge of managing both the level of social impact and the financial performance, which adds to the challenge of handling the dual identity of the venture (Tracey and Phillips, 2007). Herein, the challenge for future entrepreneurship education is to develop creative ways in which to help students come with ideas that serve the dual purpose of venture growth and providing greater societal value.

Experiential learning

With regard to pedagogical theories, the two dominant approaches (experiential learning and competency-based), have proven their effectiveness (Haase and Lautenschläger, 2011; Robinson and Josien, 2014). Entrepreneurship educators are increasingly using the lean-start up methodology to encourage students to 'get out of the building' and talk to potential customers. The value of lean start-up methodology lies in its ability to force students to experience starting a business and talking to customers to test their ideas and pivot (i.e. refine their ideas) based on customer feedback. Nonetheless, educators still debate on the best ways to implement the start-up methodology. Based on the results of our study, we suggest that educators emphasise the process rather than the final product. We believe that as promoters of entrepreneurs, we need to encourage students to experience the process of starting a business, and focus less on the quality of the product. This is not to argue that quality is irrelevant, but to accept that in reality many students with start-up ideas need experience to develop their ideas into high quality businesses. By focusing on the process, rather than the product, we as educators can provide students with the value of acquiring the tools and knowledge of starting a business that they can later apply to other business ideas. One way to emphasise the process, rather than the product, of start-up methodology is to leverage the use of technology by encouraging students to take pictures, record interviews, and use social media to post their questions and then submit these materials – perhaps in the form of a portfolio – as the final project, as well as requiring students to articulate what they learned during the process.

Another valuable tool to encourage competency based and experiential learning is to collaborate with entrepreneurship institutions outside of the university and within different universities. As Winkel (2013) noted, an important next step in entrepreneurship education is to move from traditional single-instructor models located within a classroom to a community of scholars and practitioners testing and practicing concepts in society. Programmes such as start-up weekends or regional school competitions provide great value by allowing students to network with others outside their university, as well as bring in a broader audience and attention to the great work many entrepreneurship institutions are currently doing. For example, Startup Weekend[3] is a U.S. not-for-profit community-based organization that provides resources to volunteers to help organise local events which bring together entrepreneurs, people interested in working in start-ups, investors, and mentors. Over a 54-hour period, entrepreneur's network, pitch their ideas to the audience, recruit team members, meet with mentors, develop their idea, and finally present to a panel of judges. Having students participate in such events as part of their entrepreneurship course can thus provide them with relevant and useful experiential learning opportunities.

Interdisciplinary programmes

Pedagogy is also changing based on a broadening market interest in entrepreneurial education. New interdisciplinary programmes use faculty teams to develop programmes for non-business students, and there is a growing trend in courses specifically designed for art, engineering and science students. Non-business students may require basic technology laboratories that focus on internet-based feasibility research, developing effective audio visual pitch presentations and creating professionally-formatted business plans. In addition to courses focused on preparing the future entrepreneur and small business manager, instructional methodologies should also be developed for those who manage entrepreneurs in organizations; potential resource people (accountants, lawyers, consultants, etc.) used by entrepreneurs; and top managers who must provide vision and leadership for corporations which must innovate in order to survive (Block and Stumpf, 1992).

International considerations

U.S.-based entrepreneurship education remains underdeveloped with regard to an international focus. While this is not surprising given the breadth of opportunities available within the U.S., the fact that less than a third of entrepreneurship education programmes have partnerships with programmes in other countries represents an untapped opportunity. Given the increasingly international nature of business, partnerships with programmes in other countries that can offer externships or practicum opportunities, as well as exposure to a different market are exciting areas that can be leveraged to further the impact of entrepreneurship education. In addition, many business schools and researchers within those schools already have close ties to their international counterparts, thereby lowering the barriers to such partnerships.

Theoretical perspectives

In addition to the need to incorporate different ontological and epistemological approaches, entrepreneurship education would also benefit from incorporating hitherto underused theoretical perspectives. We highlight two such perspectives that we feel are particularly promising: sensemaking and emotional regulation. Sensemaking is a socially-driven process where an individual retrospectively evaluates discrepancies and environmental cues to create their own understanding of their situation (Weick, 1995). Since entrepreneurs often work in disruptive and chaotic environments, needing to make critical decisions with limited information, sensemaking is an important tool for an entrepreneur. Accordingly, it is also a tool that will be of use to future entrepreneurs in college courses (Williams Middleton and Donnellon, 2014). By helping students understand their own processes of sensemaking, educators can better prepare them for the inevitable challenges that lie ahead.

The other theoretical area is emotional regulation. Emotional regulation is "the processes by which individuals influence which emotions they have, when they have them, and how they experience and express these emotions" (Gross, 1998, p. 275). Entrepreneurship is an intensely emotional process (Baron and Tang, 2011), and increasingly researchers are adopting emotional regulation approaches to understand how emotions affect entrepreneurial processes and outcomes. However, entrepreneurship education has still to fully embrace this approach. While traditional entrepreneurship education has focused mostly on cognitive effects, combining affective components into an experiential learning approach holds much promise for entrepreneurship educators, trainers and professional consultants in the field (Robinson and Josien, 2014).

Need for greater use of technology

In addition to these future trends, entrepreneurship education can improve by greater adoption of online technology. Although the use of technology has increased in terms of the use of social media and web-based activities, the field can still improve in terms of offering online courses to reach a broader audience. For example, computer simulations provide entrepreneurial students "with multiple experiences of simulated new venture decision-making" (Van Clouse, 1990, p. 51). The use of computer simulations described by Brewer *et al.* (1993) affords students realistic entrepreneurship experiences that develop skills in complex decision-making and offer instant feedback. One particularly interesting area for future entrepreneurship programmes is their ability to provide experiential learning in an online form. We believe that those programmes who are leaders and innovators in this new trajectory will have great impact in entrepreneurship education.

The greater adoption of technology can be tied in with the need for more interdisciplinary programmes in the future, as indicated by entrepreneurship educators. For example, many of the technologies and innovations come from outside the school of business, such as the art or engineering departments. Similarly, Public Health Schools are turning to entrepreneurial activities to create innovative solutions to the rising concerns over health care in the United States. Overall, integrating different schools into the entrepreneurship programme provides greater exposure to the students joining entrepreneurship programmes, allowing for guest speaker discussion with practicing entrepreneurs that are experts in the field in technology, as well as providing more experiential and hands on experience for students by allowing them to work outside their primary area of discipline and be a part of a team with diverse backgrounds (Duval-Couetil, 2013; Rideout and Gray, 2013; Solomon and Matthews, 2014).

Student resources

Ten years ago, entrepreneurship education was primarily driven by three resources: case discussions, business plan competitions and talks by guest speakers (Solomon *et al.*, 2002). In the intervening years since then, resources available for students have mushroomed. While business plan competitions are still de rigueur in many schools, colleges are moving swiftly to provide students with resources such as entrepreneurship clubs, hatcheries/incubators and campus-based business offices that not only help them learn, but which can also partner in student ventures. In addition, resources such as internships/practicums, feasibility studies, computer simulations and blogs provide students with more ways in which to engage with entrepreneurship education. However, even today, the tried-and-true methods (e.g. case studies) dominate the landscape of educational resources. While such methods can be very effective in helping students understand the basics of entrepreneurship, the dichotomy between the orderly world of case studies and classroom discussions, and the frenzied, unpredictable world of entrepreneurial businesses may account, in part, for why some studies fail to find significant outcomes as a result of entrepreneurship education. Incorporating real-time advice and helping students navigate the tricky world of entrepreneurship through resources such as blogs and incubators helps better prepare students for entrepreneurial success (Gendron, 2004). We expect this trend of incorporating innovative resources into entrepreneurship education to continue, and in fact, accelerate in the years to come.

Conclusion

To further enhance the field of entrepreneurship education it would be helpful to: (1) generate greater dialogue between the schools on the most effective and innovative methods they have adopted, either through blogs or more traditional face-to-face conferences; and (2) increase flexibility in teaching entrepreneurship by being more responsive to the new trends in both research and periodicals. For example, despite the findings in research that most new business is started by teams rather than individuals, or that entrepreneurs do not have a certain personality style, these findings are not reflected in teaching entrepreneurship. Specifically, we did not find that research taught students on how to build effective teams, and we continue to see a dominant focus on teaching the topic of entrepreneur's personality. Similarly, the rise in technology and its importance in the business world have not been reflected in our entrepreneurship education, despite the high demand for such topics from students. Entrepreneurship educators should be aware of the changing trends of the world and leverage different resources and experts to provide students the opportunity to learn about these trends in the classroom.

Despite these challenges, entrepreneurship education has evolved considerably since the first National Survey of Entrepreneurship Education. In the first survey, only eight entrepreneurship-related course options were available to college students, with only classes on small business management, introduction to entrepreneurship and new venture creation being offered by more than 10 per cent of the programmes. Today, that number has doubled, with 16 courses offered by more than 10 per cent of colleges, and three other courses rapidly approaching that benchmark. We fully expect this trend to continue. As entrepreneurship education matures and expands, we expect growth both in related courses such as social entrepreneurship, as well as the adoption of entrepreneurship pedagogical approaches in other areas such as engineering, medicine and the arts. In fact, given the wide applicability of the entrepreneurship competencies taught in many programmes, we believe these tangential offerings have the potential to outstrip growth from traditional entrepreneurship-related courses. We hope that greater collaboration between entrepreneurship educators and with others outside entrepreneurship education will bring further advancement to the

46 *G. Solomon* et al.

field of entrepreneurship education. Finally, with the maturation of the field of entrepreneurship education, the time has come to move beyond unidimensional measures of the field. Future research in this area that adopts a triangulation approach and compares perspectives on entrepreneurship from various stakeholder groups (e.g. students, businesses, governments and academics) holds great promise in helping move this field forward.

Notes

1 Entrepreneurship clubs refers to student-led clubs or societies formed under the aegis of the institution (often under the mentorship of a faculty member) that bring together students interested in entrepreneurship from across the university (Pittaway, Rodriguez-Falcon, Aiyegbayo and King, 2011).
2 Hatcheries/incubators and campus-based business offices are for-profit institution based and sponsored offices that provide support in the form of infrastructure, mentoring, training and sometimes even finance to current students as well as alumni to help them develop and implement new venture ideas, in return for an ownership or investment stake in the business (Bager, 2011; Culkin, 2013).
3 https://startupweekend.org.

References

Aldrich, H. (1999). *Organizations Evolving.* Sage: Thousand Oaks, CA.
Amezcua, A.S., Grimes, M.G., Bradley, S.W. and Wiklund, J. (2013). Organizational sponsorship and founding environments: A contingency view on the survival of business-incubated firms, 1994–2007. *Academy of Management Journal,* 56, 1628–1654.
Arbaugh, J.B., Desai, A., Rau, B. and Sridhar, B.S. (2010). A review of research on online and blended learning in the management disciplines: 1994–2009. *Organization Management Journal,* 7, 39–55.
Bae, T.J., Qian, S., Miao, C. and Fiet, J.O. (2014). The relationship between entrepreneurship education and entrepreneurial intentions: A meta-analytic review. *Entrepreneurship Theory and Practice,* 38(2), 217–254.
Bager, T. (2011). Entrepreneurship education and new venture creation: A comprehensive approach. In K. Hindle and K. Klyver, eds. *Handbook of Research on New Venture Creation.* Cheltenham, UK: Edward Elgar Publishing, pp. 299–315.
Baron, R.A. and Tang, J. (2011). The role of entrepreneurs in firm-level innovation: Joint effects of positive affect, creativity, and environmental dynamism. *Journal of Business Venturing,* 26, 49–60.
Beard, C.M. and Wilson, J.P. (2006). *Experiential learning: A best practice handbook for educators and trainers.* London: Kogan Page Publishers.
Beard, C. and Wilson, J. P. (2013). *Experiential learning: A handbook for education, training and coaching.* London: Kogan Page Publishers.
Bergmann, J. and Sams, A. (2012). Flip your classroom: Reach every student in every class every day. Washington, DC: International Society for Technology in Education.
Blank, S. and Dorf, B. (2012). The startup owner's manual Vol. 1: The step-by-step guide for building a great company. California: K&S Ranch, Inc.
Blenker, P., Korsgaard, S., Neergaard, H. and Thrane, C. (2011). The questions we care about: Paradigms and progression in entrepreneurship education. *Industry and Higher Education,* 25, 417–427.

Block, Z. and Stumpf, S.A. (1992). Entrepreneurship education research: Experience and challenge. In D.L. Sexton and J.D. Kasarda, eds. *The state of the art of entrepreneurship.* Boston, MA: PWS-Kent Publishing, pp. 17–45.

Brawer, F.B. (1997). Simulation as a vehicle in entrepreneurship education. *ERIC Digest,* 97, 433–469.

Brewer, B., Anyansi-Archibong, C. and Ugboro, I.O. (1993). *Using computer simulation technology in entrepreneurship and small business education.* Proceedings of the International Council for Small Business, Las Vegas, NV, 217–229.

Brophy, M. and Kiely, T. (2002). Competencies: A new sector. *Journal of European Industrial Training,* 26, 165–176.

Charney, A. and Libecap, G.D. (2000). *Impact of entrepreneurship education.* Kansas City, MO: Kauffman Center for Entrepreneurial Leadership.

Cooperrider, D.L. and Srivastava, S. (1987). Appreciative inquiry in organizational life. *Research in organizational change and development: An annual series featuring advances in theory, methodology and research,* 1, 129–169.

Culkin, N. (2013). Beyond being a student: An exploration of student and graduate start-ups (SGSUs) operating from university incubators. *Journal of Small Business and Enterprise Development,* 20, 634–649.

Davis, C., Hills, G.E. and LaForge, R.W. (1985). The marketing/small enterprise paradox: A research agenda. *International Small Business Journal,* 3, 31–42.

Donckels, R. (1991). Education and entrepreneurship experiences from secondary and university education in Belgium. *Journal of Small Business and Entrepreneurship,* 9, 35–42.

Driver, M. (2012). An interview with Michael Porter: Social entrepreneurship and the transformation of capitalism. *Academy of Management Learning & Education,* 11(3), 421–431.

Drucker, P.F. (1985). *Innovation and entrepreneurship practices and principles.* New York: Harper & Row.

Duval-Couetil, N. (2013). Assessing the impact of entrepreneurship education programs: Challenges and approaches. *Journal of Small Business Management,* 51, 394–409.

Edelman, L.F., Manolova, T.S. and Brush, C.G. (2008). Entrepreneurship education: Correspondence between practices of nascent entrepreneurs and textbook prescriptions for success. *Academy of Management Learning & Education,* 7(1), 56–70.

Fayolle, A. and Gailly, B. (2008). From craft to science: Teaching models and learning processes in entrepreneurship education. *Journal of European Industrial Training,* 32, 569–593.

Fayolle, A. and Liñán, F. (2014). The future of research on entrepreneurial intentions. *Journal of Business Research,* 67, 663–666.

Fayolle, A., Gailly, B. and Lassas-Clerc, N. (2006). Assessing the impact of entrepreneurship education programmes: A new methodology. *Journal of European industrial training,* 30, 701–720.

Finkle, T.A., Kuratko, D.F. and Goldsby, M.G. (2006). An examination of entrepreneurship centers in the United States: A national survey. *Journal of Small Business Management,* 44, 184–206.

Foote, D. (19 April 1999). Show us the money! *Newsweek,* 43–44.

Frese, M. and Gielnik, M.M. (2014). The psychology of entrepreneurship. *Annual Review of Organizational Psychology and Organizational Behavior,* 1, 413–438.

Friga, P.N., Bettis, R.A. and Sullivan, R.S. (2003). Changes in graduate management education and new business school strategies for the 21st century. *Academy of Management Learning & Education,* 2, 233–249.

Gartner, W.B. (1988). "Who is an entrepreneur" is the wrong question. *American Journal of Small Business,* 12, 11–32.

Gartner, W.B. and Vesper, K.H. (1994). Experiments in entrepreneurship education: Successes and failures. *Journal of Business Venturing,* 9, 179–187.

Gartner, W.B., Bird, B.J. and Starr, J.A. (1992). Acting as if: Differentiating entrepreneurial from organizational behavior. *Entrepreneurship Theory & Practice,* 16, 13–32.

Gendron, G. (2004). Practitioners' perspectives on entrepreneurship education: An interview with Steve Case, Matt Goldman, Tom Golisano, Geraldine Laybourne, Jeff Taylor, and Alan Webber. *Academy of Management Learning & Education,* 3, 302–314.

Gibb, A.A. (1996). Entrepreneurship and small business management: Can we afford to neglect them in the twenty-first century business school? *British Journal of Management,* 7, 309–321.

Godfrey, N. (August 2015). Business not as usual: The millenial social entrepreneur. *Forbes.* Retrieved from: *www.forbes.com/forbes/welcome/?toURL=www.forbes.com/sites/neale godfrey/2015/08/23/business-not-as-usual-the-millennial-social-entrepreneur/.*

Gorman, G., Hanlon, D. and King, W. (1997). Some research perspectives on entrepreneurship education, enterprise education, and education for small business management: A ten-year literature review. *International Small Business Journal,* 15, 56–77.

Gross, J.J. (1998). The emerging field of emotion regulation: An integrative review. *Review of General Psychology,* 2, 271–299.

Haase, H. and Lautenschläger, A. (2011). The 'teachability dilemma' of entrepreneurship. *International Entrepreneurship and Management Journal,* 7, 145–162.

Hills, G.E. (1988). Variations in university entrepreneurship education: An empirical study of an evolving field. *Journal of Business Venturing,* 3, 109–122.

Hills, G.E. and Welsch, H.P. (1986). Entrepreneurship behavioral intentions and student independence characteristics and experiences. In R. Ronstadt, J.A. Hornaday, R. Peterson and K.H. Vesper, eds. *Frontiers of entrepreneurship research.* Wellesley, MA: Babson College, pp. 73–186.

Hood, J.N. and Young, J.E. (1993). Entrepreneurship's requisite areas of development: A survey of top executives in successful entrepreneurial firms. *Journal of Business Venturing,* 8, 115–135.

Jones, C. and English, J. (2004). A contemporary approach to entrepreneurship education. *Education + training,* 46(8/9), 416–423.

Katz, J.A. (2003). The chronology and intellectual trajectory of American entrepreneurship education: 1876–1999. *Journal of Business Venturing,* 18, 283–300.

King, S.W. (2001). Entrepreneurship education: What the customer values. In: *Proceedings of the 46th International Council for Small Business, Taipei, Taiwan.*

Klatt, L.A. (1988). A study of small business/entrepreneurial education in colleges and universities. *Journal of Private Enterprise,* 4, 103–108.

Kolb, D. (1984). *Experiential Learning.* Englewood Cliffs. NJ: Prentice-Hall.

Kozlinska, I. (2011). Contemporary approaches to entrepreneurship education. *Journal of Business Management,* 4, 205–220.

Kuratko, D.F. (2005). The emergence of entrepreneurship education: Development, trends, and challenges. *Entrepreneurship Theory & Practice,* 29, 577–598.

Leschke, J. (2013). Business model mapping: Application and experience in an introduction to entrepreneurship course. *Journal of Entrepreneurship Education,* 16, 77–92.

Lima, E., Lopes, R.M., Nassif, V. and Silva, D. (2015). Opportunities to improve entrepreneurship education: Contributions considering Brazilian challenges. *Journal of Small Business Management,* 53, 1033–1051.

Maritz, A. and Brown, C.R. (2013). Illuminating the black box of entrepreneurship education programs. *Education+ Training*, 55, 234–252.

Martin, B.C., McNally, J.J. and Kay, M.J. (2013). Examining the formation of human capital in entrepreneurship: A meta-analysis of entrepreneurship education outcomes. *Journal of Business Venturing*, 28, 211–224.

Matlay, H. (2008). The impact of entrepreneurship education on entrepreneurial outcomes. *Journal of Small Business and Enterprise Development* 15(2), 382–396.

McMullan, W.E. and Long, W.A. (1987). Entrepreneurship education in the nineties. *Journal of Business Venturing*, 2, 261–275.

McMullan, W.E., Long, W.A. and Wilson, A. (1985). MBA concentration on entrepreneurship. *Journal of Small Business and Entrepreneurship*, 3, 18–22.

Mitchell, R.K. and Chesteen, S.A. (1995). Enhancing entrepreneurial expertise: Experiential pedagogy and the new venture expert script. *Simulation and Gaming*, 26, 288–306.

Mwasalwiba, E.S. (2010). Entrepreneurship education: a review of its objectives, teaching methods, and impact indicators. *Education+ Training*, 52, 20–47.

Ollila, S. and Williams-Middleton, K. (2011). The venture creation approach: integrating entrepreneurial education and incubation at the university. *International Journal of Entrepreneurship and Innovation Management*, 13, 161–178.

Oosterbeek, H., Praag, M.V. and Ijsselstein, A. (2010). The impact of entrepreneurship education on entrepreneurial skills and motivation. *European Economic Review*, 54, 442–454.

Neck, H., Greene, P. and Brush, C. (2014). Practice-based entrepreneurship education using actionable theory. In M.H. Morris, ed. *Annals of entrepreneurship education and pedagogy*. Cheltenham, UK: Edward Elgar Publishing, pp. 3–20.

Pittaway, L., Rodriguez-Falcon, E., Aiyegbayo, O. and King, A. (2011). The role of entrepreneurship clubs and societies in entrepreneurial learning. *International Small Business Journal*, 29, 37–57.

Plaschka, G.R. and Welsch, H.P. (1990). Emerging structures in entrepreneurship education: Curricula designs and strategies. *Entrepreneurship Theory & Practice*, 14, 55–71.

Powell, B.C. (2013). Dilemmas in entrepreneurship pedagogy. *Journal of Entrepreneurship Education*, 16, 99.

Raffiee, J. and Feng, J. (2014). Should I quit my day job?: A hybrid path to entrepreneurship. *Academy of Management Journal*, 57, 936–963.

Rankin, N. (2004). The new prescription for performance: The eleventh competency bench marking survey. *Competency and Emotional Intelligence Benchmarking Supplement*, 2004/2005. London: IRS.

Rideout, E.C. and Gray, D.O. (2013). Does entrepreneurship education really work? A review and methodological critique of the empirical literature on the effects of university-based entrepreneurship education. *Journal of Small Business Management*, 51, 329–351.

Ries, E. (2011). *The lean startup*. New York: Crown Publishing Group.

Robinson, P. and Josien, L. (2014). Entrepreneurial education: Using 'the challenge' in theory and practice. *Journal of Entrepreneurship Education*, 17, 172.

Robinson, S., Neergaard, H., Tanggaard, L. and Krueger, N.F. (2016). New horizons in entrepreneurship education: From teacher-led to student-centered learning. *Education + Training*, 58, 661–683.

Ronstadt, R. (1987). The educated entrepreneurs: A new era of entrepreneurial education is beginning. *American Journal of Small Business*, 11, 37–53.

Ronstadt, R. (1990). The educated entrepreneurs: A new era of entrepreneurial education evolves. In C.A. Kent ed. *Entrepreneurship education.* New York: Quorum Books, pp. 69–88.

Schumpeter, J.A. (1934). *The theory of economic development: An inquiry into profits, capital, credit, interest, and the business cycle* (Vol. 55). New Jersey: Transaction publishers.

Schumpeter, J. (1942). *The process of creative destruction (capitalism, socialism and democracy).* NewYork: Harper and Row.

Scott, M.G. and Twomey, D.F. (1998). The long term supply of entrepreneurs: Student's career aspirations in relation to entrepreneurship. *Journal of Small Business Management,* 26, 5–13.

Sexton, D. and Bowman, N. (1984). Entrepreneurship education: Suggestions for increasing effectiveness. *Journal of Small Business Management,* 22, 18–25.

Shane, S. and Venkataraman, S. (2000). The promise of entrepreneurship as a field of research. *Academy of Management Review,* 25, 217–226.

Shepherd, D.A. and Douglas, E.J. (1997). Is management education developing, or killing, the entrepreneurial spirit? In: *Proceedings of the 1997 USASBE Annual National Conference Entrepreneurship: The Engine of Global Economic Development, San Francisco, California.*

Sirelkhatim, F. and Gangi, Y. (2015). Entrepreneurship education: A systematic literature review of curricula contents and teaching methods. *Cogent Business & Management,* 2, 105–2034.

Solomon, G. (2007). An examination of entrepreneurship education in the United States. *Journal of Small Business and Enterprise Development,* 14, 168–182.

Solomon, G.T. (2014). The National Survey of Entrepreneurship Education: An overview of 2012–2014 survey data. *George Washington University Center for Entrepreneurial Excellence,* 29.

Solomon, G.T. and Fernald Jr, L.W. (1991). Trends in small business management and entrepreneurship education in the United States. *Entrepreneurship Theory & Practice,* 15, 25–39.

Solomon, G.T. and Fernald Jr, L.W. (1993). Innovative approaches to meeting entrepreneurial informational needs: SBA enters the XXI century. *Journal of Creative Behavior,* 27, 103–111.

Solomon, G.T. and Matthews, C.H. (2014). The curricular confusion between entrepreneurship education and small business management: A qualitative analysis. In M. Morris, ed. *Annals of entrepreneurship education and pedagogy.* Cheltenham, UK: Edward Elgar Publishing, pp. 91–115.

Solomon, G.T., Duffy, S. and Tarabishy, A. (2002). The state of entrepreneurship education in the United States: A nationwide survey and analysis. *International Journal of Entrepreneurship Education,* 1, 65–86.

Solomon, G.T., Weaver, K.M. and Fernald, Jr L.W. (1994). Pedagogical methods of teaching entrepreneurship: A historical perspective. *Gaming and Simulation,* 25, 67–79.

Solomon, G.T., Weaver, K.M. and Fernald Jr L.W. (2005). Pedagogical methods of teaching entrepreneurship: An historical perspective. In: R.V.D. Horst, S. King-Kauanui and S. Duffy, eds. *Malden keystones of entrepreneurship knowledge.* MA: Blackwell Publishing Inc.

Stumpf, S.S., Dunbar, L. and Mullen, T.P. (1991). Simulations in entrepreneurship education: Oxymoron or untapped opportunity? *Frontiers of Entrepreneurship Research,* 11, 681–694.

Tracey, P. and Phillips, N. (2007). The distinctive challenge of educating social entre-preneurs: A postscript and rejoinder to the special issue on entrepreneurship education. *Academy of Management Learning & Education*, 6, 264–271.

Truell, A.D., Webster, L. and Davidson, C. (1998). Fostering entrepreneurial spirit: Integ-rating the business community into the classroom. *Business Education Forum*, 53, 28–29.

Unger, J.M., Rauch, A., Frese, M. and Rosenbusch, N. (2011). Human capital and *entre-preneurial success: A meta-analytical review. Journal of Business Venturing*, 26, 341–358.

United States Association for Small Business and Entrepreneurship (USASBE). (2017). Member benefits (para 1). Retrieved from: www.usasbe.org/?page=memberbenefits& hhSearchTerms=%22largest+and+independent%2c+and+professional%2c+and+acade mic+and+organi%22.

Van Clouse, G.H. (1990). A controlled experiment relating entrepreneurial education to student's start-up decisions. *Journal of Small Business Management*, 28, 45–53.

Valerio, A., Parton, B. and Robb, A. (2014). *Entrepreneurship education and training programs around the world: dimensions for success*. Washington, DC: World Bank Publications.

Vesper, K.H. and McMullan, W.E. (1988). Entrepreneurship: Today courses, tomorrow degrees? *Entrepreneurship Theory & Practice*, 13, 7–13.

Weick, K.E. (1995). *Sensemaking in Organizations*. Thousand Oaks, CA: Sage.

Williams Middleton, K. and Donnellon, A. (2014). Personalizing entrepreneurial learn-ing: A pedagogy for facilitating the know why. *Entrepreneurship Research Journal*, 4, 167–204.

Winkel, D. (2013). The changing face of entrepreneurship education. *Journal of Small Business Management*, 51, 313–314.

Winslow, E.K., Solomon, G.T. and Tarabishy, A. (1999). Empirical investigation into entre-preneurship education in the United States: Some results of the 1997 National Survey of Entrepreneurial Education. Paper presented at the 1999 USASBE conference.

Zeithaml, C.P. and Rice, G.H. (1987). Entrepreneurship/small business education in American universities. *Journal of Small Business Management*, 25, 44–50.

3 Reflections and evaluation of Chinese enterprise education

The role of institutions from the perspective of learners

Weili Teng and Jason J. Turner

The development of higher education in China, remains at a very low level compared with developed and quite a number of developing countries in the world (Bie and Yi, 2014: 1500). The Chinese education system takes a surface learning approach and teaching is content-oriented whereby students are heavily involved in direct classroom teaching. In such a system, students believe that everything a teacher says is correct, and many do not challenge the teacher's knowledge base, thereby failing to develop their creativity, an element considered essential to enterprise and entrepreneurship. The foundations of the education system in China are founded in the Chinese culture (i.e. Confucianism) and as this chapter will investigate the culture can encourage entrepreneurial activity but not necessarily entrepreneurial and enterprise thinking. The chapter will investigate student perceptions of Chinese education and the role it plays in encouraging or discouraging enterprise and entrepreneurship among learners and the changes that are perhaps required to take Chinese enterprise education forward.

Learning approaches

Learning is about how we perceive and understand the world and about making meaning (Marton and Booth, 1997). "Learning may involve mastering abstract principles, understanding proofs, remembering factual information, acquiring methods, techniques, recognition, debating ideas, or developing behaviour appropriate to specific situations" (Fry *et al.*, 2009: 8*)*. Many researchers are interested in studying learning styles, such as dependent learning and independent learning (Marshall and Rowland, 1998). However, from our experience of different systems, it can be suggested that the education system is another influential factor on students' learning, and education systems should not be treated separately from culture. A related issue to learning styles is that understanding may be affected by context. It is argued that understanding can enhance students' learning outcomes and improve their performance (Marton and Saljo, 1997). The two main types of understanding are argued to be target understanding and personal understanding (Entwistle and Smith, 2002).

To understand different learning approaches, it is necessary to appreciate the meaning of learning. According to Marton (1975: 13), learning is "the grasping of what is signified (what the discourse itself is), i.e. understanding what a written or spoken discourse is about". Barnett (1992b: 4) states "learning is a human process which has an effect on those understanding it". Marton (1975) and Barnett (1992ab) believe that understanding is critical to learning because understanding would enable students to not only 'know' but also to perform well via articulating what they were taught. Learning is thus seen as a process of understanding not just knowing and deep learning is essential to knowing.

Deep vs surface learning

The two approaches of deep and surface learning have been well researched (Fry *et al.*, 1999; Marton, 1975). Deep learning has been one of the most influential constructs to emerge in the literature on effective learning in higher education (Boyle, Duffy and Dunleavy, 2003). The deep learning approach is typified as an intention to understand and seek meaning and leads students to attempt to relate concepts to existing experience, distinguish between new ideas and existing knowledge, and critically evaluate and determine key themes and concepts. Deep learners actively try to understand meaning by working out relationships between concepts, relating new material to previously known information and adopting a critical attitude to information. In short, the deep learning approach results from the students' intention to gain better understanding from their studying (Fry *et al.*, 1999). The deep learning approach appears to be more broadly accepted as effective learning in the literature (Entwistle and Smith, 2002) in contrast to the surface learning approach.

The surface learning approach is typified as an intention to complete the task, memorise information, and making no distinction between new ideas and existing knowledge (Fry *et al.*, 1999) the approach highlights the routine use of rote memorisation. Students who take the surface approach believe that their achievement is through superficial levels of cognitive processing (Brown, Bull and Pendlebury, 1997). The link between memorisation and the surface approach has, however, proved to be an oversimplification (Kember, 1996). Memories can also be used, for example, to master unfamiliar terminology by initial rote learning, as a first step towards developing understanding, or when committing an understanding to memory. Where memorisation involves meaningful learning, it has been described as deep memories (Tang, 1991) and therefore implied learning beyond the superficial. The deep approach is therefore not entirely separate from surface learning approach, deep learners also need to memorise what they were taught so that they could make sense of it. While two learning approaches are studied, understanding inevitably needs to be addressed because learning is about deeper understanding (Brown, Bull and Pendlebury, 1997) and experiential learning could be a way towards deeper understanding linking to employment.

Experiential learning

Similarly to the debate over surface and deep learning there is discussion in academia over experiential learning and its appropriateness in education and to the employment market. Currently researchers question the role of education to furnish young learners with the necessary set of skills to compete in the employment market (Belwal, Balushi and Belwal, 2015; Hytti and O'Gorman, 2004; Jones *et al.*, 2008; Lewis and Massey, 2003; OECD, 2014; Parinduri, 2014; Strauss, 2014; Svitak, 2015; Van Damme, 2014; Vukovic, 2015; Wright, 2013) and the necessity to better prepare learners for the real world by including more business engagement in the curriculum through internships, work based learning, real-world assessment and knowledge-evaluating projects, collectively known as 'learning by doing'.

Learning by doing is argued to make an individual more employable, providing graduates with the necessary skills to compete whether that is working for an organisation or working for one's self. The phrase, 'enterprising' could have two connotations, to have the necessary skills to work in an enterprise or to work as a self-employed employee, to be more entrepreneurial. When we discuss the skills necessary to be entrepreneurial, arguably there needs to be creativity and innovation (Schumpter, 2008), in contrast, the skills considered necessary to be enterprising are creativity and innovation but also collaboration, communication, confidence, problem-solving, decision-making, leadership, resolving conflict, reflection, organisation and management (Barbar, 2014; Chell, 2013; Fiala, Gertler and Carney, 2014). Can such skills be taught in the classroom or through engagement with business? If we are to accept the argument of Vesper and Gartner (1997) and Drucker (1985ab), entrepreneurship can be learned. However, McClelland (1999) and Hills (1988) argue that it is difficult to train someone to be entrepreneurial. It requires a certain mindset, with a certain attitude towards risk. Although these skills can be taught to a degree through work based learning, placements, real-world business engagement (Turner and Mulholland, 2017) with any combination of external (outside the classroom) engagement able to develop "positive mistake-making, calculated risk-taking, creative problem-solving and interaction with the outside world" (Jones and Iredale, 2010: 12), being enterprising or entrepreneurial essentially means being employable, with a wider range of options and opportunities in any number of countries.

Chinese culture and education system

Culture has a number of meanings, as derived from literature. Trompenaars and Hampen-Turner (1997: 3) argued that "the essence of culture is not what is visible on the surface. It is the shared ways groups of people understand and interpret the world". In the literature, culture, theoretically speaking, is a set of values and beliefs shared by people in a social community (Schein, 1985). Trompenaars and Hampen-Turner (1997: 6) emphasise "culture is the way in which a group of people solves problems and reconciles dilemma". Hofstede (1980) views culture as the collective programming of the mind that distinguishes the members of one human group from another. The function of culture is to establish modes of conduct, standards of performance and ways of dealing with interpersonal and environmental relations that reduce uncertainty, increase predictability, and thereby promote survival and growth among the members of any society (Ahmed and Li, 1996). For example, Chinese culture, especially Confucianism, advocates the importance of commitment and patience, orders relationships by status, requires respect for tradition, frugality in consumption, reciprocation of greeting, favours and gifts, and imbues a sense of shame through its construction of the concept of 'face' (*mianzi* 面子). Within this cultural setting, the function of culture is to establish modes of conduct, standards of performance and ways of dealing with interpersonal and environmental relations that reduce uncertainty, increase predictability, and thereby promote survival and growth among the members of any society. 'Correct' interpersonal behaviour is determined by gender, age and position in society. Chinese culture also stresses group harmony, trust, sensitivity and social cohesion. It encourages complex hierarchically based interrelationships and interdependencies (Redding, 1980). Members within a group are required to co-operate and trust each other. At times, this requirement makes it necessary for the individual to subordinate self-interest, or even the truth, in order to maintain group harmony. Wang *et al.*, (2005) shares some of Redding's view and stresses five major aspects of Confucianism, which are (1) hierarchy and harmony; (2) group orientation; (3) guanxi networks (relationships); (4) mianzi (face) and (5) time orientation. These five characteristics are seen as core in Confucianism-based culture. All these characteristics, to some degree, may be reflected in the Chinese education system.

The education system in China

One of the most influential phrases in Chinese history was 'Wan ban jie xia pin wei you du shu gao' (万般皆下品, 惟有读书高). This means that only people who were educated could be in the top echelon in society and had power over others. Position was somehow determined by education level and result of exams with only education able to change people's position, illustrated by the Chinese imperial exams, which appoint civil service positions not through special or inherited privilege, but through an individual's own abilities. These included *Six Arts* (music, archery and horsemanship, arithmetic, writing and knowledge of the rituals and ceremonies of both public and private life) in the first generation exams and later the curriculum was extended to the *Five Studies* (military strategies, civil law, revenue and taxation, agriculture and geography) in addition to the Confucian classics. The exams had three levels (i.e. local, provincial and national) and those who passed the local level exam and then the provincial level exam became *juren* (举人) or a recommended man and were eligible for the national level exams. Those who passed the national exams became *jinshi* (进士) or a so-called 'presented scholar'. These were highly prestigious special exams for scholars who were occasionally assessed by Imperial Decree, the exams lasted up to 72 hours and each individual was set and examined separately from others. For those who passed all the exams and were selected for administrative positions, it meant that their clans or families also rose in social prestige and wealth, however only a small proportion of candidates were selected.

"Although the imperial examination system set up in the seventh century was abolished in 1911, candidates continued to strive for exam success in order to better themselves" (Chan, 1999: 297). "This served to reinforce the fact that academic achievement and hard work were seen by many as the main way of moving up the social ladder for the Chinese" (Chan, 1999: 297). Therefore, pursuing higher education is still seen even now as a better way to achieve success. The annual national examination in China is the biggest event to those families who have children entered for the exam, especially to those families that only have one child.[1] Those children start to prepare for the examination from primary school using surface learning and targeted understanding techniques, focusing on the retention of knowledge learned from classes. Students have to remember as much as they can in order to receive better marks, therefore the surface learning approach is reinforced through the assessment and in fact rewarded by better marks. A further dimension to the way student learn is that pupils are located in a fixed classroom and study alongside the same group of students, sitting in the same seat for 45 minutes, not allowed to move during this time and refraining from discussing with others in the classroom. This disciplined and regulatory approach is compounded by pupils believing that their teacher is 100 per cent correct and they therefore rarely challenge their teachers, which has implications for creativity and independent thinking, linked to enterprising and entrepreneurial behaviour. Students may not wish to question and staff may not wish to be questioned because of the variable of 'losing face', which although outside the scope of this chapter, its importance to the learning process cannot be ignored. The crucial point here is the Chinese education system encourages a 'surface' approach to learning, which is not necessarily a viable breeding ground for enterprising thinking.

In the Chinese education system, during 12 years of study from primary to secondary school, children become skilled at memorising and taking exams. If successful, they then have the opportunity to enter a university in China where the surface approach to learning is reinforced. Universities in China reflect a similar approach of rewarding performance in examinations based on memory and memorising, which influences a student's choice of module and programme, selecting those subjects where they are more likely to achieve good results.

The curriculum at primary, secondary and tertiary educational levels has changed little over the years, with teachers not required to change their teaching structure and content. As a result teachers use the same methods – didactic, one way delivering at all levels of education, and typically a teacher may use teaching materials for more than ten years without any change. Assessment is almost 100 per cent closed paper exams towards the end of the term or year, and exam questions are designed based upon one single textbook. The education system appears not to encourage change, and this applies to teachers and students. Teachers expect students to have the same knowledge as they do, therefore students have to remember what the teacher has said in the lecture and answer the question in the exam with the same answer. Otherwise students would receive no mark on that particular question, although some subjects require students to have their own thoughts, such as Chinese composition. This, however, is unusual and untypical of most subjects where rote learning and regurgitation of facts is rewarded.

Having described the general basis of Chinese education, and the traditional approaches to student learning, the chapter now moves on to illustrate the research methodology upon which this chapter was based, explaining how the data was gathered from Chinese students studying in China and the UK before examining their perspectives of enterprise learning and entrepreneurial behaviour and the role of educational institutions in this learning.

Methodological approach to the study

Using an interpretivist approach (Saunders, Lewis and Thornhill, 2000), the research employed two focus group discussions and in-depth interviews with Chinese students who studied in a UK university for a postgraduate degree. All the participants had more than seven years of working experience and some of them already had a postgraduate degree from Chinese universities. The aim of the focus group discussions and the interviews were to understand the impact of different cultural and educational backgrounds on their learning outcomes in their learning and whether entrepreneurial skills could be developed in universities. The focus group discussion lasted for between two and half and one and a half hours with 31 students spread over two groups. The face-to-face interviews took on average 45 minutes. All the data was collected just before the students were leaving the UK to return to China, as it was considered that at this stage the students would be able to reflect on their learning experience in the UK and make a comparison between China and the UK.

Critical thinking

Critical thinking is seen as a useful learning approach to widen the students' perspectives, hence the requirement in western education for this practice to underpin teaching and assessment to encourage evaluative and critical practices. However, as we have seen earlier in the chapter this practice is not practised in Chinese education and therefore the practice is not straightforward to Chinese students, particularly at the beginning of their respective course. When students in the focus groups and interviews were asked how they found the experience of critical thinking, the majority found it a rather unique experience but one they learned from, a typical response from the interview was:

> When I wrote the first essay I used a lot of quotations from textbooks and journal articles as well as published government documents to explain how the NHS system here works. I was very pleased with my writing and expected a good result for the assignment. I was shocked when I received the essay back as it was a very low mark. After reading the comments I realised that I need to evaluate it critically not just simply present the

information quoted from others. I thought the information written in the coursework is useful to my job and I should remember them for my practice.

This respondent perspective reflects the Chinese surface learning approach, which highlights routine use of rote memorisation (Fry *et al.*, 1999). The majority of students argued that their previous learning experiences at Chinese institutions influenced their perceptions of critical thinking at UK universities and their initial ability to tackle such an approach to teaching and learning. A typical response from the focus groups and interviews from a respondent who has experienced both undergraduate and postgraduate education in China was:

This was how l learned from an MBA programme at one of the top universities in China. I used to prefer learning new ideas and new information and try to remember the details so that I could use (show to others) it when I need. This is a habit and developed from my life. It is probably not just me but also my colleagues in the course feel the same.

This perspective regarding the surface learning approach experience in Chinese education was confirmed by the majority of respondents who had experienced only undergraduate education in China. Those respondents explained that in China they had to remember everything that either the teacher taught in the classroom or what was written in the assigned textbook in order to get a good mark in the exam, which would usually be closed book and the only assessment, taken at the end of the term or year. A typical response was:

We only had one text book for one module and it was like a Bible. We had to learn everything written in the book. Otherwise I would not get a good result. In addition the tutor gave us a revision session and covered most exam questions. Therefore, everybody could pass and it was difficult for anyone to fail ... [teaching] was content driven and there was no space to think. Teachers hoped to tell everything they know and did not consider the other way.

The role of teachers in the learning experience and critical thinking was developed by a minority of respondents with a typical response being:

Teachers in Chinese universities normally introduce big theories but we felt that we have learned a lot of knowledge more from the teaching/delivering here [in Nottingham]. Now I recall what I had learned and feel that the knowledge stored in my brain has gradually disappeared and the knowledge I had learned appears to be very superficial or background information. Chinese teachers generally prepare and teach carefully and seriously about the theories themselves. We used to believe what they taught was 100 per cent correct. Thus, we first (normally) accepted it without questioning. For example two Chinese universities of A and B I studied at previously are very famous in China and the programme seems to be well designed. But I feel that I learned much more here [in Nottingham] because the education system here encourages critical ways of thinking ... the term 'critical' appears to be a serious term from a Chinese perspective but it is so popular here in the UK, like cookies on the table.

The role of teachers and the reliance on one textbook in the learning experience and critical thinking was developed by a minority of respondents with a typical response being:

Twenty years ago when I was doing the degree in a Chinese university, the teachers taught a very complicated equation, and one of my classmate asked why is it like this? The teacher said "that is what I have learned from my teacher". Teaching one textbook and assessing the memory of the book at the end of the term. There is no need to read other references. [surface learning approach].

The reliance on a single text book for a module was further evidenced by a respondent in the focus group who stated:

I felt very sad when I failed one module at the beginning of the programme [MPA]. I did read the textbook and used some quotation from the book. But one of the comments I got was "very descriptive" and limited understanding and reading. I used to be a very good student in my class in China and I had never failed any module.

Clearly we can see the impact of the Chinese educational system on the way students approach their learning, with rote learning, a lack of critical thinking and the reliance on one main textbook and teachers whose practices of teaching purely theory without being questioned by students, the identified themes by respondents. The different systems of teaching and learning in the UK and China affected the student learning experience, with respondents not only 'accepting' the surface learning approach but had it already embedded in their learning.

As we have seen earlier, the Chinese education system has a standardised approach to learning and assessment where teachers historically prepare students for exams so that they could get good jobs if they had good exam results. The system itself, however, does not encourage tutors to adopt innovative way of teaching and therefore teachers are reluctant to take risks in case there are negative outcomes associated with adopting a new approach, for example, lower pass rates. The issue of pass rates has further implications for a lack of creativity in the teaching and learning approach from teachers and Chinese institutions. There are many examples where students who failed a module complained that the teaching was the problem for their failure resulting in the staff member receiving a bonus reduction or no promotion/upgrading. There appears to be no incentive to encourage academic staff to do things differently in the Chinese education system. As one student said: "In the university's rewards and promotion system teachers do not consider this element [new approach of teaching] so it does not encourage undertaking innovation". Both teachers and students are reluctant to take the risk of failing an assessment through being innovative (both arguably key enterprising qualities) preferring instead to repeat the same thing over and over again. This is in direct contrast to the UK education system, which appears to take a more personal and independent approach to learning as a means to enhance their understanding (Fry *et al.*, 1999).

Unequal relationships

The standardised approach to learning and conformity is embedded in Chinese culture and does not sit well with independent thinking and challenging authority, which in this case is teaching staff and the educational apparatus. Chinese culture encourages complex hierarchically based interrelationships and interdependencies (Redding, 1980), although it also stresses group harmony, trust, sensitivity and social cohesion. There were five hierarchical relationships derived historically from Chinese Confucianism. These five relationships and their characteristics are: sincerity between father and son, righteousness between ruler and subjects, distinction or separate functions between husband and wife, order between older brothers and younger brothers, and faithfulness among friends (Chen, 1995). These five cardinal relationships are based upon a differentiated order among individuals (ibid) and the five relations are called *Wu Lun* (五论). "Although there have been changes given the dramatic development achieved in China some of these five principles still play a role in people's behaviours, such as sovereign and subject"(Teng, 2015: 212) and is still seen in the rather imbalanced relationship between teachers and students in China. To illustrate the point one of the students cited the example when Tony Blair, the former UK Prime Minister was challenged by an academic about the Third Way Philosophy. The student said in the focus group:

> When Tony Blair proposed 'The Third Way and' it raised a lot of different voices from academics who criticised him from different angles (i.e. not new, not suitable to the current situation etc.). It was the time when Tony Blair was still in his most respected period. It would certainly not be the case in China. For example if the central government implements a new policy, academics would be reluctant to challenge the central government although different voices may be helpful to the government to form a better policy although there were often discussions taking place before the policy was finalised. There was a mentality which limits people's critical thinking as they are concerned about the leaders' opinions. If their leader said one thing there would be hardly any second voice about it.

The Chinese education system appears to lack a mechanism to encourage people to think differently because of its culture and the specific interplay between student and teacher. This trend does not show any immediate signs of change given people still strongly respect the values of Confucianism. The role of the teacher in a student's learning in China is a recurring theme, with respondents referring to the power distance between them and the staff member and also the focus of institutions themselves, being faculty rather than student centred, a typical response was:

> The university seems to be teacher-centred and they always have absolutely top authority above students. Teachers are not willing to accept the critical thinking/challenge from students.

A minority of respondents compared the Chinese and UK teaching approaches, further underlining the role teachers have in the learning experience of Chinese students, a typical response was:

> In the UK teachers and students seem to be at an equal position. Students are allowed and encouraged to challenge teachers. This is because they (teachers) believe this would develop students' creativity and also they are aware that students come from different backgrounds and experiences and could be able to demonstrate different views on an issue from them. We were often encouraged to say different opinions in the classroom here in the UK. However, we feared to say different things at the beginning of the course as we used to believe that teachers were always right as they have much more knowledge than we do.

A respondent who had experienced both undergraduate and postgraduate education in China developed the theme of not challenging teachers by developing the aspect of respect:

> I always respected my MBA supervisor at a Chinese university when I was doing my MBA. We had a very close relationship. He supervised a few students and we often went to see him, especially during the Chinese Spring Festival. We still carry the belief of being a teacher one day and being a father for life (一日为师, 终生为父).

This quote in particular reflects the unequal relationship between student and teacher (father and son), where the student (son) always has to obey the teacher (father) and not challenge the teacher (father) because he was above them all, i.e. beyond reproach. This theme reveals another aspect of Chinese culture, the loss of face which was identified by the majority of respondents, with a typical response being:

> Teachers are always right. Also teachers are frightened if students ask a lot of challenging questions. This is because they may lose face if they had no answers to the questions.

Chinese culture, especially requires respect for tradition, frugality in consumption, reciprocation of greeting, favours and gifts, and instils a sense of shame through its construction of the concept of 'face (*mianzi* 面子) (Teng, 2003). Everybody is concerned about their 'face', i.e. how other people perceive them. In the Chinese educational context this is not just an issue for teachers but also for students, both parties are concerned about their respective faces. This 'dual loss of face' was acknowledged by the majority of respondents, with a typical response being:

> Before the exam the teacher asked students if they liked a closed exam paper or an open one. (Interestingly the form of the paper had not been decided in advance.) Most students were happy to have an open paper. It is simply because students would easily get a pass so that both teachers and students had good 'face' because of no failure. It would be different if they took a closed paper which both teachers and students 'face' a difficulty if some students fail.

To protect the 'face' of stakeholders in the Chinese education system students are 'taught' to pass their respective exams, which influences the approach to teaching, surface learning. On the one hand the teacher provides students with the knowledge they know and on the other hand students remember the knowledge imparted by the teachers. When those students studied in the UK this 'loss of face' presented an obstacle to their learning with students reluctant to challenge teachers, with the majority of respondents fearing they would ask the wrong question, a typical response was:

> I was not willing to ask any questions, especially in the first two modules. There were a couple of reasons. First, I thought my English was not good enough and I wondered whether the teacher would understand my question. Second, there are many of my colleagues who have better English than mine and they may laugh at me if I say something wrong, such as grammar and pronunciation. Speaking in the whole group with some mistakes I would have no 'face' although my colleague may not say so directly but I was scared.

Another 'face' issue relating to not only teaching and learning but independent and creative thinking was in the approach towards academic referencing. It was unpopular in Chinese academic writing to use many references, due to the belief that the author would appear to be less knowledgeable, i.e. the practice of referencing impacts on the loss of face. In the UK appropriate referencing of others people's work is a requirement to avoid plagiarism, and this issue was a real concern to all respondents with a typical response being:

> I did not want to write many references in my paper as this could devalue my paper in China. However we learned from the UK that we have to

acknowledge other people's work in the assignment otherwise we would fail the module. I also know that more references used in the paper could be seen as more 'critical' as more views could be drawn into the paper. Importantly I would not lose 'face' if I do so. In contrast I may get good 'face' by having a good mark from the assignment by using more references appropriately.

Enterprise learning

From interpreting responses and themes to emerge from the focus groups and interviews it would appear that Chinese culture, particularly Confucianism has a direct impact on the learning of students, whether they followed an under-graduate and/or postgraduate programme in China because of the approach to teaching across primary, secondary and tertiary education. By the time respondents entered the tertiary sector the practices of surface learning, not challenging teachers and conformity were already embedded in their psyche. It has been noted that student learned by 'following' whether that was a textbook or a teacher, which has clear implications for creativity and independent learning as these students are not learning by doing, they are rote learning. As discussed in the literature, experiential learning may add value to a student's employment prospects and future career development. What is interesting from the responses is that there was an appetite for this type of learning with the majority of respondents understanding the need for engagement with business practice and hoping that they would get this experience in a UK university, as articulated by one respondent:

> We have learned knowledge about the UK public administration from the classroom but we have not had the opportunity to work or even shadow in the work environment. It would be helpful so that we could have a better understanding of the theories thoroughly and dapperly and apply them in a Chinese context.

All respondents acknowledged the need for business engagement but when it came to being enterprising and entrepreneurial the majority of respondents were of the opinion that to be enterprising cannot be taught, that is has to come from within the individual, with a typical response being:

> entrepreneurship can be cultivated but can be inspired. I believe every one has some spirit of entrepreneur in his or her heart but all one needs is some opportunities to open up that spirit and to know what he or she really want to do.

These responses support the work of McClelland (1999) and Hills (1998) and conflict with the research of Drucker (1985ab) and later by Vesper and Gartner (1997) that entrepreneurship can be learned, meaning that entrepreneurs can be motivated to becoming entrepreneurial (Jensen, 2008). With regards to the skills necessary to be both entrepreneurial and enterprising all respondents thought universities should teach students the necessary skills to compete in the employment market, with a typical response being:

> Universities can help students develop most of the skills necessary to be employed by enterprises.

However the majority of respondents did not think these employability skills should simply revolve around being creative and innovative (Schumpter, 2008). Respondents made the distinction between being enterprising i.e. to work for an enterprise and have the skills necessary to work for others and being entrepreneurial, i.e. working for oneself. To be enterprising requires a graduate to be collaborative, able to communicate, have a degree of confidence, able to problem solve, make decisions, lead, resolve conflict, be able to reflect, organise and manage (Barbar, 2014; Chell, 2013; Fiala, Gertler and Carney, 2014). Many of these skills were identified by the majority of respondents, in particular the skills of creativity, being analytical (problem-solving), team working (collaborative) and able to communicate, with a typical response being:

> There are five capabilities (skills) that can be developed at university, learning ability, creative capability, analytical research, team work capability and communication capability.

All respondents thought a university should teach both the so called hard skills (project management, communication, creative thinking, problem-solving and leadership) as well as the softer skills (confidence, communication and reflection), (Barbar, 2014; Fiala, Gertler and Carney, 2014; Jones and Iredale, 2010). But Chinese culture and the education system focused only on the skills necessary to pass the module and the final examination, which although taking into account some of the hard skills, did not necessarily prepare them particularly well for the employment market. A typical response was:

> Chinese universities focus more on hard skills that works may need, such as MS offices, writing skill, etc. Students are trained to master these skills in class. However, only a small amount of these skills are used in actual jobs. Additionally, many students forget them only a short time after finishing the class because they do not think they are important. They learn these skills just to pass the modules (surface learning). UK universities are different, in terms of the skills they prepare students for the workplace. They focus on both hard and soft skills by using classes, lectures and group discussions to help students develop them. Soft skills may include communication skill, the way of professional thinking and behaviour, etc. Both hard and soft skills are very important for jobs and sometimes soft skills are even more important for career development.

All respondents acknowledged the importance of learning the softer skills to gaining suitable employment, but they emphasised the point that such skills would assist them in gaining employment as a manager, i.e. working for someone else and not being entrepreneurial, with a typical response being: "soft skills can help an employee to develop into a good manager".

Although it is acknowledged that some students will go on to become entrepreneurial and enterprising, setting up a business on their own, what this research illustrates is that the Chinese educational system potentially limits students' opportunities. Through a standardised, more surface learning approach, students are more likely to be adverse to taking risk, which is a characteristic deemed important for working for oneself (Jones and Iredale, 2010). Respondents acknowledged the need and indeed desired certain hard and soft skills but given the culture did not receive these skills while in the Chinese education system nor would they challenge the system and request such skills be embedded into the curriculum. This creates a vicious circle, similar to the one relating to the loss of face with staff and students.

Conclusion

From the responses of students who have experienced both Chinese and UK education, it is clear that Chinese culture influences its education system, and as a result the teaching and learning strategy of institutions and the students' learning experience. The Chinese education system is well established, built on Confucianism culture which appears to create barriers to a student's employment choices. Students had little opportunity or a platform to develop their creativity and critical thought process due largely to unequal relationships between teachers and students and the persistence of both surface learning and the culture of 'face'.

This chapter presents an interesting insight into the role of Chinese culture on the learning experience of students and their entrepreneurial and enterprising intentions. The discussion highlight the ways in which Chinese universities might alter existing teaching and learning approaches, assessments and learning outcomes to develop students' creativity, innovation and the softer skills which would not only better prepare them for the employment market but also enable them to manage the transition to other institutions outside China. The importance of culture to an education system suggests that the culture not only of learners but of the way a particular country learns should be a major consideration in the designing of curriculum and preparing the student for the employment market.

Note

1 A national policy in China to manage the population.

References

Ahmed, P.K. and Li, X. (1996). Chinese culture and its implications for Sino-Western joint venture management. *Strategic Change*, 5, 275–286.

Barbar, N. (2014). Five reasons for teaching entrepreneurship, [online]. *SAIS*, Available at: www.sais.org/news/205092/Five-Reasons-for-Teaching-Entrepreneurship.htm [accessed 13 December 2016].

Barnett, R. (1992a). *Improving higher education*. Buckingham: SRHE and Open University Press.

Barnett, R. (1992b). *Learning to effect*. Buckingham: SRHE/Open University Press.

Belwal, R., Al Balushi, H. and Belwal, S. (2015). Student's perception of entrepreneurship and enterprise education in Oman. *Education + Training*, 57(8/9), 924–947.

Bie, D. and Yi, M. (2014). The context of higher education development and policy response in Chin, *Studies in Higher Education*, 39(8), 1499–1510.

Boyle, E.A., Duffy, T. and Dunleavy, K. (2003). Learning styles and academic outcome: The validity and utility of Vermont's Inventory of Learning Styles in a British higher education setting. *British Journal of Educational Psychology*, 73(2), 267–290.

Brown, G., Bull, J., Pendlebury, M. (1997). *Assessing student learning in higher education*. London: Routledge.

Chan, S. (1999). The Chinese learner – a question of style. *Education + Training*. 41(6/7), 294–305.

Chell, E. (2013). Review of skill and the entrepreneurial process. *International Journal of Entrepreneurial Behaviour and Research*, 19(1), 6–31.

Chen, M. (1995). *Asian management systems*, London: Routledge.

Drucker, P.F. (1985a). The practice of innovation. *Innovation and Entrepreneurship Practice and Principles*. New York: Harper & Row.

Drucker, P.F. (1985b). Entrepreneurial strategies, *Innovation and Entrepreneurship Practice and Principles*. New York: Harper & Row.

Entwistle, N. and Smith, C. (2002). Personal understanding and target understanding: Mapping influences on the outcomes of learning. *British Journal of Educational Psychology*, 72, 321–342.

Fiala, N., Gertler, P. and Carney, D. (7 November 2014). The role of hard and soft skills in entrepreneurial success: Experimental evidence from Uganda. *AEA RCT Registry*.

Fry, H., Ketteridge, S. and Marshall, S. (1999). Understanding student learning. In S. Marshall, ed. *A Handbook for teaching & learning in higher education: Enhancing academic practice*. London: Kogan Page.

Hills, G.E. (1988). Variations in university entrepreneurship education: An empirical study of an evolving field, *Journal of Business Venturing*, 3(1), 109–122.

Hofstede, G. (1980). *Culture's consequences: International differences in work-related values*. Newbury Park, CA: Sage.

Hytti, U. and O'Gorman, C. (2004). What is 'enterprise education'? An analysis of the objectives and methods of enterprise education programmes in four European countries. *Education + Training*, 46(1), 11–23.

Jensen, E. (2008). *Brain-based learning: The new paradigm of teaching*. 2nd ed. Corwin Press, Thousand Oaks, California.

Jones, B. and Iredale, N. (2010). Enterprise education as pedagogy, *Education + Training*, 52(1), 7–19.

Jones, P., Jones, A., Packham, G. and Miller, C. (2008). Student attitudes towards enterprise education in Poland: A positive impact. *Education + Training*, 50(7), 597–614.

Kember, D. (1996). The intention to both memorise and understand: Another approach to learning. *Higher Education*, 31, 341–354.

Lewis, K. and Massey, C. (2003). Delivering enterprise education in New Zealand. *Education + Training*, 45(4), 197–206.

McClelland, D. (1999). *The achieving society*. The Free Press: New York.

Marshall, L. and Rowland, F. (eds). (1998). *A guide to learning independently*. Buckingham: Open University Press.

Marton, F. (1975). On non-verbatim learning – 1: Level of processing and level of outcome. *Scandinavian Journal of Psychology*, 16, 273–279.

Marton, F. and Booth. S. (1997). *Learning and awareness*, Mahwah, New Jersey: Laurence Erlbaum Associates.

Marton, F. and Saljo. R. (1997). Approaches to learning. In N.J. Entwistle, ed. *The experience of learning*. Edinburgh: Scottish Academic Press.

Parinduri, R.A. (2014). Do children spend too much time in schools? Evidence from a longer school year in Indonesia, *Economics of Education Review*, 41, 89–104.

OECD. (April 2014). How much time do primary and lower secondary students spend in the classroom, *Education Indicators in Focus*, 1–4.

Redding, S.G. (1980). Cognition as an aspect of culture and its relation to management processes: An exploratory view of the Chinese case. Preview by. *Journal of Management Studies*, 17(2), 127–148.

Saunders, M., Lewis, P. and Thornhill, A. (2000). *Research methods for business students*. Harlow: FT/Prentice Hall.

Schein, E. (1985). *Organizational culture and leadership*, San Franciso: Jossey-Bass Publishers.

Schumpter, J.A. (2008). *Capitalism, socialism and democracy*. 3rd ed. London: Harper Perennial Modern Classics.

Strauss, V. (2014). 10 things wrong with what kids learn in school, [online]. *Washington Post*, Available at: www.washingtonpost.com/news/answer-sheet/wp/2014/04/02/10-things-wrong-with-what-kids-learn-in-school/ [accessed 15 September 2016].

Svitak, A. (2015). Does school prepare students for the real world? This teen speaker says no, [online]. *TEDEd*, Available at: http://blog.ed.ted.com/2015/08/25/does-school-prepare-students-for-the-real-world-this-teen-speaker-says-no/ [accessed 15 September 2016].

Tang, C. (1991). *Effect of different assessment methods on tertiary students' approaches to studying*, Hong Kong: University of Hong Kong.

Teng, W. (2013). Trust in innovation process: Cases in China and Europe. PhD thesis submitted to Nottingham Trent University, Nottingham. http://ethos.bl.uk/Order Details.do?did=1&uin=uk.bl.ethos.271783.

Teng, W. (2015). Developing senior leaders and managers in the public sector: The case of the MPA for Chinese local government leaders. In: *The 41st EIBA Annual Conference, Rio de Janeiro, Brazil, 1–3 December 2015*.

Trompenaars, F. and Hampden-Turner, C. (1997). *Riding the waves of culture: Understanding cultural diversity in business*. London: Nicholas Brealey.

Turner, J.J. and Mulholland, G. (2017). Enterprise education: Towards a framework for engaging with tomorrow's entrepreneurs, *Journal of Management Development*, 36(6), 1–18.

Van Damme, D. (2014). Is more time spent in the classroom helpful for learning? [online]. *Education & Skills Today*, Available at: http://oecdeducationtoday.blogspot.my/2014/05/is-more-time-spent-in-classroom-helpful.html [accessed 15 September 2016].

Vesper, K.H. and Gartner, W.B. (May 1997). Measuring progress in entrepreneurship education. *Journal of Business Venturing*, 403–421.

Vukovic, R. (2015). Are schools preparing kids to be future entrepreneurs? [online]. *EducationHQ*, Available at: http://au.educationhq.com/news/32397/are-schools-preparing-kids-to-be-future-entrepreneurs/ [accessed 15 September 2016].

Wang, J., Wang, G.G., Ruona, W.E.A. and Rojewski, J.W. (2005). Confucian values and the implications for international HRD. *Human Resource Development International*, 8(3), 311–326.

Wright, S. (2013). Academic teaching doesn't prepare students for life, [online]. *Powerful Learning Practice*, Available at: http://plpnetwork.com/2013/11/07/obsession-academic-teaching-preparing-kids-life/ [accessed 15 September 2016].

4 Entrepreneurship education effectiveness

What we can learn from education and organisation studies

Joseph Tixier, Michela Loi, Sandrine Le Pontois, Mohsen Tavakoli and Alain Fayolle

Introduction

Entrepreneurship education has very different definitions, goals,[1] organisations, content,[2] targets, depending on whether it is given by academics, economists, professionals and policy makers (Fayolle, 2013; Fayolle and Gailly, 2015). Entrepreneurship education can be better understood using three analytical levels, which entail different sets of objectives, contents and targets. It relates to fostering an entrepreneurial mindset or culture in nations and organisations such as companies and universities. It also relates to developing entrepreneurial knowledge, skills and competencies which enables entrepreneurial behaviours. These two levels have transferable impact and not only serve the entrepreneurial agenda. The last level is about creating more exposure to entrepreneurship situations through teaching methods and/or setting up a context which is conducive to creating new values, developing innovations in a company or organisations. This last level is much more entrepreneurship oriented, in that it focuses on the core of entrepreneurship's new value creation and opportunity orientation (Fayolle, 2013). Fostering entrepreneurial competencies can also be important for corporations to revitalise strategy and improve financial performance (Byrne *et al.*, 2016).

In literature there is agreement about the need to improve studies' robustness with respect to the methods used to assess entrepreneurship education (Gielnik *et al.*, 2015). Some authors have also stressed the concept that more complex phenomena should be investigated by looking, for example, at those variables that act as moderators in the relationship between education and outcomes (Fayolle and Gailly, 2015); and that new outcomes ought to be explored apart from personal attitudes and intentions (Nabi *et al.*, 2017). We extend these suggestions by claiming that researchers should also reflect on the theoretical lenses that could drive the formulation of future hypotheses on entrepreneurship education evaluation. Current works, in fact, rarely make reference to evaluation models to guide an assessment study. In the late 2000s, there was a lack of research focusing on the evaluation of entrepreneurship education programmes (Pittaway and Cope, 2007). The problem is that assessments of specific programmes in entrepreneurship education are only limited to local empirical studies and illustrate the role of essential factors such as institutional strategies, infrastructure, people and relationships, in the diversity of implementation and level of success. This called for more rigorous research designs for entrepreneurship education evaluation, which would include both ex-ante and ex-post interventions measures, treatment and control group comparisons, correlation tables, the addition of moderators such as age, gender, type of course, background of teachers, teaching methods, etc. (Gielnik *et al.*, 2015; Martin *et al.*, 2013). Moreover, entrepreneurship education and its evaluation should be grounded in strong intellectual and conceptual frameworks, drawing from the fields of entrepreneurship and education, and more complex phenomena should be investigated by looking, for example, at those variables that can act as moderators in the relationship between education and outcomes (Fayolle and Gailly, 2015).

Recent meta-analysis and literature reviews point towards entrepreneurship education's influence on students' entrepreneurial perceptions and behaviours (Bae *et al.*, 2014; Nabi *et al.*, 2017). In these studies, the effect size of this impact depends on previous entrepreneurial experiences and previous intentions; its effects varies across countries depending on their cultural values; and the pedagogical guidelines behind these activities have also a role in stimulating or hindering the entrepreneurial outcomes (Piperopoulos and Dimov, 2015). In the literature there is agreement about the need to improve the studies' robustness with respect to methods (Gielnik *et al.*, 2015); and that new outcomes should be explored (Nabi *et al.*, 2017).

Researchers should also reflect about the theoretical lenses that might drive the formulation of future hypotheses. Current works, in fact, rarely make reference to the evaluation models that might guide an assessment study (Duval-Couetil, 2013; Nasr and Boujelbene, 2014; Shinnar *et al.*, 2014). Therefore, with this work we intend to present key theoretical points in the direction of stimulating a debate on the assumptions that might drive future empirical and theoretical works on entrepreneurship education assessment.

In line with this claim, we propose to look at what models the educational and organisation studies have developed to understand what constitutes effectiveness of education and training activities. The starting point of our concern is that these fields can offer interesting insights for enhancing our knowledge regarding the evaluation process in entrepreneurship education. These disciplines, in fact, have an important tradition in terms of empirical research and theoretical propositions regarding the evaluation topic (Salas and Cannon-Bowers, 2001).

Specifically, we perform an analysis of the literature by focusing attention on reviews and meta-analyses with the aim of addressing three important questions: (1) which models have these disciplines developed to assess and evaluate both education and training activities? (2) which theoretical points emerge as crucial for assessing education and training programmes? (3) which mistakes should be avoided and how the methodological and theoretical rigour can be improved?

As main results, the analysis allowed us to highlight three main key points that should be taken into consideration. First, a great deal of contributions has carefully addressed the epistemological issues that are inherent to the assessment practice. The major claim is that these issues impact the assumptions, procedures and methods of an evaluation process. For this reason they should be taken into account before approaching the assessment topic. Second, we have recognised two principal models driving the assessment research, with interesting developments that, especially in recent times, have been proposed to amend them. Finally, we inferred key aspects that scholars suggest as possible inputs to improve assessment research and practice. All these observations taken together, lead us to discuss important implications for assessing entrepreneurship education programmes.

In this chapter we first illustrate the methodological steps we followed to carry out our analysis of the literature. Then we present our major results followed by the discussions regarding the implications for entrepreneurship education.

Methodology

In order to review the literature on training and education assessment, we set up a list of keywords that best fitted with our research objectives. In particular, we concentrated our attentions both on training and education in order to have a wide view on the assessment processes. We will not attempt to define what education is as this would be too much of a contentious claim. This chapter aims at reaching a wider audience, regardless of the epistemological positioning regarding education. However, we used education as a key word as to not be limited by the context of training, to include all processes facilitating learning for attaining a higher level or stage of development in adulthood (Kohlberg and Mayer, 1972). We define training as a purposeful action taken by an organisation and its members to give participants a set of knowledge, skills and attitudes used in professional contexts. In contrast to education, whose context and goals are more general or societal, training is meant to increase the performance of the organisation implementing it (Aguinis and Kraiger, 2009).

First, we decided to concentrate our attention on systematic literature reviews and meta-analyses in order to gather the condensed knowledge developed so far. Literature reviews explore a field of research to acknowledge its main topics, ongoing dialogues, ideas, gaps depending on their specific purposes (Creswell, 2014), while "meta-analysis allows researchers to arrive at conclusions that are more accurate and more credible than can be presented in any one primary study or in a non-quantitative, narrative review" (Rosenthal and DiMatteo, 2001: 61). The fact we based our analysis on reviews and meta-analyses ensures that we are able to take into account most of the points of view that have animated the field. For this reason, we included in our list only 'Review' and 'Meta-analysis'.

Second, we crossed the keywords 'Training' and 'Education' with a set of synonyms of assessment and evaluation, by relying on previous works of literature reviews (e.g. Aguinis and Kraiger, 2009; Burke and Hutchins, 2007; Salas and Cannon-Bowers, 2001): 'training effectiveness', 'education effectiveness', 'transfer of training', 'training transfer', 'training outcomes', 'learning outcomes', 'training evaluation', 'education evaluation', 'educational assessment', and 'assessment + learning outcomes'.

This research resulted in 689 articles from ISI Web of Knowledge. Among them 88 papers were manually selected on the basis of their relevance to the subject and if they were indeed a meta-analysis or a literature review. This first selection was then refined to only keep papers focusing on the evaluation itself and excluding those focused solely on specific training characteristics (such as the use of a specific method in a specific context) or personal characteristics. This further selection yielded 29 papers to be retained that we analysed following an abductive reasoning, which is concerned with generating hypotheses about the observations or with reasoning to the best explanation (Cohen *et al.*, 2010).

We chose to proceed with an abductive reasoning going back and forth between what seemed to be important topics in the literature and a preliminary codebook based on our research question (Gioia *et al.*, 2013). This first analysis compared the summaries independently and was prepared by the authors of this chapter and colleagues working on the same body of papers to check its validity and avoid bias. In addition to this work, we compiled the selected literature's main findings, which we presented as an annexed table and summarise herein.

Results

Our analysis provided three main issues to be selected as crucial in the current debate on training and education assessment. First, we clearly noticed the importance of looking at the epistemological issues, as a necessary step to the comprehension of education effectiveness assessment. These considerations received particular attention by scholars working on evaluation, and we will highlight their implications in this chapter. Second, we found the main models in the literature, that we will discuss in chronological order, in an attempt to demonstrate how they respond to one another and to the subject matter of entrepreneurship education. These models have also received several amendments to correct their limits and inform scholars on how they could be implemented in research and practice. Third, our analysis leads us to identify key implementation issues these models face, in terms of measurement the use of indicators. Regarding this methodological point, we also touch upon the potential endogeneity issue of education effectiveness assessment models.

Preliminary epistemological considerations

Education assessment models are interesting in that they provide different lenses through which education can be looked upon and influence our perspective of education and training themselves. However, carefully reading the literature has unveiled the tension points and the deeper reflections underlying education research. It is then important for entrepreneurship education research to take a step back and consider what evaluation and assessment is really about and what is at stake for researchers, practitioners, and policy makers. We will thus first address the notions of evaluation and assessment themselves in training and education. Then we highlight how the way in which a construct is defined can completely alter the way the models that employ them are used and perceived. We take as an example the importance attributed to knowledge as a training evaluation criterion. Finally, we will reflect on the epistemological positioning of the researcher or practitioner, pointed out by scholars as crucial to assess training and education activities.

Assessment types and objectives

Education assessment has become very important for policy makers (Shephard, 2009), and should be relevant to all stakeholders (Coates, 2016). For instance, it could be rejected if baring a top-down mandate in a formal accreditation process, or if it limits faculty freedom regarding course content (Buchan *et al.*, 2004). This illustrates the first distinction which needs to be made when considering the purpose of education assessment. Assessment can be summative, a stock taking exercise, usually with a high stake for the learner or the institution[3] and taking place at the end of a course or programme; or formative, an exercise which aims at informing the education design and delivery process, usually taking place throughout the education process or through cohort monitoring (DeLuca, 2011). These different types of assessment have goals of their own, which have been judged by some scholars as incompatible to supporting learning as they could fail to provide students with individual and targeted guidance for improvement (Delandshere, 2002). For example, standard test theories associated with summative assessment take on a behaviourist perspective, in which learning is understood as an accumulation of knowledge. Testing this accumulation of knowledge, even when done through psychometric methods, would give little insight to the occurring learning processes and neglects the much more complex description of knowledge's nature more recent cognitive theories brought up (Delandshere, 2002).

Assessed constructs and their definitions

Whatever the goal or timing, assessment measures a set of criteria dealing with the acquisition, retention and transfer of knowledge, skills and attitudes. As for the concept of assessment itself, all these criteria are complex and debated in the literature, and for good reasons. It is important for scholars and practitioners to have robust definitions when collecting data for education assessment implementation or research (Melton, 1996). Here, we do not claim to give definitive recommendations, but to raise awareness on these issues to encourage debate and future research from fellow scholars in the entrepreneurship education field. We will thus consider 'knowledge' as an example of the complexity of each of these concepts mobilised by the model we present herein. Knowledge can be conceptualised in different levels of understanding which can be organised in how knowledge is recalled[4] or how it is structured and processed[5] (Entwistle and Smith, 2002). Assessing knowledge requires considering these subtleties and to acknowledge the difference between programmes' targeting understanding and the learner's personal understanding which is linked to the idiosyncratic or constructed nature of knowledge (Arthur Jr *et al.*, 2003; Entwistle and Smith, 2002).

Epistemological positioning of researchers and practitioners

Authors such as Lam (2016) brought up the importance of different epistemological positioning in the selection and use of assessment methods. For instance, in behaviourist paradigms, assessment aims to measure students' achievement in specific learning outcome targets, which can be useful to inform on compliance to standards but lacks the ability to gather progression or the learners' individual differences (Melton, 1996). Hermeneutic paradigms for example support assessment as an integral part of the learning process in foreign language education (Lam, 2016). Finally, socio-constructivist paradigms support the use of assessment beyond decision-making[6] regarding the student as a tool to support learning. This illustrates how the epistemological positioning of scholars and practitioners have shaped the way learning outcomes are assessed, resulting in methods which can be mutually incompatible.

Models of education and training effectiveness and evaluation

The models we will discuss in the next sections should be considered as complementary to each other as they represent two distinct perspectives of evaluation (Salas and Cannon-Bowers, 2001). On the one hand, the framework of Kirkpatrick (1967) offers a taxonomy of training criteria that helps understand whether, and to what extent, trainees have achieved specific training objectives. On the other hand, the model of Baldwin and Ford (1988) looks at training from a macro perspective as it aims to understand the reasons why an intervention works. Accordingly, it identifies variables and surrounding dynamics that connect training inputs and outcomes. Many empirical studies relying on the Baldwin and Ford model have included the Kirkpatrick's taxonomy as evaluation criteria, contributing to highlight some pros and cons regarding its wide application (Arthur Jr *et al.*, 2003). Kirkpatrick's model allows us to pinpoint the level at which education or training is effective. Moreover, the transition from the outcome level to the behaviour level described below can be assimilated to the transfer mechanisms described in Baldwin and Ford's (1988) model (Arthur Jr *et al.*, 2003).

By looking at recent developments it is worth noticing that these two models maintain their relevance in the literature (Bell *et al.*, 2017), and that contemporary attempts are focused on integrating different models into a unique perspectives. This provides evaluation scholars and practitioners rely on to gain a more systemic view and evaluative perspective.

Kirkpatrick's (1967) four level assessment model

Kirkpatrick's model was developed gradually from 1959 to 1996 and focuses on the different levels of outcome. It is, with Baldwin and Ford's model arguably one of the most cited assessment models (Arthur Jr *et al.*, 2003) which has influenced the development of other models (Fayolle and Gailly, 2015; Giangreco *et al.*, 2010). This model is often referred to as goal oriented as the training programme is based on targeted outcome at different levels (Gilibert and Gillet, 2010). As suggested in the title, Kirkpatrick's model is structured around four incremental levels of assessment, with each level being wider and of longer term than the previous one.

The *reaction* level focuses on the immediate effect the programme or course has on trainees. It seeks to analyse the affective response and perception of the trainee on the course itself, regardless of any knowledge or skills acquired. This level can be assimilated to a satisfaction analysis, with indications how to collect such information through surveys. Kirpatrick's (1967) own work provides possible questions to ask trainees at the end of the course, which inquires about the presentation and implementation of objectives, how the trainer presented the content in a pleasing and interesting fashion, complemented with illustrations to clarify the concepts. At this level, trainees are asked to give impressions on the preparedness of the trainer and the perceived quality of the sessions/course/programme, with the debated assumption that a high level of satisfaction will positively influence the upper levels.

The *learning* level focuses on the knowledge and skills acquired and retained during the course or programme. This level can be associated with summative, end-term assessment of the trainee, regardless of what is at stake (i.e. if the certification/degree depends on the result of this assessment). The model suggests the utilisation of a multitude of assessment methods, all aiming at measuring the knowledge and skills trainees have acquired during the course. Still according to Kirkpatrick's (1967) work, this can range from classroom performance to traditional pen and pencil tests before and after the training programme, including self-assessment methodologies.

The *behaviour* level aims to assess whether the acquired knowledge and skills during the training programme are applied beyond the training's end (Kirkpatrick, 1967). This links back to the notion of learning outcome transfer detailed in Baldwin and Ford's (1988) model, making those two models relatively complementary. This level's assessment calls for ex-post studies with a long enough delay between the end of the training programme and the actual measure. It is suggested in Kirkpatrick's (1967) work to delay the measurement by several months after the course or programme has ended. Assessing this level requires setting behaviour targets before the training takes place for comparison purposes, which links back to training design elements. The assumption underlying such assessment, similar to the previous level, is that a high level of learning will positively correlate to the observation of desired behaviours.

The *result* level, the last of Kirkpatrick's (1967) four level assessment model, could be considered by organisations as a crucial as it consists of assessing the results of the training programmes in terms of its overarching objectives. Kirkpatrick's (1967) four-level assessment model was intended for organisational training, of which the overarching objectives are an expected reduction of costs, turnover, absenteeism and/or grievances, and an increase in production quantity and quality (Fayolle and Gailly, 2015).

Baldwin and Ford (1988) model of learning outcome transfer

Baldwin and Ford's (1988) model focuses on the transfer of training outcome(s), that is, the generalisation and application of knowledge, skills and attitudes in the context other than training and maintaining this knowledge, these skills, and attitudes over time (Baldwin and Ford, 1988). This model focuses on training (as opposed to education) and is the case with Kirkpatrick's model, which is arguably the most frequently cited model of training transfer (Blume *et al.*, 2010). The model has been developed through an extensive review of empirical studies of training transfer before 1987 contemporarily to Noe's (Noe and Schmitt, 1986) work on training transfer (Cheng and Hampson, 2008). We discussed previously the necessity to better define constructs as transfer of training. However, at the time Baldwin and Ford (1988) developed their model, the literature offered little explanation as to what influences training transfer (Cheng and Ho, 2001).

The Baldwin and Ford (1988) model structures the transfer of training outcome in an input/output process with additional conditions which are more or less conducive to the generalisation and maintenance of training outcomes. The training inputs, namely the trainee characteristics, work environment and training design are suggested to influence training outputs (defined as learning and retention of learning), with the two former influencing training transfer directly as well as opposed to the latter's influence which is thought to transit though the outputs. Baldwin and Ford (1988) give a detailed description of the different inputs and conditions which have an effect on transfer, with particular attention given to the training design.

Training design characteristics proposed by the model pertain to the capacity of the programme to enhance the potential of trainees to acquire and retain knowledge skills and attitudes which are applicable to other contexts (Baldwin and Ford, 1988). Education design can expose the student to situations which are similar to 'real life situations' in which they can make effective use of their newly acquired knowledge skills and attitudes. These *identical elements* are thought to increase the retention of competencies and their generalisation into different context. The use of *general principles* in teaching, that is, the general rules and theoretical principles underlying the content presented throughout the programme, arguably enables deeper cognition and meta-cognition in trainees. This in turn enables the generalisation of the specific skills and knowledge acquired through the training programmes content and activities. The training design can also be analysed in terms of *stimulus variability*, that is, the multiplication of different training stimuli such as using several examples for the same concept. Empirical evidence suggests that a stimulus variability correlates positively with learning outcomes (Baldwin and Ford, 1988). A last category of training design mentioned in the model is the *condition of practices*, which pertains to the more logistical aspects of training. Condition of practice includes the delivery of training into distributed segments or in a massed practice, the former having empirical evidence to nurture the retaining of the outcome(s). Training can be practised by presenting the whole content and ramifications to trainees or in parts, with the former being more advantageous provided trainees have high abilities. Practice is distributed with low complexity. Feedback and overlearning (providing trainees with content which exceeds targeted knowledge levels) are also a condition of practice which can be conducive to increasing the learning outcome and its transferability.

The model considers trainees as an input to the training and transfer process as their characteristics can influence the level of learning and retention on the one hand, and the generalisation and maintenance of training outcomes on the other hand. These trainee characteristics include their pre-training abilities and aptitude, concepts which are not sufficiently defined nor given enough empirical evidence to support a link to trainability. Personality traits, such as the locus of control and pre-training motivation are also important contenders as influencing training outcome and transfer. Motivational factors more specifically have received much attention from the education assessment literature as an important factor influencing many aspects of training and education effectiveness, regardless of the assessment model considered (Baldwin and Ford, 1988).

Adaptations and evolutions of the Kirkpatrick (1967) model

Kraiger Ford and Salas 1993's work stems from Kirkpatrick's (1967) original model and the subsequent comments in the literature. Despite basing their model on Kirkpatrick's work (1967), the authors have criticised the model as not sufficiently defining what learning outcomes are and how they should be assessed (Kraiger *et al.*, 1993). They therefore propose a framework for analysing the different types of learning outcomes, breaking them down in cognitive, skill-based or conative, and affective outcome. This framework contains the types of outcomes emerging from training as well as gaining an indication on how to assess them in a practical setting.

Cognitive outcomes refer to the knowledge acquired by the trainee, their structure and inter-relations, as well as the awareness of the trainee of having acquired and organised this knowledge (referred to as *meta-cognition*). In Kraiger, Ford and Salas's (1993) publication, verbal knowledge includes declarative knowledge, procedural knowledge and tacit knowledge with the emphasis on the former. Declarative knowledge focuses purely on the amount of information retained during the programme, its accuracy when recall is asked and the speed at which this recall occurs. This type of outcome is arguably the most commonly assessed, for instance during pen and pencil, summative tests. The model prescribes the assessment of the organisation of knowledge, that is, the interconnection of knowledge elements and they hierarchical ordering. This knowledge organisation and hierarchical structure is what the authors refer to as mental models and is assessed through free sorts and structural assessment methods for instance. Last in the cognitive outcome category is the trainees' awareness of their own mental models (self-insight) and voluntary regulation strategies (meta-cognitive skills). These are grouped under the cognitive strategies category. The authors propose several method of testing ranging from probed protocol analysis to self-report to account for the diversity of cognitive outcomes' nature in their model.

Skill-based learning outcomes[7] concerns the ability to display technical or motor behaviours, derived from knowledge or abilities. Using skills to link cognitive outcomes to behaviours resemble what other authors, such as Baldwin and Ford (1988), defined as transfer and might hint at a possible compliment to these models. Skills can be developed through initial acquisition, which can be seen as transitioning from declarative knowledge to procedural knowledge, skill compilation and automaticity. Skill-based learning outcomes in Kraiger, Ford and Salas's (1993) model concerns the compilation and automaticity of skills. Compilation stems from the proceduralisation of skills, a process by which students build domain specific production or routines from small and discrete behaviour which are seemingly unrelated. This can also be directly linked to the generalisation of outcomes described in Baldwin and Ford's (1988) model. Simultaneously, compilation stems from the composition of incremental steps requiring specific skills into a more complex production process. Kraiger, Ford and Salas (1993) have proposed several observational methods to assess the compilation of skills which make use of more qualitative approaches such as behaviour observations and interviews. Automaticity is usually thought of as the stage following compilation, described by the authors as an unconscious completion of tasks or behaviour display. The student is, at this stage, incapable of verbalising the intended behaviour, in an automatic processing. This automatic processing is followed by tuning phases whereby the behaviours gain in precision and the ability to reduce the attention need for the completion of a task. The authors illustrate these phases with the example of a skilled driver being able to perform other tasks while driving such as conversing with passengers and monitoring the road without losing control of the mechanical aspects of driving.

Affective outcomes refers to the attitudinal and motivational changes involved with the training programme. Attitudes can be addressed in training through setting targeted attitudes such as sociability, creative individualism and/or tolerance for diversity. This category of affective outcome is particularly elusive as measurements are much more complex. Measurements should consider the expression of a particular attitudinal trait as well as the intensity of such a trait. Motivational outcomes are measured through motivational dispositions, that is, the concern for increasing competencies (referred to as mastery orientation) and an intention to perform a task well (referred to as performance orientation) (Kraiger *et al.*, 1993). Moreover, this category of affective outcome is composed by self-efficacy, a recurring personality characteristic in education literature as well as entrepreneurship literature which is arguably tied to the application of learning outcomes beyond the context of training. Motivation is, according to the literature reviewed by Kraiger, Ford and Salas (1993), linked to the ability to set goals which increases the like-lihood of learning outcomes to be transferred into behaviours.

As stated above, Kraiger's model sheds light on the different types of outcome expected out of training programmes and provides the guidelines to assess them. However this model cannot be isolated from more general models to understand the diversity of impact that a training programme can offer an organisation or society (Gilibert and Gillet, 2010). This discrepancy in both Kraiger *et al.*'s (1993) and Kirkpatrick's (1967) model called for a combined effort similar to the Beech and Leather (2006) attempt. Beech and Leather (2006) argued that Kirkpatrick's (1967) model was outdated and needed to include findings from more recent models. To do so, the authors have included Kraiger, Ford and Salas's (1993) typo-logy of learning outcomes at both Kirkpatrick's (1967) learning and behaviour levels. They however separated each category depending on whether they pertain to learning or to behaviour results. This meant including verbal knowledge and knowledge organisation at the learning level and knowledge organisation and cog-nitive strategies at the behaviour level. Regarding skill-based outcome, compilation skills have been added to the learning level as this describes the organisation of learning outcomes and automaticity to the behaviour level to give a level of detail on whether the behaviour is consciously manifested or not. Finally, affective out-comes have been added in their entirety of both learning and behaviour levels. In addition to incorporating Kraiger, Ford and Salas's (1993) typology of outcome into Kirkpatrick's model of impact levels, Beech and Leather followed on Phillips' work (1996) to add a cost/benefit analysis of the training programme. Another con-tribution from Beech and Leather (2006), arguably the most interesting (Gilibert and Gillet, 2010), concerns the timing of training results assessments whereby lower levels of impact, namely reaction and learning are assessed immediately after the training's end and the following levels at longer term.

Another notable model which addresses the context and resources of a train-ing programme has been developed by Warr, Bird and Rackham (1979). This model considers the Context, Inputs, Reaction and Outputs of a training pro-gramme, and is referred to by its acronym CIRO. In this model, reaction and outcome corresponds to the definitions provided in Kirkpatrick's model, with the addition of the outcome typology provided by Kraiger, Ford and Salas (1993) (Beech and Leather, 2006; Gilibert and Gillet, 2010). The main addition of Warr, Bird and Rackham (1979) has been to add two distinct levels of analysis which take into consideration the context, including the training needs assessment, and the resources available for the training, including finances, time and competen-cies. An interesting aspect of Warr, Bird and Rackham's model is that it con-siders needs assessment as an integral part of the training design and assessment and posits that the training's quality is dependent on this needs assessment (Gilibert and Gillet, 2010). This is particularly important as previous works suggest that the valence, that is the trainers' belief that the learning outcome is desirable or fit their expectations, influences the motivation to learn and to transfer learning outcomes (Colquitt *et al.*, 2000).

Reflection on assessment models

Over the years, empirical evidence using Kirkpatrick's (1967) model has been provided regarding the impact of training on the different outcome levels. The evidence suggest a more pronounced effect for learning level outcomes but less so at reaction level (Arthur Jr *et al.*, 2003). This could be explained by the presence of other factors influencing reaction levels (such as pre-training motivation and self-efficacy) and the heterogeneity in reaction types themselves which blur the link between reaction and outcome (Zietsma and Lawrence, 2010). However, if Kirkpatrick's (1967) model helps understand the level at which training impacts outcomes, it suffers from several limitations and has sparked much debate. This is perhaps due to its simplicity, which might have eased its diffusion but triggered accusations of oversimplifications and incompleteness. Scholars have argued that the sequential organisation of levels haven't been backed up by sufficient empirical evidence (Cheng and Hampson, 2008; Holton *et al.*, 1997). Contextualisation is deemed important in education, yet Kirkpatrick's (1967) model insufficiently describes the contextual conditions interacting with the different outcome levels (Gilibert and Gillet, 2010). The model has been amended with the addition by Phillips (1996) of a fifth indicator in parallel to the result level taking into consideration the cost of training (Cheng and Hampson, 2008). This indicator, often assimilated to a return on investment (ROI), contributes to the formulation of a four-plus-one assessment model. Adding to the theoretical limitations, empirical evidence gathered from 1952 through to 2002 has suggested very little improvement of training effectiveness amongst programmes using the model's assessment guidelines (Skylar Powell and Yalcin, 2010).

Baldwin and Ford's (1988) model, like the ones described herein, attempts to assess how the learning outcomes result in a behavioural change beyond the training context, linking it to a behaviourist approach of education. Scholars such as Cheng and Ho (2001) have found several limitations which are linked to semantics and the methodological operationalisation of an assessment using this model. Specifically, this model is limited by the definition of training transfer itself, its operationalisation and timing of measurement; the lack of models describing which trainee and environmental characteristics influence training outcome transfer and how to operationalise them; and the low complexity of the tasks and training design elements used to examine the transfer of training outcomes (Cheng and Ho, 2001).

At this point it seems also relevant to stop and consider the importance motivation has been given in the existing literature as an important variable to education assessment. Motivation has been found to be a powerful mediator and moderator in the effect personal characteristics (such as the locus of control, conscientiousness, anxiety, age, cognitive ability, self-efficacy, valence, job involvement) and situational characteristics have on training outcome. This result, stemming from Noe and Schmitt's 1986 work on trainees' attitude and motivation, uncovered in a large meta-analytic study by Colquitt, LePine and

Noe (2000) and led Naquin and Holton to define a specific indicator of motivation to improve work through learning (MTIWL). This indicator is a function of the motivation to train, defined as the desire to learn the content of a programme, and motivation to transfer these learning outcomes into everyday practice. It provides an interesting construct of motivation and how it can affect learning outcomes.

Key points from the literature and for education assessment implementation and assessment research

The selected literature on education and training effectiveness is unanimous on the positive correlation between education or training[8] and an increased human capital or job performance. From an organisational perspective, this translates into a positive return on investment in terms of financial indicators and their stability (Aguinis and Kraiger, 2009). We will present here the main findings in the extant literature using the Baldwin and Ford (1988) model as a structure for factors influencing education and training effectiveness. In this model, the factors are grouped into educational/training characteristics, personal characteristics and environmental characteristics. Similarly, we will refer to Kirkpatrick's (1967) model for the level at which educational and personal characteristics have an effect.

Education/training characteristics or design includes the different teaching methods used, content, as well as the tacit and explicit objectives of the programme. The choice of a teaching method isn't neutral to the reaction and learning outcome of a training or education programme (Salas and Cannon-Bowers, 2001) and scholars have been exploring the effect different methods have on different outcome types. For example, as a consequence of the rise in the use of technology, scholars have explored the effect this approach has on learning and its assessment with contradicting results (Perrotta, 2014). In contrast to the teaching method, the effective content of training, such as the trained skill or tasks characteristics, could be more correlated to the behaviourial outcome (Arthur Jr *et al.*, 2003). Entrepreneurship being closely related to context and interactions with it (Bruyat and Julien, 2001), entrepreneurship education research should focus on interactions and the psycho-cognitive processes which play a role in individual learning and pedagogical strategies (Béchard and Grégoire, 2005). In contrast to the teaching method, the effective content of training, which can be specialised or generalist; and approached from a learning or a teaching paradigm (Béchard and Grégoire, 2005); could be more correlated to the behaviour outcome (Arthur Jr *et al.*, 2003). Research in graduate entrepreneurship (GE) has examined the role of various supports or interventions (Blizzard, 1996; Flemming, 1994), assessed mechanisms for promoting GE as a career option (Fletcher, 1999); explored the factors that influence the start-up process (Macfarlane and Tomlinson, 1993), and has developed model processes to turn virtual projects into real business, and finally has tracked the performance of graduate-led enterprises. Entrepreneurship education and training, linked with the notion human capital assets, provides (1) entrepreneurial knowledge and skills; (2) positive perceptions of entrepreneurship; (3) intentions to start a business (Martin *et al.*, 2013). Educational characteristics also include the design phase, which include assessing needs, antecedent and pre-training conditions, and setting objectives and instructional strategies. The need assessment phase is useful for organisations to analyse the task requirements and organisational requirements which could be addressed by a training programme. We argue that this assessment can be done outside organisation boundaries, for instance in the design of a national curriculum. Although arguments have been made in favour of needs assessment (Salas and Cannon-Bowers, 2001), with some scholars arguing that its correlation to education effectiveness hasn't been robustly tested throughout the literature (Arthur Jr *et al.*, 2003). The objectives underlying an education programme has been scrutinised as well in the literature. For instance, Blume, Ford, Baldwin and Huang (2010), have conducted a meta-analysis on the effect of certain aspects of training characteristics on its effectiveness. They found that open training objectives correlate more strongly to effectiveness than closed training objectives. This means that training programmes aiming at giving students broader skills could be more effective than those focusing on skills and tasks to be transferred identically in professional contexts. In the same study they found that training programmes aiming at having an effect at the learning level would be more correlated to effectiveness than those aiming at behavioural targets.

Personal characteristics have received their share of attention by education assessment scholars as well (Baldwin and Ford, 1988; Colquitt *et al.*, 2000; Noe and Schmitt, 1986). The main question being 'which of these characteristics are correlated to education effectiveness, and the direction of this correlation?'. On the one hand, personal characteristics arguably influence how learners react to training (Salas and Cannon-Bowers, 2001), which in turn could influence a higher level of outcome (Kirkpatrick, 1979). Other characteristics such as cognitive abilities, conscientiousness and ambition, to strive for achievement can be correlated directly to learning and behaviour levels of training outcome (Cheng and Ho, 2001). On the other hand, education and training has the obvious capacity to influence personal characteristics as well, but Kirkpatrick's (1979) model allows a finer analysis of the phenomenon. There is a strong body of evidence that the student's reaction to education or training can have an effect on motivation (Blume *et al.*, 2010; Cheng and Hampson, 2008; Cheng and Ho, 2001), and self-efficacy (Salas and Cannon-Bowers, 2001). Other personal characteristics, which correlate to education effectiveness, belong to the relationship itself learners have with the training or education programme. These personal characteristics describe how the learner perceives the training to fulfil their expectancy, its relevance to the learner as well as the learner's readiness for the programme (Knyphausen-Aufseß *et al.*, 2009).

Implementation of education and training assessment and assessment research

Our literature review also unveiled a certain number of hot topics which could be addressed in entrepreneurship education as well. These topics pertain to the practical implementation of education or training assessment and research regarding this assessment. The first concerns how the purpose of the assessment is tied to contextual elements and informs policy makers on the amplification of effective education programmes. Should assessment be implemented top-down or at classroom level? Should it consider a course, programme, education system? Should it serve a stock-taking, high stake, purpose or be an integral part of the learning process? All these questions should be taken into consideration in terms of future research.

Another source of scholarly discussion concerns the impact of the assessment itself – the actual measurement of education outcomes – has on the education process. This discussion is particularly crucial and is tied to the question mentioned above on whether assessment should serve a stock-taking purpose or be embedded in the education process. This also informs on the potential source for endogeneity in empirical work concerning the use of models.

A last point we wish to put forward for our future discussion in entrepreneurship education effectiveness concerns the methodological aspects of assessment. We touched upon this issue at the beginning of this chapter with a reflection on the epistemological positioning of assessment scholars and practitioners. However, there is an important discussion going on in the education literature on the potential methodological biases the assessment exercise inherently holds.

The context in which assessment is implemented isn't neutral in the interpretation of results and subsequent actions taken by practitioners and policy makers. For instance, poor feasibility of data collection, analysis and reporting might lead to focusing on outcome rather than resources and take time away from education or research, and eventually the rejection of assessment results (Buchan *et al.*, 2004; Coates, 2016). Assessments might be rejected as well when they contradict teachers' traditional epistemological positioning (Buchan *et al.*, 2004), or if it deters their independence, creativity or enthusiasm (Melton, 1996; Perrotta, 2014). All these arguments have a strong contextual dimension, similar to any education assessment endeavour. Researchers have pointed out the danger of national or international assessment practices aiming to set standards without considering context or the latest development in cognitive theories (Delandshere, 2002). The context in which assessment is implemented isn't neutral to the researchers' community either. Considering the importance of education policies in political debates, the rise of stock-taking assessment holding those policies accountable and its impact at various scales (DeLuca, 2011), led scholars in education science to taint current research with a sense of urgency and pressure. This deters rigorous research on learning and its assessment, which seems to focus more on stock taking than truly understanding the nature of knowledge, acquisition processes and outcomes (Buchan *et al.*, 2004; Delandshere, 2002). Qualitative methods have been used to include and provide support to the influence cultural attributes and evaluation systems has in learning outcome assessments (Kells, 1999). The geographical or cultural distance, in the case of international assessments, can also introduce bias if the researcher or the assessor is from a different country than the one considered (Elliott and Greatorex, 2002). This is particularly crucial in international comparison including developed and developing economies (Little, 1996). These issues of the implementation of assessment, its origin and context should be taken into consideration in future research and by scholars in their research practice as well.

Another aspect of looking at *how* assessment is researched and implemented relates to its operationalisation. Indeed, the way education assessment is operationalised has an effect on its results and their validity (Coates, 2016). When providing a grade based on targeted learning outcomes, assessment can lack the detail in describing the individual students' real understanding (Melton, 1996). Assessing learning outcome transfer through the use of acquired skills or assessing it through the *effectiveness* in using such skills have very different implications (Blume *et al.*, 2010). Scholars in education science have been lamenting the lack of a proper theoretical framework in outcome and transfer measurement (Baldwin and Ford, 1988; Noe and Schmitt, 1986). Assessment models have thus been introduced into the literature and presented herein. They include and use the relevant theoretical concepts, but concerns are still raised regarding the validity of measurements in subsequent model testing (Cheng and Ho, 2001; Coates, 2016). This links to the latest evolution of validity theory and the shift from purely quantitative measures and positivistic approaches towards multiple inquiry methods, interpretation or hermeneutic processes (Delandshere, 2002; DeLuca, 2011; Noe *et al.*, 2014). The arguments and questions of this paragraph point out the inherent obtrusive nature of assessment and the difficulty to operationalise assessment practice and research. Education assessment isn't a neutral task. It has political and policy implications, contextual dimensions, and has arguably an impact on what it is trying to measure.

The last argument we wish to put forward regarding the implementation of assessment relates to the collection of data for assessment or research purposes and how it is a potential source of bias and endogeneity. Assessment has a significant impact at classroom level on the teaching and learning processes through the effect it has on students' motivation; and at national and system level through the political and policy making effects described herein (DeLuca, 2011). Researching on the assessment of learning outcomes thus calls for the understanding of the special place assessment has in education. For this reason, scholars have even separated assessment of learning from other processes such as assessment as or for learning, which aims at increasing the student's independence and has arguable effects on meta-cognitive learning outcomes through self-assessment and increased self-efficacy (Lam, 2016). Method variance, in particular the time taken between the programme's end and the transfer measurement, also has been pointed out as the source of assessment variance in general (Blume *et al.*, 2010). This bias source is in fact so important that the authors called for a moratorium on studies using a same source and same measurement context methodology[9] (Blume *et al.*, 2010). Meta-analysis, provided the considered studies report on reliability and validity, can improve models and variable interactions measurements (Huang *et al.*, 2015). Unlike most of the articles included here, future research and assessment attempts should include more details in the methodology used, such as the presence of a control group, timing of assessments (ex-ante and ex-post), and the evaluation method itself (Skylar Powell and Yalcin, 2010). Another way to improve the validity of measurement and reduce potential biases is to use multiple assessment methods (Perrotta, 2014). These methods involve multiple stakeholders, such as moderated and collaborative assessment (Coates, 2016). These arguments point at the potential source of endogeneity and biases the methodology used for assessment represents, as they influence learning outcomes and the precision of their measurement.

Discussion: linking education and training literature to the field of entrepreneurship

Throughout our chapter, we have outlined the important aspects of education and training assessment literature. Our contributions are multiple. First, relying on an in depth literature analysis, we have shed light on the ontological and epistemological aspects of education and assessment. Then we proceeded to cast light on the different models used to assess education outcomes and their transfer. These models are responding to one another and have evolved over time, as we attempted to demonstrate. In a logical subsequence of steps, we delved into the practical aspects of education assessment. Drawing from the literature's main result, we pointed out some key correlations in education effectiveness, linking them to the different main models presented herein. All these results can be useful to understand entrepreneurship education effectiveness assessment for researchers and practitioners. We, therefore, provide some suggestions in this direction by recognising the need of focusing our attention on three main issues related to delimiting concepts, contents and methodology. (Figure 4.1 summarises our contribution to entrepreneurship education assessment.)

Due to the inherent complexity of education and its assessment, and to their multiple and fragmented nature, our analysis suggests that we should carefully reflect on their possible meaning in entrepreneurship education. Our analysis of the literature has revealed that education and its assessment are strictly tied to the contexts, people involved in training or educational activities, and secondary stakeholders of these activities. First and foremost, this implies the need to identify the different natures of entrepreneurship education. In other words, we need to have an idea of what entrepreneurship education should achieve and to what purpose before implementing a course in a specific context and before designing a 'protocol' of evaluation.

Concerning the need to delimiting the concept of assessment as a research process, our analysis has shown that it can have different functions. Specifically, we can recognise two main evaluative roles that can apply to entrepreneurship education: on the one hand the assessment process is set to understand the impact and the effectiveness of a specific entrepreneurship programme, where a principal distinction is between a summative and formative evaluation; on the other hand the assessment process can be seen as a protocol by which experimenting and developing new training approaches and designs better sustains entrepreneurial learning.

Furthermore, the entrepreneurship education impact can be analysed from different levels of analysis, which span from the individual, course, university/institution and state level. For each level we can set different outputs and protocols of evaluation, and each of them contributes to defining and delimiting the concept of entrepreneurship education.

Regarding the content, Baldwin and Ford (1988) have pointed out in their model that complex dynamics surround the processes of learning and transferring, all these processes implies a set of mutual interactions among personal, training and environmental characteristics. These dynamics should be carefully scrutinised in future assessment studies on entrepreneurship education, with the

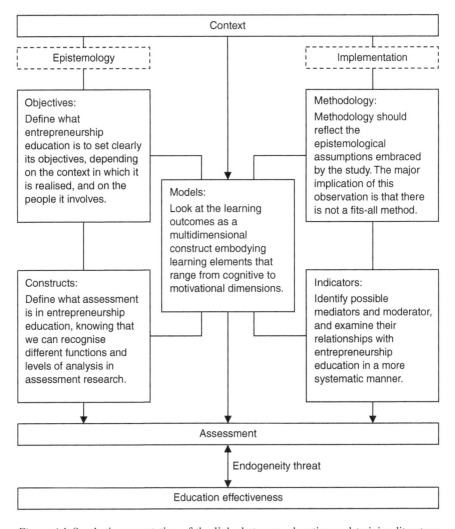

Figure 4.1 Synthetic presentation of the links between education and training literature and the field of entrepreneurship.

aim of identifying possible mediators and moderators that can contribute to hindering or fostering the role of entrepreneurship education.

The literature also suggests embracing a broader conception of learning, seen as a multidimensional construct embodying elements ranging from cognitive to motivational dimensions. In entrepreneurship education studies, we should then reflect on these dimensions to figure out how to examine the entrepreneurship programmes' impact at the individual or group level.

Methodological issues are key elements in evaluation (Aguinis and Kraiger, 2009), as they reflect the epistemological assumptions of a study, by ensuring its robustness. By looking specifically at the research approaches, we can recognise two main designs of conducting an assessment research, one is based on quasi-experiment or experiment, oriented to evaluate specific goals (Sackett and Mullen, 1993); the other one is known as goal-free, more adapted to discover unexpected results (Jonassen, 1992). The analysis of the literature suggests that there is not a unique research approach that fits-all assessment studies, rather there is a need to identifying an evaluation protocol that mirrors training peculiarities (e.g. target and objectives), assessment functions and levels of analysis.

Conclusion

This chapter provides an overview of the literature on education and training assessment with the aim of enriching the debate on assessment in the field of entrepreneurship education. In reviewing literature reviews and meta-analyses, grounded on education and organisational studies, we describe (1) the models these fields of inquiry have developed to assess and evaluate both education and training activities; (2) the theoretical points that emerge as crucial for assessing education and training programmes; (3) the elements that this body of research suggest as key elements to avoid mistakes while improving the methodological and theoretical rigour in assessment practice.

Based on these reflections we highlight a set of key points that we believe should be considered to enhance the evaluation practices of entrepreneurship education: (1) identifying the different natures of entrepreneurship education by clearly defining its purposes; (2) taking into account the complex dynamics surrounding the processes of learning and transferring, stemming from mutual interactions among personal, training and environmental characteristics; (3) embracing a multidimensional conception of learning, embodying elements ranging from cognitive to motivational dimensions; (4) consider multiple methodological approaches; (5) understanding of different assessment goals and (6) different levels of analysis.

Notes

1 Entrepreneurship education's objective range from increasing start-up rates to nurturing an entrepreneurial mindset, promoting entrepreneurship as a viable career option.
2 Entrepreneurship education's content can be about the nature of entrepreneurship as well as the process of entrepreneurship, and the teaching methods can vary from experiential learning to traditional frontal teaching.

3 The stake can be the selection of a candidate, or the accreditation of a course/curriculum (Delandshere, 2002).
4 Such as in Peel's levels of mentioning, describing and explaining (1975).
5 Such as in Biggs and Collis's taxonomy of pre-structural, multi-structural, relational and extended abstract levels (1986).
6 What is often referred to as 'high stake assessment' and is perceived as being tied to a positivist paradigm.
7 Sometimes referred to as conative outcomes in other publications (Gilibert and Gillet, 2010).
8 This include personal development programmes.
9 Evidence suggest that same source and same measurement context (or SS/SMC) methodologies inflate the relationships between variables, where for instance the measurement of input factors and outcome factors of transfer is done with the same self-assessment method and at the same point in time (Blume *et al.*, 2010).

Bibliography

Aguinis, H. and Kraiger, K. (2009). Benefits of training and development for individuals and teams, organizations, and society. *Annu. Rev. Psychol.*, 60, 451–474. doi:10.1146/annurev.psych.60.110707.163505.

Arthur Jr, W., Bennett Jr, W., Edens, P.S. and Bell, S.T. (2003). Effectiveness of training in organizations: A meta-analysis of design and evaluation features. *J. Appl. Psychol.*, 88, 234.

Bae, T.J., Qian, S., Miao, C. and Fiet, J.O. (2014). The relationship between entrepreneurship education and entrepreneurial intentions: A meta-analytic review. *Entrep. Theory Pract.*, 38, 217–254.

Baldwin, T.T. and Ford, J.K. (1988). Transfer of training: A review and directions for future research. *Pers. Psychol.*, 41, 63–105.

Béchard, J.P. and Grégoire, D. (2005). Entrepreneurship education research revisited: The case of higher education. *Academy of Management Learning & Education*, 4(1), 22–43.

Beech, B. and Leather, P. (2006). Workplace violence in the health care sector: A review of staff training and integration of training evaluation models. *Aggress. Violent Behav.*, 11, 27–43.

Bell, B.S., Tannenbaum, S.I., Ford, J.K., Noe, R.A. and Kraiger, K. (2017). 100 years of training and development research: What we know and where we should go. *Journal of Applied Psychology*, 102(3), 305–323.

Biggs, J.B. and Collis, K.F. (1982). *Evaluating the quality of learning: The SOLO taxonomy*. New York: Academic Press.

Blizzard, D. (1996). Promoting entrepreneurship as a career option and providing business start-up support for students and graduates – experiences of graduate enterprise. *International Small Business Journal*, 14(3), 104–106.

Blume, B.D., Ford, J.K., Baldwin, T.T. and Huang, J.L. (2010). Transfer of training: A Meta-Analytic Review. *J. Manag.*, 36, 1065–1105. doi:10.1177/0149206309352880.

Bruyat, C. and Julien, P.A. (2001). Defining the field of research in entrepreneurship. *Journal of Business Venturing*, 16(2), 165–180.

Buchan, V., Rodenhiser, R., Hull, G., Smith, M., Rogers, J., Pike, C. and Ray, J. (2004). Evaluating an assessment tool for undergraduate social work education: Analysis of the Baccalaureate Educational Assessment Package. *J. Soc. Work Educ.*, 40, 239–253.

Burke, L.A. and Hutchins, H.M. (2007). Training transfer: An integrative literature review. *Human Resource Development Review*, 6(3), 263–296.

Byrne, J., Delmar, F., Fayolle, A. and Lamine, W. (2016). Training corporate entrepreneurs: an action learning approach. *Small Bus. Econ.*, 47, 479–506. doi:10.1007/s11187-016-9734-9.

Cheng, E.W.L. and Hampson, I. (2008). Transfer of training: A review and new insights. *Int. J. Manag. Rev.*, 10, 327–341. doi:10.1111/j.1468-2370.2007.00230.x.

Cheng, E.W. and Ho, D.C. (2001). A review of transfer of training studies in the past decade. *Pers. Rev.*, 30, 102–118.

Coates, H., 2016. Assessing student learning outcomes internationally: Insights and frontiers. *Assess. Eval. High. Educ.*, 41, 662–676. doi:10.1080/02602938.2016.1160273.

Cohen, T., Schvaneveldt, R. and Widdows, D., 2010. Reflective random indexing and indirect inference: A scalable method for discovery of implicit connections. *J. Biomed. Inform.*, 43, 240–256. doi:10.1016/j.jbi.2009.09.003.

Colquitt, J.A., LePine, J.A. and Noe, R.A. (2000). Toward an integrative theory of training motivation: A meta-analytic path analysis of 20 years of research. *J. Appl. Psychol.*, 85, 678.

Creswell, J.W. (2014). Research design: Qualitative, quantitative, and mixed methods approaches. 4th ed. Los Angeles: Sage publications.

Delandshere, G., 2002. Assessment as inquiry. *Teach. Coll. Rec.*, 104, 1461–1484.

DeLuca, C., 2011. Interpretive validity theory: Mapping a methodology for validating educational assessments. *Educ. Res.*, 53, 303–320. doi:10.1080/00131881.2011.598659.

Duval-Couetil, N. (2013). Assessing entrepreneurship education programs: Challenges and approaches. *Journal of Small Business Management*, 51(3), 394–409.

Elliott, G. and Greatorex, J. (2002). A fair comparison? The evolution of methods of comparability in national assessment. *Educ. Stud.*, 28, 253–264. doi:10.1080/0305569022000003670.

Entwistle, N. and Smith, C. (2002). Personal understanding and target understanding: Mapping influences on the outcomes of learning. *Br. J. Educ. Psychol.*, 72, 321–342.

Fayolle, A. (2013) Personal views on the future of entrepreneurship education. *Entrepreneurship & Regional Development: An International Journal*, 25(7–8), 692–701.

Fayolle, A. and Gailly, B. (2015). The impact of entrepreneurship education on entrepreneurial attitudes and intention: Hysteresis and persistence. *J. Small Bus. Manag.*, 53, 75–93. doi:10.1111/jsbm.12065.

Fleming, P. (1994). The role of structured interventions in shaping graduate entrepreneurship. *Irish Business and Administrative Research*, 15, 146–157.

Fletcher, M. (1999). Promoting entrepreneurship as a career option – the graduate enterprise programme. *Journal of European Industrial Training*, 23(3), 127–139.

Giangreco, A., Carugati, A. and Sebastiano, A. (2010). Are we doing the right thing? Food for thought on training evaluation and its context. *Pers. Rev.*, 39, 162–177. doi:10.1108/00483481011017390.

Gielnik, M.M., Frese, M., Kahara-Kawuki, A., Katono, I.W., Kyejjusa, S., Ngoma, M., Munene, J., Namatovu-Dawa, R., Nansubuga, F., Orobia, L., *et al.* (2015). Action and action-regulation in entrepreneurship: Evaluating a student training for promoting entrepreneurship. *Acad. Manag. Learn. Educ.*, 14, 69–94.

Gilibert, D. and Gillet, I. (2010). Revue des modèles en évaluation de formation : approches conceptuelles individuelles et sociales. *Prat. Psychol.*, 16, 217–238. doi:10.1016/j.prps.2009.03.006.

Gioia, D.A., Corley, K.G. and Hamilton, A.L. (2013). Seeking qualitative rigor in inductive research: Notes on the Gioia methodology. *Organ. Res. Methods*, 16, 15–31.

Holton, E.F., Bates, R.A., Seyler, D.L. and Carvalho, M.B. (1997). Toward construct validation of a transfer climate instrument. *Hum. Resour. Dev. Q.*, 8, 95–113. doi:10.1002/hrdq.3920080203.

Huang, J.L., Blume, B.D., Ford, J.K. and Baldwin, T.T. (2015). A tale of two transfers: Disentangling maximum and typical transfer and their respective predictors. *J. Bus. Psychol.*, 30, 709–732. doi:10.1007/s10869-014-9394-1.

Jonassen, D.H. (1992). Evaluating constructivistic learning. In: Thomas M. Duffy and David H. Jonassen, eds. *Constructivism and the technology of instruction: A conversation*. Abingdon: Routledge, pp. 137–148.

Kells, H.R. (1999). National higher education evaluation systems: Methods for analysis and some propositions for the research and policy void. *High. Educ.*, 38, 209–232.

Kirkpatrick, D.L. (1967). Evaluation of training. In: R.L. Craig and L. Bittel, eds. *Training and development handbook*. New York: McGraw Hill, pp. 87–112.

Kirkpatrick, D.L. (1979). Techniques for evaluating training programs. *Train. Dev. J.*, 33, 78.

Knyphausen-Aufseß, D. Zu and Smukalla, M., Abt, M. (2009). Towards a new training transfer portfolio: A review of training-related studies in the last decade. *Ger. J. Hum. Resour. Manag.*, 23, 288–311. doi:10.1177/239700220902300408.

Kohlberg, L. and Mayer, R. (1972). Development as the aim of education. *Harv. Educ. Rev.*, 42, 449–496. doi:10.17763/haer.42.4.kj6q8743r3j00j60.

Kraiger, K., Ford, J.K. and Salas, E. (1993). Application of cognitive, skill-based, and affective theories of learning outcomes to new methods of training evaluation. *J. Appl. Psychol.*, 78, 311–328.

Lam, R. (2016). Assessment as learning: examining a cycle of teaching, learning, and assessment of writing in the portfolio-based classroom. *Stud. High. Educ.*, 41, 1900–1917. doi:10.1080/03075079.2014.999317.

Little, A.W. (1996). Globalisation and educational research: Whose context counts? *Int. J. Educ. Dev.*, 16, 427–438.

Macfarlane, B. and Tomlinson, K. (1993). Managing and assessing student enterprise projects. *Education + Training*, 35(3), 33–37.

Martin, B.C., McNally, J.J., and Kay, M.J. (2013). Examining the formation of human capital in entrepreneurship: A meta-analysis of entrepreneurship education outcomes. *J. Bus. Ventur.*, 28, 211–224. doi:10.1016/j.jbusvent.2012.03.002.

Melton, R. (1996). Learning outcomes for higher education: Some key issues. *Br. J. Educ. Stud.*, 44, 409–425.

Nabi, G., Liñán, F., Krueger, N., Fayolle, A. and Walmsley, A. (2017). The impact of entrepreneurship education in higher education: A systematic review and research agenda. *Acad. Manag. Learn. Educ.* amle.2015.0026. doi:10.5465/amle.2015.0026.

Nasr, B.K. and Boujelbene, Y. (2014). Assessing the impact of entrepreneurial education. *Procedia – Social and Behavioural Sciences*, 109, 712–715.

Noe, R.A. and Schmitt, N. (1986). The influence of trainee attitudes on training effectiveness: Test of a model. *Pers. Psychol.*, 39, 497–523. doi:10.1111/j.1744-6570.1986.tb00950.x.

Noe, R.A., Clarke, A.D.M. and Klein H.J. (2014). Learning in the twenty-first-century workplace. *Annu. Rev. Organ. Psychol. Organ. Behav.*, 1, 245–275. doi:10.1146/annurev-orgpsych-031413-091321.

Peel, E.A. (1971). *The nature of adolescent judgement*. London: Staples Press.

Perrotta, C. (2014). Innovation in technology-enhanced assessment in the UK and the USA: Future scenarios and critical considerations. *Technol. Pedagogy Educ.*, 23, 103–119. doi:10.1080/1475939X.2013.838453.

Phillips, J.J. (1996). How much is the training worth? *Train. Dev.*, 50, 20–24.

Piperopoulos, P. and Dimov, D. (2015). Burst bubbles or build steam? Entrepreneurship education, entrepreneurial self-efficacy, and entrepreneurial intentions. *J. Small Bus. Manag.*, 53, 970–985.

Pittaway, L. and Cope, J. (2007). Entrepreneurship education: A systematic review of the evidence. *International Small Business Journal*, 25(5), 479–510.

Rosenthal, R. and DiMatteo, M.R. (2001). Meta-analysis: Recent developments in quantitative methods for literature reviews. *Annu. Rev. Psychol.*, 52, 59–82.

Sackett, P.R. and Mullen, E.J. (1993). Beyond formal experimental design: Towards an expanded view of the training evaluation process. *Pers. Psychol.*, 46, 613–627. doi:10.1111/j.1744-6570.1993.tb00887.x.

Salas, E. and Cannon-Bowers, J.A. (2001). The science of training: A decade of progress. *Annu. Rev. Psychol.*, 52, 471–499. doi:10.1146/annurev.psych.52.1.471.

Shephard, K. (2009). *e* is for exploration: Assessing hard-to-measure learning outcomes. *Br. J. Educ. Technol.*, 40, 386–398. doi:10.1111/j.1467-8535.2008.00927.x.

Shinnar, R.S., Hsu, D.K. and Powell, B.C. (2014). Self-efficacy, entrepreneurial intentions, and gender: Assessing the impact of entrepreneurship education longitudinally. *The International Journal of Management Education*, 12, 561–570.

Skylar Powell, K. and Yalcin, S. (2010). Managerial training effectiveness: A meta-analysis 1952–2002. *Pers. Rev. 39, 227–241.* doi:10.1108/00483481011017435.

Warr, P., Bird, M. and Rackham, N. (1979). Evaluation of management training: A practical framework, with cases, for evaluating training needs and results. Westmead U.A.: Gower Press.

Zietsma, C. and Lawrence, T.B. (2010). Institutional work in the transformation of an organizational field: The interplay of boundary work and practice work. *Adm. Sci. Q.*, 55, 189–221.

5 In search of relevance

The value of work based learning

David Devins and Martin Reynolds

Introduction

It is a stimulating exercise for those working in higher education (HE) to reflect on where leaders, managers and workers learn the knowledge and skills necessary to succeed in the world of work. The most frequent finding will be that they say that they learn them at work rather than by way of reference to any formal education undertaken. Of course on reflection, many workers will recognise that the basic skills of literacy and numeracy that laid the foundations for later learning are acquired largely in the classroom. However, the finding that much relevant learning is informal and occurs in the workplace is a good reason to reflect on the teaching and learning strategies adopted in HE. At a time of increasing social, cultural and technological complexity, the workplace is both an outcome that many HE students strive to succeed in and a site of learning for those who seek to progress in their careers. In this chapter we explore the implications of this through the development of work based learning (WBL) as a response to the imperative for more relevant HE in today's economy.

The first part of this chapter reviews the context that drives work oriented pedagogical developments in HE. A context where universities are increasingly expected to drive productivity and economic growth whilst at the same time ensuring that their students are well equipped to make the transition from education to the workplace and succeed in their careers. The second part of the chapter sketches out some theoretical foundations highlighting pragmatic, problem-solving and reflective approaches that lie at the heart of WBL pedagogy and the challenges that these bring to the traditional curriculum that universities offer. Whilst we locate the narrative in the chapter to the challenges facing business schools, many of the issues discussed are relevant to other disciplines and fields of study. Two case studies introduce very different forms of WBL: one describing a prevalent form of WBL founded upon project-based work placement as part of a course curriculum and another outlining a whole course representing a more radical challenge to the traditional academic curriculum delivered in the classroom. The next part of the chapter reflects on the case studies and wider literature to consider some key questions associated with the nature of WBL, the structure of such programmes of study, the integration of academic and practitioner knowledge and some factors that influence the adoption of WBL in HE. The chapter concludes with a challenge to traditional curriculum and a call for disruption and innovation through the introduction of more WBL in the HE sector.

Context

The dynamic nature of economies and labour markets are key drivers of change in the HE sector (EC, 2012; OECD, 2007; Warshaw and Hearn, 2014). For example, there are more and more jobs both now and forecast in the future which require high level qualifications; globalisation is widening, deepening and speeding up connections across national borders; digital disruption is changing the nature of the labour market and developments in information and communications technologies present ever more significant opportunities for flexible and distance learning and employers of all sizes are increasingly seeking competitive advantage through a range of partnerships and strategic alliances with universities (DBIS, 2013).

Add to this a policy context where the role that universities play in achieving wider social and economic development objectives is increasingly recognised in many countries and the context for WBL can be viewed as more favourable than it has ever been in the past. Education policy in countries as diverse as the United States, Scandinavia, Thailand, South Africa and Australia has been encouraging the development of WBL for a number of years, calling for the use of innovative pedagogies to support workforce development and innovation (see various OECD Reviews).[1] In the UK, the Witty Review of universities and growth highlighted a range of interventions to maximise the impact of universities including the role of student placements, access to facilities and joint working with business as key contributions to be made to economic growth by the university sector (DBIS, 2013).

At the same time, central to employment and skills policy in many countries is smoothing the transition between education and the world of work. The Organisation for Economic Cooperation and Development (OECD) refers to widespread opportunities that combine learning and work for young people as one of the key features of successful transition between education and work in a variety of national contexts (OECD, 2000). Increasingly complex work practices, greater job flexibility and interaction with consumers mean that employers are looking for a range of general skills to accompany technical skills. These 'employability skills' combine hard skills (project management, communication, creative thinking, problem-solving and leadership) and soft skills (confidence, communication and reflection) of learners (DBIS, 2015; Draycott and Rae, 2011; Jones and Iredale, 2010) and are increasingly important because the labour market is intensely competitive and employers in all sectors are looking for people who are flexible, able to act on initiative, work in teams, have the ability to solve problems and undertake a variety of tasks in different cultural and work contexts. The way in which new university graduates are absorbed in the labour market has changed radically over the years with a decrease in the use of national mass recruitment programmes and an increase in non-traditional graduate routes into work including self-employment or employment in small and medium sized enterprises (Personnel Today, 2015a, 2015b; Pollard *et al.* 2015). As a consequence of this, there has been a steady rise in appreciation of the role that work based learning can play in pursuing policy goals in the UK, and the introduction of an employer levy in 2017 is sure to promote the development and delivery of WBL through a range of HE apprenticeships (Universities UK, 2016).

The rates of innovation and change both now and in the future demand a more flexible and ongoing relationship between industry and universities to ensure that organisations and economies remain competitive in the global economy. One of the trends apparent in educational reforms across Europe is enrichment of programmes meaning that the number of parameters addressed by university curricula is increasing. Whereas curricula traditionally tended to reflect a body of disciplinary knowledge to be transmitted, they are now increasingly perceived as policy instruments setting a framework for education and training stakeholders, including not only lecturers and learners but other stakeholders from industry and professional bodies for example (Carswell *et al.*, 2010; Psifidou, 2010).

Finally, in framing the context for WBL in this chapter, it is important to recognise two key institutional factors that influence WBL in different nations. First, that HE systems at the national level are comprised of a range of universities with differing foci typically (but not restricted to) research-intensive and applied universities which may influence the attention paid to WBL development at the micro level of the organisation. The second factor is the role that the national regulatory framework plays in supporting or constraining the development of WBL in universities. In some nations, such as Finland for example, Universities of Applied Science are required by law to provide WBL experiences as part of the curriculum for all learning programmes. In others such as Spain, the requirements of a centralised system and an emphasis on traditional forms of education can make WBL difficult to design and implement. In the UK, universities have considerable local autonomy, and those institutions supportive of WBL can design processes to facilitate and encourage the development and implementation of WBL. Our case studies are both drawn from the UK and reflect this dynamic environment.

Theory/definitions

The theoretical foundations for WBL can be traced back to the influential educational thinker John Dewey (1859–1952). His ideas sprang from a philosophy of pragmatism where a central tenet of education is its relevance to the lives of learners. For Dewey, learning is viewed as primarily an activity that arises from the personal experience of grappling with a problem. His view contrasted with the conventional view of learning at the time that was based on students receiving knowledge that was packaged by teachers, often in the form of textbooks and learnt largely by rote. This is echoed in the distinction between academic and practice based knowledge that has informed discussions and literature on the nature of business schools and the tension between the requirement for a robust, scientific approach to the production of knowledge and the requirement for practice based and relevant knowledge (Bennis and O'Toole, 2005; Mingers, 2015; Thomas and Cornuel, 2012).

Learning theories are embedded explicitly or implicitly in all curricula, but how these theories are applied depends on the larger social, cultural, economic and political contexts within which HE is situated. These broader contexts privilege some theories at the expense of others, determining what knowledge, which methods of instruction, assessments and learning objectives will dominate (Devins *et al.*, 2015). The contexts and pedagogies show some similarities and differences both within and between nations and institutions. Complex questions related to how learning theories translate into educational practice are beyond the scope of this chapter, and we choose to pursue a focus on intellectual problem-solving activities and the development of cognitive skills to support further knowledge acquisition and active learning (Fink, 2003; Garrison and Archer, 2000). Through this lens, the educator is responsible for structuring a learning environment and facilitating collaborative learning with others rather than transferring codified academic knowledge. Teachers remain subject experts but also facilitate problem-solving by their students who are expected to think in a live work context where ambiguities and dilemmas provide a rich and dynamic learning environment. This perspective embraces notions of self-directed learning, recognition of prior learning and flipped classroom within a context of a more fundamental emergent WBL-related mindset in HE (Boud and Soloman, 2001).

Traditional campus based degrees in the business and management field are predominantly anchored around knowledge drawn from the scientific disciplines (academic theory). However, there is also a general understanding that there is a mode of knowledge relating to management practice. Management practice knowledge tends to be seen as implicit knowledge that manifests itself more often than not in the actual practice of management (Shin *et al.*, 2001; Van De Ven, 2006). One of the challenges facing business schools who wish to blend academic knowledge and management practice in curriculum design is how to give a 'scientific basis' to articulated management practice knowledge. This leads some academics to focus on the integration of academic knowledge and management practice knowledge in curriculum design (Khurana and Spender, 2012).

However, integration is no simple task and there is no settled definition of either WBL or an integrated curriculum. The definitions are often highly dependent upon historical circumstances, pedagogical approaches and national contexts (Costley and Armsby, 2007; Foster and Stephenson, 1998; Graf, 2016). A wide range of terms are used interchangeably for the concept of WBL in HE across the globe. These include co-operative education, work-integrated learning, workplace learning, work-related learning, vocational learning, flexible learning, experiential learning, situated learning, competence-based learning, problem-based learning, problem-solving and many more. Each term embraces a range of variations and subtleties, the explanation of which are beyond the scope of this chapter. Nevertheless, these terms capture the rich landscape of WBL whilst they also lead to some confusion associated with what WBL means in certain contexts and the form that WBL should take to achieve its learning outcomes. In order to illustrate some of the variations in form we draw on research undertaken for the Higher Education Academy in the UK which suggests several different models of WBL as in Table 5.1.

Whilst there are many forms of WBL, the concept of curriculum has become broader, increasingly changing from a static document indicating the subject knowledge to be acquired at the completion of an academic year, towards a more dynamic framework embracing, for example, occupational standards and defining learning outcomes, assessment, teaching and training methods (Psifidou, 2010). This leads to considerable differences between a traditional approach to curriculum where the learner has a largely passive role as a recipient of knowledge provided by the academy and WBL approaches to curriculum in HE where the learner has a more active, participative and reciprocal learning context. Several of the differences between traditional and WBL curriculum are summarised in Table 5.2, which provides an insight into some implications for pedagogy and curriculum in HE.

In order to illustrate the nature of WBL curriculum more clearly we consider examples of two models introduced in Table 5.1. The first one represents a form of the most common mode of WBL i.e. placements within a programme of study (IES/IRS/BIBB, 2012). The second example illustrates an institutional approach that provides a context for whole WBL programmes. Both cases focus on developments in WBL in undergraduate degree programmes that were first introduced in the early 2000s and have proved to be successful and enduring examples. The first case reflects WBL as a module that can be used within several undergraduate programmes to provide experience of working with external organisations whilst the second case provides an insight into a more radical work based degree where the whole curriculum is delivered to learners who are in full-time employment.

Case 1: project-based, work placement – the undergraduate consultancy project

This case study has been chosen to illustrate an approach that blends work-related and work based learning in an undergraduate degree module. It is not an example of a typical placement with a single employer and it reflects an orientation towards an economy where non-standard employment (fixed-term, project or task-based) is becoming a significant feature of employment in many nations. The module was introduced in 2004 and is a core element in several Leeds Business School programmes and an elective in others. Typically more than 800 undergraduate students participate annually in the first and second semesters of

Table 5.1 Different models of work based learning

Model	Typical attributes
Work based studies degree	Content negotiated with learner (which may have some employer input), part-time degree whilst in full-time employment
Degree in cohorts with thesis based on work project	Content designed with contribution of employer and learner, part-time degree, full-time employment
US/Canadian model	First year in HEI and subsequent years in work with content negotiated with employer and learner
Sandwich year, work placement, work experience, project-based, internship within programme of study	Content designed with employer, full-time degree, temporary work with employer (variable duration)
In-house training/education	Accredited short courses influenced by employer/professional standards
Conventional degree programme to support work role (e.g. MBA)	Content designed by HEI, often part-time degree, full-time employment

Source: adapted from Costley and Dikerdem, 2011.

Table 5.2 Differences between traditional and WBL curriculum

	Traditional	WBL
Location	Mainly university campus	Often employer's workplace
Mode of delivery	Mainly face to face academic–student	Often academic and practitioners, facilitation and blended (combination of distance and face-to-face) learning
Focus	Mainly academic and–disciplinary	Linking theory and practice
Nature of curriculum	Significant theoretical and conceptual elements determined by HE	Significant practice based elements determined by employer/learner
Recognition of prior learning	Limited	Can be substantial
Teaching staff	Mainly full- and part-time academic staff	Mixture of university academics, employer trainers and third party tutors
Teaching materials	Developed and owned by the university	Often shared between university and employer
Learner support	Primarily university	University and employer
Assessment	Primarily academic knowledge assessed by university	Mix of academic and practice knowledge Jointly assessed with employer/student/university

Source: adapted from Carswell et al., 2010.

year 3 (September to April). The module runs in several countries through franchise agreements in countries such as Hong Kong, Sri Lanka, Singapore and the UK. Students are usually assigned to a small group to work together on a complex open-ended problem facing an external organisation. The module leader at Leeds Business School suggests that "this module is one of the most challenging and rewarding that students will study at the University".

The Business Consultancy Module provides an opportunity for students to learn some of the theory underpinning consultancy and to put into practice knowledge gained in other academic modules though a live problem or opportunity located in a specific organisational setting. It also provides an opportunity for students to develop key employability skills by learning informally from the experience of undertaking a project through collaborating with their peers and working with an external organisation. The first four weeks of the module engage the student body through traditional lectures drawing on work-related consulting theory designed to transmit multi-disciplinary knowledge. Students are subsequently assigned to a small group of 4–8 learners to identify and engage a potential client organisation within which to deliver a consultancy project. The group then work with the client to develop a project suitable for study at undergraduate level which is formalised in a project proposal agreed with the external organisation and the academic tutor assigned to the group. There is no syllabus underpinning the module beyond the requirement to reflect on the need to consider the stages involved in conducting a consultancy project and the adoption of an appropriate research methodology. Academic tutors work in a facilitative rather than teaching mode of instruction to support the learning experience. These tutors are expected to have experience of consultancy, research and project management as well as specific subject knowledge.

Students are expected to select projects that provide a context to apply theoretical models or frameworks gained from other academic modules in their course curriculum. The projects are particularly suited to the application of business and marketing strategy, communications and a variety of forms of process innovation in organisations. This provides a rich canvas for curriculum content, and a wide range of consultancy projects in terms of aims, nature and site of learning occur each year. Organisations providing a site of learning for students include high profile companies such as Disney, Morrisons and Balfour Beatty along with local small and micro independent enterprises in a range of industrial and voluntary sectors. Examples of consultancy projects include market analysis and recommendations to increase brand awareness of a family firm (Johnson Motors), recommendations for the development of brand presence for a leading clothing retailer (Jack Wolfskin) and the development of a digital marketing strategy for a leading health charity in the UK (The Children's Heart Foundation).

The module aims to develop the high level hard and soft skills necessary to initiate, coordinate, organise and manage a project addressing complex open-ended problems. It provides an opportunity to implement and test academic knowledge related to a range of disciplines and consultancy, project management, research methods and evaluation. Students typically encounter a variety of real world situations that include the challenges of specifying complex problems, clients that change their minds, managing stakeholder expectations and team-performance related issues. The module engenders a high level of independence as students are expected to identify and be responsible for their own learning needs and strategies. Specific learning outcomes include the ability to communicate effectively in a variety of situations and to make practical recommendations based on a rigorous and analytical approach to consultancy. The learning strategy also requires students to reflect on their own and others' performance and to offer feedback on this to each other. This peer assessment and the content of the consultancy report provided to the employer provide the foundation for the assessment of the module. Students receive a group mark, an individual mark and client-informed feedback on the performance of the consultancy project.

The module provides an opportunity for students to select a learning context that is relevant to future career aims. A survey conducted at the end of the module (100 respondents) reveals that students report a relatively high level of relevance and satisfaction with the learning experience. Almost 90 per cent of students undertaking a consultancy project report that the module was relevant and a similar proportion report that the content was appropriate. More than 80 per cent report enjoying the learning experience with a similar proportion reporting overall satisfaction with the module (higher than the average over business-related programmes more generally). The students value the practical knowledge that they generate and recognise the value of the soft skills they develop. For example, one student reflected that

> the consultancy project allowed me to develop written and verbal communication skills as a lot of communication with the client as well as group members was involved. I have also learnt what working in a team is like and how to solve problems and take leadership and ownership of certain situations.

Another student noted

> The project definitely helped me develop my group work skills, I would also say creative thinking as we tried to make as many innovative ideas as possible that the company would like. I also developed my leadership skills as usually I take a back seat but in this situation I had to take the lead role to push the project forward.

These experiences help the students to build the employability skills that will be valuable in making the transition from education to work and subsequent progression in their careers. Anecdotal evidence suggests that by obtaining references from client organisations students are often able to build and strengthen their CVs by demonstrating the value of their placement experience.

Employers often value the business benefits related to student placement activity. They point to the fresh ideas they can bring into the workplace and an additional resource for specialist projects. More often than not, employers see the placement as an opportunity to assess the potential of students as future employees once they graduate. They also point to the wider benefits of working with a university. For example IKEA, a leading multinational furniture retailer employing around 10,000 people in the UK offers a range of opportunities for student placements and graduate jobs. The General Manager at IKEA in Leeds suggests that:

> We have been working with Leeds Business School for six years now. In that time students at the university have given us ideas about how we can improve the way we do business and develop our service to better match customers' needs. In part, our success in the Leeds community has been because of Leeds Business School.

This case demonstrates the value of an innovative project-based placement opportunity where students are encouraged to apply academic knowledge and work together on a complex problem within a specific work context. It illustrates elements of curriculum design and learning outcomes that help to equip the student apply academic knowledge in a practical situation and develop the knowledge and skills likely to help them to succeed in the world of work. As importantly, it provides practical experience of high level consultancy that they can use to demonstrate their value to employers when they seek to gain work. The module is not without its challenges that require careful leadership and management; efforts are required to align employer and student expectations; there are times when projects may not present the opportunity to develop the higher level critical analysis skills required by HE and there can be tensions between group members associated with work distribution and individual contribution. Nevertheless, the relatively high level of relevance and satisfaction reported by both students and enterprises participating in the module provide a firm foundation for its sustainability and further development.

Clearly the consultancy project is not representative of placement oriented WBL in HE more generally. Some programmes may specify placements for one or two days each week for a set time period (e.g. semester or academic year) whilst others may be completed and assessed entirely in the workplace. Some may introduce placements in year one whilst others may schedule them at various times throughout the learning programme. A common variation appears to be for students to spend the third of a four-year programme of study in a placement with a single employer. However, there does not appear to be a single 'best way' of harnessing the value of placements with the design of this form of WBL contingent upon a range of local conditions. Whilst placements are generally recognised as a valuable means of developing a range of graduate employability and enterprise skills, for some proponents of WBL seeking greater immersion in the workplace and integration of practical and academic knowledge, other forms of WBL may be preferred as illustrated in our second case below.

Case 2: work based studies degrees in UK university business schools

Work based degrees address the 'whole course' learning experience in contrast to individual module initiatives illustrated in our first case example. The narrative for our case illustration is drawn specifically from a UK business school context using the 'Degrees for Work' initiative at Anglia Ruskin University; the university has won many awards for its work based degrees all of which involve significant partnership with local and national employers.[2] While work based degree models are by no means the 'norm', there are good examples of such degrees offered by other UK universities including Nottingham Trent University; Northumbria University; Manchester Metropolitan University; Durham University; Bradford University and Middlesex University.

Anglia Ruskin's work based degree with retail banker Barclays has now been running for over ten years and this scheme has recently aligned itself to the UK Government's apprenticeship scheme for funding. The three-year BA Business and Management Leadership degree involves A level students being recruited by the sponsoring employer (in this case Barclays) and then enrolled on Anglia's work based degree. The whole three-year learning experience for the degree is defined by work experience blended with six one-week study blocks (two per academic year). In sum, work experience is not an 'add-on' but core to how academic knowledge is introduced in the degree and most importantly in defining learning tasks that involve the student in blending academic knowledge and management practice knowledge through work based tasks. The design principle behind this model is simple. It integrates work based problem-solving as a key learning mechanism that adds integrity and rigour to the knowledge synthesis activity of the students involved in the generation of solutions to complex 'real world' problems. Students become highly engaged in the notion of being able to describe their learning in terms of 'solving' complex problems rather than simply knowing academic subject matter. It is important to emphasise that students on work based degrees still study academic subjects but the real learning happens in the knowledge synthesis work undertaken during work based problem-solving and thereby ensuing measurable and tangible outcomes. In this way the practical learning context rather than academic knowledge is the defining characteristic of the curriculum and pedagogy.

Anglia's work based degree is fundamentally different from a conventional sandwich degree. The first obvious difference is the time spent in work effectively being equivalent to a full apprenticeship. More important is the pedagogic difference enabled in work based degrees by anchoring a significant proportion of the learning around knowledge synthesis activity (through making explicit the blending of academic knowledge and management practice knowledge). By way of contrast, conventional campus based degrees, including one-year sandwich degrees, present limited opportunities for knowledge synthesis based learning by students.

It is easy to see the major advantage of immersive work based degrees such as the BA Business and Management Leadership degree at Anglia Ruskin.

Students graduate after three years with a degree and three years' work experience. Moreover, as the work experience period on the degree develops it is associated with students undertaking a range of different problem-solving activities that place considerable value on not just spending time in an organisation but developing the ability to gain organisation traction and making an impact through problem-solving. The integration of these problem-solving tasks into the assessment of the degree ensures students perceive high relevance of their studies to working as a future practising manager. It is perhaps not surprising to find that graduates of such work based degrees significantly outperform conventional campus based graduates in the graduate job market.[3] Indeed, a major motivation for both the sponsoring company and the student is the expectation that their management career will continue in the host company post graduation.

Anglia's Degrees for Work initiative also includes a number of variations of the work based degree design and delivery methods described above. Another well-known example is the work based degree in retail with arguably London's most prestigious store – Harrods. Unlike the Barclay's model this involves Harrods placing existing employees on a 'top-up' final year for a retail degree. This model reflects the experience and qualifications of the targeted cohort of employees in Harrods. An equally interesting aspect of the Harrods top-up degree is the way the work based design involves blending Harrods' own internal 'practice based training and learning' activities within the validated degree design. This is explicit recognition in the course design for this degree that academic knowledge and management practice knowledge (acquired through internal training activities) can be brought together in course validation. This is indicative of an important feature of work based degree designs where academic knowledge is not necessarily the core anchor of the course design.

Both the Barclays and Harrods programmes are examples of single company work based degrees. There are examples of consortia based models where multiple companies participate in offering full placement degrees e.g. the BA Business and Management degree at Nottingham Trent. Single company schemes allow the opportunity for a higher degree of bespoking in terms of student assessments and project work focusing on one company. Consortia schemes work well where a company may only wish to take say, one to three placement students; single company schemes like Barclays run multiple cohorts of *c*.20 students per cohort. The primary motivation for participating companies in the type of work based degrees described above is to recruit 'work ready graduates'. The investment costs required of companies participating in such work based degrees (essentially a placement salary plus a degree of course fee sponsorship) compares favourably with conventional graduate recruitment costs. However, the most important benefit is the opportunity provided by the work based degree for the company to 'assess' a potential recruit over a three-year placement and also knowing they have three years of highly relevant work experience of their organisation upon graduation.

In terms of course and curriculum design practice work based degrees offer the opportunity to create modules that blend traditional academic knowledge with 'management practice' knowledge drawn from the participating companies. This is particularly important in the common use of 'empty' project based modules that characterise such degrees. Indeed, you can see that some work based degrees have as much as a third of their content driven from company based project modules. This involves the team of university academics designing and validating any degree scheme working closely with key managers in the participating placement companies.

The characteristics of the course and its relevance in terms of the development of soft skills are reflected in the testimonials provided by graduates on the Anglia website. For example, graduates report the benefits of the course, which include "giving me a breadth of knowledge about retail in lots of different areas which I was unaware of before starting", "developing my confidence and presenting skills" and "sharing knowledge with my colleagues and director of the business". Several of the graduates point to the application of specific theoretical knowledge with one graduate drawing attention to the benefits of applying knowledge associated with the psychology of the sales module on the shop floor. From the corporate perspective, the Learning and Development Manager at Harrods suggests that the main benefits for the organisation lie in the recognition that the organisation is looking after and nurturing their sales team which helps the organisation retain the best talent and offer world class sales service to their customers.

Qualitative statements by students, tutors and companies that have been involved in work based degrees are numerous and can be easily accessed on web based and other marketing materials communicated by the business schools delivering such programmes. A few examples are illustrative of both the content and tone of messaging from students who have studied on immersive work based degrees. There appears to be two common themes. First is the value attached to work experience as part of their degree studies – enriching the learning experience. For example, a student from the work based BA Business Management degree at Nottingham Trent University talks about blending work experience with completing university coursework

> It gives you the opportunity to combine academic theory with practical experience and helps you to understand how organisations work.[4]

The second theme is students connecting the work experience gained on their degree with the career and job opportunities available upon graduation. For example, students from a work based degree at Anglia Ruskin state:

> I was a Sales Assistant and now I am a Store Manager. Since I got my degree my salary has doubled.

> During my interview … they pointed to my CV and said … "you'll bring something new to the business" … they were pointing to my [work based] BA Sales degree.[5]

For companies the major benefits highlighted in work based degrees focus on the relevance of the degree content to the development of (future) employees and second the recruitment of high calibre graduate talent. For example, a participating manager on the University of Bradford's BSc Management and Business degree for Morrisons states that the degree will have far reaching consequences by "creating a highly-skilled workforce at the top of the business."[6] Similarly, a senior Barclays' executive argues that the Anglia Ruskin work based degree apprenticeship developed in partnership "supports our vision of allowing anyone who has the right attitude and aptitude to progress and develop their career no matter what background they are from."[7]

Discussion

Two important and interwoven themes are highlighted in this chapter for developing our understanding of WBL and its practice in HE. First, is the broader institutional context that encourages or inhibits the development and implementation of WBL. Second, is the theoretical understanding and variety of pedagogical practices that underpin it. WBL has a long tradition in many countries and has been a central element in areas of HE such as medicine and teaching for many years. In some countries it is well established in multi-disciplinary areas (such as business) but in other countries it is far less prevalent. In the current UK context and in countries as diverse as Finland, South Africa and Australia we are seeing increasingly active government policies driving new WBL practices in universities. At the time of writing, the UK Government policy is encouraging a more radical approach to WBL in HE with incentives being offered through new apprenticeship frameworks likely to foster significant growth in WBL. In the current context, WBL is premised on the view that a university degree can and should focus on preparing a graduate for the world of work. However, it is important to realise that any discussion and comparison of WBL with traditional campus based learning needs to acknowledge the difference in purpose of these contrasting educational models. Clearly both models of learning can and do co-exist within institutions and across a national HE sector/system (see for example OECD, 2014).

Traditionally many UK universities would see their teaching and learning models premised on the purpose of a degree as being to develop the knowledge and minds of students along the lines of 'reading for a degree', and there are a number of philosophical, social, economic and cultural objections to WBL which continue to hamper its development and implementation in some HE systems. For many in HE, disciplines lie at the core of academic activity and the traditional emphasis on pedagogy as a means to transmit the knowledge that students are to master remains a dominant focus for curriculum design. This view is underpinned by the ascendency of the academic, campus based model of learning where students develop knowledge of disciplines through engaging with subject knowledge and academic tutors. This maintains a longstanding intellectual high ground that favours traditional academic knowledge based degree design. The model for undergraduate degrees founded on academic knowledge where the majority of the learning is undertaken in the classroom and predominantly delivered by career academics can nonetheless be challenged through the introduction of WBL. This can be achieved through an evolutionary approach, with elements of WBL being introduced into parts of the traditional curriculum (through placements for example) or through the introduction of WBL degrees that represent a more radical challenge to the equilibrium model in business schools.

A departure from the equilibrium model is not to the detriment of the learning experience, rather WBL is a necessary component to prepare the student for the life of work. WBL may be considered as an inferior form of HE and continues to be viewed negatively by some in the academic community. This appears to be influenced by wider prejudices associated with the esteem attributed to academic and vocational learning and a nervousness associated with ceding greater influence over the curriculum to employers. However, adding engagement with the workplace environment both physically and academically should not be seen as dumbing down HE, rather as a necessary move to reflect the needs of students and employers.

The case studies in this chapter provide an introduction to two successful and enduring examples of WBL that illustrate contrasting models of learning design whilst at the same time sharing common philosophical positions. They illustrate learning and teaching strategies that join the worlds of academia and work and the different levels of influence that the two worlds exert on WBL pedagogy. The influences provoke transformations in curriculum, as academics implement more active methods of teaching, research, learning and assessment to integrate student, employer and policy interests. The first case study represents a variation on the typical placement model with a single employer to provide an illustration of a model that reflects an orientation towards problem-solving whilst working in non-traditional (i.e. project-based, temporary) employment. The second case provides an illustration of a more radical whole programme approach to WBL. Both approaches bring challenges for academics and have implications for pedagogic practitioners. For example, WBL often necessitates a need for a multi-disciplinary approach to address real-world problems and this can challenge some academics with a strong single disciplinary orientation. At the same time, WBL necessitates the tutor role changing from a traditional approach founded on the transmission of academic knowledge to facilitation of learning that reflects the interests of the academe, learners and employers to varying degrees. The academic tutor may be required to collaborate with employers or learners to specify learning outcomes and negotiate a pluralistic assessment with peer review, collaborative written reports, reflective reviews and oral feedback from the external organisation providing a portfolio of inputs. The tutor also has an important role to play in ensuring a productive and positive relationship develops and is maintained between the participating organisation, students and the university. WBL requires all stakeholders engaged in the process; learners, tutors and those providing administrative or pastoral support to develop shared beliefs and behaviours that contribute towards successful WBL development and delivery (Devins *et al.*, 2015). Some academics and stakeholders may resist these changes, and innovative ways to engage and reward them may be required to encourage participation and develop the capability to deliver WBL effectively.

Studies identify a range of barriers to the development of WBL in HE including a lack of senior management strategy and support, staff capability, inflexible quality assurance systems, assessment practices, employer engagement, responsiveness and lead-in times (Medhat, 2008; Tallantyre, 2010). Perhaps as a consequence of this, linking with the world of work practice is generally not seen as a priority in the design of university degrees, and few universities have developed a compelling theoretical narrative around the knowledge synthesis learning activity undertaken by students on WBL degrees (see for example Bennis and O'Toole, 2005; Khurana and Spender, 2012). As opposed to academic knowledge being seen as the primary design anchor and management practice knowledge being loosely coupled with the curriculum, learning in the work environment can drive whole course design and implementation, increasing the relevance of provision whilst maintaining academic rigour. A core purpose of WBL degree designs is to enable learning whereby students blend/integrate academic knowledge and practice knowledge. This knowledge synthesis activity is not without a knowledge outcome. That knowledge outcome relates to learning that takes place in 'solving' complex and messy real world problems. In sum, it is both a theoretically derived and context specific knowledge artefact that has been defined elsewhere as 'practice intelligence' (Minocha and Reynolds, 2013). In practice, intelligent management practitioners evolve their practice intelligence as they gain experience of solving problems in many and varied contexts. WBL offers the opportunity for students to not only learn about discipline based academic knowledge but also to develop their practice intelligence through problem based learning activities that take place in the workplace. Arguably, it is the student's experience i.e. their acquired practice intelligence – that makes them highly employable to employers. The offer of real-life learning experiences through WBL enables HE to provide an effective link between education and employment and enhance its relevance to the economy. There is considerable evidence associated with the positive role that WBL plays in the personal and professional development of undergraduates and in measurable employment benefits for graduate students in terms of level of job, job satisfaction and salary on leaving HE (Blasco *et al.*, 2002; Gault *et al.*, 2010; Wilton, 2008). However, as Mason *et al.* (2009) note, "it is difficult to say whether work experience makes students more employable or whether the more employable students are more likely to choose, find and successfully complete work experience opportunities" (p. 23). Nevertheless, the balance of the evidence is in favour of the positive contribution that WBL can make to the employability of students. In addition, a number of studies have highlighted the benefits associated with a period of work experience and the positive influence this has on academic progress and achievements of learners (Green, 2011; Mandilaras, 2004).

Although other models of WBL exist we selected a work based degree design in the business and management field to illustrate key principles and themes underlying disequilibrium models of curriculum. The structure of these degrees typically involves the learner spending the majority of their degree working in-company and attending intense study blocks at the University. These degrees provide an illustration of the flipped classroom where the majority of the programme curriculum is developed and delivered in the workplace with students problem-solving whilst in work and the university campus playing a relatively small role as a site of learning (Lage *et al.*, 2000). This highlights one of the first principles of such degrees where typically 80 per cent plus of the degree involves learning in the work context and a much reduced level of learning in the classroom. This shift from 'content to context' means these degrees stand out from the normal three-year campus based degree and ensure students develop a graduate employability offering that gives a distinct advantage in the market for graduate talent.

In some instances, the introduction of a work-based degree has led to a business school offering a full set of work based variations where one, two or all three years of the degree are in the workplace.[8] While there are nuances and variations between these models at Anglia Ruskin and other successful examples in the UK (see for example; Northumbria, Middlesex, Chester and Durham) there are design similarities that inform them all. These include pedagogies that seek to develop and apply new knowledge, collaboration across academic disciplines and across different domains of practice and partnership working with employers. In terms of the choices of methodologies underpinning WBL provision, these do not tend to be different to those that might be used in conventional academic offerings in similar contexts, and there is an understandable inclination to use action based methods to focus on work based problems and to build conceptual models, develop interventions and evaluate impact. These include problem-based learning, action research, action learning, inquiry based learning, case study, ethnography, co-operative learning and reflective practice (Costley and Armsby, 2007; Van Gyn and Grove White, 2004). However, WBL assessment processes often differ from those associated with more traditional pedagogies where assessment mainly requires reproduction of the prescribed curriculum content with a low level of application (Fink, 2003). More recently, it is becoming increasingly unusual for WBL not to be formally assessed in some way, particularly if it is seen as a means of demonstrating attainment of National Occupational Standards or satisfying the membership requirements of a professional association. Assessment is increasingly associated with reflecting on action (Schon, 1983) and encouraging an exploration of thoughts and feelings; looking for insights; and maximising self-awareness. A wide range of artefacts can be used including reflective essays, learner portfolios, diaries, industrial and academic supervisor reports (Helyer, 2015; Helyer and Kay, 2015).

A final comment we would like to make relates to the drivers of WBL in HE. Many WBL innovations have been encouraged through a variety of funding mechanisms often provided by government or their associated agencies. Critics of 'sluggish UK universities' in terms of university-business engagement would argue that certain areas (including business and management) could find their traditional classroom based degrees seriously challenged by the introduction of the Apprenticeship Levy in April 2017. As a result it is reported in the press that half of employers are planning to turn their graduate recruitment schemes into apprenticeship programmes in order to reclaim money from the Levy (*The Times*, 9 February 2017). This could represent the biggest single injection of funding to support WBL that the HE sector has seen in the UK. However, other innovations have been prompted by private sector initiation and co-production in the past. For example the School of Management at the University of Bradford has a long standing BSc Management and Business degree developed and delivered in partnership with a private sector company – the retail store chain Morrisons. Indeed, the retail supermarket sector in the UK has been a significant driver of WBL related HE activity with for example, Tesco and Asda also partnering with UK universities (Manchester Metropolitan University and Middlesex University respectively) to establish similar work based degree models. As can be seen from both university and corporate websites for these degrees, a theme at the heart of work based degrees is their relevance to the businesses in the economy and the emphasis given to blending theory and practice by having students develop and apply their knowledge in the workplace context.

Conclusions

In conclusion, it is important to acknowledge that the discussion in this chapter reflects our particular understanding of what WBL is in HE and also the varied practice models of WBL in different institutional contexts. Both of the case studies have universities at the centre of the discussion and we have not critically questioned the assumption about the role and purpose of universities. Authors such as Jarche (2013) offer a different perspective arguing that 'work is learning and learning is work' and present a philosophy of learning that might be radically at odds with the traditional models of what universities do. Furthermore, our case studies are not representative of the wide range of WBL activity either in the UK or in many countries across the globe. The nature and prevalence of WBL within and between countries is difficult to capture and a limited and partial picture of activity often emerges. This is partly due to the conceptual ambiguity of WBL and the fact that it not reported on as a distinct entity in strategic documents guiding HE policy. Where WBL does feature, the reported data does not allow a full understanding of its nature in the HE context nor its incidence, funding or impact.

Protagonists for WBL not surprisingly straddle the evolution–revolution spectrum illustrated in our two case studies. They can draw on an increasing evidence base highlighting the benefits of WBL in terms of the development of employability and enterprising skills-sets, graduate employment and careers as well as productive employer–university partnerships. However, WBL can involve change and innovation where student, university and employer have various and often new roles to play in learning. Consequently, whilst the benefits in terms of student employability and closer university–industry relationships can be realised, it may require pedagogical innovation and investment in programmes that may be more expensive to design and deliver than traditional forms of HE. Rigorous assessments of the cost-benefit of WBL appear to be largely absent and an area ripe for further research and development.

Our final point considers that WBL, in terms of thinking and its practice, continues to evolve across different education systems. In large part we cannot understand this development without reference to the institutional context. Leadership from national governments and their relevant departments has a key role to play in providing a vision and incentivising change within national systems. HE policy and funding need to clearly identify and reward the different roles and expectations of institutions, so that missions, strategies and funded practice reflect policy priorities. Currently, an interesting case in the formative stages of implementation lies with the UK Government's policy on apprenticeships through to 2020. This is unambiguously a call by government for universities to work with companies to establish a significant number of undergraduate and masters level degrees that are work based and in contrast to traditional three-year campus based degrees. Leeds Beckett University has recently designed and launched Degree Apprenticeships in the areas of Digital and Technology solutions and Business Management Practice with more planned to follow. Time will tell if this marks a new dawn for WBL in HE or a minor disturbance to the equilibrium curriculum.

Notes

1 Various OECD Reviews are available at www.oecd.org/edu/skills-beyond-school/oecd reviewsofvocationaleducationandtraining-learningforjobs.htm.
2 Readers interested in a more detailed account can visit www.anglia.ac.uk/business-employers/professional-courses/degrees-at-work.
3 Illustrations of enhanced career opportunities for graduates from work based degrees can be found at, for example, Nottingham Trent: see www4.ntu.ac.uk/nbs/courses/undergraduate/work-based-degrees/index.html. Anecdotally work based degrees were found to result in over 95 per cent retention on graduation compared with over 60 per cent retention for conventional placement/sandwich degrees.
4 See NTU website: www.ntu.ac.uk/study-and-courses/courses/our-students-stories/business/ug-profiles/aidan-keyworth.
5 See ARU website: https://distancelearning.anglia.ac.uk/courseDetail.php/sales-136/.
6 See the University of Bradford website: www.bradford.ac.uk/management-and-law/our-people/students-and-graduates/undergraduate/management-and-business-morrisons-plc/nigel-boyle/.
7 See ARU website www.anglia.ac.uk/business-employers/professional-courses/degrees-at-work/who-we-are-working-with/barclays.
8 See Nottingham Trent University for example www4.ntu.ac.uk/nbs/courses/undergraduate/work-based-degrees/index.html.

References

Bennis, W.G. and O'Toole, J (May 2005). How business schools lost their way. *Harvard Business Review*, 83(5), 96–104.

Blasko, Z. with Brennan, J., Little, B. and Shah, T. (2002). *Access to what: An analysis of factors determining graduate employability*. Bristol: Higher Education Funding Council for England.

Boud, D. and Solomon, N. (eds). (2001). *Work-based learning: A new higher education?* Buckingham. Society for Research into Higher Education and the Open University Press.

Carswell, M., Maguire, D. and Mooney, M. (2010). Developing the ability of academic staff to work successfully with employers: enhancing expertise and creating opportunities. In: F. Tallantyre, ed. *University management of work-based learning*. York: The Higher Education Academy.

Costley, C. and Armsby, P. (2007). Work-based learning assessed as a field or mode of learning, *Assessment and Evaluation in Higher Education*, 32(1), 21–33.

Costley, C. and Dikerdem, M. (2011). *Work based learning pedagogies and academic development*. A research project funded by the HEA Subject Centre for Education, ESCalate, Institute for Work Based Learning, Middlesex University, London.

DBIS (2013) *Encouraging a British invention revolution: Sir Andrew Witty's Review of Universities and Growth*. Department for Business Industry and Skills. London. Crown Copywrite [online]. Available at: www.gov.uk/government/uploads/system/uploads/attachment_data/file/291911/bis-13-1241-encouraging-a-british-invention-revolution-andrew-witty-review-R1.pdf [accessed March 2017].

DBIS (2015). *Entrepreneurship skills: Literature and policy review*. BIS Research Paper, No 236 [online]. Available at: www.gov.uk/government/uploads/system/uploads/attachment_data/file/457533/BIS-15-456-entrepreneurship-skills-literature-and-policy-review.pdf [accessed June 2017].

Devins, D., Ferrandez-Berrueco, R. and Kekale, T. (2015). Educational orientation and employer influenced pedagogy practice and policy insights from three programmes in Europe, *Higher Education, Skills and Work-Based Learning*, 5(4), 352–368.

Dewey, J. (2009). *Democracy and education: An introduction to the philosophy of education*. New York, NY: WLC Books (original work published 1916).

Draycott, M.C. and Rae, D. (2011). Enterprise education in schools and the role of competency frameworks, *International Journal of Entrepreneurial Behaviour and Research*, 17(2), 127–145.

EC (2012). *Rethinking education: Investing in skills for better socio-economic outcomes*. Communication from the Commission to the European Parliament, the Council, the European Economic and Social Committee of the Regions. Strasbourg.

Fink, L.D. (2003). *Creating significant learning experiences. An integrated approach to designing college courses*. San Francisco, CA: Jossey-Bass.

Foster, E. and Stephenson, J. (1998). Work-based learning and universities in the UK: A review of current practive and trends. *Higher Education Research and Development*, 17(2), 155–170.

Garrison, D.R. and Archer, W. (2000). *A transactional perspective on teaching and learning: A framework for adult and higher education*. Oxford: Pergammon-Elsevier Science.

Gault, J., Leach, E. and Duey, M. (2010). Effects of business internships on job marketability: The employers' perspective. *Education and Training*, 52(1), 76–88.

Graf, L. (2016) .The rise of work-based academic education in Austria, Germany and Switzerland. *Journal of Vocational Education & Training*, 68(1), 1–16.

Green, J.P. (2011). The impact of a work placement or internship year on student final year performance: An empirical study. *International Journal of Management Education*, 9(2), 49–57.

Helyer, R. (2015). Learning through reflection: The critical role of reflection in work-based learning (WBL*). Journal of Work-Applied Management*, 7(1), 15–27.

Helyer, R. and Kay, J. (2015). *Building capabilities for your future*. In: R.Helyer, ed. *The work-based learning student handbook*. 2nd ed. London: Palgrave, pp. 31–50.

High Flyers. (2017). *The graduate market in 2017. Annual review of graduate vacancies and starting salaries at Britain's leading employers* [online]. Available at: www.high fliers.co.uk/download/2017/graduate_market/GMReport17.pdf [accessed June 2017].

IES/IRS/BIBB (2012). *Study on a comprehensive overview of traineeship arrangements in Member States* [online]. Available at: http://ec.europa.eu/social/main.jsp?catId=738 &langId=en&pubId=6717 [accessed June 2017].

Jarche, H. (2013). *Learning is the work* [online]. Available at http://jarche.com/2013/10/learning-is-the-work-2/ [accessed June 2017].

Jones, B. and Iredale, N. (2010). Enterprise education as pedagogy, *Education and Training*, 52(1), 7–19.

Khurana, R. and Spender, J.C. (2012). Herbert A. Simon on what ails business schools: More than 'a problem in organizational design'. *Journal of Management Studies*, 49(3), 619–639.

Lage, J., Platt, G.J. and Treglia., M. (2000). Inverting the classroom: A gateway to creating an inclusive learning environment. *The Journal of Economic Education*, 31(1), 30–43.

Mandilaras, A. (2004). Industrial placement and degree performance: Evidence from a British higher institution, *International Review of Economics Education*, 3(1), 39–51.

Mason, G, Williams, G. and Cranmer, S. (2009). Employability skills initiatives in higher education: What effects do they have on graduate labour outcomes? *Education Economics*, 1, 1–30.

Medhat, S. (2008). *The progress of work-based learning strategies in higher education engineering programmes* [online]. Available at: www.heacademy.ac.uk/system/files/wblreportfinalv4.pdf [accessed March 2017].

Mingers, J. (2015). Helping business schools engage with real problems: The contribution of critical realism and systems thinking. *European Journal of Operational Research*, 242, 316–331.

Minocha, S. and Reynolds, M. (2013). The artistry of practice or the practice of artistry embodying art and practice in a business school context. *Journal of Management Inquiry*, 22(2), 173–192.

OECD (2000). *From initial education to working life: Making the transition work*. Paris: Organisation for Economic Cooperation and Development.

OECD (2007). *Higher education and regions. Globally competitive, locally engaged*. Paris: Organisation for Economic Cooperation and Development.

OECD (2014). *The state of higher education 2014*. Paris. Organisation for Economic Cooperation and Development.

Personnel Today (2015a). Graduate recruitment: The end of the milk round? January [online]. Available at: www.personneltoday.com/hr/graduate-recruitment-the-end-of-the-milk-round/ [accessed March 2017].

Personnel Today (2015b). Graduates shunning regular work for freelancing and self-employment October [online]. Available at: www. today.com/pr/2015/10/graduates-shunning-regular-work-for-freelancing-and-self-employment/. [accessed March 2017].

Pollard, E., Hirsh, W., Williams, M., Buzzeo, J., Rosa Marvell, Tassinari, A., Bertram, C., Fletcher, L., Artess, J., Redman, J. and Ball, C. (2015). Understanding employers' graduate recruitment and selection practices. Research Paper 231. London. Department for Business, Innovation and Skills.

Psifidou, I. (2010). *Learning outcomes approaches in VET curricula: A comparative analysis of nine European countries*. Luxembourg: European Centre for the Development of Vocational Training.

Schon, D.A. (1983). *The reflective practitioner: How professionals think in action.* New York, NY: Basic Books.

Shin, M., Holden, T. and Schmidt, R.A. (2001). From knowledge theory to management practice: Towards an integrated approach. *Information Processing and Management,* 37(2), 335–355.

Tallantyre, F. (2010). *University management of work-based learning*. York: The Higher Education Academy.

Thomas, H. and Cornuel, E. (2012). Business schools in transition? Issues of impact, legitimacy, capabilities and re-invention. *Journal of Management Development,* 31(4), 329–335.

Universities UK (2016). The future growth of degree apprenticeships [online]. Available at: www.universitiesuk.ac.uk/policy-and-analysis/reports/Pages/future-growth-degree-apprenticeships.aspx [accessed March 2017].

Van De Ven, A.H. and Johnson, P.E (2006). Knowledge and practice. *Academy of Management Review*, 31(4), 802–821.

Van Gyn, G. and Grove-White, E. (2004). Theories of learning in education. In: R.K. Coll and C. Eames, eds. *International handbook for cooperative education. An international perspective of the theory, research and practice of work integrated learning.* Boston, MA: World Association for Cooperative Education, pp. 27–36.

Warshaw, J.B. and Hearn, J.C. (2014). Leveraging university research to serve economic development: An analysis of policy dynamics in and across three U.S. states. *Journal of Higher Education Policy and Management*, 36(2), 196–211.

Wilton, N. (2008). Business graduates and management jobs: An employability match made in heaven? *Journal of Education and Work*, 21(2), 143–158.

6 Work placements and sandwich programmes

The case of MacEwan University's Supply Chain Co-op programme

Rickard Enström

Introduction

Discussions around the value of integrated curricula, future work skills and graduates' work readiness has become a centrepiece in contemporary business education research (Daly, 2013; Jackson and Chapman, 2012a, 2012b). Adding to the debate, are frequent reports on a gulf between formal business education and actual experienced success in business (Pfeffer and Fong, 2002), fuelling the never-ceasing discussion about the role of a 'university'. In a response to these concerns, many post-secondary institutions are reconsidering their business models and putting substantial efforts into improving students' learning experiences. The hope is that these improvements will provide a better alignment with those skills that are requested by the market and also provide those students with a competitive edge and enhanced employability (Lichy and Enström, 2015). Particular efforts have been spent on the furthering of professional skills such as team work, critical thinking, presentation and the use of technology (Benson and Enström, 2017). Other approaches have sought to bridge the gap between academia and industry through the external world having a presence within the university or the university participating in the external world. These approaches therefore span having students being mentored by industry professionals, students and professors working on industry-initiated research projects, industry professionals as guest speakers, experiential learning inside and outside the classroom, and internships and co-operative education (Boulocher-Passet, Daly and Sequeira, 2016).

Of the different approaches, co-operative education is probably the most resource demanding and complex to administer. To ensure that learning outcomes are met and experiential learning happens, it requires an integration and coordination of three parties: the institution, the employer and the student. Likewise, it poses a number of challenges with regards to building relationships with the industry and finding employers willing to take on and supervise co-op students, setting up a support infrastructure to monitor and guide students and finding appropriate ways of evaluating them. Even so, co-operative education has seen a revitalisation and has been taken up as a viable option by many business schools around the world. With this chapter, we take a closer look at co-operative education and illustrate the discussion by examining the co-op programme in Supply Chain Management at MacEwan University, Canada. All students declaring this major, after first taking a pre-employment seminar,[1] undertake a total of 12 months of relevant industry work interlaced with the academic terms in a structured way with reflective pieces, effectively making this a 4.5 year BCom programme. The aim is that students will further their learning by applying their knowledge from the classroom and positively impact on how the work is being done on site as well as bringing their experiences back to the university to pollinate the in-class discussions. In telling this story, we revisit the fundaments of the co-op idea and position within the world of enterprise education before turning to the Canadian context, sizing up the curriculum and programme procedures, and listening to the narratives from the MacEwan's Supply Chain Management Co-op programme.

Enterprise education

The concept of enterprise education has arisen as one of the more discoursed pedagogical orientations in twenty-first century post-secondary business education (Jones and Iredale, 2010; Pittaway and Hannon, 2008; Rae, 2010; Rae, Martin, Antcliff and Hannon, 2010). A seminal example is the formation of The Association of Private Enterprise Education, originating from the installation of the Chair of Private Enterprise at Georgia State University in 1963, with its ambitious mission "to put into action accurate and objective understandings of private enterprise" and focus on a "future of innovation, productivity, fairness, and ever improving standards of living for all people" (The Association of Private Enterprise Education, 2017). Other examples from around the world are the explicit recommendations in Wilson (2012) to create greater opportunities in the UK for university students to gain relevant work experience through sandwich degree programmes and internships. Specifically, it is emphasised that "every full-time undergraduate student should have the opportunity to experience a structured, university-approved undergraduate internship during their period of study" (Wilson, 2012: 12). In the European Union, there is also mounting concern that the lack of innovativeness and entrepreneurship is affecting the economy negatively, with a much lower ratio of people preferring self-employment than in the USA and China. New enterprises also grow more slowly in Europe than in the USA or emerging economies (European Commission, 2013). This has caused the European Union to formalise an action plan for the furthering of the entrepreneurial mind-set among EU citizens. It is specifically emphasised that "education should be brought to life through practical experiential learning models and experience of real-world entrepreneurs" and that "partnerships with businesses can ensure that education and training curricula are relevant to the real world" (European Commission, 2013, n/p).

Even so, the concept of 'enterprise education' has remained largely disjointed in terms of the meaning, scope, purpose and anticipated benefits, with frequent simultaneous and ill-defined references to both 'enterprise education' and 'entrepreneurial education' and a variety of programmatic approaches (Gibb, 1993; Hytti and O'Gorman, 2004; Pittaway and Cope, 2007) In terms of the learning process, it is often noted that 'action learning' or 'experiential learning' are desirable and qualifying characteristics of 'enterprise education'. While drawing on UK examples, Gibb (1993) has illustrated the variety of ways the term 'enterprise' is used and notes the often occurring mix-up and overlap of enterprising behaviour and entrepreneurial behaviour. From this point of departure, a model of enterprise education with three components is established: (1) an essence of enterprise in the classroom; (2) decision-making under uncertainty; and (3) opportunities for self-discovery. It is furthermore stressed that enterprise learning is about learning by doing, learning under pressure to achieve goals, learning by problem-solving, learning by discovery, and learning from each other. Moreover, enterprising learning is primarily intended to instil a feeling of self-reliance. Other researchers have pointed out that enterprise education can achieve much more than serving as a preparation for entrepreneurship or being entrepreneurial (Hytti and O'Gorman, 2004), with programme objectives ranging from the cultivation of skills needed for the management of small businesses and preparation for work life to shaping people's general enterprising behaviour in regards to self-reliance and management of one's life and career in a society fraught with change. In juxtaposing enterprise and entrepreneurship education, Jones and Iredale (2010: 9) stressed that "enterprise education assists, develops and improves links between education and business and brings greater coherence to their activities". In a direct comparison between the two concepts, it is accentuated that while the focus of entrepreneurship education concerns the planning, launching and managing of a new business or joint venture, the focal point of enterprise education is instead active, experiential, or work-related learning centred around the development of knowledge, personal skills and behaviours to function as a citizen, consumer, employee and self-employed person in a market economy fraught with change. Similar sentiments are provided by The Higher Education Academy, where it is stated that "employers expect graduates to be innovative, adaptable, resilient, flexible and have an enterprising mind-set" and "enterprise education supports employability by enabling students to develop the characteristics, attributes and skills that will enable them to make effective contributions to the economy and society" (Owens and Tibby, 2014: 3). Last, through the lens of Dewey's philosophy of experience, it is emphasised that claims of enterprise education should come with opportunities for a plan and purpose of action, an undertaking of the action to receive the experience, and an enlacing dialogue between action and reflection (Lewis and Williams, 1994; Matlay and Pepin, 2012).

Thus, based on what has been learned about enterprise education and enterprising behaviour, one can make the case that the co-operative education curriculum needs to be designed in such a way that ample opportunities are provided to students to partake in experiential learning where self-discovery, goal setting, time management and decision-making under uncertainty are naturally occurring.

In terms of the work placements, this translates into ensuring that the work placements encompass relevant work assignments with real problem-solving components and that the employer offers a supportive environment allowing for a trial and error approach. The co-operative work terms then need to be followed by reflective evaluation assignments permitting the student to juxtapose and contrast subject matter knowledge acquired in class with knowledge acquired through the work placements and how these experiences have impacted them.

The co-op idea

An over century-long seasoned educational orientation, co-operative education is perhaps more forward-looking than ever before. With inspiration derived from existing examples of apprenticeships, sandwich programmes, and informal observations that students with prior work experience did better in courses than students without this experience, co-operative education has since experienced a massive resurgence (Barbeau, 1973; Haddara and Skanes, 2007; Zegwaard and Coll, 2011). The essence of co-operative education lies in the idea that, in particular, for studies in professional fields such as medicine, engineering and commerce, the in-class training alone is insufficient for preparing graduates for their work. It therefore has to be complemented with relevant work experience so that theory and practice can be bridged. Co-operative education therefore conforms to the idea of an integrated curriculum with anticipated benefits beyond mere subject matters (Benson and Enström, 2017) and can be embraced as a response to the skills gap in much the same way as the endorsement of generic professional skills (Daly, 2013; Davies, Fidler and Gorbis, 2011; Harder, Jackson and Lane, 2014).

One of the corner stones of enterprise education is the reliance upon experiential learning as the mode of learning where new knowledge is brought about through a transformation of the person's experience in consecutive steps (A.Y. Kolb and D.A. Kolb, 2005; D.A. Kolb, 1976; Lewis and Williams, 1994; Mainemelis, Boyatzis and Kolb, 2002). For this to happen, a learner must first have concrete experiences. Following this, the learner then reflects on the experiences; this phase also allows the learner to contrast and reconcile the in-class content with the out-of-class experience. In the final step, the learner forms conceptualisations leading to generalisations and heuristics. Comprising a personal toolkit, these newly acquired principles are at the learner's disposal when engaging in more venturous actions, followed by additional learning cycles. Thus, essential for co-operative education is the structured interlacing and juxtaposition of academic work and relevant work experience and students' critical reflection pieces of their experiences to enable their sense-making and integration of theory and practice (Harvey, Coulson, Mackaway and Winchester-Seeto, 2010). This permits co-operative education to fill the role as an experiential learning vehicle (Billett, 2007; Haddara and Skanes, 2007).

In terms of common denominators of the term co-operative education across definitions, often mentioned characteristics include integrated curricula, a learning derived from a practical work experience, opportunities for ongoing support and a formalised and structured coordination of experiential learning (Groenewald, 2003; Haddara and Skanes, 2007; Zegwaard and Coll, 2011). Nevertheless, several challenges have been pointed out with regards to administering co-operative education programmes. These challenges encompass the vast resources they require in terms of staffing to allow for coordination of the institution, students and industry partners, and assessment of co-op students; managing the inherent tension between academic rigour and workplace practical relevance; and cultivating and expanding upon the institution's relationship with industry stakeholders (Lazarus, Oloroso and Howison, 2011; Zegwaard and Coll, 2011).

As for the presumed benefits of co-operative education in learning outcomes and personal development, the literature has provided mixed messages (Haddara and Skanes, 2007). Part of the problem is likely to be the challenge presented in measuring and isolating the effects of co-operative education itself, while at the same time accounting for self-selection bias among students choosing to participate in a co-operative education programme in comparison with students preferring a traditional programme (Ballantine and McCourt Larres, 2007). In other words, these two groups may be systematically different in terms of characteristics and abilities prior to their choice of educational programme, something that could drive some of the empirical findings. Nonetheless, in a study by Blair, Millea and Hammer (2004), an assessment was made of the impact of co-operative education on academic performance and salary for engineering majors. Through a regression analysis of students' GPA (Grade Point Average) upon enrolment in a co-op programme, while controlling for demographics and eligibility, a statistically significant effect of co-op upon GPA was found. As well, by using a two-stage Heckman estimation it was found that a successful completion of the co-operative education programme had a positive impact on starting salary. When investigating to what extent students' co-op experience translated into enhanced maths, verbal and academic self-concept, Drysdale and Mcbeath (2012) found that co-op students had significantly higher scores on the maths and academic self-concept but significantly lower on the verbal self-concept. For tacit knowledge, and unconventional knowledge rooted in procedural action and common sense (Seidler-de Alwis and Hartmann, 2008), the results instead point to the conclusion that non-co-op students perform better (Drysdale and Mcbeath, 2012). The authors, however, caution against drawing too much on the results as it is hard to establish the causal direction.

Looking instead through the eyes of the co-op students, there are some indications that they deem the co-op experience useful in terms of developing their professional skills (Ballantine and McCourt Larres, 2007). Furthermore, students partaking in programmes saw an increase in their work self-efficacy over the course of their programme, whereas non-co-op students experienced a decrease (Raelin *et al.*, 2014). It appears specifically that the student perceived usefulness to the organisation, the opportunity to be part of a work team, and the extent to which the co-op experiences exposed students to applications in their majors played a significant role in students' growth in work self-efficacy. Students' career self-efficacy was also found to be positively impacted by co-op place- ments that offered rich opportunities for performance feedback. There are, however, eminent threats to the usefulness of co-operative education and student satisfaction. Often, students are not sufficiently versed in critical reflection and critical incident analysis for experiential learning to occur, leading to low satis- faction with the co-operative programme and students simply not seeing the purpose of doing it (Fleming and Martin, 2007). It is therefore necessary to provide appropriate support to facilitate and enhance their reflection from simply noticing to sense making. Of key importance are structured assignments that provide sufficient context and guidance to students, an antecedent which will be investigated later in the chapter.

MacEwan and the Supply Chain Management Co-op programme

MacEwan University started as Grant MacEwan University Community College in 1971 to provide a learner-centred experience with a focus on undergraduate education. In this regard, it emphasises research-informed teaching with small class sizes (MacEwan University, n.d.). MacEwan has since evolved from being primarily a transfer institution to a university, offering a comprehensive set of undergraduate degrees. Today MacEwan offers eight four-year bachelor pro- grammes, two applied degrees and several diploma and certificate programmes. It has a student body of close to 20,000 full-time and part-time students (MacEwan University, n.d.).

In 2006, the Alberta provincial legislation granted several colleges the right to become universities and offer degree programmes. For the School of Busi- ness, this materialised into a systematic process of designing a Bachelor of Com- merce programme where administration and faculty took an active part in developing the curriculum. The purpose of this process was to address how the new Bachelor of Commerce programme would be accepted by the provincial programme and other universities and, most importantly, how it would be differ- entiated from other Bachelor of Commerce programmes in the province and Canada to provide a competitive advantage. An important role was played by the Business Advisory Council, an ad hoc advisory board comprised of Canadian business executives who provided inputs into how MacEwan School of Business should be positioned to become a leader in business education. Essential out- comes of these deliberations were liberal arts requirements, small class sizes, experiential learning focus and community involvement. It was also determined that the seven professional skills of Team Work, Presentation, Critical Thinking, Research, Technology, Ethics and Writing were to be formally integrated and assessed in the curriculum (Benson and Enström, 2017).

The current Bachelor of Commerce Major in Supply Chain Management Co-op arose from an earlier applied degree in Supply Chain Management with directed field studies components instead of formal co-op work terms. Building upon these experiences, and in consultation with representatives from the supply chain industry and the Supply Chain Management Association of Canada, it was recognised that supply chain students, in much the same way as accounting students, need strong technical preparation with both theoretical and practical components integrated into their studies to be successfully prepared for a career in supply chain management. It was furthermore identified that supply chain professionals are tasked with managing the flow of materials and services along with the business relationships necessary to move products through complex integrated value networks. Hence, the core areas of the supply chain curriculum were identified as procurement and supply management, production and operations management, and logistics and distribution. These core substantive areas are also fused by courses covering aspects of e-business and technology strategy, which are essential to the supply chain operation. The firm advice provided by supply chain professionals at the time, and subsequently implemented in the curriculum by MacEwan School of Business, were education components that develop students' critical thinking skills and general business courses that provide a general well-roundedness in general business skills such as marketing, strategy, finance and operations. The discipline-specific courses in supply chain management then foster students' analytical and problem-solving skills in supply chain management. With the co-operative education component, students are provided with the linkage to the industry and opportunities to operate as a learner and worker conjointly. This allows students to develop not only discipline-specific skills but also generic professional skills such as the ability to assess and communicate their knowledge to potential co-op employers, interview successfully, develop time management skills and personal responsibility, work in diverse teams, develop problem-solving skills in a real work environment and manage information. Several of these skills have been identified by Conference Board of Canada as 'employability skills' (n.d.) and have also been identified by post-secondary institutions and organisations around the world as desirable learning outcomes beyond specific subject matter knowledge (Benson and Enström, 2017). Thus, this curriculum sets students up to be both business generalists and specialists. All students in this major take courses in the three core supply chain areas of procurement and supply management, production and operations management and logistics and distribution. Students can then take senior-level optional courses in these disciplines.

In Canada, the voice and interest organisation for co-operative education is The Canadian Association for Co-operative Education (CAFCE). It was founded in 1973 as a non-profit organisation representing employers, federal and provincial governments, students and educators involved with co-operative education. As part of their mission, CAFCE develops recommended standards and procedures for Canadian co-op programmes and also promotes co-operative education (CAFCE, n.d.). According to their definition, "co-operative education is a program that formally integrates a student's academic studies with work experience with participating employers" (CAFCE, 2005, n/p). Further, CAFCE stresses that the co-operative education curriculum should normally require students to alternate the periods of academic study with work experience in suitable fields of business, industry, government and social services. The idea is that the interlaced structure allows for a stronger linkage between academia and work and an educational environment where the students can enjoy continuous learning through the integration of classroom and applied work-based learning. Also, the interlaced structure allows for career exploration, multiple reflections and exposure to several work environments in the student's discipline. This interlaced set-up also permits the student to bring the experience from the classroom to the workplace and the experience from the workplace to the classroom in several successive rounds for heightened learning. CAFCE also sets forth criteria stressing that the co-op work is to be recognised by the institution as a relevant learning opportunity, that the student is fully immersed in productive work rather than observing, the student receives remuneration for the co-op employment, the educational institution is involved by following up on the student's progress during the co-op employment, co-op students are supervised and evaluated by the co-op employer, and finally, the time spent in co-op employment should be at least 30 per cent of the time spent in academic study. Last, CAFCE emphasises that the co-op approach to education rests upon a three-way partnership between the student, the employer and the institution, where the successful outcome depends upon the co-creation of all three parties.

When designing MacEwan's Bachelor of Commerce Major in Supply Chain Management, it was decided to align with CAFCE's recommended standards for co-operative education. Accordingly, beyond the classroom coursework, master course syllabi, learning outcomes, and assessment and evaluation procedures had to be developed for the co-op work terms. In doing so, MacEwan also considered how best to prepare students for their co-op journey. The result of these deliberations was a suite of three co-op work term courses: COOP 295, COOP 395 and COOP 495. As a preparation for the work terms, a pre-employment seminar course was created, COOP 290.

In COOP 290, the supply chain students prepare for the work integrated learning by learning about the co-op idea and co-operative education guidelines and requirements. As students are responsible to find their own co-op employments, they prepare for their upcoming job search by conducting self-enquiry into career plans and write up professional documents such as resumes and cover letters. Students are also taught employment search techniques and networking strategies and develop their interview skills. There are also recurring in-class discussions about workplace issues such as etiquette, professionalism and conflict resolution. The class features several guest speakers from the industry, some of them former MacEwan graduates, who speak to their formative experiences as well as professional head-hunters who discuss the recruitment process. Normally, the pre-employment seminar is taken in the semester before the commencement of the work term, and this is also when students would normally start to search for co-op jobs.

The sequence of the work terms starts with COOP 295 and continues with COOP 395 and COOP 495 interlaced with the academic semesters. Each work term lasts for four months and students cannot take more than two work terms consecutively to maintain the interlaced requirement of work terms and academic semesters in the co-operative education. The four-month work terms commence in January, May or September. As the work terms are meant to be full time, students are not allowed to be enrolled in any courses while on work terms, and the student's last term in the programme must be an academic semester. Figure 6.1 presents a typical course sequence for a Supply Chain Management Co-op Major student at MacEwan University. Upon entering the Bachelor of Commerce programme, students will typically take courses in economics, probability and statistics, business law and general business courses. In the second year, students will normally declare their major and take introductory courses in accounting, marketing, finance, management, accounting, operations management and a senior course in probability and statistics. For supply chain students, they then take the pre-employment seminar and do the first four-month work term starting in May. In the third and fourth year, students will primarily concentrate on courses in supply chain management interlaced with the second and third work terms.

Each of the three work terms has their own set of learning outcomes and reflective pieces with increasing complexity. Hence, for the first work term, students are asked to describe the requirements of an entry-level position in their field and assess their preparedness to assume those responsibilities. They are also asked to develop professional learning objectives for their work term and negotiate these with their work supervisor and reflect on and assess their professional skills and abilities related to the requirements of their job and the implications for their career path. For their second work term, the requirement is that students find a work placement at a more advanced level in supply chain

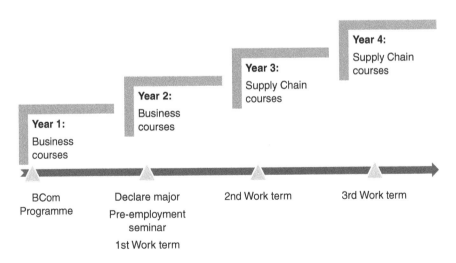

Figure 6.1 Course sequence for a Supply Chain Management Co-op Major student at MacEwan University.

management, and it is also expected that students in their reflective pieces show evidence of more insightful knowledge and discourse. Thus, when assessing students' reflective pieces, a grading rubric constructed with Bloom's Taxonomy of Learning as a centrepiece is used. Consequently, the final work term, COOP 495, is regarded as the capstone work term. What is common across the three work terms is that MacEwan maintains contact with the student throughout their work term and also arrange site visits where a MacEwan representative meets up with both the student and their employer to discuss their progress. Both the employer and the student complete separate reports upon completion of the work term.

Upon graduation with a Bachelor of Commerce with a major in Supply Chain Management from MacEwan University, students have an advanced standing when working toward the Supply Chain Management Professional designation (SCMP) offered by the Supply Chain Management Association (n.d.). As Canada's largest association for supply chain management professionals, the Supply Chain Management Association (SCMA) represents over 7000 members working in the fields of sourcing, procurement, logistics, inventory and contract management (SCMA, n.d.) and greatly benefits not only the employability of graduates but their personal development.

Co-op learning: views of students and employers

Even though the rationale and theoretical underpinnings of a programme may be sound, theory does not necessarily replicate practice. It is therefore crucial to the viability and success of the programme to take into consideration the participants' perspectives. Looking at students' thoughts about their co-op experience at MacEwan, some of their responses revolve around the theme of the added learning acquired through their workplace engagement, with sentiments such as "I probably learned ten times as much in my different jobs than I actually have studying textbooks" and "a lot of learning takes place not in the classroom; it takes place in the co-op". When commenting on the difference between students who have completed one or several work terms and those who have not, a student put forth that "many professionals notice the difference between students who have completed it and who have not".

There are, however, some notable negative aspects of co-op learning that students have mentioned in their feedback. Some of these comments centre on struggles with finding suitable work placements. As the 'finding' of a suitable placement that the institution is likely to approve resides with the student, this could delay their graduation: "it's a concern for many students here that their graduation will be pushed back because of co-op". On occasion students also encounter work placements that turn out to be unsatisfying, with representative responses such as "I've worked in supply chain for six years before coming to school. I worked for an employer who had offered one position to 200 students. I have past experience and I don't really think co-op is adding much to my degree."

From the industry side, employers have frequently indicated the added value they see in the co-operative education component, with one employer saying that "each business culture is going to be unique and wherever you work, you take a piece of that … students are very well prepared and ready to contribute from day one. The part that they need is the practical experience." Another employer points out that the co-op experience provides an added way for students to prosper: "Sometimes a student doesn't blossom in the education system. They blossom in the real world." Employers also often comment on the inferential value a co-op degree provides when hiring new staff: "GPA doesn't give me any indication of what they're going to be like. Give me a co-op and I know exactly what I'm getting when they graduate." Some of the negative feedback from employers touches on the dilemma of students having to return to university after completing their work term, with one employer articulating that "the company wanted that student but they had to go back to school and then they lost momentum on the project they were working on" and "sometimes we find the students who we have for eight months work well with the team and we would like to extend it for another four months".

These perspectives of students and employers highlight some of the key challenges associated with operating a successful co-op programme. Following an analysis of the main themes to emerge, there are generally five types of challenges to be encountered while developing and overseeing the Supply Chain Management Co-op Major: forming and cultivating the necessary close relationships with industry partners, attaining rigour in the co-operative curriculum, students not understanding the requirements of the co-operative curriculum, co-op employers not understanding the requirements of the co-operative curriculum and students not finding appropriate work placements. Tackling such challenges has taken a number of years to address and perfect, with the first fundamental challenge being the handling of co-operative partners. A co-operative programme cannot exist without industry partners, and the most straightforward point of departure is to reach out to alumni, former graduates who now have become mid-level professionals and executives. Through the personal experience of staff engaged with the programme, employers are generally very keen to be involved. However, the process of engagement needs to be transparent and robust. To formalise the initial contact with prospective employers, it has been useful to create an ad hoc advisory board consisting of industry professionals and representatives from the appropriate designation-granting body. These parties can then serve as the first point of contact for additional industry consultation but also for identifying potential co-op employers and opportunities for students. Over the academic year, it has been found to be useful to host a variety of events on campus where potential co-op employers can network and interview students or arrange panel discussions about future career opportunities.

When developing the co-op curriculum, one cannot overemphasise the importance of putting great thought into the design of the pre-employment seminar. This seminar prepares students for work placements and introduces them to the concept of experiential learning. The design of the sessions are vital so that students 'buy in' and see a real purpose with setting their personal learning objectives and contemplate their learning in the reflective pieces. Students also need to receive communication early on about the co-operative education requirements so that they understand that the co-op brings additional requirements and that it is their responsibility to find work placements but that the institution needs to approve these positions based on the job descriptions. This two-way relationship between student and employer is enhanced through institutional communication whereby employers and students are informed about the co-operative requirements and responsibilities. The development of comprehensive co-op handbooks which delineate the responsibilities of both students and employers is essential when managing expectations and reducing negative outcomes for stakeholders. The co-op handbook is supported by cultivating trust and belief in the co-operative education model. Specifically, it is crucial to recognise that all parties understand that the programme is resource demanding and requires designated staff and faculty members to coordinate and maintain contact with students and employers, including site visits, throughout the co-op. Having stakeholders who believe in the merits of the programme is an essential ingredient in the success of the programme as the co-op is not for everyone.

Note

1 In the pre-employment seminar, students prepare for the work integrated learning component by learning about co-operative education guidelines and requirements. Students also prepare for their job search by developing career plans, resumes and cover letters. Important components are employment search techniques, networking strategies and interview skills. In addition, students discuss workplace issues such as office protocol, professionalism and conflict resolution.

References

The Association of Private Enterprise Education. (2017). Welcome to APEE [online]. Available at: www.apee.org/ [accessed 29 October 2017].

Ballantine, J. and McCourt Larres, P. (2007). Cooperative learning: A pedagogy to improve students' generic skills? *Education + Training*, 49(2), 126–137.

Barbeau, J.E. (1973). Cooperative education in America: Its historical development, 1906–1971. Boston: North Eastern University.

Benson, L. and Enström, R. (2017). Deliberate institutional differentiation through graduate attributes: Implementing professional skills at MacEwan School of Business. *Journal of Management Development*, 36(6), 817–827.

Billett, S. (2007). Cooperative education: Supporting and guiding ongoing development. *Journal of Co-operative Education and Internship*, 41(2), 37–44.

Blair, B.F., Millea, M. and Hammer, J. (2004). The impact of cooperative education on academic performance and compensation of engineering majors. *Journal of Engineering Education*, 93(4), 333.

Boulocher-Passet, V., Daly, P. and Sequeira, I. (2016). Fostering creativity understanding: Case study of an exercise designed for a large undergraduate business cohort at EDHEC Business School. *Journal of Management Development*, 35(5), 574–591.

CAFCE – Canadian Association for Co-operative Education. (n.d.). About CAFCE. Retrieved from http://scma.com/en/about-scma.

CAFCE – Canadian Association for Co-operative Education. (2005). Co-operative Education Manual: A guide to planning and implementing co-operative education programs in post-secondary institutions. Retrieved from www.cafce.ca/_Library/_documents/coopmanual.pdf.

Conference Board of Canada. (n.d.). Employability skills 2000+. Retrieved from www.conferenceboard.ca/topics/education/learning-tools/employability-skills.aspx.

Daly, P. (2013). Future work skills: Employers' view and business school implications. In *20th EDiNEB Conference: Future Skills for Competitive Business Education*, pp. 27–34.

Davies, A., Fidler, D. and Gorbis, M. (2011). *Future work skills 2020*. California: Institute for the Future for the University of Phoenix Research Institute.

Drysdale, M. and Mcbeath, M. (2012). Self-concept and tacit knowledge: Differences between cooperative and non-cooperative education students. *Asia-Pacific Journal of Cooperative Education*, 13(3), 169–180.

European Commission. (2013). Entrepreneurship 2020 action plan: Reigniting the entrepreneurial spirit in Europe. Retrieved from http://eur-lex.europa.eu/LexUriServ/LexUriServ.do?uri=COM:2012:0795:FIN:en:PDF.

Fleming, J. and Martin, A. (2007). Facilitating reflective learning journeys in sport cooperative education. *Journal of Hospitality, Leisure, Sport and Tourism Education*, 6(2), 115–121.

Gibb, A.A. (1993). Enterprise culture and education: Understanding enterprise education and its links with small business, entrepreneurship and wider educational goals. *International Small Business Journal*, 11(3), 11–34.

Groenewald, T. (2003). Growing talented people through cooperative education: A phenomenological exploration. *Asia-Pacific Journal of Cooperative Education*, 4(2), 49–61.

Haddara, M. and Skanes, H. (2007). A reflection on cooperative education: From experience to experiential learning. *Asia-Pacific Journal of Cooperative Education*, 8(1), 67–76.

Harder, C., Jackson, G. and Lane, J. (2014). *Talent is not enough: Closing the skills gap*. Calgary: Canada West Foundation.

Harvey, M., Coulson, D., Mackaway, J. and Winchester-Seeto, T. (2010). Aligning reflection in the cooperative education curriculum. *Asia-Pacific Journal of Cooperative Education*, 11(3), 137–152.

Hytti, U. and O'Gorman, C. (2004). What is 'enterprise education'? An analysis of the objectives and methods of enterprise education programmes in four European countries. *Education + Training*, 46(1), 11–23.

Jackson, D. and Chapman, E. (2012a). Non-technical competencies in undergraduate business degree programs: Australian and UK perspectives. *Studies in Higher Education*, 37(5), 541–567.

Jackson, D. and Chapman, E. (2012b). Non-technical skill gaps in Australian business graduates. *Education + Training*, 54(2/3), 95–113.

Jones, B. and Iredale, N. (2010). Enterprise education as pedagogy. *Education+ Training*, 52(1), 7–19.

Kolb, A.Y. and Kolb, D.A. (2005). Learning styles and learning spaces: Enhancing experiential learning in higher education. *Academy of Management Learning & Education*, 4(2), 193–212.

Kolb, D.A. (1976). Management and the learning process. *California Management Review*, 18(3), 21–31.

Lazarus, F.C., Oloroso, H.C. and Howison, S. (2011). Administering cooperative education programs. In Richard K. Coll and Karsten E. Zegwaard, eds. *International handbook for cooperative and work-integrated education: International perspectives of theory, research and practice*. Boston: World Association for Cooperative Education, pp. 180–191.

Lewis, L.H. and Williams, C.J. (1994). Experiential learning: Past and present. *New Directions for Adult and Continuing Education*, 1994(62), 5–16.

Lichy, J. and Enström, R. (2015). Rethinking business models for 21st century higher education: A European perspective. *International Journal of Higher Education*, 4(4), 119–127.

MacEwan University. (n.d.). Facts and figures. Retrieved from www.macewan.ca/wcm/Discover/OurStory/FactsandFigures/index.htm#.

MacEwan University. (n.d.). Our story. Retrieved from www.macewan.ca/wcm/Discover/OurStory/FactsandFigures/index.htm#.

Mainemelis, C., Boyatzis, R.E. and Kolb, D.A. (2002). Learning styles and adaptive flexibility testing experiential learning theory. *Management Learning*, 33(1), 5–33.

Matlay, H. and Pepin, M. (2012). Enterprise education: A Deweyan perspective. *Education+ Training*, 54(8/9), 801–812.

Owens, J. and Tibby, M. (2014). *Enhancing employability through enterprise education: Examples of good practice in higher education*. York: The Higher Education Academy.

Pfeffer, J. and Fong, C.T. (2002). The end of business schools? Less success than meets the eye. *Academy of Management Learning & Education*, 1(1), 78–95.

Pittaway, L. and Cope, J. (2007). Entrepreneurship education: A systematic review of the evidence. *International Small Business Journal*, 25(5), 479–510.

Pittaway, L. and Hannon, P. (2008). Institutional strategies for developing enterprise education: A review of some concepts and models. *Journal of Small Business and Enterprise Development*, 15(1), 202–226.

Rae, D. (2010). Universities and enterprise education: Responding to the challenges of the new era. *Journal of Small Business and Enterprise Development*, 17(4), 591–606.

Rae, D., Martin, L., Antcliff, V. and Hannon, P. (2010). *The 2010 survey of enterprise and entrepreneurship in higher education*. Retrieved from http://ncee.org.uk/wp-content/uploads/2014/06/ISBE_Report.pdf.

Raelin, J.A., Bailey, M.B., Hamann, J., Pendleton, L.K., Reisberg, R. and Whitman, D. L. (2014). The gendered effect of cooperative education, contextual support, and self-efficacy on undergraduate retention. *Journal of Engineering Education*, 103(4), 599–624.

SCMA – Supply Chain Management Association. (n.d.). About SCMA. Retrieved from http://scma.com/en/about-scma.

SCMA – Supply Chain Management Association. (n.d.). SCMP Designation Program Retrieved from http://scma.com/en/education-accreditation/scmp-designation-program.

Seidler-de Alwis, R. and Hartmann, E. (2008). The use of tacit knowledge within innovative companies: Knowledge management in innovative enterprises. *Journal of Knowledge Management*, 12(1), 133–147.

The Association of Private Enterprise Education. (n.d.). Retrieved from www.apee.org.

Wilson, T. (2012). *A review of business-university collaboration*. London: Department for Business, Innovation and Skills.

Zegwaard, K.E. and Coll, R.K. (2011). Exploring some current issues for cooperative education. *Journal of Cooperative Education and Internships*, 45(2), 8–15.

7 Digital transformation at the *New York Times*

The usefulness of the live case intervention method

Peter Daly and Isabelle Sequeira

Introduction

The pace of digital consumption is increasing with the vast majority of Americans getting their news in some digital format, either from a desktop/ laptop (82 per cent) or a mobile device (54 per cent) (Pew Research Centre, 2013). The press media has faced increased competition from new online aggregators such as the *Huffington Post, US News and World Report,* the *Independent* (in the UK), and as a result, find themselves having to adapt in order to reach readers on various social platforms and mobile devices beyond the traditional formats. As well as digital reach, there are many other challenges facing press media such as how to drive traffic, boost revenues, increase subscriptions as well as protect subscription renewals. Bloomberg (2014: 1) expressed this issue as follows: "Newspapers are dead. People won't pay for news any more. Millennials don't read the news. Media companies, especially newspapers, struggle with digital transformation". The issue of how to reach millennials, a group who are the greatest influencers on the digital economy and who trust user-generated content (UCG) more than traditional media (Crowdtap/IPSOS, 2014), is the focus of this particular research. The *New York Times* (hereafter NYT) is a typical case of a tradition media facing these issues and that is why they first of all published an Innovation Report (Benton, 2014) and then a Digital Strategy Memo (CNN, 2015) in order to guide their reflection on the strategies they should take to ensure greater digital reach and audience engagement. Some of the questions that they asked included: how to simplify subscriptions to reach the younger readers (between 20 and 30 years old)?; how to improve advertising and sponsorship?; how to optimise their content for different media?; as well as how to extend their international reach? It is with all of these questions in mind that the International Senior Vice President of the *New York Times* contacted EDHEC Business School to see if our students would be interested in reflecting on this strategic issue. An EDHEC Business School alumnus, he was very familiar with this type of live case as he experienced this pedagogical technique during his studies at the business school where the use of the live-case and CEO intervention method is common across a number of modules. The request for students to reflect on digital transformation within the NYT coincided with the issue of a strategy memo by the NYT (CNN, 2015) on Wednesday 7 October, which outlined the steps they must undertake to double their digital subscription revenue (to reach $800 million per year by 2020) and become mobile-first.

In this chapter, we first, report on research into the CEO intervention method, we then position this method within an experiential learning approach and within enhanced student engagement. Second, we outline the design and delivery of a creativity seminar at a French business school involving the NYT who themselves are facing a pressing strategic issue, namely how to encourage millennial readers to pay for digital subscriptions in return for access to quality articles. Third, we discuss this study contextualised through the perspectives of identified stakeholders, the students, the CEO and the seminar facilitators to provide insight and implications on the appropriateness of the CEO intervention method and offer suggestions on how to improve the impact on the learner experience.

Literature review

The CEO intervention method in business education dates back to Harvard Business School in the early 1920s whereby businessmen were invited to present a strategic issue: "a problem from their desk". A few days later, "each student handed in a written report embodying his analysis of the problem and his recommended solution" (Copeland, 1954: 33), which the CEO subsequently discussed with teams of students. Rashford and Nieva de Figueiredo (2011) see this experiential approach as more global and cross-disciplinary in nature in that it builds on previously acquired knowledge from a range of disciplines, it incorporates the existence of various stakeholders, enables students to understand how to effect lasting change that is both acceptable and beneficial to all stakeholders and develops key soft skills such as research skills, teamwork, proposal presentation and decision-making, among others. Based on our extensive experience of using the LCS method since the late 1990s and on the case study and discussion literature (Brookfield and Preskill, 1999; Christensen, 1987; Rashford and Nieva de Figueiredo, 2011) for the CEO intervention method to work effectively, some key principles need to be aligned: (1) the case study needs to be a real strategic issue that an external corporate partner is facing and for which he/she is looking for a solution; (2) the person that intervenes needs to be a high-ranking member of the management team of the company, either the CEO or general manager/president or vice-president with the power to implement and evaluate the course of action suggested by the students; (3) the intervention is both in-class and out-of-class and integrated within an overall pedagogical framework that builds on previously covered material in a programme or module; and 4) the intervention should create value for the CEO/management of the company but also for the students working on the case.

It is helpful to position the CEO intervention model within experiential learning (Beard, 2010; Beard and Wilson, 2013; Kolb, 1984; Kolb and Kolb, 2005, 2010). Live case pedagogies have extremely high experiential learning potential as they move beyond the instructor/student dyad to include the client; have a whole-person emphasis to include behavioural, cognitive and affective dimension; involve contact with real world environment that is variable and uncertain; include student evaluation of the experience; and incorporate both process and outcome feedback (Gentry, 1990). Beard and Wilson (2013) experiential learning framework, the Learning Combination Lock[1] can be used to conceptualise the CEO intervention method which is the focus of this research. First, concerning the learning environment (the 'belonging' dimension of Beard and Wilson's [2013] framework), it is stimulated through the direct and personal interaction between the CEO and the students; the student interaction with company representatives and the peer student interaction. Therefore, the students navigate different physical and virtual spaces in order to solve the problem posed by the CEO: classroom space; company space; virtual space, hence extending the learning environment beyond the classroom alone. Second, as regards the experiential learning activity itself (the 'doing' dimension), it is embodied via the meeting with the CEO, who tells the story of the strategic issue and asks the students to provide a specific deliverable within a given timeframe. Third, the sensory experience (the 'sensing' dimension of the model) is operationalised via the images, videos and language used by the CEO to make sense of the to-be-solved strategic issue. Students are afforded a unique interaction with a CEO and they can get inside his/her head in order to evaluate their thought processes and how they perceive the world of business. This kind of privileged contact with someone at that managerial level of the company is not something that is usual even when working inside the company, and the students are positioned as co-creators of the knowledge solution that shifts their learning from an acquisition model to a participation model and makes them a partner with the CEO in finding a solution to the problem encountered. The three premises of partnership (respect, reciprocity and responsibility) as outlined in Cook-Sather *et al.* (2014) are relevant here in that the students are called upon to respect and take the strategic issue seriously, be open and receptive to the problem, willing to consider different experiences in a quest to find a solution and withhold their own judgment. They are also required to exercise reciprocity in their exchanges with the CEO and fellow students so that the CEO as well as the students gain from the experience albeit in different ways. Students must also take responsibility for not only their own learning but also the solutions they present to the CEO, all of this while making sense of the issue at hand. Fourth, meeting a CEO is an emotional experience (the 'feeling' dimension of the model) when the CEO connects emotionally with the students and expresses his/her fears and doubts given the uncertainty, ambiguity and complexity of the future of a given market. The students also connect emotionally with the CEO, a personality they normally would not have access to. Finally, the CEO in this example appeals to the student's experience, knowledge and intelligence (the 'knowing' dimension of the model) as he/she engages the students on a digital transformation Millenial question that is relevant to them. It is hoped that through this CEO intervention, the experience will be a learning experience for the students as they alter their assumptions and beliefs about creativity and digital transformation in the press media.

While many have lauded the advantages of this live-case method (Burns, 1990; Culpin and Scott, 2012; Daly, 2013; Elam and Spotts, 2004; Markulis, 1985; Wassermann, 1994), there are also limitations of this approach such as the extra work and motivation required from students (Camarero *et al.*, 2009), the messy nature of the information provided (Kennedy *et al.*, 2001) and the time-consuming nature of this method for instructors (Simkins, 2001). Rashford and Nieva de Figueiredo (2011) is the only article to discuss the CEO intervention method, which they use as a capstone experience with MBA and Executive MBA students. This research builds on the work of Rashford and Nieva de Figueiredo (2011) by providing further insight into the use of this method in the context of an undergraduate BBA (Bachelor in Business Administration) pro-gramme as opposed to a postgraduate MBA programme. This chapter also extends the analysis to the various stakeholders of the CEO intervention method namely, the CEO, the students and the faculty member(s).

Design and delivery of live case CEO intervention

The CEO intervention method was integrated into a creativity seminar for 560 final year undergraduate BBA students on two campuses at EDHEC Business School. The creativity seminar was a nine-hour seminar over two days with the following objectives: (1) better appreciate the rules, principles, definitions, phases of creativ-ity as well as the creative process; (2) provide students with a creativity methodol-ogy and toolbox to manage creativity within future corporate projects; (3) offer new ideas/recommendations on a problematic and strategic corporate issue which would be more difficult using conventional rational methods; and (4) deal with a real strategic issue a CEO is currently facing in their company. The seminar[2] involved three phases: (1) introduction to creativity – awareness raising of creativ-ity as a concept and using exercises to enhance creative thinking; (2) divergence – involving exercises to enable students to let their imagination run wild through various brainstorming techniques; (3) convergence – exercises to formalise the recommendations and provide the deliverables for the corporate partner – the NYT. The four principles outlined above were integrated into the seminar in that a real strategic issue was posed (1) by the high-ranking CEO; (2) involving both in-class and out-of-class work to operationalise prior experience; (3) creating value for the CEO but also for the students.

The NYT provided the students with a strategic issue namely: "What would motivate young people (20–30 year olds) to accept to pay for digital subscriptions to quality press articles that are only available on their mobile phones?" The NYT Senior Vice President in charge of International Operations presented the strategic issues and asked the question in a four-minute video that was imbedded in the crea-tivity seminar slides. The seminar was run by ten facilitators (mainly adjunct faculty who are both academics and practitioners) in Lille and by ten in Nice.

The deliverables included a five-minute pitch of the recommendations of the group (24 students in each group) and a one-page summary of the main ideas and an advertisement of the idea.

The pedagogical design differed slightly between the Lille and Nice campuses due to timetabling constraints. For the Nice group (293 students), the CEO went to give a lecture and interacted with the students prior to the creativity seminar, whereas on the Lille campus, the CEO was present when they worked on their solution and on the final jury panel to evaluate the student solutions. Students on the Lille campus watched the live broadcast of the CEO's lecture in Nice and he was represented by one of his NYT colleagues in Nice for the final jury panel. This ensured that all students received the same content and that a representative from the company was on the jury for the final presentations. This learning activity reveals that it is possible to create large-scale student learning experiences for significant numbers of undergraduate students in real-time through a well planned and executed design. Later in the chapter we will discuss the implications and lessons learned, which should prove useful to those academics and practitioners wishing to run similar type learning events.

Research design and analysis method

Data was collected from 560 final year BBA students, from the CEO himself and from 20 creativity facilitators. The evaluation of the seminar was obligatory; hence, all students completed the qualitative evaluation. We decided to collect quantitative data rather than qualitative data as we wanted to have student feedback that would enable us to reflect better on the redesign of the creativity seminar and the use of the CEO intervention method. Data analysis was inspired by Miles and Huberman (1994) who suggests their three-step analytical framework: (1) data reduction; (2) data display and (3) drawing conclusions and verification. Data reduction involved the transcription of the CEO interview after the live case study intervention and the interviews from the 20 creativity facilitators, who were asked to provide specific feedback on the CEO intervention method. Data display involved reading the data, colour coding and developing categories. Verification and drawing conclusions, the final stage, was conducted to confirm the themes and patterns identified. Data analysis was ongoing and non-sequential but occurred in a simultaneous, cyclical and iterative manner. The most common themes are discussed in the findings section below.

Findings and discussion

Students reported five main positive themes around five lexical collocations: (1) real life; (2) novel; (3) soft skills; (4) learn differently; (5) structured framework; with four negative themes extracted from the coded data: (1) exploitation; (2) lack of time; (3) lack of guidance; (4) lack of visibility. Common themes from the CEO involved: (1) fitting the corporate issue into the creativity seminar; (2) the quality of the work produced; (3) the difficulty of finding one question; and (4) the provision of in-depth contextualised information. The most common themes from facilitators revolved around: (1) the concrete nature of the learning activity; (2) how the seminar changed student vision of creativity; (3) how students took the work seriously; and (4) the relevance of the deliverable to students and the 'desiloising' effect of this seminar. We will discuss the three stakeholders below.

Student evaluation of CEO-intervention method

In the qualitative data collected from students on the CEO intervention method with the NYT, students appreciated the applied, novel and relevant nature of the pedagogy employed which enabled them to acquire soft skills and learn differently. The majority of students appreciated the real and concrete nature of the case study during the seminar with no recognisable differences in responses between the centres. Typical responses from both the Nice and Lille campuses were "creativity case that was real and not just invented"; "working on a real case for the *New York Times*"; "interesting seminar with a concrete project"; "group work project that is interesting an concrete". This is in line with research by Burns (1990), where he attests that the key ingredient of the live case study is realism. The majority of students from both campuses also liked the novel topic that was relevant to them with a typical response being "interacting to reflect on the creation of a project within a group of 25 students in a limited timeframe on a topic that concerns us directly within a structured creativity framework". This comment points to the professional relevance debate within business education (Bennis and O'Toole, 2005; Pfeffer and Fong, 2002) and the need to match the practitioner's expertise to the to-be-taught class (Clinebell and Clinebell, 2008). The students also appreciated the opportunity to develop their soft skills that included presentation skills on a real subject in front of the CEO with typical responses from the majority of students from both campuses: "challenged by the final presentation in front of all students on a real project with the presence of the corporate partner"; "presenting in front of an audience helped me overcome my stress due to presence of CEO"; "public speaking in front of a real audience" with a typical response from both campuses being how they learnt differently: "very interesting project with pure creativity techniques that enabled us to go beyond ordinary learning". This activity reflects how millennials learn, their preference to work on team projects, and how they expect to be challenged in the classroom situation (Howe and Strauss, 2003). Most students enjoyed the structured creative framework to accompany the strategic issue with a typical response from students on both campuses being: "specific stages of the seminar to construct the case response bit by bit with activities at each stage". While a structured creativity may seem like an oxymoron, many creativity experts suggest a structured framework within which students develop creativity (Liedka and Ogilvie, 2011; Raison, 2014), a statement illustrated by this live-case and CEO intervention method.

The main four criticisms expressed by students concerning the live-case study CEO intervention method were: (1) the CEO involvement on both campuses and student perceptions that they are being exploited in some way; (2) the CEO does not put in the time; (3) more guidance during the process; and

(4) the CEO does not come back later to provide them with feedback on how their ideas have been used in the company. A minority of students from both campuses, not just the Nice campus, felt they were being exploited by the NYT with typical responses being from both campuses being: "they make us work for free for the NYT"; "we worked for the NYT, not for ourselves". These are comments we have often heard following a live case at a business school, and there is an expectation on behalf of the students to win a prize for the best ideas, which is why we always integrate a prize within the CEO intervention method. The majority of students from both campuses regretted the lack of time to really interact with the CEO whether they had direct access to the CEO or not, and students from both campuses felt they could have had more CEO interaction around the issues raised by the assessment, with typical responses being: *"did not have enough time to deal with the strategic issue presented"*; *"should extend the seminar over several days as too condensed to exercise our creativity on issue"*; *"have more time to fine-tune the project before we hand it in to CEO".* This is paradoxical in that on the one hand, the CEO does not have time to interact with every student personally given his schedule, and on the other hand, the Millenial student expects individual attention when completing an exercise (Howe and Strauss, 2003). The majority of students from both campuses also felt that they had not enough guidance on the solution process of how to find a solution with a typical response being: "more directions and support during the process of the project"; "would have liked to have more company contact to get inside the company". This has also been identified as one of the challenges when teaching Millenial students (Howe and Strauss, 2003), i.e. their neo-traditional nature where they want to 'live by the rules', which is not always compatible with a creativity seminar and even less so with the CEO intervention method, where students are expected to break the rules and be creative, albeit within a framework. A final criticism by a minority of students from both campuses was the lack of visibility on what happens next "so what happens to our ideas and solutions, where is the follow-up?" as one student from the X campus put it. Students expect detailed feedback on what happens to their ideas and how they are used by the CEO. This was provided by email to the students, but we believe that a better approach would be for the CEO to return a few months later or organise a Skype to address all students on how the ideas were or could be operationalised with the NYT.

Therefore, students evaluated the experience positively as the CEO case study is relevant, real and concrete to their lives, helps them to develop their soft skills and learn differently as well as acquire a creativity methodology that they can use later on in brainstorming activities in their future companies. The student criticisms point to the need to manage student expectations to ensure that they do not feel they are being exploited, that their ideas matter and that they are validated completely. More guidance needs to be provided from the company via a hotline or a virtual platform for example, and students need to have a prize for the most creative ideas and also be provided with feedback on what happens next.

Corporate partner evaluation of CEO intervention method

First, similar to the student responses, the corporate partner was predominantly positive about the experience and he was positively surprised with the compatibility of the strategic issue being discussed and the choice to integrate this issue into a creativity seminar. Second, the corporate partner was also pleased with the quality of the work produced by the students despite their difficulty in finding a question initially. Third, the corporate client was mindful of the fact that the NYT could have provided the students with more contextualised information about press media and that this would have been very beneficial to the students. Below we discuss the main themes to emerge from the qualitative responses.

The NYT senior vice president felt that there was a good fit between the strategic issue raised, i.e. the motivation of young people to pay for digital subscriptions to quality press articles on mobile devices, and a creativity seminar as creativity is at the heart of what the NYT are all about: "creativity is everything in NYT and is part of our DNA, we cannot work without it. If we are not creative, we are dead". He goes on to explain how creativity is important in marketing, communication, journalistic content provision, in digital media delivery and speaks about the pervasiveness of creativity in the press media. Hence, he found that positioning this particular question within a creativity seminar was very relevant as not only did the students get to acquire key creativity tools and methodologies but they also worked on a topic that was implicitly creative. By couching a strategic CEO question within a structured learning framework in the creativity seminar, this experiential learning experience attended to the whole-person whereby the six philosophical considerations as outlined by Beard and Wilson (2013) are enacted.

The corporate partner was very surprised and pleased with the quality of reflection and the deliverables as well as the degree of creativity from certain teams: "This work gave us insight into the motivations of young international and European students as our research to date has been very America-centric. It will enable us to test premium offers for students". Therefore, the student output provided food for thought for the NYT executives and the corporate partner intended to discuss the ideas with top management and with the digital marketing section of the NYT to action some of the student suggestion, such as the integration of Twitter feed from war correspondents and the provision of background information regarding key figures in the media via click-through video content.

While the NYT found that the students were an ideal group to reflect on digital transformation in the press media in order to acquire fresh ideas from a group of European undergraduates, they had limited experience with the CEO intervention method. The question was even more difficult as the generation in question are used to free content on the Internet and do not pay to read the press. The most challenging part of the question, therefore, was linked to how you entice young people to pay for quality press and how to find a payment model that is adapted to the consumption habits of this generation. "Indeed the only people who can answer this type of question are those who read regularly on digital platforms. The pleasure and ease of reading is not the same with paper and on a digital platform". The NYT really needed to access young digital natives who do not share their mobile phones and have a different approach to reading and consuming the press media. According to the corporate partner:

> Statistics show that 1 copy of a newspaper is read on average by 6 people ... the same is not true on a mobile as if you have 1 million mobile subscribers, there is only 1 million readers as you do not share your mobile with someone else.

Another challenge in the formulation of the question is the type of content that this generation wants. The NYT assumed that they wanted interactive content and in fact the students corroborated this by making proposals, which included video, audio alerts, zapping options, background information on a topic such as timelines, click-through links to provide extra information on countries, organisations, personalities, etc. as well as virtual reality and live video streaming, Twitter feed, personalisation of content, all of which moved away from a push strategy to a pull strategy whereby the reader decides.

In hindsight, the CEO believed that he should have provided the students with more in-depth information with regards to the context, perhaps putting more restraining parameters on the assignment brief: "We maybe should have given the students a memo on press media and on the major sociological challenges facing the press media today". Therefore, moving forward and when using the CEO intervention method in the future, we would ask the company and CEO to provide more concrete background information on the issues, and in this case, the issues facing the industry and the digital considerations necessary when you move from a paper to a digital content model. The CEO explained that the profession and organisational culture has changed dramatically within the NYT and that many digital technology positions have been created since October 2015. They now recruit a very particular profile: digitally aware; agile project teams with marketers, technology experts and journalists, which engage in quick 'try and buy' strategies (i.e. develop and test a product, get people to buy it, get reader feedback) that do not have set hours but work intensively on projects similar to many technology companies. This kind of live feed of insider information would have been beneficial to help students better conceptualise the digitalisation of the press and possible create greater ownership of the experience as it would reflect a real life working environment.

Therefore, the corporate partner was pleased with the compatibility between his strategic issue and a creativity seminar as well as with the quality of the work produced. However, he had difficulty finding the right question and deciding on the proper amount of contextual background information to provide to students so that they could answer his question. This points to the need to align the current company strategy and culture, the strategic issue, and the course content and student relevance and requires a lot of prior preparation and negotiation between the course coordinators, the CEO and the seminar facilitators.

Seminar facilitator evaluation of CEO intervention method

A total of 20 facilitators worked together on this seminar. They each had a group of 25 students. Similar to the other stakeholders as mentioned earlier, they believed that the CEO intervention method has many advantages. First, all believed that the method goes beyond the classical teaching model to introduce a systemic approach involving many stakeholders (business school, permanent faculty, adjunct faculty, company, CEO and other employees) to enable students to work on a concrete and strategic issue that is totally embedded in an economic and corporate environment, a typical response from both campuses was: "this is the introduction of a pedagogical approach in teaching around a real project that makes students work on concrete topics that are aligned to the economic environment".

Second, like the students and the CEO, the facilitators thought that problem/issue proposed by the CEO exemplifies the importance of creativity in a company to enable the various teams to understand the inherent role of creativity in most project work in corporate environments. This also helps the students to surpass the assumption that creativity is only for artists and that only some people are creative, a typical response from respondents at both campuses was: "The creativity aspect got the students in the right space and helped the students buy into the project". They also believed that the students took the seminar seriously as there was a real deliverable set by a real CEO that is looking for their feedback and ideas in order to solve a strategic issue within the company, a representative quote from respondents from both campuses was: "An external project is great as it ensures that the students take the work seriously".

Third, the importance of relevance in business education as outlined by various researchers (Bennis and O'Toole, 2005; Clinebell and Clinebell, 2008; Pfeffer and Fong, 2002) is present in the comments of all the facilitators. They appreciated the relevance of the strategic issue – the digital transformation of press media, albeit unique to the NYT at a particular moment in time, is transferrable to a range of industries and professions as many will confront digital transformation in their future jobs as managers in a variety of sectors. A typical response from respondents at both campuses was: "Digital transformation is ubiquitous in companies today and even if students will not work in the media industry, the challenges faced are transferrable to other industries". Hence, the majority of facilitators felt that the NYT CEO intervention brought timely, up-to-date, relevant content to the seminar, which enabled student collaboration and capitalised on the student's digital awareness and literacy to solve a strategic issue. The usefulness of using both a relatable and contemporary issue was summarised by the quote: "I appreciated the explicit link to digital media, which is a key competence of our students". They appreciated the importance of the financials in the question as it de-siloised business disciplines by including many disciplines such as marketing, finance, communication, creativity within a complex problem, with a typical response from respondents of both campuses being: "The students had to use their transversal knowledge of business to solve the issue given by the CEO". They also appreciated the prestige and the international focus of the corporate partner and the personality of the CEO, with a representative quote from respondents of both campuses being: "The CEO was very charismatic and approachable, which is helpful in this kind of exercise".

The facilitators, however, did point out some weaknesses to a CEO intervention. The facilitators believed that it would be better to have the company CEO and partners interact more with the students doing the exercise with a typical response from respondents at both campuses being: "The CEO or his staff could be present throughout the exercise and go from group to group". The facilitators realised that a CEO may not have had time to spend two days on each campus talking to students and believed that this was one of the major constraints of the CEO intervention method. Rashford and Neiva de Figueiredo (2011) point to the importance of managing the CEO and maximising the time spent with him/her to ensure that the CEO's thought process is experienced.

In line with the feedback from the CEO, the facilitators also believed that the students should have engaged more readily with the contextual background of the case prior to the event and have the client provide additional CEO intervention by providing them with even more contextual information on the company, the industry challenges and the sector. While the majority of the facilitators saw the relevance of creativity and a CEO intervention method, some felt that there was a possible disconnect between a creativity seminar, which is supposed to liberate ideas for the future, and the very strict project requirement to provide rational, concrete, directly applicable ideas for the NYT with a typical response from respondents at both campuses being: "If we are working on creativity and imagining the future, it is difficult to ask students to rationalise their project and think about the financials. We should have stayed on the creative part of envisioning the future". Some respondents suggest a two-phase approach: (1) liberation of ideas; and (2) concrete implementation of ideas, which would be separated by a time lag. The advantage would be that students would not be constrained creativity by the need to implement the idea and hence, not censure their creative ideas.

The majority of facilitators from both campuses called for students to be more immersed in a creative project bubble rather than in a familiar environment (their business school) as they were not necessarily on-task for the entire two days with a typical response from respondents being: "We need to break the routine of the classroom by bringing students elsewhere". They suggest a contained environment, possible outside the school, within a creativity lab that provides everything students need – food, beverages and internet access. This questions the learning environment being only the classroom and the possible borders that we as educators often create for ourselves in business education (Mintzberg and Gosling, 2002). We should look beyond the classroom to other environments, which could provide equal or even better learning opportunities for business students.

The majority of facilitators from both campuses felt that the CEO needs to provide more visibility to the students on what happens to their ideas – which ideas were taken up; which were less appreciated and why; and possibly have access to the next stage – the further development and implementation of their ideas. A typical response from respondents were: "The students, I feel, need more feedback on the outcome of the project, otherwise they feel frustrated. The CEO should come back and provide a report on the ideas chosen, developed and implemented". Elam and Spotts (2004) suggest that extensive debriefing is required with a live case study to ensure that the learning process of an experiential exercise is completed and links to a theme to emerge from the students following completion of the learning activity.

Therefore, facilitators appreciated the relevance of the topic, the student-centred approach, the choice of CEO and the teaching methodology employed but felt that more interaction from the company and more contextualised information on the company would have facilitated learning and impacted the final deliverable. Some questioned the disconnect between a creativity seminar to liberate ideas and a deliverable that required a concrete outcome and would appreciate more visibility and feedback from the CEO on the ideas provided.

Implications

For those interested in implementing a CEO intervention method in their pedagogy within business education, we outline below some lessons learned from using this approach through discussing the themes to emerge from perspectives of stakeholders individually and collectively.

Adopt a cross-disciplinary student-centric approach at the end of a programme of study

One of the major challenges faced by the CEO was formulating a strategic question that was sufficiently interesting yet doable. In this particular situation, digital transformation was very pertinent to the target student population in that it enabled students to discover a new industry and espoused a cross-disciplinary approach to find a solution. Therefore, we suggest that a cross-disciplinary student-centric method be adopted that capitalises on student knowledge and experience. In order to be a useful learning experience for both the CEO and the students, this method needs to be positioned at the end of a programme of study when students have mastered certain theoretical concepts and have some work experience. This explains why Rashford and Neiva de Figueiredo (2011) use this method as a capstone course so that students can utilise the skills acquired during their studies.

Develop soft skills via the CEO intervention method

All the stakeholders agreed that the creativity seminar was the appropriate vehicle for the CEO intervention method due to the importance of creativity in the corporate world and necessity to have a structured creativity framework, which enables the development of this competence amongst undergraduates (Boulocher *et al.*, 2016) as well as key soft skills such as conversing and listening (Brink and Costigan, 2015). In addition to providing a glimpse into the dynamics of a company leader's strategic issue, we would advise that the instructor organising a CEO intervention method also considers what soft skills can be developed by the students beyond the problem-solving process that is customarily associated with this type of learning activity and embrace other soft skill development.

Offer a realistic context that is ambiguous, messy and incomplete

The CEO intervention method is more in line with a pedagogical tradition that emphasises conceptual development and critical thinking of 'wicked problems' in an uncertain, complex and protean environment rather than a vocational skill-based tradition that involves managers making controlled interventions in a safe environment as outlined by Rippin *et al.* (2002). Although students requested more guidance and more time, we believe that for students to understand the complex reality of management practice and the applicability of their insights on specific corporate settings as well as the conflicting goals and values therein, the real life strategic issues must be diverse, complex and noisy. Hence, students should be provided with a rich array of materials such as videos, meetings, interviews, original documents, website information in a virtual learning environment that are conflicting, messy and incomplete as this mirrors real management complexity. Students could also be provided with increased exposure to the corporate space if that is feasible given the proximity of the company to the business school and the number of students involved. The CEO could provide more exposure to the company by having a contact person within the company to provide additional information. This we believe would enhance student's belonging (Beard and Wilson, 2013) by extending the learning environment beyond the classroom to the corporate space. This proximity with the strategic issue we think is crucial to help students make greater sense of the project and their role within the project.

Ensure that the CEO returns to provide detailed feedback

Rashford and Neiva de Figueiredo (2011: 645) write:

> the fact that the CEOs go through the process of articulating the issue they are facing in detailed terms to outsiders to understand it and subsequently go through a systematic process of addressing the respective issue has been mentioned as a significant benefit from the process.

We believe that by encouraging the CEO to find a strategic issue, getting a fresh vision of this issue from undergraduates and also by coming back to see the students a few months later, the CEO can benefit even more from the process as they can see the progression to the end. Students would also appreciate having feedback on their ideas and this would curb student criticisms that they are being exploited and that they lack visibility on the implementation of their ideas. We would, therefore, advise instructors to invite the CEO to return to the classroom with their feedback to discuss the applicability of the ideas proposed by students as well as provide a prize for the best and most feasible, original and creative ideas.

Conclusion

In this chapter we looked at the CEO intervention method from three perspectives: from the perspective of the BBA undergraduate students who experienced this method during a creativity seminar at a French business school; from the point of view of the CEO and the seminar facilitators. All stakeholders appreciated the real, concrete, novel and relevant nature of the method, which capitalised on the prior student knowledge and experience within a student-centric, cross-disciplinary approach. All parties saw the relevancy of couching the CEO intervention method within a creativity seminar, which enabled students to acquire a structured creativity framework and develop critical thinking as well as other other soft skills and also enabled creativity to be brought to life given its importance within the contemporary corporate world. Beard and Wilson's (2013) experiential learning model was used to explicate the belonging created via the learning method that enabled students to create an emotional link with a CEO grappling with a strategic issue that required fresh, reasoned and intelligent ideas from undergraduate students who enacted a change in their vision of the challenges faced by a CEO.

For those intending to use this method, five considerations are outlined: (1) this method is best employed at the end of a programme with the strategic issue involving a cross-disciplinary, student-centric approach that is relevant to the student population you are teaching; (2) the instructor should consider the soft skills development of the students to go beyond the simple problem-solving skills normally associated with this type of method and embrace other competencies and skills; (3) the instructor should provide a real-life context that incorporates wicked, messy and noisy strategic issues that mirror real-life management practice rather than trying to control the learning environment; they should provide increased exposure to the corporate space as well as the requisite background information to enhance students ownership; and (4) the instructor should ensure that the CEO returns to discuss the feasibility and applicability of the students' ideas a few months after the intervention (if possible) so as to avoid student frustration.

The CEO intervention method is time-consuming and complex but if you can bring a real strategic issue to the classroom offered by a high-ranking CEO that provides a challenging learning experience for your students and creates value for a CEO as well as for your students, then this experiential technique is well worth the trouble.

Notes

1 Beard and Wilson (2013) developed an experiential learning framework based on information processing, which they used as a basis for the design of a metamodel – the Learning Combination Lock (LCL).
2 For more information on the description of the creativity seminar and some ideas on the types of exercises used with a mass student audience and the challenges faced in undergraduate business education, please refer to Boulocher *et al.* (2016).

References

Beard, C. (2010). *The experiential learning toolkit: Blending practice with concept.* London: Kogan Page.

Beard, C. and Wilson, J. (2013). *Experiential learning: A handbook for education, training and coaching.* 3rd ed. London: Kogan Page.

Bennis, W.G. and O'Toole, J. (2005). How business schools lost their way. *Harvard Business Review*, 27, 43–62.

Benton, J. (2014). The leaked New York Times innovation report is one of the key documents of this media age. Nieman Lab. Retrieved from www.niemanlab.org/2014/05/the-leaked-new-york-times-innovation-report-is-one-of-the-key-documents-of-this-media-age/.

Bloomberg, J. (5 November 2014). Digital transformation in action at the Financial Times. *Forbes Magazine.* Retrieved from www.forbes.com/sites/jasonbloomberg/2014/11/05/digital-transformation-in-action-at-the-financial-times/#2715e4857a0b249071d67446.

Boulocher, V., Daly, P. and Sequeira, I. (2016). Fostering creativity understanding: Case study of an exercise designed for a large undergraduate business cohort at EDHEC Business School, *Journal of Management Development*, 35(5), 574–591.

Brink, K.E. and Costigan, R.D. (2015). Oral communication skills: Are the priorities of the workplace and AACSB-accredited business programs aligned? *Academy of Management Learning & Education*, 14(2), 205–221.

Brookfield, S.D. and Preskill, S. (1999). *Discussion as a way of teaching.* New York: NY: Jossey Bass.

Burns, A.C. (1990). The use of live cases in business education: Pros, cons and guidelines. In: J.W. Gentry, eds. *Guide to business gaming and experiential learning.* London: Kogan Press, pp. 201–215.

Camarero, C. Rodriguez, J. and San José, R. (2009). A comparison of the learning effectiveness of live cases and class projects. *International Journal of Management Education*, 8(3), 83–94.

Christensen, C.R. (1987). *Teaching the case method.* Boston MA.: Harvard Business School Press.

Clinebell, S.K. and Clinebell, J.M. (2008). The tension in business education between academic rigor and real-world relevance: The role of executive professors. *Academy of Management Learning and Education*, 7(1), 99–107.

CNN (2015). *The New York Times strategy memo.* New York: CNN. Retrieved from http://money.cnn.com/2015/10/07/media/new-york-times-strategy-memo/.

Cook-Sather, A., Bovill, C. and Felten, P. (2014). *Engaging students as partners in learning and teaching: A Guide for Faculty.* San Francisco: Jossey-Bass.

Copeland, M.T. (1954). The genesis of the case method in business instruction. In M.P. McNair and A.C. Hersum, eds. *The case method at Harvard Business School: Papers by present and past members of faculty and staff.* New York: McGraw-Hill, pp. 25–33.

Crowdtap/IPSOS (2014). *Social influence: Marketing's new frontier*. New York: Crowdtap. Retrieved from http://go.crowdtap.com/socialinfluence.

Culpin, V. and Scott, H. (2012). The effectiveness of a live case study approach: Increasing knowledge and understanding of 'hard' versus 'soft' skills in executive education. *Management Learning*, 43(5), 565–577.

Daly, P. (2013). The live case study approach in business education. In: E. Doyle, P. Buckley and C. Carroll, eds. *Innovative business school teaching: Engaging the Millennial generation*. Abingdon: Routledge, pp. 70–80.

Elam, E.L.R. and Spotts, H.E. (2004). Achieving marketing curriculum integration: A live case study approach. *Journal of Marketing Education*, 26(1), 50–65.

Gentry, J.W. (1990). What is experiential learning? In: J.W. Gentry, ed. *Guide to business gaming and experiential learning*. London: Kogan Page, pp. 9–20.

Howe, N. and Strauss, W. (2003). *Millennials go to college: Strategies for a new generation on campus*. VA: Lifecourse Associates.

Kennedy, E.L., Lawton, L. and Walker, E. (2001). The case for using cases: Shifting the paradigm in marketing education. *Journal of Marketing Education*, 23(2), 141–151.

Kolb, D.A. (1984). *Experiential learning: Experience as the source of learning development*. Upper Saddle River: NJ: Prentice Hall.

Kolb, A.Y. and Kolb, D.A. (2005). Learning styles and learning spaces: Enhancing experiential learning in higher education. *Academy of Management Learning and Education*, 4(2), 193–212.

Kolb, A.Y. and Kolb, D.A. (2010). Learning to play, playing to learn: Case study of a ludic learning space. *Journal of Organizational Change Management*, 23(1), 26–50.

Liedka, J. and Ogilvie, T. (2011). *Designing for growth: A design thinking tool kit for managers*. NY: Colombia Business School Publishing.

Markulis, P.M. (1985). The live case study: Filling the gap between the case study and the experiential exercise. *Developments in Business Simulation & Experiential Exercises*, 12, 168–171.

Miles, M.B. and Huberman, A.M. (1994). *Qualitiative data analysis: An extended sourcebook*. 2nd ed. Thousand Oaks, CA: Sage Publications.

Mintzberg, H. and Gosling, J. (2002). Educating managers beyond borders. *Academy of Management Learning & Education*, 1(1), 64–76.

Pew Research Centre (2014). Key indicators in media and news. Retrieved from: www.journalism.org/2014/03/26/state-of-the-news-media-2014-key-indicators-in-media-and-news/.

Pfeffer, J. and Fong, C.T. (2002). The end of business schools? Less success than meets the eye. *Academy of Management Learning and Education*, 1, 78–95.

Raison, M. (2014). *Oser la créativité: inspirez-vous des pratiques des entreprises innovantes*. Limoges: Vitrac Editeur.

Rashford, N.S. and Neiva de Figueiredo, J. (2011). The live in-class CEO intervention: A Capstone experiential technique for leadership development. *Journal of Management Education*, 35, 620–645.

Rippin, A., Booth, C., Bowie, S. and Jordan, J. (2002). A complex case: Using the case study method to explore uncertainty and ambiguity in undergraduate business education. *Teaching in Higher Education*, 7(4), 429–441.

Simkins, B.J. (2001). *An innovative approach to teaching finance: Using live cases in the case course*. Working Paper, Oklahoma State University, Stillwater, OK.

Wassermann, S. (1994). *Introduction to case method teaching. A guide to the galaxy*. Columbia University, New York: Teachers College Press.

8 International short-term study programmes

An institutional roadmap to sustainable student engagement

Bernhard Herold

International short-term programmes in the form of dual foreign exchanges (Dual International Programmes/Duale Auslandsprogramme), predominantly one-way exchanges represent a unique selling point of the Business Administration degree at DHBW Karlsruhe, not only setting the institution apart from its competitors but giving its graduates a set of employability skills, setting them on the path to successful careers in a number of top companies in Germany. From its introduction in 2009, with students going to Abertay University, Dundee, Scotland, the Dual International Programmes have seen more than 500 students from the Management in Commerce degree programme participate in such programmes across the globe including Hong Kong, China and India. The author of this chapter is Head of Department Business Administration – Management in Commerce at the DHBW Karlsruhe and was both one of the designers and managers of these programmes, leading at least 1–2 programmes a year.

Background to the institution

The DHBW was founded as a Cooperative State University and is the largest university of Baden-Württemberg and one of the largest in Germany, with around 35,000 students at nine locations. It attracts high-school graduates with particularly good school grades and as such occupies a special position in the German university landscape. Initiated by leading German companies in the 1970s, the study concept to be discussed in this chapter is a consistent transfer of the successful German dual educational concept to a university. During the three-year study period, the students switch to a Bachelors degree in an average of three months between university and practice, which requires a training contract with an accredited partner of DHBW. In addition to the good career prospects, the monthly wage payments granted by the training companies over the period of three years, there are also other important incentives. During the course of studies, the programme usually allows for students to be not only employment ready but financially independent.

The concept of duality – Dual International Programmes of DHBW Karlsruhe

In line with the duality of studies at the DHBW, the Dual International Programmes also has the blended learning approach of theory and practice, that is, lectures at universities and practice in the companies. In the Management in Commerce degree, the Dual International Programmes connects academic and practitioner input through student projects where students have to produce an industry related project report which contributes towards their final grade. The concept of duality includes three parts. Lectures at a local university about specialities of the local market to get a structured view into the market and the competitive environment, visits to local companies to get a feeling for the specific challenges and range of circumstances facing the company and the project which encourages active engagement with the business, interpretation of current strategy and the making of justified recommendations. The modules 'Intercultural Competences' and 'Country, target group and value specific peculiarities' are specific examples of the concept of duality and how academic content compliments the world of work and are the modular basis upon which our discussions take place.

The cross empowerment element of the module 'Country, target group and value specific peculiarities' is that students have acquired skills to identify and analyse intercultural issues. They are thus able to develop strategies with which trade and service companies can react in a targeted manner to the identified country-specific and target-specific peculiarities. They are able to define relevant tasks, to work independently and to coordinate those tactics and strategies.This cross empowerment theme is reflected in the aim of the Dual International Programmes, where students are expected to recognise that there are differences between countries especially in buying behaviour, retail marketing/management and consumption development stage. They should learn that this depends on various factors (such as culture, ideals, income, prices, competition) so that they are able to have a clear perspective, once in industry, on impact and influencing factors as well as having more tolerance for other ways of thinking and doing.

Offer of Dual International Programmes in the course of business management Karlsruhe

The study programme Management in Commerce has developed into the largest course at DHBW Karlsruhe. Within the last ten years, companies' demand for study places has already nearly trebled resulting in a continuous expansion of the offered Dual International Programmes. The choice of countries is extremely important for the course management in commerce and is therefore very targeted. The focus is on the commerce-oriented use and thus also the usefulness of the gained knowledge for students and commercial enterprises.

The first Dual International Programme started in 2009 with Abertay University Dundee, Scotland. It was initiated by Management in Commerce and was exclusively reserved for those students. Great Britain is considered to be extremely innovative in new marketing strategies and technologies. In the UK, Tesco is one of the leading European trading companies. At the same time, Great Britain is one of the largest growth markets for the German food discounters Aldi and Lidl. Dundee in particular was selected for two reasons, the first is historical. Wm Low, was based in Dundee and purchased by Tesco to gain a foothold in the Scottish retail market and second, the concentration of Tesco retail formats in Dundee with an express, a metro, a superstore and extra, not to mention the fact that Dundee is also home to a Tesco call centre and until 2006 a Tesco distribution centre. Nine student groups with a total of around 250 students were able to participate. After the programme proved so successful, and with so many applications already submitted in the second year the programme had to be offered twice, in 2011 the additional Dual International Programme Hong Kong at Polytechnic University Hong Kong, China started, later extended to Guangzhou, China. Hong Kong, was and is considered very important for the procurement of trade. Apart from trade companies, which focus on food and drug products, Hong Kong is the bridgehead to the procurement market of China. Many German trading companies have their own purchasing offices in Hong Kong. At the same time, China is developing into one of the most interesting expansion areas for German and international trading companies. The Dual International programme has been in operation since 2011, sending two groups and a total of over 60 students in the first year. In 2013, the Dual International Programme India followed in co-operation with the IGTC in Mumbai, an initiative involving the courses Management in Commerce and Business Engineering. India, too, was considered of great importance as a procurement market and is also one of the largest potential sales markets.

The Dual International Programme Turkey with the Yeditepe University in Istanbul has not yet gone beyond two pilot projects in 2013 and 2015 due to the tense security situation. Turkey is an important procurement market, not just for the textile trade. At the same time, Turkey is a large potential market for German trading companies with the close cultural connection between Germany and Turkey appealing to German trading companies.

The US was also discussed when setting up target countries for the Dual International Programmes given its prominence in the retail sector and range of successful companies. However the US seemed to only have a minimum level of attractiveness for students, and as such no programme with the US has been set up to date. Currently, initial discussions are taking place with a partner university, in order to be able to offer such a programme from 2018/2019. These discussions surround a two-way exchange, similar to that of the India programme where students are given topics suited to their respective programmes of study and the host institution expertise. In this case students of the DHBW are offered a trade-oriented programme in the USA and the American students are given brand management of German premium brands.

In other words the rationale behind the selection of country is because of its strategic importance to German retail and commerce. The choice of city and institution is more related to the variety of the retail offer and negotiations with the specific institutions to establish a relationship. The issue of language also influences the selection of institution, particularly in China where courses taught exclusively in English was not necessarily the norm. However the main reasons for the strategic educational alliances are outlined in the next section.

The checklist for educational partnerships

When selecting educational partners it is not just the students at the home university who are considered, it is also the partner institution. Due to the duality of the DHBW, the opportunity for collaboration and exchanges are considered to enhance the experiences of participants as well as enhancing their employment skills set, specifically the ability to work in multi-national groups and share knowledge. The availability of partner companies is also a consideration when selecting a partner. Due to the participants engagement with a company in Germany as part of their studies, it is an advantage to get the same or similar company in these partner countries to allow continuity of industry engagement. In order to evaluate the value of the Dual International Programmes for the individual participants, a cost-benefit analysis is offered with the ideal situation being where all identified stakeholders benefit from the partnership experience.

Students

The core needs, which can be satisfied by the dual programmes abroad include:

Expanding a student's own horizons, encouraging curiosity, the opportunity to experience adventure, stimulating and discovering new insight into solving business problems.

Improving professional opportunities, improving the linguistic knowledge, providing insight into the hitherto unfamiliar cultures and peculiarities of the target country and making professional contacts.

To stand out positively from the majority of students, through illustrating their commitment to extra-curricular studies, able to provide a contrast to their familiar economic and social environment.

A change from the highly structured studies at the DHBW, able to gain insight into other teaching and learning practices and learning spaces, the opportunity to work in teams and collaborate with students from other countries.

As a 'dry-run' for future foreign engagement, international semesters of study abroad, working abroad, postgraduate studies and international collaboration.

Despite the numerous benefits, one must remain vigilant to possible obstacles and limitations which include:

The costs associated with the programme.

The image and perceptions of target countries and partner institutions.

The timing of the programme and orientation during the initial period of the programme. Recognition of the achievements and grades attributed to the activities undertaken during a student's time on the Dual International Programme.

Past experiences of participating students.

Partner companies

The benefit for the partner companies of Dual International Programmes is not only the ability to gain insight into the potential of future employees it is also an opportunity to 'sell themselves' to graduates. Germany currently suffers from an increasing lack of potential school and university graduates resulting in young people having more choice, and many training courses and graduate positions remaining unfilled. The required knowledge of the language spoken by the customers does not open up alternatives for retailers, thus aggravating the situation. This situation forces companies to increase their recruitment efforts and brand attractiveness so as to improve their ability to acquire graduates.

As a result, the provision and support of Dual International Programmes can become a competitive advantage to companies in the labour market.

The partner companies can also benefit from the knowledge gained by the students in the framework of Dual International Programmes. This knowledge can directly impact on improvement processes in the company or indirectly serve as the basis for a company-oriented Bachelors thesis.

There is a risk however that dual foreign programmes could lead to an over-qualification of students, which could make graduates even more employable and therefore encourage the individual to change jobs and pursue opportunities with other employers either at home or abroad.

Home university

The home university, in this case the DHBW Karlsruhe, is able to increase its attractiveness to students, companies and teaching staff through the range of Dual International Programmes it offers. Dual International Programmes can thus become a clear demarcation from other universities. Surveys among the graduates regularly confirm that Dual International Programmes are one of the strongest positive memories of their study, in addition to one semester abroad. The programmes also ensure positive PR and marketing materials for prospective students and promote the institution in general. Engagement with programme also create valuable contacts and possible collaborative research projects, publications, guest lectures and the sharing of networks. Such Dual International Programmes, however, also bind capacities at the home university and can lead to conflicts in the allocation of resources.

Partner university

Increasingly, universities see so called 'special' programmes for student groups from other universities as a source of income, especially during the semester breaks where there is often an unused capacity and infrastructure available. Foreign student groups can also contribute to the image of a partner university through adding to the diversity and options available for host students to also study abroad.

Host businesses and organisations

There are two types of business involved: partner businesses which have been explained earlier and those businesses who are involved in the programme as hosts and/or the focus of the assessment. The engagement with international students opens up opportunities not only for image enhancement for the businesses through visits. Such engagement could also lead to new perspectives in terms of their businesses products and services, because the students at the DHBW all have experience of operational practice in their respective placement company. Visits from those international students can also create new contacts, which may prove the basis for future institutional or business engagement or partnerships.

It should be noted however that for those businesses, the time and cost factors associated with the visit of student groups could be a potential barrier to involvement.

A student perspective of their experiences on the Dual International Programmes

Dual International Programmes and student semesters abroad can arguably be in competition with each other. A recent survey of interested students at an information event of DHBW Karlsruhe 2017 has shown that especially students who already have foreign experience are looking for a semester abroad, where students who have no or little experience prefer the Dual International Programmes as a comfortable and safe pathway to gain initial experience abroad. In some cases, Dual International Programmes are also being used to prepare students for the semester abroad. When students are asked after they returned from a Dual International Programme or semester of study abroad, the decision taken is considered the right one afterwards. Students who used both options considered them both equally useful, giving them useful insight into business practices abroad, which they felt enhanced their employment skills and employability.

One of the student's exhortation:

> Through my semester abroad in Scotland, I was able to prove my English language skills, by my participation in the Dual International Programme Hong Kong/China and my interest and openness to the Asian culture. That's why I was offered an interesting job in the international purchasing of my company.

Intention and perceived benefits of Dual International Programmes

In a survey of interested parties, the push and pull factors which influenced students to study on Dual International Programmes or a semester of study abroad were the pull of extending personal benefit, which was cited as the number one factor in their decision The second most important factor was the improvement of professional opportunities. With regards to the push factors, the main factors were the duration of the foreign stay, the country, followed by the costs. Strikingly often, the behaviour of fellow students also seems to influence the decision. However, the wishes of the placement company do not seem to play a role in the students' decision, which is perhaps surprising.

The survey conducted among 114 students of the 2017 final year, regardless of the extent to which they participated in a Dual International Programme and/ or a semester of study abroad, has shown that both options have been classified as equally good for extending a student's personal horizon. According to the German school number system, 1 stands for a very good performance and 6 for inadequate. The Dual International Programmes were rated with a mean value of 1.93 (= good), in contrast a semester of study abroad was rated at a mean value of 1.95 (= good). This is an interesting result, as international semesters with an average of 12 weeks compared with around two weeks for Dual International Programmes would be expected to have a higher degree of influence on a student's personal horizon, with greater opportunity for integration into local student life. A partial explanation for this result could be that students on the Dual International Programme enjoyed the fact that there was more pressure to fully engage with the host country given the rather tight time constraints, a further explanation could be down to the comprehensive nature of the Dual International Programmes, where participants get involved with a whole range of activities, mixing theory with practice and coverage similar to that of study abroad as a result of its intensive nature. Students who have used both the Dual International Programme and the study abroad semester and thus can assess the suitability of both options gave them both a mean value of 1.0 (= very good). Students who have not used either one of the two options evaluate the suitability of Dual International Programmes with a mean value of 2.16 (= good), with a semester of studying abroad gaining a slightly better mean value of 2.11 (= good). This result is also interesting as it illustrates how students perceive the two alternatives. With students who have not experienced either the Dual

International Programme or a semester of studying abroad considering the semester studying abroad as more beneficial, which would make sense as this is a program of 12 weeks or so in length. However the finding is in contradiction to those students who have participate in both programmes, with participants viewing both programmes as equally viable and beneficial.

Students did not couch their opinions solely in terms of personal horizons, they also discussed it in terms of the prospects for improved career opportunities. A semester studying abroad received a mean value of 2.34 (= good), in contrast the Dual International Programmes receiving a mean value of 2.74 (= satisfactory). A similar level of distance between the two international alternatives can be seen in the responses of those students who have used both options. Those students rated the suitability of Dual International Programmes with a mean value of 1.8 (= good), with a semester of study abroad receiving a mean value of 1.2 (= very good). A reason for the difference in score could be how students perceive the impact of the academic transcript with the performance during a semester's study abroad documented in the diploma, whereas in the Dual International Programme, although there is an assessment and grade attributed to student performance on the programme, it is not documented in the final academic transcript. In addition, the presentation in the CV is usually more prominent. A further reason could be the length of study on the respective programmes, with students perceiving that employers would put more value on a longer period of engagement in another country at least on a superficial level.

Despite the overall positive student perceptions of the programmes, with the majority of participants considering participation on the Dual International Programme as beneficial to their employability skills and future employment, the participation rate in the course, Management in Commerce did not exceed 50 per cent in recent years. For almost all graduates the associated costs and their limited financial resources were cited as the main obstacles. Only a few placement companies grant their students comprehensive financial support, which is disappointing given the mutual benefit participation in these programmes bring to both the employer and the student and is something institutions should attempt to encourage to ensure better take-up rates of the international opportunities available.

For the transferability of knowledge, it would be interesting to know how students from other countries assess the usefulness of dual international programmes, also in comparison with foreign semesters. This was followed by a survey among the participants of the Dual International Programme Karlsruhe 2017, which was offered by IGTC in Mumbai India. Some 18 students from India took part in the survey.

The students from India also stated that the two most important goals were to expand their personal horizons and improve their career prospects. The assessment of the suitability of Dual International Programmes and one semester abroad has a strikingly high similarity with the results from the graduate survey at DHBW. This should at least be an initial indication of the international applicability of the results.

The suitability of Dual International Programmes for the extension of personal horizon was with a mean value of 2.06 (= good); the suitability of a foreign semester with a mean value of 1.89 (= good), roughly equal to the average of German students with 1.93 and 1.95. Very interesting is the different view of those Indian students, who are in an executive programme, they are older and have the appropriate professional experience. Students from the executive programme evaluate the suitability of Dual Foreign Programmes for the extension of personal horizon with a mean value of 1.37 (= very good), much better than the suitability of a semester abroad with a mean value of 2.13 (= good). The reason for this may lie in a larger life experience, but also in the felt time shortage. Accordingly, this is in contrast with the responses of the younger students, a semester abroad has scored significantly better with a mean value of 1.22 (= very good) than the Dual International Programme with a mean value of 2.78 (= satisfactory).

In order to achieve the goal of improving job opportunities, Dual International Programmes are rated as slightly lower by the Indian students with a mean value of 3.0 (= satisfactory) than by the German students with a mean value of 2.74 (= satisfactory). The suitability of a semester abroad, on the other hand, is assessed more positively with a mean value of 2.00 (= good) versus a mean value of 2.34 (= good) of German students. It is striking that students from executive programmes assess the suitability of a semester abroad much more critically than the younger Indian students and approach the level of German students. The students from the executive programme rate 0.25 grades better than the younger Indian students, which is still slightly worse than the German students.

Characteristics and decision-making behaviour of the participants

The 2017 survey of interested DHBW students suggests that the choice for a Dual International Programme or an international semester abroad could depend on the extent of existing international experience. Also there is the presumption that age and professional experiences influences the decision of participants to join a foreign exchange programme. What is noticeable is the level of enthusiasm for both options at the beginning of a student's studies, however this enthusiasm appears to decline as the student progressed through their degree programme with the main obstacles of financial burden as well as a the limited recognition by the placement company as reasons for non participation.

Although popular, as a result of the decision to cancel the subsidy of the Dual International Programmes, with students now having to bear the full costs themselves, the initial high growth rates are no longer sustainable. However due to the integral position of the Dual International Programmes in the course of Management in Commerce, their existence is ensured. This integral position is however reliant on the popularity of the partner country and the individual(s) at the host institution. Countries such as Great Britain, China and others in Asia continue to prove popular among students. However it should be noted that further expansion into Great Britain is made more difficult by their decision to exit the European Community. The experience has also shown that Dual International Programmes are strongly aligned on individual persons and are also dependent on them. Such a relationship can lead to a number of research and collaborative spin offs. However it can also lead to a dependency on individual persons, whose withdrawal could endanger the continuity of the respective Dual International Programme.

The role of the academic and the academic structure are also not to be under-estimated and while they are usually the instigators and supporters of such pro-grammes they could also be potential obstacles. With regard to academics, as the engagement with such programmes increases the academics' interest may dissi-pate, often experiencing conflict with family commitments, particularly as the Dual International Programme Hong Kong, for example, falls during the school holidays. In terms of the academic structure, the Dual International Programme Hong Kong, China and formerly also Dundee, Scotland are firmly integrated into the fourth semester. This is commonly known as the theoretical phase just after the examinations, and if students wish to participate in the programme they would potentially miss lectures and have to negotiate with their placement company and course leader. This should not present a huge barrier in theory but in practice it is a reason given by students not to engage with the programme, despite its benefits and opportunities for enhanced employability.

Two different examples of Dual International Programmes

The manifestations, developments, peculiarities and challenges can be illustrated through two examples of Dual International Programmes. The sequence is by no means a valuation, but takes place in the order of introduction.

One-way programme and two-way exchange programme

The Dual International Programme Hong Kong, China is a one-way programme, because only DHBW students go to Hong Kong, China, with no reciprocal pro-gramme offered at DHBW Karlsruhe for students from Hong Kong, China. Reasons for the comparatively low attractiveness of Germany for students from Hong Kong is arguably the perceived language barrier. As the benefit for the stu-dents of the host university is limited, the university is almost exclusively a service provider. The university in Hong Kong focuses on the organisation of lecture rooms, lecturers, accommodation in student residences, access to the can-teens and bus transfers. The situation in Guangzhou is similar. This is a special challenge for the International Dual Programmes, which often results in limited contact between the universities and the companies to be visited. As a result, visits to companies/institutions are organised by DHBW, which does not present a huge problem because of the company network DHBW has through its partner business and years of international experience. International experience and engagement is therefore key to the continued success of international programmes such as the Dual International Programme.

In contrast to Hong Kong, China, the Dual International Programme, Mumbai, India is aimed at a two-way exchange. A student group from DHBW visits IGTC in Mumbai for almost two weeks in January, and in return a student group from IGTC visit DHBW for almost two weeks in October, and since 2017 in July. Participants of the last and following programme meet the guest students to provide mentoring and support. Through joint activities between students from both institutions, the shared cultural experience is deepened which in turn improves the benefit to the student and the added value of the programme. The programmes in Mumbai, India and Karlsruhe are similar, in that they consist of lectures and practical elements. The organisation of the lectures, practical elements, accommodation and transfers is completed by the host university and works well, which underlines the importance of 'getting the right partner' in order to grow the success of any international programme of study.

Initial contact

The Dual International Programme Hong Kong, China relationship was based on contact made between the international office of DHBW Karlsruhe and the Polytechnic University Hong Kong. Alternative platforms for contact could be special international fairs, such as the conference of the EAIE (European Association for International Education), the conference of the APAIE (Asia-Pacific Association for International Education) and the DAAD (Deutscher Akademischer Austauschdienst), one of the world's largest funding organisations for the international exchange of students and scientists, as well as the respective individual networks between the individual international offices of universities.

The basis for the development of the Dual International Programme Mumbai, India were personal contacts. At the time, the Head of Department Industrial Engineering at DHBW Karlsruhe was the founding director of the IGTC (Indo-German Training Centre) in Mumbai. The institution is also affiliated to the AHK (German Foreign Trade Chamber) in Mumbai and thus has excellent contacts not only to German companies in India.

Check of suitability

Following initial consultation between the respective international offices, a delegation of two professors, including a representative of the course in Management in Commerce, explored the possibilities for co-operation on site in Hong Kong, China. The demand on the part of the students was so great that the pilot project in 2011 had to be started with two groups totalling more than 60 students. One group of students was from the Faculty of Technology, supervised by a professor from the Faculty of Technology. The second group of students was from the faculty of economics, mostly from the course in Management in

Commerce, supervised by the author. Polytechnic University Hong Kong took over the organisation of accommodation in student halls, lectures, lecturers, visits to state and local organisations. A major challenge for the author and his colleagues was the organisation of specific company visits for the respective groups. In concrete terms, this means that every day, following the official programme at the Polytechnic University, the possibilities for a visit or a lecture and the benefit for the students had to be assessed by means of telephone contacts and personal meetings with companies in Hong Kong. It was not only the DHBW networks, the contacts of the students within their placement organisation, but also the local German community, which had to be used.

The same delegation as in Hong Kong also travelled to Mumbai to negotiate the finer details of the exchange and after a lead time of about two years, the Dual International Programme Mumbai, India started with the first group of students from DHBW travelling in 2013. In the same year, the first reciprocal visit of Indian students arrived at DHBW Karlsruhe. The close and regular communication between IGTC and the DHBW prove to be beneficial in the coordination and design of the programmes with no major issues revealed and the organisation of site visits and schedules both academic and extracurricular organised by the host institution.

Procedure

Because the Dual International Programmes Hong Kong, China and Mumbai, India are offered throughout a student's course of studies, the International Office at the DHBW Karlsruhe assumes an essential coordinating task between the individual courses at DHBW Karlsruhe and with the foreign partner universities, in the case of these illustrative examples, the Polytechnic University Hong Kong, China, the Jinan University Guangzhou, China and IGCT Mumbai, India. For the students, this includes the invitation letter associated with the Dual International Programme being sent by mail on the registration of the applications and specially for Hong Kong, China up to the completion of the visa process, in addition the conclusion of the framework agreements with the foreign institutions and schools, the booking of accommodation for students and accompanying tutors, and the development of the academic schedule.

The focus of the courses of studies, in this case the course of Management in Commerce, is on the content design. This includes the content of the lectures, as far as possible the choice of lecturers, the maintenance of contacts with companies and institutions, the selection of practical visits and guest lectures. In addition, a variety of other practical components could be established by partner companies of the course, current and former students and other networks. This includes, in particular, leading institutions and companies from the German market, in addition to the purchasing departments of German non-food dealers, the sales branches of German industrial companies, German start-ups in the Chinese and Asian regions, logistics service providers, Chinese trading houses, as important suppliers not only of German companies and production sites for

German companies. The economic interests and support mechanisms, such as the AHK (German chambers of commerce), are also extremely valuable.

The Dual International Programme Hong Kong, China covers two weeks. When it was launched in 2011, the programme was limited to two weeks in Hong Kong combined with a one-day practice element in the People's Republic of China. Since 2011, the proportion of time spent in the People's Republic of China was extended, culminating in 2014 in the programme consisting of one week in Hong Kong and one week in Guangzhou, China. At both locations there was the tried and tested combination of lectures, in particular to obtain the necessary background information on the political, societal and economic framework conditions, and practical elements to assess the impact of the economy on (German) companies.

In terms of organisation and processes, the Dual International Programme Mumbai is similar to Hong Kong, China, with organisation of the programme in Mumbai, India largely carried out by the IGTC. The IGTC plans the lectures, visits to companies and institutions, accommodation, on-site transfers and catering. During the visit to Karlsruhe the DHBW takes over these tasks. The Dual International Programme Mumbai India covers ten days and not 14 days like the combined programme Hong Kong and Guangzhou/China. Experiences have shown that in the case of more than ten days at one city, students begin to experience fatigue. The charm of the city is reduced, and the limits imposed on a student's personal liberties become more obvious. To address issues of academic fatigue, the programme is reviewed based on feedback from staff and students with amendments, where necessary, made to lectures, visits and assessments.

Programme structure

In order to increase the benefit for the students on the programme, they are divided into groups, to work on a specific project on site and to present their results on the last day of their programme. The presentations are held before the plenary session and before an examination team of host academics and industry practitioners with the mark included in the module 'Country, target group and value specific peculiarities'. Attributing a mark to the work performed in the Dual International Programme motivates the students to be more involved with the programme, encouraging them to conduct market analysis and empirical research which are important skills when they move into the employment market. However, as alluded to earlier, the grade only contributes to the overall grade which, in contrast to the semester of study abroad does not receive full recognition on the academic transcript.

Before embarking on the Dual International Programme, students are inducted with at least one meeting of the group at DHBW. In addition to providing general information on the process, rules of behaviour (including dress code), accommodation and advice and guidance on the host country and university, students are furnished with the group project assignment. Examples of group projects for Hong Kong, China include, 'Brand and origin as sales argument in

Hong Kong and China', and 'Innovative concepts of easy shopping in Hong Kong and China'. The project assessed not only a student's ability to search for answers on the market, but also to evaluate the transferability or utilisation of recommendations and outcomes for German companies in Germany and abroad. To further student learning and understanding, from 2016 competence groups have been established to encourage student discussion on topics related to the host country. The topics cover contemporary issues in health, infrastructure and social and economic activity, with students having the ability to choose the competence group they want to participate in.

The arrival and departure of students takes place individually with a sufficient time window of approximately 3–4 days allocated for the arrival, so that the students have the possibility to customise the airline and route according to their budget and wishes. The accommodation is usually available from Saturday/Sunday and the programme starts on Monday morning. On Sunday there is usually a 'pre-program briefing session' to clarify any questions and to prepare students for the following day and time on the programme.

The lectures and programme components take place from Monday to Friday, mornings through to afternoons and on the weekends the students are free to travel in the region, sight see and/or prepare for the assessed project. Each student has to create a daily diary during their time on the programme, which although not assessed is submitted upon completion of the course. This allows the academic team the opportunity to gain an insight into participant perspectives and gain feedback beyond the end of the programme survey.

On the last day of the programme, the results of the group projects are presented. This requires at least one preliminary presentation, in which an academic panel representative provides feedback and identifies potential areas for improvement. On the last day, the closing ceremony will take place at the respective host university with the awarding of the participation certificates, followed by a party initiated by the students. The accommodation is still available for a further day to allow students to transition home or onward to another destination.

Special challenges presented by the Dual International Programme

Language

The success and failure of dual foreign programmes are linked to specific challenges related to the host country, the most important challenge is language. Due to its history as a British colony, Hong Kong is still strongly influenced by the English language, making it a widely spoken language. However, the importance of the English language in everyday life is decreasing. In schools, English is increasingly being replaced by Mandarin. Nevertheless, wide areas of everyday life are still opened up to the students through English.

It is quite different in the People's Republic of China. During the week spent in Guangzhou, communication became a challenge due to the low frequency and level of spoken English. Among others things, this makes the organising of company visits sometimes a little difficult. In Mumbai, India there was no problem with language with English being the official language.

Date of yearly implementation

A particularly challenge in Hong Kong, China was where it was integrated in the curriculum, and thus impacted on the offer of teaching and practice elements as well as accommodation. In terms of time, the Dual International Programmes have to be placed in the theoretical phases at DHBW. An offer outside the theoretical phases would mean that students would have to apply for a holiday which could create, as mentioned earlier, difficulties with their placement company, which has a negative impact on participation. For the Dual International Programmes and its relationship with the Management in Commerce course, module content was mapped so that any missing module material at DHBW was partially addressed at the host university, but there was still specific material on the modules 'Country, target group and value-specific peculiarities', which was required to be 'caught up' by students upon their return to DHBW. This approach was successfully implemented and piloted with Abertay University Dundee, Scotland, during the first half of August but like any strategy there is risk associated to it, with students benefitting from the international exposure but having to do a degree of 'double work' upon their return to DHBW.

In order to give the students the opportunity to create their own individual follow-up programme the Dual International Programme was deliberately placed at the end of the semester. Students added in additional itinery on the return leg of their journey with low additional flight costs. Many students took the opportunity to continue studies in preferred destinations such as China, Thailand, Vietnam, Dubai, Indonesia, Australia and New Zealand.

The availability of rooms and lecturers as well as the possibilities for the organisation of the lectures are also strongly influenced by the date of the Dual International Programme. During the lecture times, the teaching staff is present and joint events with students of the host university are possible. However, the availability of suitable lecture rooms and organisational capacity is often restricted. A position outside the normal operating hours allows greater flexibility with regard to the position of the individual lectures, but leads, among other things, to a limitation of the staff available and the possibility of a limited student life experience at the host university because of a lack of contact with local students. Since the Dual International Programme takes place in the first half of August, it is held outside the lecture times. However due to a good working relationship and communication with the institution in Hong Kong, China there were no such time restrictions on the course.

Accommodation is relatively expensive in Hong Kong. The use of student residences is a way to keep the costs for the participants as low as possible and as it is August, during the semester break at the Polytechnic University, the student residencies are open in principle. However, during semester breaks, there is usually conversion/renovation work being performed in the residences which restricts or excludes availability. This has led in the past to relatively short term changes and one time to change the student residence during the programme. The student residences are usually well equipped, with a wide range of fitness and leisure facilities, and panoramic terraces with views over the sea of Hong Kong and sometimes even residents' private pools.

In Mumbai the climate influences the timing of the programme. The visit had to run in January, one of the coolest months in Mumbai, which made it more difficult for students to attend because most students were in the practical phase of their programme at DHBW. That meant students had to agree with their placement company and take leave. If they were in the theoretical phase, when they participate in the Hong Kong visit, it would only be necessary to 'catch up' on missed lectures. This is a major reason why the number of participants in the Mumbai programme is lower than in Hong Kong.

Costs and government regulations

As the students who want to participate in the Dual International Programme Hong Kong, China have to bear the costs themselves, DHBW not only strives to keep the costs for the students as low as possible, they also provide several grants and scholarships through the Förderkreis der DHBW Karlsruhe, which is an association of sponsorships and grants several scholarships to students. For the students, it is important in this context that the costs associated with participation are manageable and can be estimated in advance. The visa requirements and costs for the People's Republic of China have proved to be a particular area of uncertainty. Short-term changes in the processing of applications, increases in fees and types of visa influence participant costs and future perspectives and participation in the programme. In the summer of 2016, for example, the cost of issuing a one-time entry visa increased from under €100 to over €170. In May 2017 the special '144 hours visa', which was cheap, was suspended for entry from Hong Kong to Canton, China, where Gunagzhou is located. In July 2017 the requirements for the passport were also changed.

The costs of living for Mumbai were lower than that of Hong Kong, China, with flights, costs associated with visas, accommodation and living all more financially viable for participants, however the lower costs were offset by the timing of the programme, which made participation more difficult. As this example illustrates, the operation of an international programme is a constant balancing act to ensure positive outcomes for students and identified stakeholders.

Conclusion

In a world of increasing globalisation, international openness and graduate mobility, a student's exposure to international opportunities has become an increasingly important addition to the student CV. The experiences from DHBW show that the students are both eager to expand their personal horizons and to improve their career prospects through an internationalised curriculum and the opportunities provided by Dual International Programmes and semesters of study abroad. Participants clearly feel Dual International Programmes have a valuable place in the curriculum, able to open up new and interesting professional perspectives in a short two-week period. The Dual International Programmes not only assess a participants hard skills (project management, communication, creative thinking, problem-solving and leadership), they also test the softer skills (confidence, communication and reflection), (Barbar, 2014; Department for Business Innovation and Skills, 2015; Draycott and Rae, 2011; Fiala, Gertler and Carney, 2014; Jones and Iredale, 2010) through exposure to other cultures, dealing with cross-disciplinary issues, reflecting on experiences and taking responsibility for themselves.

The Dual International Programme appears to have a double impact on the employability of graduates, not only do they consolidate and enhance the employability skills set of participants through employer engagement, exposure to different teaching and learning methodologies and pedagogies and cultural experiences, they also encourage other companies to get involved as a means to 'sell themselves' to participants. As was discussed earlier, in Germany graduate positions are becoming increasingly difficult to fill so participants on these programmes increase their employability two-fold through participation. Participating companies see participation as a significant contribution to their ability to secure mature, yet young talent. In summary, it could be argued that the inclusion of an international dimension is a necessity for any programme and institution not only to attract and produce better students but to enhance the employment prospects of graduates and make them better global citizens, more rounded, more resilient and tolerant of other attitudes and behaviours.

References

Barbar, N. (2014). Five reasons for teaching entrepreneurship [online]. *SAIS*. Available at: www.sais.org/news/205092/Five-Reasons-for-Teaching-Entrepreneurship.htm [accessed 13 December 2016].

Department for Business Innovation and Skills (2015). Entrepreneurship skills: Literature and policy review [online]. *BIS Research Paper*, No. 236, 1–50.

Draycott, M.C. and Rae, D. (2011). Enterprise education in schools and the role of competency frameworks. *International Journal of Entrepreneurial Behaviour & Research*, 17(2), 127–145.

Fiala, N., Gertler, P. and Carney, D. (November 2014). The role of hard and soft skills in entrepreneurial success: Experimental evidence from Uganda. *AEA RCT Registry*, 7.

Jones, B. and Iredale, N. (2010). Enterprise education as pedagogy. *Education + Training*, 52(1), 7–19.

9 Learning-apprenticeship methodologies

Virtuous relation between international entrepreneurial teaching and entrepreneurial attributes

Luísa Cagica Carvalho, Iara Yamamoto and Adriana Backx Noronha Viana

Introduction

Nowadays entrepreneurship is considered as a key factor to promote economic activity (European Commission, 2003) attending to their capacity to influence positively the fall in unemployment levels (Audretsch, 2002) and to stimulate economic development and employment (Mitra, 2008). Entrepreneurial education assumes a particular role of increasing the entrepreneurial attitudes of people (Potter, 2008). The literature identifies several variables that determine the individual's decision to start a venture and presents different perspectives in respect to the methodologies used over the years (Gartner, 1989; Rauch and Frese 2007). Cognitive approaches paid special attention to the entrepreneurial intention (Autio *et al.*, 2001), capacity of personality traits (McClelland, 1961) or demographic characteristics such as age, gender, origin, religion, level of studies, labour experience, etc. (Reynolds *et al.*, 1994).

The empirical studies about entrepreneurial education face some limitations and problems. Entrepreneurs are a highly heterogeneous group of people that defies a common definition and, consequently, common predictors. A so called 'average entrepreneur' does not exist and, therefore, an average personality profile of entrepreneurs cannot be determined (Gartner, 1985). Nevertheless, Rauch and Frese (2007) propose that some specific traits may be linked to certain entrepreneurial tasks. Another perspective is that the intention to create a firm is a voluntary and conscious activity (Krueger *et al.*, 2000), and entrepreneurial intention would be a prior and determinant element towards performing entrepreneurial behaviours (Fayolle and DeGeorge, 2006). In this sense more favourable attitudes would make the intention of carrying entrepreneurial activity more feasible. Similarly, the 'attitude approach' would be preferable to those used traditionally in the analysis of the entrepreneur, such as the traits or the demographic approaches (Krueger *et al.*, 2000). As a consequence, attitudes would measure the extent to which an individual's values positively or negatively impact on entrepreneurial behaviour (Liñán, 2004).

Given the current gap in the literature with regards definitions of an 'entrepreneur', there is also a need to clarify the conceptualisation of relationships between entrepreneur, entrepreneurial activity and entrepreneurial education, the impact of new technologies, the development of competencies and the construction of suitable methodologies. Also, the linkage between learning and active participation methods to achieve outcomes from entrepreneurial education needs to be better explained. This chapter aims to discuss these pertinent topics and present some remarks and suggestions for a better development of higher education in higher education institutions (HEI).

Entrepreneurial education in higher education institutions

Around the world it is agreed that there is a relationship between entrepreneurship and economic growth. This tendency implies the development of public policies suitable to the small business, due the prevalence of small and medium enterprises in the economies. Supported by government policies that encourage small business growth, higher education provides more and more training programmes for small business owner-managers (Zhang and Hamilton, 2010).

Entrepreneurship education is possibly at present more pertinent than ever before (European Commission, 2016; Fayolle, 2010; Matlay, 2008). Several authors report the huge growth in entrepreneurship education programmes (Kuratko, 2005; Matlay and Carey, 2007; Penaluna, Penaluna and Jones 2012), particularly since the 1960s. However the effects of entrepreneurship education are still poorly understood. Some studies find a positive impact of entrepreneurship education courses or programmes at universities on perceived attractiveness and the feasibility of new venture initiatives or even on actual start-up activity (Fayolle *et al.*, 2006; Souitaris *et al.*, 2007), but others find evidence that the effects are negative (Oosterbeek *et al.*, 2010). Similarly to definitions of entrepreneur and entrepreneurship, there is a lack of consensus regarding the effectiveness of entrepreneurial education which requires a framework with possible milestones and effective measures to assist the effectiveness and measurement of entrepreneurial education (European Commission, 2016; Graevenitz *et al.*, 2010; Nabi *et al.*, 2016). We believe that collectively the studies developed about enterprise and entrepreneurship education could facilitate a better understanding about entrepreneurial education in HEI.

A review of the literature on enterprise and entrepreneurship education (Gorman *et al.*, 1997), in particular entrepreneurship programmes (McMullan *et al.*, 2002) provides evidence that these programmes encourage entrepreneurs to start a business. The literature hypothesises that entrepreneurship education has the potential to engender the necessary skills and mind-set among learners to be able to turn creative ideas into entrepreneurial action. This perspective connects with personal development and employability due to the possibility of developing some key skills considered as essential to becoming an entrepreneur. This perspective is connecting with personal development and employability.

The European Union supports the perspective that entrepreneurial education is also relevant across "the lifelong learning process, in all disciplines of learning and to all forms of education and training (formal, non-formal and informal) which contribute to an entrepreneurial spirit or behaviour, with or without a commercial objective" (European Commission, 2016: 19).

Among the limited number of studies who have investigated the area there is arguably the limitation that such studies do not engage control groups or a form of stochastic matching (Block and Stumpf, 1992). Basic controls as pre- and post-testing are not used, and most studies survey participants with an existing predisposition towards entrepreneurship, skewing the results in favour of educational interventions (Gorman *et al.*, 1997). The studies by Souitaris *et al.* (2007); Oosterbeek *et al.* (2010) and Rosendahl Huber *et al.* (2012) are notable exceptions, using pre-test-post-test control group designs. Souitaris *et al.* (2007) used a pre-test/post-test, quasi-experimental design to test the effect of entrepreneurship education and training directed at science and engineering students, finding that participation in such educational initiatives raised entre- preneurial attitudes and intentions. Oosterbeek *et al.* (2010) used a difference- in-difference framework to evaluate the effects of a Junior Achievement Company Programme targeted at Dutch junior college students, whose loca- tional choice was used as an exogenous instrument. They did not obtain any significant effect on students' self-assessed entrepreneurial skills but did find a negative effect on entrepreneurial intentions, i.e. after the programme maybe students become aware of the risk and hard work to become an entrepreneur, and their entrepreneurial intentions decrease in opposite to the expected. Rosendahl Huber *et al.* (2012) applied a randomised field experiment to measure the effects of the programme 'Bizworld', which focuses on develop- ing the competencies pertinent for future entrepreneurship among children aged 11 to 12. They found no effect on cognitive competencies, such as calculus or reading ability, but a positive effect on non-cognitive competen- cies, such as persistence, creativity and forward-looking behaviour in consen- sus to the research developed by Souitaris *et al.* (2007).

Entrepreneurial intention in the context of entrepreneurial education in HEI requires further discussion, and using the two main theories entrepreneurial event theory and planned behaviour theory this chapter will investigate this rela- tionship between education and intention developing understanding of the role of providers and impact of educational providers.

Entrepreneurial education theories

Although there is a lack of appropriately controlled studies on entrepreneurial education, there is an area which has received attention, the theoretical underpin- ning of the phenomena. This section presents the two theories: entrepreneurial event theory and planned behaviour theory.

Entrepreneurial event theory (Shapero and Sokol, 1982) believes that the firm creation is a result of the interaction among contextual factors, influencing individual's perceptions. The consideration of the entrepreneurial decision would take place as a consequence of some external change, as a precipitating event that influences people perceptions (Peterman and Kennedy, 2003). There are two basic kinds of perceptions:

- Perceived desirability refers to the degree to which an individual feels attraction for a given behaviour (to become an entrepreneur).
- Perceived feasibility is described as the degree to which individuals consider themselves personally able to carry out certain behaviour (to become an entrepreneur). The existence of role models, mentors or partners would be a crucial element in creating the individual's entrepreneurial feasibility level (Peterman and Kennedy, 2003).

Both types of perceptions are determined by cultural and social factors, through their influence on the individual's values system (Shapero and Sokol, 1982).

Planned behaviour theory (Ajzen, 1991) develops a psychological model named 'planned behaviour'. It is a theory that may be applied to nearly all-voluntary behaviours, and it provides quite good results in very diverse fields, including the choice of professional career (Ajzen, 2001). This theory (Ajzen, 1991) captures three motivational factors that influence behaviour:

- Perceived behavioural control, which is defined as the perception of the easiness or difficulty in the fulfilment of the behaviour of interest (becoming an entrepreneur). Bandura (1997) define this concept as self-efficacy.
- Attitude towards the behaviour, which refers to the degree to which the individual holds a positive or negative personal valuation about being an entrepreneur.
- Perceived social norms which measures the perceived social pressure to carry out (or not) the entrepreneurial behaviour.

These theories provide different perspectives about 'how entrepreneurship can happen'. On the one hand, entrepreneurial event theory argues that entrepreneurship depends on cultural and social factors, through their influence on the individual's values system and perceptions. On the other hand, planned behaviour theory considers entrepreneurship as a result of a planned behaviour. Both theories provide some insights to the study of entrepreneurial intentions as a result (or not) from the entrepreneurial education. The literature about entrepreneurial education examines the factors associated with entrepreneurial intentions such as individuals' personality traits that influence their intentions to start a business (Koh, 1996; Mueller and Thomas, 2001; Robinson *et al.*, 1991). The next section, presents a summary of the development of concepts related to these intentions or traits, including entrepreneurial traits, personality traits and education, reflecting upon their impact on entrepreneurial education.

Entrepreneurial intentions, personality traits and education

The entrepreneurial intentions could be shaped by some factors, such as personality traits and education (De Jorge-Moreno *et al.*, 2012; Sánchez, 2011). According to some studies, not all individuals have the potential to start a new venture, it is the personal characteristics or traits which define an individual's potential to become an entrepreneur (Learned, 1992; Sánchez, 2011).

Personality traits

Past research on entrepreneurship can be categorised into three major genres; functional, personality and behavioural approaches (Cope, 2005). While the functional approach studies rational outcomes of entrepreneurship within economic theory, the personality approach deals with the characteristics of entrepreneurs' psychological traits. In contrast, the behavioural approach investigates the process of how an entrepreneur perceives and acts on present opportunities (Nga and Shamuganathan, 2010). This study by Koh (1996) is positioned on the personality approach, and the linkage between entrepreneurial inclination and some psychological characteristics.[1] Arguably, to study entrepreneurial potential it is fundamental to analyse the following traits: need for achievement, locus of control, propensity to take risks.

Research developed by McClelland (1961), associated need for achievement with entrepreneurial behaviour. Based on the results of his series of studies on need for achievement, McClelland (1961, 1965) argued that such behaviours or behavioural traits correlate strongly with 'entrepreneurial' success. The need for achievement is one of the most frequently cited entrepreneurial traits in the literature (Gurol and Atsan, 2006; Ryan *et al.*, 2011), and it is the strongest predictor of entrepreneurship (de la Cruz del Río-Rama *et al.*, 2016; Pillis and Reardon, 2007).

Another recurrently cited entrepreneurial psychological variable is the internal locus of control, defined as the ability of the individual to influence events of his/ her life. Several research results propose that the internal locus of control is an entrepreneurial characteristic (Koh, 1996; Mueller and Thomas, 2001; Robinson *et al.*, 1991) due the influence of this feature on the behaviour of the entrepreneur in some situations such as risk-taking or decisions. Additionally, Gurol and Atsan (2006: 30) suggest that entrepreneurship is historically associated with risk-taking, and Gurel *et al.* (2010), Gurol and Atsan (2006) and Koh (1996), demonstrate that entrepreneurially inclined students have significantly higher scores in risk-taking than non-entrepreneurially inclined students. In other words there are a number of key measures which indicate a pre-disposition to be entrepreneurial.

Education

According to Nga and Shamuganathan (2010: 259), "Personality traits are partly developed by innate nurturing, socialization and education." Education in general plays a crucial role in predicting and developing entrepreneurial traits.

However, to develop entrepreneurial competencies a school's curricula should focus on encouraging independence, innovation, creativity and risk-taking, the pedagogical approach should encourage children to make decisions, accept mistakes and learn from them (Ibrahim and Soufani, 2002). Laukkanen, (2000) highlights that in business schools around the world, rather than being educated for entrepreneurship, students are educated about entrepreneurship and enterprise. In the fact most of the programmes provide enterprise training not entrepreneurial training. Entrepreneurial training requires the development of skills and competences such as, need for achievement, locus of control, propensity to take risk, tolerance of ambiguity, self-confidence and innovativeness.

Since the 1960s, research into the impact of education on entrepreneurial behaviour has increased, however the research findings are arguably contradictory. Some researchers claim that formal education lessens the entrepreneurial desire of the individual (Shapero, 1980), others argued that people's entrepreneurial intentions actually increase with education (Davidsson and Honig, 2003). Some authors alleged different effects according with education level and advanced business education seems to increase an individual's propensity towards entrepreneurship (Davidsson and Honig, 2003; Goedhuys and Sleuwaegen, 2000), these authors report that while primary education does not have a significant impact on the probability of being an entrepreneur, this effect increases progressively for higher levels of education and becomes more significant.

A different perspective provided by Wu and Wu (2008) report that respondents with a diploma and undergraduate degree demonstrate higher interest in starting a business than those with a postgraduate degree, i.e. students with higher levels of education might have more employment options and thus have less intention to be entrepreneurial. Several authors (Ertuna and Gurel, 2011; Fallows, 1985; Shapero, 1980; Ronstadt, 1984) claims that formal education decreases curiosity and vision and increases risk aversion because traditional education leads to conformity and decreases tolerance for ambiguity, thus lowering students' abilities in creative thinking, an indispensable characteristic of entrepreneurship.

Some authors state that business schools traditionally teach their graduates to be too analytical, problem-conscious and risk-averse, they scare students away from establishing new business ventures (Laukkanen, 2000) with formal education in general not encouraging entrepreneurship because it generally trains students for jobs in corporations and suppresses creativity and entrepreneurship (Peterman and Kennedy, 2003; Robinson, 2006; Turner and Mulholland, 2017).

Mindset for a trial model for the twenty-first century: classes, technology and extracurricular activities

Although some authors argue that formal education cannot encourage entrepreneurship, educational institutions wishing to train and develop human talent for business management need to organise themselves with new training and teacher training proposals. The youth of today is embedded in what Bauman (2001) called 'Liquid Modernity' – characterised by the inconstancy and immediacy prevalent in this generation, where the world of information is within the reach of most people. The search for something is performed through Google, with the platform providing access to data and information, however the training necessary for critical thinking cannot necessarily be found online or by using online platforms rather it has to be learned through doing, which is why appropriate training and teaching of students to be critical, creative and reflective becomes even more important today.

In the era of continued transformation whether that be digital or non-digital, the modus operandi of students through global communication at the click of a button, both our daily life and our thinking is changed due to the context in which we live. In such an environment, entrepreneurship must be inserted into an ever changing social context, can the same be said of the teacher's role? Undoubtedly the teacher becomes the great agent responsible for the human development of the students in their care.

In addition, it must be taken into account that the act of learning is not transferable, only the individual can do it and no one can learn in the place of another; interest can be encouraged through the exploring of student enhanced learning opportunities using hybridisation, which is the mixture of techniques and tools that help and stimulate learning through the combination of classroom and virtual teaching environments. (Alheit, 2013; Charlot, 2010; Demo, 2009; Freire, 2002; Heron, 2013), but it cannot work in isolation and the voluntary participation of the individual. An educational project has several actors involved; among them we can highlight the educational institution, teachers and students, each with its responsibility in this process.

The important focus on improving education is not about what teachers do, but about what and how students learn in order to align appropriate teaching methods and project assessment tasks that will allow a judgment of how well students learn. Although students' motivation for learning is intrinsic and hence dependent on the individual, external factors such as passing, gaining their qualification or diploma, are often desired by them and can be a source of motivation, according to Biggs (1999).

Repositioning the role of the teacher

As a result of external market changes the way students learn and the skills they require from their learning have changed, which now requires not only curriculum changes but also an attitudinal change which involves encouraging rather than discouraging students to consider an entrepreneurial path. Teachers and teaching play a prominent role in this shifting in light of active methods.

Teaching methods that promote social interaction at higher levels have shown themselves able to increase knowledge and skill development in business students (e.g. Burke, Salvador, Smith-Crowe, Chan-Serafin, Smith and Sonesh, 2011; Siegel, Khursheed and Agrawal, 1997; Specht, 1991; Taylor, Russ-Eft and Chan, 2005).

These active or problem based methods favour greater student participation, providing them with the means to maintain a deeper interaction with both the content and the teacher; as well as with their peers through the awakening of student's curiosity. They are incorporating theorisation and new approaches through the use of problem based method as a strategy of teaching-learning. It is a teaching strategy that leads students to realise their full potential and the potential of teaching, changing from 'content transmitter' to learning enabler. (Charlot, 2010; Demo, 2009; Freire, 2002).

Great attention in literature is also given to experiential learning, originally introduced by John Dewey and resumed by David Kolb and many other researchers and has been a key issue in the discussions about learning since the late 1980s. According to Blikstein (2010), an educational system that stimulates students' interest and creativity, so that they might become able to produce and have a real impact on the lives of their own as well as those of their communities cannot look like a prison or a factory but rather as an intellectually vibrant as well as emotionally healthy space; as an atelier, as a research centre, so as not to be a breeding ground for what already exists, with bureaucratic, disciplinary and punitive schemes as complicated as the criminal code of a country.

Danish author Bente Elkjaer (2013) holds the chair of learning theory at the University of Aarhus in Denmark and is the editor-in-chief of *Management Learning Magazine*. Her main focus is learning in professional life with her theoretical approach inspired by Dewey's work on professional learning, which reflects his view of the continuous encounters of individuals in experiential and playful environments. Elkjaer associates the interaction between individuals and the environment (school, community, family and culture) as the main factor for learning, evidencing the students' experience as an active exchange, based on Dewey's proposal, in which the student is portrayed as protagonist in the progress of local, social and world society changes, and the act of teaching captures methodologies and appropriate didactic resources. According to Dewey, as quoted by Elkjaer, "education and teaching is a way of supporting, through research, the direction of experience" (Elkjaer, 2013: 99).

In this context, active methodologies can contribute to a meaningful student experience, where, guided by their teachers, they take pleasure in the search for knowledge, with the clear notion that the learning function does not end when they leave school and that they will always be ready to face new problems as well as conduct innovative projects (Blikstein, 2010).

In a study conducted by Yamamoto (2016), factors that support the use of active methodologies to increase students' performance for meaningful learning have been analysed. According to the researcher, the introduction of the method success is directly related to the importance of the involvement of all the actors of the process, such as educational institutions, teachers and students, and the predominant characteristic of one of the studied groups was the motivation of obtaining a diploma/career (66.6 per cent) aiming to get a good job. Charlot (2002), confirm this idea, and reports that approximately 75 per cent to 80 per cent of the students who engage in this approach towards their studies progress to good jobs.

Paulo Freire (1994) describes in his research that the more one works with problems with learners, as beings in the world and with the world, the more one will feel challenged. The more one is challenged, the more the learner will be forced to respond to the challenge and understand the interconnected nature of the problem, becoming increasingly critical and courageous, provoking new understanding of new challenges which emerge from the responding process, i.e. a deeper commitment to self learning. Figure 9.1 shows this cycle.

Such engagement in the development of competences is based on the construction of conceptual, procedural and attitudinal knowledge and is considered essential for entrepreneurial education (Zabala, 1998, 2002). Conceptual knowledge is developed through the understanding of concepts and techniques, which generate know-how. (Coll, 2003; Pozo and Crespo, 2009). Procedural knowledge is provided by the ability to perform, which generates know-how. Attitudinal knowledge is configured in the posture and way of acting and living, which culminates in the knowing of how to be. The application of these three associated axes determines competence. Figure 9.2 presents this competencies/ knowledge relationship in a framework.

Explore new learning opportunities, more student-centred, more flexible and mobilising, more capable of sustaining processes of authorship and autonomy is becoming of the utmost importance for business education. When something makes sense, one learns better, such an understanding is shared by many

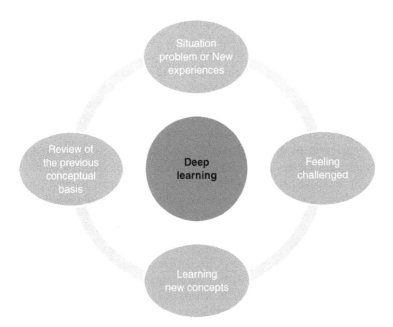

Figure 9.1 Cycle for deep learning.
Source: Carvalho, Yamamoto and Backx.

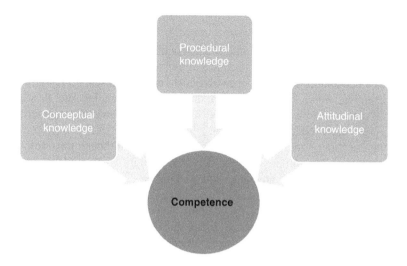

Figure 9.2 Competence and associated strategic axes.

Source: Carvalho, Yamamoto and Backx.

researchers (Alheit, 2013; Ausubel, 2000; Charlot, 2010; Crooks, 1988; Demo, 2009; Freire, 2002; Heron, 2013; Jarvis, 2013; Mezirow, 1998). Ausubel (2000) in particular states that meaningful learning is enjoyable, familiar, sharpens the curiosity and people tend to work harder and feel much more motivated when the learning activity makes sense.

This is reason why the concept of active learning methodologies is presented. As there is no formal concept about active learning methodologies, the challenge is to bring authors and elements together that can be useful in their contextualisation. Active learning methodologies can be described as a principle, in that it has evolved generalised thoughts on teaching and learning nature (Adler, 1982; Biggs, 1999; Chickering and Gamson, 1987; Ericksen, 1984; Kane, 2004). It is also closely associated with the implementation of practical teaching methodologies, in which numerous examples of activity types as well as of pedagogical techniques are provided to be explored by teachers when facing different learning situations, encompassing a multiplicity of disciplines and formal and informal educational, efforts. These concepts are based on the premise that genuine learning is active, non-passive, which takes place through a process of students being discovered as the main agent, (Adler, 1982; Biggs, 1999; Chickering and Gamson, 1987; Ericksen, 1984; Kane, 2004).

Kane (2004) also explores Denicolo *et al.*'s (1992: 3) concept: "The active and participative learning methodology is a generic term for expressing a wealth of ideas. There is no single definition, it takes different meanings and different degrees of emphasis, in different areas and for different groups of students" (as cited in Kane, 2004: 276).

According to Kane (2004), some of the main characteristics of active and participatory learning methodology are:

1   It seeks to encourage students to independent and critical thinking.
2   Encourages students to take responsibility for what they learn.
3   Involves students in a variety of open activities (projects, discussions, simulation exercises among others) to ensure that they play a leading role, thus a much less passive role when compared with that in 'knowledge transfer'. Both process and product are important.
4   Takes into account how important the educator role is, although not exclusive, to organise appropriate learning activities though which students can explore and develop their knowledge and thinking base.

High learning goals can remain at the rhetoric level in case the assessment process is not adequate. Students may be discouraged when they are required to participate in an assessment system, purely based on accumulated knowledge tests, forcing them to memorise content.

The problem concerns the goals and objectives for learning promoting. It must be made clear to the student what we want them to learn with clear objectives that indicate the level of understanding required followed by an evaluation according to an aligned instruction system. A criteria reference system, in which the objectives define what to teach, teaching methods that will accomplish those objectives and evaluation tasks so that one can test what they have learned. The teacher's fundamental task is to get students involved in learning activities that are likely to result in these outcomes (Biggs, 1996, 1999; Shuell, 1986).

For many schools of active learning methodology, the process is as important as the product. The active learning methodology is designed to promote the spirit of research by encouraging critical thinking, as educators have certain leverage on students as they feel they are also responsible for the process. In the experience of Kane (2004) and supported by Biggs (1999), Demo (2009), Kane (2004), it seems that the active learning methodology is simply seen as a more efficient method to lecture or teach, which requires caution as the main purpose is the actual learning objective.

Figures 9.1 and 9.2 summarise the ideas surrounding the construction of conceptual, procedural and attitudinal knowledge and suggests some possibilities of active methodologies, such as:

•   problem-solving;
•   problem-based learning;
•   learning portfolio;
•   jigsaw technique;
•   blended learning;
•   flipped learning;
•   case method;
•   study of the environment/experiential practices, among others.

These methods can work in collaboration because they are tools that help and stimulate learning that can have the combination between face-to-face and virtual teaching environments, always in consonance with previous planning so that the context in which students learn is understood; from this point strategies that give meaning to each situation are chosen. Planning has to be aligned with tangible learning objectives, clearly described in a teaching plan, relating the relevant learning and teaching strategies to assessment and self-assessment tasks.

Problem-solving is a teaching and learning strategy in which the subject is presented with a task that, when seeking to solve it, does not come to a solution immediately or automatically. This learning process is the true objective of problem-solving, which takes place when the obstacle is overcome in the accomplishment of the task. The student engages in a process of reflection and decision-making resulting in a certain sequence of steps to be followed (Nuñes *et al.*, 2004; Onuchic, 1999; Peduzzi, 1997).

One of the challenges for this strategy is the problem elaboration – when formulated, it should consider social reality observation, starting from a contextualised study topic, that allows students to identify problems, which will be transformed into hypotheses, which in turn will be tested through data analysis to show solutions. Considerations in consonance with Blikstein (2010); Freire, (1994, 2002); Demo (2009); Crooks (1998); Morin (2015); Gardner (2000).

PBL (problem-based learning) is a methodology of teaching and learning widely used in higher education and in other educational levels. Conceived in the late 1960s, PBL employs real-life problems (real or simulated) to initiate, motivate and focus the learning of conceptual, procedural and attitudinal knowledge; stimulating development and critical thinking, and problem-solving skills; and the acquisition of fundamental concepts in the area of knowledge in question (Ribeiro, 2008).

PBL is a sequence of problem situations with different levels of depth. In general, students begin by reading the problem, then by making an individual reflection, followed by the discussion, initially in the group and in then the whole class, in order to define investigative next steps (possibly through the inclusion of extra classes or homework). Finally the teacher makes the closing remarks, summarising the main points. The objectives are to get students to solve the problems they will encounter in their professional careers – the teaching method is to present problems for them to solve; The evaluation is based on how well they solve them (Biggs, 1999; Ribeiro, 2008).

Learning portfolio is a progressive and creative compilation of work developed by students during a subject or course, which reconstructs their experiences and reflections throughout the learning process, encouraging awareness of their advances and setbacks, as an agent of their learning. (Baker, Gearhart, Herman, Tierney and Whittaker, 1991; Biggs, 1999; Calfee and Perfumo, 1992; Camp, 1990; Condon and Hamp-Lyons, 1991; Tierney, Carter and Desai, 1991; Valencia and Calfee, 1991). The approach may include abstracts or text and article files, registration of visits, research projects, among other activities, thus integrating the appropriate knowledge obtained along the course and gathered in a portfolio for later evaluation; this becomes a tool to help the teacher analyse the singularity and peculiarity of how each student has developed academically. According to Gardner (2000), a portfolio is not reduced to a collection of works carried out by the learner during a certain period, but, it constitutes a project that records the best works selected by the student to represent his or her production within a certain period of time. For Villas Boas (2004), the portfolio is a collection of productions, which present the learning evidences, organised by the student him or herself so that he/she and his/her teacher together may monitor progress, thus allowing the students to participate in the formulation of the specified learning objective(s) as well as assessing progress. The learner is therefore an active participants in the assessment, selecting the best samples of his/her work to be included into the portfolio.

For Anastasiou and Alves (2003) the most important point in this technique is the construction of teacher and student knowledge throughout the module/ semester period and not only at the end, facilitating procedural evaluation, because the teacher is able to identify the learning process as well as students' difficulties, guiding in a unique way. This strategy requires a differentiated assessment, which should be discussed with the students, the institution and other teachers to ensure transparency and gain engagement in the process.

The Jigsaw method is based on a co-operative learning technique developed in the early 1970s by Elliot Aronson and his students at the University of Texas and the University of California. According to The Jigsaw Classroom (2017) website, as in a puzzle, each piece – each student's part – is essential for the completion and for full understanding of the final product. Students are divided into groups to help each other learn, with greater encouragement for co-operation and reflection on the part/whole relationship. In the puzzle, each member of a group is assigned a different part of the material. So, all students from different groups who have the same material get together in a 'group of experts' to discuss with each other, until all of them master the material. Later, the students return to their original group to pass the materials on to the other members of their group. After the whole process, each group have to present the result of their study in a plenary forum, which may be, depending on the strategy of each teacher, a solution to a specific and practical problem (Perkins and Saris, 2001; Walker and Crogan, 1998).

Following the application of this theory on a group of Applied Masters in Technology Entrepreneurship at the University of São Paulo – USP – Faculty of Economics, Administration and Accounting – FEA, in April 2017, the majority of participants enjoyed the experience, with key themes to emerge being the application of theory to practice, encouraging creativity and deeper understanding of the subject, with representative quotes including:

> Found interesting the case applied in the social area in which a solution should be quickly bought up; in real world, the need is urgent.

Enjoyed the technique, especially the part when experts are joined together in order to deepen a knowledge.

Talking about creativity is about getting people involved in the process, driving entrepreneurship to a higher level, especially when using a social case. I think the methodology was well suited as it was able to encompass all this.

These findings provide some initial insight into perspectives of the approach which will be further interrogated so as to address issues of generalisability and validation. What the results show is that participants felt that the jigsaw method not only encouraged the application of theory to practice but instilled creativity and deeper understanding of subject matter, results which are supported by the literature (Perkins and Saris, 2001; Walker and Crogan, 1998).

Blended learning or b-learning – there is no single definition in literature for the term, however the definition from the Clayton Christensen Institute, 2007, following the cataloguing of over 100 models of hybrid education would appear to be the most appropriate: "formal education program in which a student learns through online teaching, with some element of student control over the time, place, mode and/or study rhythm, and through in school classroom instruction", (Bacich, TanziNeto and Trevisani, 2015: 52). In this context, the learning environment is considered both democratic and diverse where the teacher may provide guided access to new data and information (and will probably provide some sort of assessment to determine outcomes or desired competencies) (Crooks, 1998; Blikstein, 2010; Demo, 2009; Freire, 1994, 2002; Morin, 2015;).

Christensen, Horn and Staker (2013) point out that b-learning is emerging as a sustained innovation in relation to the traditional classroom, as an attempt to offer 'the best of both worlds', being able to obtain the advantages of online education combined with all the benefits of the traditional classroom.

According to Demo (2009), students can find in the virtual learning environment, mediated by new technologies, the expectation of a breadth of horizons, as a free world, without hierarchy, without 'vigilance', without parents and teachers imposing instructions, even if this idea is illusory, it provides a sense of freedom, as it does not offer restrictions inherent in the physical world. There are different ways of combining face-to-face and distance learning activities through ICT, the flipped learning described below is one of them.

Flipped learning – according to the Flipped Learning Network (FLN, 2017), it is a pedagogical approach in which direct instruction moves from the group learning space to the individual learning space, with the group space transformed into a learning environment which is dynamic, interactive and creative in which the educator guides students on how to apply concepts and actively participate in discussions and practices. One of the pioneers of this method are Bergmann and Sams (2013) who have their entire course available in videos, allowing each student to advance in different rhythms, in a free manner. Bergmann and Sams (2013) advise students to focus on the video, pause, take notes of questions and summarise. The authors verified that students learned in greater depth, accepted the responsibility of their own learning, thus becoming autonomous learners. It is convenient for the teacher to keep moving through the class in a non-linear manner, providing immediate feedback to students. This links back to the earlier point in the chapter – it is not just the teacher, it is the classroom environment, the modular and programme content, the assessment and the feedback – they have to work together to create the learning experience.

Yamamoto (2016) used this strategy in his research, structuring the discipline in the following way: in the first week of school, students were told that they were part of a study about the importance of the learning process and the use of new methodologies. It was also emphasised what were the learning objectives and their relevance to the process, the reason for choosing an online course, and how it was to be used in the discipline. Subsequently, the content was discussed in the classroom in order to explore the interaction between the students and the teacher during the lesson. The activities were varied every week, for example: (1) solving quizzes for a review of concepts and to verify if the students followed the course in the MOOC platform; (2) use of problem situations; (3) case method. The proposed method increased the performance of all the evaluated students, as evidenced by the result provided by the final average. The difference between the methods is knowing which one will make sense for each situation by considering the student's history to understand how the subject learns and the question of the importance of the evaluation processes that conditions the student's judgment of what is important to learn (Charlot, 2002; Crooks, 1998; Kane, 2004).

The case method consists of an educational strategy with the purpose of exploring relationships between scenarios or organisations, observing changes over a period of time, leading students to reflect on situations presented in the case. It may involve decision-making about the studied episode, with the intention to develop some specific skills in students, such as analytical, decision-making and teamworking. The objective of the technique is to present a problem to students, causing them to analyse and reflect on the subject. The method is not restricted to the use of a single type of case, there are several approaches, each of which presents peculiarities that should be considered in class planning, according to Ikeda, Veludo-de-Oliveira and Campomar (2005).

The case method is a 'to-do' tool type that allows the learner to transform knowledge into skills and attitudes, as discussion is conducted, it provides a strong evaluative and analytical potential among students, contextualising content, furnishing them with meaning, thus favouring meaningful learning through the closure of the case, establishing a connection with the rest of the discipline. Real-life situations are presented to students with the purpose of indicating what the problem is when asking the questions, through a set of recommendations to solve the case. A teacher who is prepared to facilitate rather than impose his or her knowledge and provide answers can develop critical and reflective skills and independence of thought in students by contextualising the reality of an organisation scenario accommodating different perspectives and recognising multiple explanations of the events contained in cases (Bridgman, Cummings and McLaughlin, 2016; Currie and Tempest, 2008; Garvin, 2003; Hammond, 2002).

The so called '**study of environment/experiential practices**' is an interdisciplinary teaching technique which promotes direct (experienced) contact between students and the phenomenon of reality object of study, aiming to produce new knowledge in a teacher-guided immersion, through technical visits (Carvalho and Freitas, 2010; Freire, 2002; Lopes and Pontuschka, 2009; Mazão, Fernandes and Cozza 2011).

Important points to be considered for the purpose of the technique are: selection of the place to be visited, formulation of the main questions to be answered in all stages of the visit, field registration, roadmap and schedule to be developed, theoretical basis written material to facilitate the observation process, interviews, procedures for collected material treatment, historical and geographical syntheses of the place or region studied, creation of a script of interviews, systematisation of data and evidence collected for structured elaboration of the final report, which is part of the curriculum to meet previously defined learning objectives (Carvalho and Freitas, 2010; Freire, 2002; Lopes and Pontuschka, 2009; Mazão, Fernandes and Cozza 2011).

It is an old practice, inspired by educators such as Francisco Ferrer and Guardia (1859–1909) and Célestin Freinet (1896–1966), aiming to have more direct contact with the studied reality, whether natural or social, the intention was for the students, when in contact with the environment (space to be studied), to become able to reflect on their dynamics (social relations, inequalities, injustices, etc.) and thus acquire conditions to present proposals for the transformation of society. (Lopes and Pontuschka, 2009; Mazão, Fernandes and Cozza, 2011).

The study of the environment involves activities in three stages: pre-field (planning and preparation of teachers and students), field (visiting chosen location and data collection) and post field (systematisation of data organisation, synthesis production, evaluation). The activity is accomplished by this immersion oriented by a certain space complexity, by the establishment of dialogue between peers and teachers, with the purpose of verifying and producing new knowledge, thus resulting in the development of the evaluation along the whole teaching and learning process (Carvalho and Freitas, 2010; Lopes and Pontuschka, 2009; Mazão, Fernandes and Cozza, 2011). A typical example of this approach is work based learning and the sandwich course that support learning through underpinning theory with immersed periods of practice where students develop a deeper understanding and knowledge of applied theory, data collection and/or processing or partial development of the experimental part of their research.

There are several methods developed for active learning, in addition to the ones evaluated in this section. What we have attempted to do is provide a holistic analysis of the most popular approaches to allow readers understanding of the varied techniques to enhance student learning and their employability skills. As important to the evaluation of these learning approaches is to consider the impact and not just the implied benefits, which we will do in this final section.

Evaluation and indicators

Crooks (1988), Bloom, Hasting and Madaus (1971), Rodrigues Junior (2009) in their respective research make reference to the matter of educational appraisal. In his review Crooks (1988) talks about the impact of evaluation practices, he finds that teachers deem important evaluative activities in teaching and learning practice, but also perceive inadequacies in their efforts to see that assessments probably do not reflect the instructional objectives stated by them that sometimes require the repetition of materials presented in the books or in the classroom, or even the fact that solutions to problems are very similar to those found during the lesson. Crooks (1988) further points out that both advocates and critics of education as Elton (1982) and Natriello (1987) agree that tests elaborated on by teachers show a tendency to lower cognitive levels differently from the goals they stated in lesson plans. The possible reasons could include the difficulty among some learners to write short answers (multiple choice quizzes), widely used to obtain statistics.

In this review, Crooks (1988) affirms that evaluations affect students in short, medium and, above all, in the long term. They perhaps impact negatively, reducing creativity and encouraging confirmity and prescriptive thinking according to the textbook and/or the assessment requirements, a question of what they need to know rather than what they should know. These issues affect both individual and group work, which although testing certain skills and encouraging the desirable outcome of active participation of all individuals it should be noted that it is also desirable to include some assessment of members' learning during the overall assessment of the group's accomplishments.

The importance of classroom assessment affects students in many different ways when guiding their judgment of what is important to learn: the assessment affects their motivation and self-perception of competence, structures their approaches to personal study time, consolidates learning, and affects the development of strategies and skills of long lasting learning. Evaluation seems to be one of the most powerful forces influencing education, therefore it deserves a more professional approach and careful planning, regular and reflective analysis of teacher evaluation practices, considerable time investment by educators, increased use of peer review procedures and considerable attention to establishing more consistent progressions of expectations and criteria within and between educational institutions (Crooks, 1988, Bloom, Hasting and Madaus, 1971, Rodrigues Junior, 2009). In other words it is not just about changing the way students are taught, it is also important to consider the way they are assessed as this directly impacts on the skills we expect them to learn to make them more employable, enterprising and entrepreneurial following completion of their course. Assessment and the evaluation of learning performance is a reinforcing mechanism which has the potential to undo all the good work of teaching and learning styles.

Bloom *et al.* (1971) show three types of evaluation and their purposes: diagnostic, formative and summative. The diagnostic type reveals students' personal and professional experiences, repertoire, vocabulary and reasoning skills, which map domains of content recognised as 'subject prerequisites'. The formative type, is a process evaluation designed to improve the evolution of educational practice: detecting learning problems, allowing immediate intervention, improving the teaching practices, feedback into the process, thus advancing in relation to educational objectives. Finally, the summative type, which is a summation balance of several stages of the formation work revealing the results achieved by the student at the end of an educational process, having as parameters the educational objectives established in the teaching and learning plan.

Fernandes and Fialho (2012), in their synthesised research of published literature during a ten-year period (2000–2009), within the field of student learning evaluation, revealed the following themes: (1) the practices of formative evaluation, using tasks such as reports, presentations, posters and other written works, are associated with the improvement of student learning; (2) self-assessment and hetero-assessment[3] practices play an important role in engaging students in the assessment process by improving learning, allowing them to regulate their own learning process; (3) the evaluation of formative and criterial nature helps the students to better understand what they need to learn, guiding and regulating their efforts in this direction; and (4) formative assessment practices contribute to developing students' more complex thinking skills.

Biggs's (1999) in his constructive alignment theory, positions an aligned instructional system, which needs to be tuned in: (1) learning objectives clearly stated to the student; (2) learning and teaching strategies; (3) evaluation tasks consistent with the objectives. This aligned instruction system increases the chances of the majority of students to actually engage with the proposed learning activities, avoiding the old stereotype: the teacher presenting information throughout the semester, with an examination or test at the end, which in general, is built to discriminate, to distinguish good students from bad in a very limited purview. Perhaps resource scarcity is a reason for limiting education to passive methods, such as mass lectures and multiple choice testing, but at the same time, resource constraints do not limit the creative options of rethinking education and assessment in large classes, but a recognition of alignment becomes necessary, according to Biggs (1999). Biggs (2001) further argues that for this to occur – education aligned with learning objectives, strategies, assessment tasks and institutional infrastructure is fundamental to prioritise education best practices.

Concluding remarks

Based on the development of academic knowledge in the research area of enterprise and entrepreneurial learning, this chapter has attempted to present a preliminary proposal of pedagogical approaches with a focus on learning, particularly active methodologies for new educational practices, which reveal:

* Consideration of the important role played by the institution – admit the importance of its own role in students' integral formation and the necessary

change in the current educational context; provide teachers with the necessary infrastructure and training so that they may organise appropriate learning activities in which students can explore and develop their knowledge and thinking base; and provide support staff for activities.

- Respect students' knowhow and their autonomy as the subject of the learning process, as the protagonist taking responsibility for what they learn.
- The teacher's understanding of his/her role in guiding the socio-educational process, in order to build knowledge in partnership with the student – mutual respect.
- Theory must be adequate to everyday practice, thus fostering curiosity, which in turn implies research and critical perception in order to modify what is conditioned but not determined, connecting elements make the thematical underpinning meaningful.
- A new conception of planning and construction of teaching plans as a key factor in aligning clearly described tangible learning objectives related to learning and teaching strategies relevant to assessment and self-assessment tasks. Less concern about content and more concern with quality of learning.
- In relation to learning and teaching strategies: instead of simply passing on information for memorising, involve students in projects, discussions, simulation exercises among others, to ensure that they have a leading role for the construction of knowledge and development of skills and attitudes to solving problems, considering previous learning, cultural and life experiences.
- Carefully consider assessment and self-assessment tasks and not necessarily rely solely on end of modules evaluation practices, whilst developing evaluation and constant feedback.
- Permission to use mobile devices, such as cell phones, smartphones, tablets, personal computers, to be used in favour or in conjunction with the teacher, research, search for data and information for knowledge construction.

Learning and active participation is designed to foster a research spirit, encouraging students' critical thinking to the extent that they feel they are also responsible for the process. According to Biggs (1999) learning takes place through active student behaviour, he/she learns what he/she does and not what the teacher does.

Since the act of learning is intrinsic to being and each individual has the potential to learn in varied connections, due to individual differences, one can transform the student into a protagonist in the process. Towards the idea of protagonism comes the principle of active methodologies in order to put teaching at the service of student learning, in which the teacher is committed to creating conditions that favour the learning process, mobilising the students for the encounter of themes within the context of his/her subject, using problematisation as a teaching strategy. The use of different pedagogical approaches makes it possible to reach more students in a more effective way, contributing to the students' critical sense, starting with doubt, through questioning and contradictions which benefits them in the employment market.

To reflect on the strategies further, it is considered more beneficial to the learning experience to avoid simply practices of memorising, or temporary relevance, because isolated details are easily forgotten. Information is better retrieved when students learn within a broader framework of meaningful interrelationships and understanding, always in line with learning objectives, according to Crooks (1988).

Increasingly organisations require professionals with multiple competences, with flexibility to adapt to complex challenges and to promote change. Entrepreneurial and enterprise education needs to combine theory with practice to empower individuals to prepare them for scenarios that will arise from workplace situations. For this, our contribution to the readers is the reflection of the educational process – respect for the student's knowhow and its autonomy as subject to and of the learning process; the teachers' understanding of the socio-educational process guiding role, in the construction of knowledge in partnership with the student, i.e. mutual respect; theory must be adequate to everyday practice, which fosters curiosity, connecting elements make the thematic more meaningful; designing teaching plans with planning and aligned with learning objectives, related to the strategies; thinking and rethinking evaluation and self-assessment tasks with constant feedback; less content and more quality of learning; engaging students in projects, discussions, simulation exercises among others, to ensure that they play a leading role in building knowledge and developing skills and attitudes to solve problems, considering previous experiences of learning, culture and life; permission to use mobile devices, so they can research, search for data and information fundamental for the construction of knowledge.

A big question that remains however is: how can all this be done when we think of international business education? In the first place, it is important to be clear about the competencies that are intend to be developed, clearly describing the conceptual, procedural and attitudinal knowledge that one intends to develop, related to the attributes of being enterprising or entrepreneurial. In continuity, define how the evaluation process adopted will allow this identification if the initial objectives were or were not reached. In other words, identify ways to follow-up and feedback the development related to the student. In this context, it is important to make an initial diagnosis (of what the student knows or not) that allows identifying points to be worked through so that the development can be followed. The idea is that the evaluation process allows connecting what one intends to develop (the competencies) with the way one intends to do. Finally, to draw strategies through active methods, which allow the facilitator to stimulate and to enable the student in its learning process, accompanied through the evaluation system designed.

In short, making an analogy of the learning process with a tree, we have flowers and fruits that are the learning objectives, the results that we want to achieve. In addition, they bring the seeds of new learning possibilities. Roots are responsible for the support, absorption, storage and conduction, and are responsible for bringing water and nutrients from the soil. In this analogy, roots are the active methods which allow the student to seek knowledge on the ground, or in a complex and information-rich world. However, in order for the student to be able to lead this new learning to the objectives initially set, the stem and branches are necessary, which are the process of evaluation, allowing to organise and bring the sap extracted from the soil to the flowers and fruits. The leaves are the feedback process, as they are responsible for photosynthesis, which allows results to be identified and to feed the tree, that is, the learning process. This analogy indicates that in the learning process all facets have a role to play and are reliant upon each other, learning methodologies are not as effective without the appropriate learning environment, facilitator or platform and assessment practice.

Note

1 Koh (1996) investigates if entrepreneurial inclination is significantly associated with the following psychological characteristics: need for achievement, locus of control, propensity to take risk, tolerance of ambiguity, self-confidence and innovativeness.

References

Adler, M.J. (1982). *The Paideia proposal:* An education manifesto. New York: Macmillan.

Ajzen, I. (1991). The theory of planned behavior. *Organizational Behavior and Human Decision Processes*, 50(2), 179–211.

Ajzen, I. (2001). Nature and operation of attitudes. *Annual Review of Psychology*, 52, 27–58.

Alheit, P. (2013). Aprendizagem biográfica: dentro do novo discurso da aprendizagem ao longo da vida. In: Knud Illeris, in collaboration with Vibeke Andersen, Pernille Bottrup, Bruno Clematide *et al.*, eds. *Teorias contemporâneas da aprendizagem.* Porto Alegre: Penso (VitalSource Bookshelf Online).

Anastasiou, L.G., Camargos and Alves, L.P. (eds). (2003). *Processos de Ensinagem na universidade*: *pressupostos para as estratégias do trabalho em aula.* Joinvilie, SC: Editora Univille.

Audretsch, D.B. (2002). *Entrepreneurship: Determinants and policy in a European-US comparison.* Boston: Kluwer Academic.

Ausubel, D.P. (2000). *Aquisição e retenção de conhecimentos*: *uma perspectiva cognitiva.* Lisbon: Plátano Edições Técnicas.

Autio, E., Keeley, R.H., Klofsten, M., Parker, G.G.C. and Hay, M. (2001). Entrepreneurial intent among students in Scandinavia and in the USA. *Enterprise and Innovation Management Studies*, 2(2), 145–160.

Bacich, L., TanziNeto, A. and Trevisani, F.M. (eds). (2015). *Ensino híbrido*: *personalização e tecnologia na educação.* Porto Alegre: Penso.

Bandura, A. (1997). *Self-efficacy: The exercise of control.* New York: Freeman & Company.

Bauman, Z. (2001). *Modernidade líquida.* Rio de Janeiro: Jorge Zahar.

Bergmann, J. and Sams, A. (2013). Flip your students' learning. *Educational Leadership*, 70(6), 16–20.

Biggs, J.B. (1996). Enhancing teaching through constructive alignment. *Higher Education*, 32, 1–18.

Biggs, J. (1999). What the student does: Teaching for enhanced learning. *Higher Education Research & Development*, 18(1), 57–75.

Biggs, J. (2001). The reflective institution: Assuring and enhancing the quality of teaching and learning. *Higher Education*, 41(3), 221–238.

Blikstein, P. (25 July 2010). O mito do mau aluno e porque o Brasil pode ser o líder mundial de uma revolução educacional. Retrieved from: www.blikstein.com/paulo/documents/books/Blikstein-Brasil_pode_ser_lider_mundial_em educacao.pdf.

Block, Z. and Stumpf, S. (1992). *Entrepreneurship education research: Experience and challenge*. In: D.L. Sexton, and J.M. Kasarda, eds. *The state of the art of entrepreneurship*. Boston, MA: PWS-Kent, pp. 17–42.

Bloom, B.S., Hastings, J.T. and Madaus, G.F. (1971). *Handbook on formative and summative evaluation of student learning*. New York: McGaw-Hill.

Bridgman, T., Cummings, S. and McLaughlin, C. (2016). Re-stating the case: How revisiting the development of the case method can help us think differently about the future of the business school. *Academy of Management Learning and Education*, 15(4), 724–741.

Burke, M.J., Salvador, R., Smith-Crowe, K., Chan-Serafin, S., Smith, A. and Sonesh, S. (2011). How workplace hazards and training influence learning and performance. *The Journal of Applied Psychology*, 96, 46–70.

Calfee, R.C. and Perfumo, P.A. (1992). *A survey of portfolio practices*. Berkeley: University of California, Center for the Study of Writing.

Camp, R. (1990). Thinking about portfolios. *The Quarterly of the National Writing Project and The Center for the Study of Writing*, 12(3), 8–14, 27.

Carvalho, G.S.D. and Freitas, M.L.A.V.D. (2010). *Metodologia do estudo do meio. Plural Editores*. Grupo Porto Editora. Colecção Universidade-Metodologias de ensino.

Charlot, B. (2002). Relação com a escola e o saber nos bairros populares. *Perspectiva*, 20, 17–34.

Charlot, B. (2010). Desafios da educação na contemporaneidade: reflexões de um pesquisador. *Educação e Pesquisa*, 36, 147–161.

Chickering, A.W. and Gamson, Z.F. (1987). Seven principles for good practice. *AAHE, Bulletin*, 39(7), 3–7.

Christensen, C.M., Horn, M.B. and Staker, H. (May 2013). *Is K–12 blended learning disruptive?: An introduction to the theory of hybrids*. Christensen Institute. Boston, Silicon Valley, 1(1), 1–1. Retrieved from www.christenseninstitute.org/publications/hybrids/.

Coll, C. (2003). *Psicologia e currículo: uma aproximação psicopedagógica à elaboração do currículo escolar*. São Paulo: Ática.

Condon, W. and Hamp-Lyons, L. (1991). Introducing a portfolio-based writing assessment: progress through problems. In: P. Belanoff and M. Dickson, eds. *Portfolios: Process and product*. Portsmouth, NH: Heineman, pp. 231–247.

Cope, J. (2005). Toward a dynamic learning perspective of entrepreneurship, *Entrepreneurship Theory and Practice*, 27(2), 93–104.

Crooks, T.J. (1988). The impact of classroom evaluation practices on students. *Review of educational research*, 58(4), 438–481.

Currie, G. and Tempest, S. (2008). Moving towards reflexive use of teaching cases. *International Journal of Management Education*, 7, 41–50.

Davidsson, P. and Honig, B. (2003). The role of social and human capital among nascent entrepreneurs, *Journal of Business Venturing*, 18(3), 301–331.

De Jorge-Moreno, J., Castillo, L.L. and Triguero, M.S. (2012). The effect of business and economics education programs on student's entrepreneurial intention. *European Journal of Training and Development*, 36(4), 409–425.

184   *L.C. Carvalho* et al.

de la Cruz del Río-Rama; Peris-Ortiz, M., Álvarez-García, J. and Rueda-Armengot, C. (2016). Entrepreneurial intentions and entrepreneurship education to university students in Portugal. *Technology, Innovation and Education*, 2, 7.

Demo, P. (2009). Aprendizagens e novas tecnologias. *Revista Brasileira de Docência, Ensino e Pesquisa em Educação Física*, 1(1), 53–75.

Elkjaer, B. (2013). Pragmatismo: uma teoria da aprendizagem para o futuro. In: Knud Illeris, in collaboration with Vibeke Andersen, Pernille Bottrup, Bruno Clematide *et al.*, eds. *Teorias contemporâneas da aprendizagem*. Porto Alegre: Penso (VitalSource Bookshelf Online).

Elton, L.R.B. (1982). Assessment for learning". In D. Bligh, ed. *Professionalism and flexibility for learning*. Guildford, Surrey, England: Society for Research into Higher Education.

Ericksen, S. (1984). *The essence of good teaching*. San Francisco: Jossey-Bass.

Ertuna, Z.I. and Gurel, E. (2011). The moderating role of higher education on entrepreneurship, *Education + Training*, 53(5), 387–402.

European Commission. (2003). Green *paper – entrepreneurship in Europe*. Brussels: DG Enterprise. European Commission.

European Commission/EACEA/Eurydice (2016). *Entrepreneurship education at school in Europe*. Eurydice Report. Luxembourg: Publications Office of the European Union.

Fallows, J. (December 1985). The case against credentialism. *The Atlantic Monthly*, 49–67.

Fayolle, A. (2010). *Handbook of research in entrepreneurship education*. Vol. 3: International Perspectives. Boston, MA: Edward Elgar.

Fayolle, A. and DeGeorge, J.M. (2006). Attitudes, intentions, and behaviour: New approaches to evaluating entrepreneurship education. In: A. Fayolle and H. Klandt, eds. *International entrepreneurship education. Issues and newness*. Cheltenham: Edward Elgar, pp. 77–89.

Fayolle, A., Gailly, B., Lassas-Clerc, N. (2006). Assessing the impact of entrepreneurship education programmes: A new methodology. *Journal of European Industrial Training*, 30, 701–720.

Fernandes, Domingos and Fialho, Nuno (2012). Dez anos de práticas de avaliação das aprendizagens no Ensino Superior: uma síntese da literatura (2000–2009). In: Carlinda Leite and Miguel Zabalza, eds. *Ensino superior: Inovação e qualidade na docência*. Porto: CIIE da Universidade do Porto, pp. 3693–3707.

Flipped Learning Network–FLN. (2017). Definition of Flipped Learning. Retrieved from: https://flippedlearning.org/definition-of-flipped-learning.

Freire, P. (1994). *Pedagogia do oprimido*. 11th ed. Rio de Janeiro: Paz e Terra.

Freire, P. (2002). *Pedagogia da autonomia*: *saberes necessários à prática educativa*. 25th ed. São Paulo: Paz e Terra.

Gardner, H. (2000). *Inteligências múltiplas*: *a teoria na prática*. Porto Alegre: Artmed.

Gartner, W.B. (1989). "Who is an entrepreneur?" Is the wrong question. *Entrepreneurship Theory and Practice*, 13(4), 47–68.

Garvin, D.A. 2003. Making the case: Professional education for the world of practice. *Harvard Magazine*, 106, 56–65.

Goedhuys, M. and Sleuwaegen, L. (2000). Entrepreneurship and growth of entrepreneurial firms in Cote d'Ivoire. *The Journal of Development Studies*, 36(3), 122–145.

Gorman, G., Hanlon, D. and King, W. (1997). Some research perspectives on entrepreneurship education, enterprise education and education for small business management: A ten-year literature review. *International Small Business Journal*, 15, 56–77.

Graevenitz, G., Harhoff, D. and Weber, R. (2010). The effects of entrepreneurship education. *Journal of Economic Behavior & Organization*, 76, 90–112.

Gurel, E., Altinay, L. and Daniele, R. (2010). Tourism students' entrepreneurial intentions. *Annals of Tourism Research*, 37(3), 646–669.

Gurol, Y. and Atsan, N. (2006). Entrepreneurial characteristics amongst university students: Some insights for entrepreneurship education and training in Turkey. *Education and Training*, 48(1), 25–38.

Hammond, J.S. (2002). *Learning by the case method*. Boston, MA: HBS Publishing Division, Harvard Business School,.

Heron, J. (2013). Ciclos de vida e ciclos de aprendizagem. In: Knud Illeris, in collaboration with Vibeke Andersen, Pernille Bottrup, Bruno Clematide *et al.*, eds. *Teorias contemporâneas da aprendizagem*. Porto Alegre: Penso (VitalSource Bookshelf Online).

Ibrahim, A.B. and Soufani, K. (2002). Entrepreneurship education and training in Canada: a critical assessment. *Education + Training*, 44(8/9), 421–430.

Ikeda, A.A., Veludo-de-Oliveira, T.M. and Campomar, M.C. (2005). A tipologia do método do caso em administração: usos e aplicações. *Organizações & Sociedade*, 12(34), 141–159.

Jarvis, P. (2013). Aprendendo a ser uma pessoa na sociedade: aprendendo a ser eu. In: Knud Illeris, in collaboration with Vibeke Andersen, Pernille Bottrup, Bruno Clematide *et al.*, eds. *Teorias contemporâneas da aprendizagem*. Porto Alegre: Penso (VitalSource Bookshelf Online).

The jigsaw classroom. (2017). Available at: www.jigsaw.org/#overview.

Kane, L. (2004). Educators, learners and active learning methodologies. *International Journal of Lifelong Education*, 23(3), 275–286.

Koh, H.C. (1996). Testing hypotheses of entrepreneurial characteristics: A study of Hong Kong MBA students, *Journal of Managerial Psychology*, 11(3), 12–25.

Krueger, N.F., Reilly, M.D. and Carsrud, A.L. (2000). Competing models of entrepreneurial intentions. *Journal of Business Venturing*, 15(5–6), 411–432.

Kuratko, D.F. (September 2005). The emergence of entrepreneurship education: Development, trends, and challenges. *Entrepreneurship Theory & Practice*, 577–597.

Laukkanen, M. (2000). Exploring alternative approaches in high-level entrepreneurship education: Creating micro-mechanisms for endogenous regional growth. *Entrepreneurship and Regional Development*, 12(1), 25–47.

Learned, K.E. (1992). What happened before the organization? A model of organization formation. *Entrepreneurship Theory and Practice*, 17(1) 39–48.

Liñán, F. (2004). Intention-based models of entrepreneurship education. *Piccola Impresa/Small Business*, 3, 11–35.

Lopes, C.S. and Pontuschka, N.N. (2009). Estudo do meio: teoria e prática. *Geografia (Londrina)*, 18(2).

Matlay, H. (2008). The impact of entrepreneurship education on entrepreneurial outcomes. *Journal of Small Business and Enterprise Development*, 15(2), 382–396.

Matlay, H. and Carey, C. (2007). Entrepreneurship education in the UK: A longitudinal perspective. *Journal of Small Business and Enterprise Development*, 14, 252–263.

Mazão, A; Fernandes, G.O., Cozza, M.M.R., eds. (2011). Estudo do meio. Editora Moderna – cópia autorizada. Retrieved from: www4.moderna.com.br/pnld2011/download/complementacao_pedagogica/geografia/estudo_do_meio.pdf.

McClelland, D.C. (1961). *The achieving society*. Princeton, NJ: Van Nostrand.

McClelland, D.C. (1965). Toward a theory of motive acquisition. *American Psychologist*, 20, 321–333.

McMullan, W., Chrisman, J. and Vesper, K., (2002). Lessons from successful innovations in entrepreneurial support programming. In: J. Chrisman, J. Holbrook and J. Chua, eds. *Innovation and entrepreneurship in Western Canada: From family businesses to multinationals.* Calgary, Alberta: University of Calgary, pp. 207–223.

Mezirow, J. (1998). On critical reflection. *Adult Education Quarterly*, 48(3), 185–198.

Mitra, J. (2008). Towards an analytical framework for policy development. In J. Potter, ed. *Entrepreneurship and higher education.* Paris: OECD – Local Economic and Employment Development (LEED).

Morin, E. (2005). Edgar Morin: o verdadeiro papel da educação. Entrevista Fronteiras do Pensamento (Porto Alegre). Retrieved from: www.fronteiras.com/entrevistas/edgar-morin-o-verdadeiro-papel-da-educacao.

Mueller, S.L. and Thomas, A.S. (2001). Culture and entrepreneurial potential: A nine-country study of locus of control and innovativeness. *Journal of Business Venturing*, 16(1), 51–75.

Nabi, G., Walmsley, A., Liñán, F., Akhtar, I. and Neame, A. (2016). Does entrepreneurship education in the first year of higher education develop entrepreneurial intentions? The role of learning and inspiration. *Studies in Higher Education*. Open Access, 1–16.

Natriello, G. (1987). The impact of evaluation processes on students. *Educational Psychologist*, 22, 155–175.

Nga, J.K.H. and Shamuganathan, G. (2010). The influence of personality traits and demographic factors on social entrepreneurship start-up intentions, *Journal of Business Ethics*, 95(2), 259–282.

Nuñes, I.B., Marujo, M.P., Marujo, L.E.L. and Dias, M.A.S. (2004). O uso de situações-problema no ensino de ciências. In: I.B. Nuñes and B.L. Ramalho, eds. *Fundamentos do ensino-aprendizagem das ciências naturais e da matemática: o novo ensino médio.* Porto Alegre: Sulina, pp. 145–171.

Onuchic, L.R. (1999). Ensino-aprendizagem de Matemática através da resolução de Problemas. In: Maria Aparecida Viggiani Bicudo, ed. *Pesquisa em educação matemática.* São Paulo: Editora da UNESP, pp. 199–218.

Oosterbeek, H., van Praag, M. and Ijsselstein, A. (2010). The impact of entrepreneurship education on entrepreneurship skills and motivation. *European Economic Review*, 54, 442–454.

Peduzzi, L.O.Q. (1997). Sobre a resolução de problemas no ensino da física. *Caderno Catarinense de Ensino de Física*, Florianópolis: UFSC, 14(3), 229–253.

Penaluna, K., Penaluna, A. and Jones, C. (2012). The context of enterprise education: Insights into current practices. *Industry & Higher Education*, 26, 163–175.

Perkins, D.V. and Saris, R.N. (2001). A 'Jigsaw Classroom'" technique for undergraduate statistics courses. *Teaching of Psychology*, 111–113.

Peterman, N.E. and Kennedy, J. (2003). Enterprise education: Influencing students' perceptions of entrepreneurship. *Entrepreneurship Theory and Practice*, 28(2), 129–144.

Pillis, E. and Reardon, K.K. (2007). The influence of personality traits and persuasive messages on entrepreneurial intention: A cross-cultural comparison. *Career Development International*, 12(4), 382–396.

Potter, J. (2008). *Entrepreneurship and higher education.* Paris: OECD – Local Economic and Employment Development (LEED).

Pozo, J.I., and Crespo, M.Á.G. (2009). *Aprendizagem e o ensino de ciências: doconhecimento cotidiano ao conhecimento científico.* Porto Alegre: Artmed.

Rauch, A. and Frese, M. (2007). Let's put the person back into entrepreneurship research: A meta-analysis on the relationship between business owners' personality traits, business creation, and success. *European Journal of Work and Organizational Psychology*, 16(4), 353–385.

Reynolds, P.D., Storey, D.J. and Westhead, P. (1994). Cross-national comparison of the variation in new firm rates. *Regional Studies*, 28, 443–456.

Ribeiro, L.R.C. (2008). *Aprendizagem Baseada em Problemas*: PBL uma experiência no ensino superior. São Carlos: EDUFSCar.

Robinson, P.B., Stimpson, D.V., Huefner, J.C. and Hunt, H.K. (1991). An attitude approach to the prediction of entrepreneurship. *Entrepreneurship Theory and Practice*, 15(4), 13–31.

Robinson, K. (2006). Do schools kill creativity? [online]. *TED Talks.* Available at: www. ted.com/talks/ken_robinson_says_schools_kill_creativity/transcript?language=en [accessed 1 September 2016].

Rodrigues, J.J.F. (2009). *Avaliação do estudante universitário*, Brasília: SENAC, 2009.

Ronstadt, R. (1984). *Entrepreneurship: Text, cases and notes*. Dover: Lord.

Rosendahl Huber, L., Sloof, R. and Van Praag, M. (2012). The effect of early entrepreneurship education: Evidence from a randomized field experiment. Tinbergen Institute Discussion Paper TI 2012–041/3.

Ryan, J.C., Tipu, S.A. and. Zeffane, R.M. (2011). Need for achievement and entrepreneurial potential: A study of young adults in the UAE. *Education, Business and Society: Contemporary Middle Eastern Issues*, 4(3), 153–166.

Sánchez, J.C. (2011). University training for entrepreneurial competencies: Its impact on intention of venture creation. *International Entrepreneurship Management Journal*, 7, 239–254.

Shapero, A. (January 1980). Are business schools teaching business? *Inc.*, 13.

Shapero, A. and Sokol, L. (1982). *Social dimensions of entrepreneurship*. In: C.A. Kent, D.L. Sexton and K.H. Vesper, eds. *Encyclopedia of entrepreneurship*. Englewood Cliffs: Prentice Hall, pp. 72–90.

Storey, D. J. (1994). *Understanding the small business sector*. London: Routledge.

Shuell, T.J. (1986). Cognitive conceptions of learning. *Review of Educational Research*, 56, 411–436.

Siegel, P.H., Khursheed, O. and Agrawal, S.P. (1997). Video simulation of an audit: An experiment in experiential learning. *Accounting Education*, 6(3), 217–230.

Souitaris, V., Zerbinati, S. and Al-Laham, A. (2007). Do entrepreneurship programmes raise entrepreneurial intention of science and engineering students? The effect of learning, inspiration and resources. *Journal of Business Venturing*, 22, 566–591.

Specht, L.B. (1991). The differential effects of experiential learning activities and traditional lecture class in accounting. *Simulation & Gaming*, 22(2), 196–210.

Taylor, P.J., Russ-Eft, D.F. and Chan, D.W.L. (2005). A meta-analytic review of behavior modeling training. *The Journal of Applied Psychology*, 90(4), 692–709.

Tierney, R., Carter, M. and Desai, L. (1991). *Portfolio assessment in the reading-writing classroom*. Norwook, MA: Christopher-Gordon Publishers.

Turner, J.J. and Mulholland, G. (2017). Enterprise education: Towards a framework for engaging with tomorrow's entrepreneurs, *Journal of Management Development* 36(6), 1–18.

Valencia, S.W. and Calfee, R. (1991). The development and use of literacy portfolios for students, classes, and teachers. *Applied Measurement in Education*, 4, 333–345.

Villas Boas, B.M. de F. (2004). A avaliação em cursos de pedagogia para professores em exercício: desenvolvendo a autonomia intelectual do professor-aluno. In: J.P. Romanowski, L.O. Martins and S.R.A. Junqueira, eds. *Conhecimento local e conhecimento universal: pesquisa, didática e ação docente*. Curitiba: Champagnat, 4, pp. 115–131.

Walker, I. and Crogan, M. (1998). Academic performance, prejudice, and the jigsaw classroom: New pieces to the puzzle. *Journal of Community and Applied Social Psychology*, 8, 381–393.

Wu, S. and Wu, L. (2008). The impact of higher education on entrepreneurial intentions of university students in China. *Journal of Small Business and Enterprise Development*, 15(4), 752–774.

Yamamoto, I. (2016). *Metodologias ativas de aprendizagem interferem no desempenho de estudantes.* Dissertação de Mestrado, Faculdade de Economia, Administração e Contabilidade, Universidade de São Paulo, São Paulo. Retrieved from: www.teses.usp.br/teses/disponiveis/12/12139/tde-22092016-121953/.

Zabala, A. (1998). *A prática educativa.* Porto Alegre: Artmed.

Zabala, A. (2002). *Enfoque globalizador e pensamento complexo: uma proposta para o currículo escolar.* Porto Alegre: Artmed.

Zhang, J. and Hamilton, E. (2010). Entrepreneurship education for owner-managers: The process of trust building for an effective learning community. *Journal of Small Business & Entrepreneurship*, 23(2), 249–270.

10 University knowledge exchange and enterprise education as a regional economic driver in the UK

Nicholas Lancaster and Mary Malcolm

Introduction

This chapter challenges university enterprise educators to consider a deeper and richer notion of 'enterprise' and to reflect upon this when designing initiatives to engender entrepreneurial attributes and skills in their students and staff, and in their engagement in knowledge exchange with external stakeholders. Through a case study of highly enterprising and impactful knowledge exchange in a modern research-active UK university, it is argued that too much of the discussion of the importance of universities on national and regional economic development is placed within a narrow focus of traditional metrics of economic impact and misses much that is relevant to the future entrepreneur and the aspiring enterprise educator. This approach does not recognise fully the contribution that UK universities make to regional economies through the breadth of their knowledge exchange, or their development of enterprising and entrepreneurial graduates.

The chapter will look in particular at the engagement gaps in enterprise development. It will examine the development of enterprise through both enterprise education (internal to the university) and enterprise and innovation development (external knowledge exchange between universities and businesses), taking the South East Midlands area of the UK as its focus. It will suggest that much of an institution's approach to enterprise education will derive from, and contribute to, its two-way knowledge exchange (KE) activities with a region's business community and many of its economic development stakeholders. Better understanding of how a university engenders successful knowledge exchange will help institutions to plan for and develop better programmes and support systems for future aspirational entrepreneurs.

Drawing from research evidence around the attitudes of regional small to medium sized enterprises (SMEs) to working with higher educational institutions (HEIs), it is suggested much work remains to be done in promoting the benefits and value of engaging with university educators and practitioners.

Universities as UK economic drivers

The importance of universities as drivers of UK growth and investment is well established. The UK's HEIs support more than 750,000 jobs, equivalent to 2.7 per cent of all UK employment, and generates a total estimated economic output of approximately £73 billion per year (Kelly, McNicoll and White, 2014: 4). HEIs are also major exporters, generating approximately £10 billion per year through export earnings (ibid.: 25).

University-led research and enterprise expertise is a crucial component of this economic impact. In terms of research outputs for example, the UK's HEIs are highly productive compared with other national competitors. A 2013 analysis demonstrated that the UK produces more research outputs (i.e. including articles, citations, downloads and patents) per researcher and per unit of R&D expenditure than China, Japan, the US or Germany (Elsevier, 2013: 9). Similarly, in 2016, an international comparison of national HEI systems found that the UK ranks second out of 50 countries for quality research output whilst only 12th for resource inputs (Russell Group, 2016). Analysis of 2014–2015 European Union (EU) funded research alone, shows that UK's HEIs received approximately £836 million in grants funding, representing 14.2 per cent of all the UK's income from research contracts for that year (Kelly, 2016: 4). This supported approximately 8,864 direct jobs, and at a broad ratio of 1 : 1 for every pound spent, £836 m of additional economic output and a contribution of nearly £577 m to the GDP of the UK (ibid.: 4). Outside the HEI sector, EU research funding to UK HEIs generated approximately 10,190 additional full-time-equivalent jobs, £1.02 bn of output and contributed a further £503 m to GDP (ibid.: 6). Such statistics demonstrate the excellence the UK's HEI sector has in producing 'impactful' knowledge, beyond and as well as generating trained graduates with the capacity to embed that knowledge in policy and practice. The income from businesses attracted by the UK's HE sector is measured by the Higher Education Business and Community Interaction Survey (HEBCIS), administered annually by the lead regulating body for higher education in England – HEFCE. Income is identified through HEBCIS as a combination of contract and collaborative research, intellectual property (IP) income through licensing and spin-out of new companies, consultancy and continuous professional development and the use of facilities and equipment.

In terms of the generation of commercial knowledge with and to business, the UK performs better than, say, Germany and France on the number of licence agreements it produces per 1000 research staff, with 16.3 licence agreements per 1000 staff versus 5.0 and 4.3 respectively (Russell Group, 2016: 7). Similarly, UK HEIs produce a similar number of spin-off companies and joint ventures to those in the United States per million pounds of research funding, and substantially more than Japanese and most European Universities (Elsevier, 2013: 88). UK HEIs also attract a higher share of their research income from industrial sources than those in the US – 7.2 per cent in the UK compared with 6.5 per cent in the US (Elsevier, 2013: 34).

As we shall see, such metrics underpin many polices, agendas and national funding streams that constitute the UK's national system of innovation between HEIs and business. It is suggested here that despite the manifest strength of UK HEIs in this area, this limited perspective on the value created through innovation generated in the HE sector potentially misses, or at least does not place full value on, other forms of knowledge created by HEIs that also have a direct and positive impact on regional economies. They do this in part through their critical role as partners in the creation of new knowledge and the exercise of innovation, but also through their enabling of an education experience that draws on the interface they provide between the requirements and practices of regional and national economies and the education of future graduates.

Universities as UK regional drivers

Within England, a substantial amount of public economic growth funding has, since the early 2000s, been channelled through Local Enterprise Partnerships (LEPs). This includes funds such as European Structural and Investment Funds (and presumably their possible replacements), local and regional growth funds as well as various devolution arrangements. In Scotland, Scottish Enterprise performs a similar role, with the Innovation Advisory Council bringing public and private stakeholders together to provide the Welsh government with direction and advice on regional innovation and enterprise policy. Political changes, including potential ramifications from Brexit, the emergence of combined authorities and elected mayors, the creation of multi-LEP areas, the development of regional identities such as the Northern Powerhouse and Midlands Engine, and other initiatives such as Catapult Centres,[1] the Smart Specialisation Hub[2] and the Science and Innovation Audits,[3] mean that innovation and enterprise policy is increasingly being shaped nationally through a better understanding of, and connection to, the capacity of universities to engage with particular business needs on a regional level.

Many universities are highly active in regional economic development. Each HEI typically interacts with many hundreds of businesses per year.[4] Often, depending on their size, mission and regional connectivity, they can provide a major foundation for regional growth strategies – beyond that of the traditional measures of commercial development such as income from licensing its intellectual property or consultancy (University Alliance, 2011). Many work closely with LEPs, local authorities and other regional economic developers and stakeholders from the public and private sector (e.g. professional representative bodies, Chambers of Commerce and public service procurers) in diverse areas such as health and social care policy, the arts and crime reduction (Taylor, 2016: 12). Similarly, HEIs often act as advisers to LEPs and other stakeholders with staff contributing to boards and committees, in many cases, writing, or at least heavily contributing to the enterprise and skills components of LEP and local authority strategic and economic plans, as well as generating graduate start-ups, work-based placements, training in industry and 'intrapreneurship' support for businesses.[5]

UK policy makers are increasingly looking for a regional voice to develop strong economic systems as a way of making a more competitive nation. While political agendas and funded business support programmes are subject to short term change, long standing and regionally focused universities typically retain and share impactful expertise over the longer term, develop long-term partnerships, and provide the critical continuity that businesses and other stakeholders require for sustained growth. This two-way transfer of 'impactful' knowledge helps drive the economic potential of regional businesses (Carberry and Driscoll, 2015). Yet the funding for research excellence found throughout the HEI sector is substantially based on international quality assessed through a combination of academic impact and non-academic impact that can be traced back directly to specific research outputs, limiting the priority given to industry collaboration at both institutional and individual levels (Dowling, 2015: 30). As the next section shows, the link between national and regional economic development strategy can therefore become disassociated.

National systems of innovation – Higher Education Innovation Fund (HEIF)

Outside core funding internal to the university and one-off external agency project based funding, perhaps the major source of longitudinal funds to support KE activity in England and Wales (Scotland has its own version – the Universities Innovation Fund)[6] comes from HEFCE funding for 'third mission' activity (the first two being the established streams for teaching and research) through the Higher Education Innovation Fund (HEIF).[7] Introduced in 1999, and aiming to "to support and develop a broad range of knowledge-based interactions between universities and colleges and the wider world, which result in economic and social benefit to the UK" (Ulrichsen, 2015: 6).

HEIF funding was intended to embed knowledge exchange activity within a University's core mission through its inclusion within the regular round of funding to institutions. From the outset, however, HEIF was awarded on a quasi-competitive basis, based on submitted plans and particular project proposals, with the aim of generating income from KE activity, support the growth of innovation and enterprise, and establish and disseminate an understanding of good practice in the sector. Altered and refocused over the years, at one point including, and subsequently dropping, an element that required multi-university collaborations, the restructuring of the funding stream in 2010 had at its core an explicit focus for the first time of helping deliver greater *impact* on the national economy by incentivising the sectors 'higher performers'. The allocation on this basis lasted for the period of 2011–2015.[8]

Current reform can be seen against a governmental agenda of both achieving economic growth and encouraging the private sector and community groups to join HEI KE activities through public and private partnerships to achieve a wider socio-economic impact.[9] Similarly, recent and wide-ranging reforms outlined in the HE White Paper 2016 and HE and Research Bill 2016–2017 include changes to other supporting structures, introducing two new bodies: the Office for Students (OfS) and UK Research and Innovation (UKRI). The expectation is that

HEFCE's KE function will fall under Research England within UKRI, and KE will be a joint co-operation between OfS and UKRI (Department for Business Innovation and Skills, 2016a: 18). As the most recent HEFCE grant letter stated:

> HEIs will continue to have flexibility to use their HEIF allocations for the full range of knowledge exchange activities in line with the policies and priorities set out in this publication. We expect institutional strategies to be based on enduring institutional and academic capabilities, long-term part-nerships, and intended outcomes and impacts and hence should not change frequently.[10]

The same letter re-emphasised a commitment to HEFCE's role in supporting KE activity, which includes HEIF, and the continued importance of developing greater links between HEIs and businesses, particularly SMEs. Similarly, the government's productivity plan reinforced the importance of government, universities, city regions, LEPs and business working in strategies to build on different regions' diverse strengths and histories to maximise the economic impact from the UK's research and knowledge base (House of Commons, 2016).

With HEIF's importance to both HEIs' KE activity and the UK's national system of innovation acknowledged and with £160 million distributed across the sector last year, HEFCE uses a variety of metrics to incentivise HEIs to engage in specific activities that fall under the broad definition of KE (HEFCE, 2016). Previously, the annual sum to each institution would be set for a number of years, but from 2017 to 2018 onwards it will be an annual re-calculation, designed to increase dynamism and reward to recent performance, but with predictability. Predictability will be achieved by confirming the yearly modera-tion factor to be applied, first between 2016 and 2017 and 2017–2018, and then annually thereafter. The yearly moderation factor provides HEIs with a planning assumption to use in drawing up their KE strategies' (HEFCE, 2017: 30–31).

There is also an adjustment to the weighting of the three years of input metrics making up the final allocation to each HEI, from 1:2:7 to 2:3:5, "to better reflect the balance of dynamism and stability in moving from a multiple year allocation to an annual year allocation".[11] A full comparison of the changes in funding formula is not possible here, but the crucial point in this context is that future allocations, as previously, will draw upon only a narrow set of annual university data of KE performance, drawn from the HEBCI survey with a maximum cap of £2.8 million and a lower cap of £250 thousand, HEIF 2017–2018 and onwards takes data sources for income; contract research; con-sultancy; equipment and facilities; regeneration; intellectual property income; non-credit-bearing courses; Knowledge Transfer Partnerships income provided by Innovate UK and income from SMEs (double weighted).[12]

In short, HEIF, through which the government incentivises HEIs to engage in KE activity, is based largely on the ability of individual institutions to generate income from research grants and leverage income from business – particular SMEs. Although individual HEIF plans do allow freedom for universities to specify their own areas in which they will use their funding, there is little emphasis on non-income value, impact or improved productivity in the region's business community, and in particular the SME community, and no direct incentive to directly seek to increase regional SME Gross Value Added (HEFCE, 2016). As we shall consider further below, a possible impact of this upon a university's mission as an enterprise educator would be to focus more upon direct income generation for the university itself rather than to seek to act as a regional catalyst for change and business support.

HEIF is considered a highly successful programme. It is estimated that HEIF brings a return of £7.30 per £1. Indeed, the ratio of additional KE income to HEIF substantially higher for the 'top six' of £21.50 per £1, high league table research institutions of £11.70, compared with medium table of £5.70 and low table institutions of £3.60 (Ulrichsen, 2015: 3). The general message is that universities with a higher emphasis on research excellence deliver higher financial returns from HEIF investments. Yet as the scheme currently operates, the metrics do not especially incentivise university enterprise educators to support entrepreneurship, start-ups, or intrapreneurship within SMEs, outside the potential for direct income generation to the university, or the many other areas of KE that have a positive effect on regional economies.

In summary, the value of the UK's HEI's as income generators – leveraging funds from both research funding agencies and businesses – is clear. Also, the value, in terms of direct and indirect employment and support to businesses is an invaluable part of the UK's national innovation system, keeping the UK competitive throughout the world. However, the role of universities as enterprise educators – particularly within a regional context is less well understood and would benefit from the application of a much deeper and richer notion of enterprise and its impact on regional economics. The systems of incentives from the UK Government, although highly successful for stimulating university income generation, perhaps does not reflect or best serve to the fullest extent a view of the role university's play in helping a regions SME business community to innovate, or indeed, to help foster the entrepreneurial aspirations of the next generation.

The next section considers the South East Midlands area, its business community and a broad understanding of the positive economic impact a modern university brings to it through its KE provision.

The South East Midlands (SEM): university to business context

A 2015 Business Survey, prepared for South East Midlands Local Enterprise Partnership (SEMLEP) by BMG Research, provides a useful insight into the strengths and challenges of businesses in the region (BMG Research, 2015). There are approximately 75,000 employing establishments across the SEMLEP area. The majority of businesses in the South East Midlands area are micro-employers with fewer than ten staff (84 per cent). This should be seen in the context of the comparative UK-wide figure of 96 per cent (Rhodes, 2016: 3), noting that both include a high percentage of companies (around 76 per cent UK-wide) of businesses that did not employ anyone aside from the owner (ibid.: 5). The BMG research (BMG Research, 2015) also indicates that just 1 per cent of all SEMLEP businesses employ 100 or more staff, and this broadly reflects the UK business population profile as a whole which is also around 1 per cent, and that the two most populous industry sectors in the SEMLEP region are wholesale and retail trade (18 per cent) and professional, scientific and technical activities (17 per cent), reflecting national levels of *c.* 14 per cent and 15 per cent nationally. Over half of SEMLEP businesses (55 per cent) are private limited companies, while 23 per cent are sole traders and 10 per cent partnerships (against 32 per cent, 60 per cent and 8 per cent nationally), with one in eight being a start-up (13 per cent), having traded for less than three years. Within the SEMLEP region there is considerable geographical variation on numbers and rates for start-ups, business deaths and survival rates, with Luton, Northampton and Milton Keynes having the highest start-up rates.

Innovation and enterprise in the South East Midlands

In 2015, approximately 12 per cent of companies in the region reported links with universities or colleges for research and development purposes (BMG Research, 2015: 17), and this figure increases to 39 per cent of businesses with 100 or more employees. Businesses within the sectors of education and health (33 per cent); manufacturing (20 per cent) and arts, recreation and other services (19 per cent) are particularly likely to have recently worked with universities or colleges (ibid.: 17). Available comparators for this interaction pattern are limited, but the SEM region compares similarly with other LEPs, for example, Leicester and Leicestershire LEP, which reports that just 17 per cent across all sectors had some form of interaction for HEIs (Brockway, 2015: 9). Similarly, this compares against the experience of the West of England LEP SMEs – which report the engagement in terms of those who have offered traineeships and/or apprentice-ships (16 per cent), providing hands-on activities (11 per cent), visits to the workplace (11 per cent) and industry projects (4 per cent), although it should be noted that these statistics include Further Education (FE) as well as HE (Wave-hill, 2016: 64).

Overall, over two-fifths of businesses in the SEM area (44 per cent) are inno-vators, based on having links with universities or colleges for R&D purposes or planning to introduce new products, services, patents or processes (BMG Research, 2015: 96). Again, although national and direct regional comparisons are challenging it is interesting to note that in the context of Brexit, it is reported that around seven in ten UK firms are planning to increase or maintain innova-tion spending, with 78 per cent of firms reporting universities as having a vital role to play in their innovation 'eco-system', reflecting companies' need for expertise and collaborative partners (CBI, 2016). Approximately 28 per cent of SEMLEP businesses can be broadly considered enterprising or innovative in that they have introduced a new product, service, patent or process in the last 12 months, increasing to more than 55 per cent with businesses with 100 or more employees (BMG Research, 2015: 17). Within the same region, 36 per cent of businesses expect to introduce new products, services, patents or new processes in the next 12 months, a substantial rise on recent years, increasing to 56 per cent for businesses with 50 or more staff. The classification of UK businesses as innovative, on these terms, is found to be associated with their deployment of the knowledge and skills associated with HE through the employment of its graduates (Department for Business Innovation and Skills, 2016b: 22).

Employment, skills shortages and skill gaps

The continuing recognition of graduates as a key output of economic value is evidenced in the continuing value of a university degree to the individual and the economy (Rich, 2015: 13). Demand for skills continues to be identified as a regional and national economic constraint. On a national level, recruitment activity in SEMLEP businesses increases with business size, but there is also an increase in the likelihood of having vacancies between businesses with fewer than ten employees and those with ten or more – 32 per cent compared with 84 per cent of those with ten to 49 and 92 per cent with 50 or more employees (BMG Research, 2015: 15). Vacancies arising from skills shortages are more likely to be evidenced within production and construction sectors than across service sectors, while lack of qualifications is most prevalent within the professional, scientific and technical activities sector (30 per cent) and lack of interest is most frequently cited by businesses within the accommodation and food services sector (41 per cent) (BMG Research, 2015: 69). Job-specific and technical or practical skills are the most frequently mentioned skills that have been difficult to obtain across all business sectors, a position strongly representative of the national picture of reported skills gaps (IFF Research, 2016). Recognising the effectiveness of higher education and the requirement for business to invest in those skills it most consistently expresses a need for, a key objective of the UK government's apprenticeship strategy seeks to expand current levels of participation in HE by combining practical and transferable skills in work-based learning programmes funded by an employer levy (Department for Education, 2017: 5).

Historically, the UK has been ambivalent towards apprenticeships, with only 15 per cent of businesses offering apprenticeships in England, compared with 24 per cent in Germany and 30 per cent in Australia (HM Government, 2015: 7). For the immediate future, the SEM region seems to compare favourably in its prospects to other LEPs, with for example, around 17 per cent of West of England LEP companies planning to offer apprenticeships in the next three years (Wavehill, 2016: 77) against a more positive 44 per cent consideration of this route to addressing skills shortages within the SEM region (BMG Research, 2015: 90). Among the latter, businesses that have links with universities, or who are innovators (a category itself associated with university links), are more likely to employ apprentices and to engage in other forms of training and placement to develop the skills they need (BMG Research, 2015: 90ff.). Universities are therefore critical to the skills development that drives innovation and enterprise in the economy, and more specifically to the UK Government's strategy for skills development through a renewed approach to apprenticeships. They do this in part through their capacity to develop the required combinations of immediate technical skill and capacity alongside generic capabilities and attributes associated with graduate status. They also accredit skills development in ways that gain employer and apprentice acceptance, and offer multi-faceted support for business engagement that allows business sectors and organisations to position their support for skills development as an element of their overall strategic development.

Business and start-up support in the South East Midlands

All of the above reflects a breadth and depth of contribution to the knowledge economy that evades the more simplistic of official definitions of success, and supports a regional economy that inevitably has specific needs and activity patterns that are legitimately more relevant to a university's approach than the drivers embedded in those definitions.

In 2014, over 9200 new employer businesses were registered in SEMLEP at a rate of 53 per 10,000, the fifth highest rate of English LEPs (Enterprise Research Centre, 2014). At around that time, 17 per cent of SEMLEP businesses were female led; 11 per cent were BME led; 15 per cent were sole traders; 22 per cent were below the VAT threshold with 56 per cent family owned (BMG Research, 2015). The SEM ranked 13th of the 39 LEPs for start-ups and 20th in survival rates. Yet across its stratified sample of just under 2000 businesses in 2015, SEMLEP (BMG Research, 2015) established that a majority (85 per cent) of businesses had used some level of advice or support in the 12 months of the survey, but this was most likely to have been their accountant (59 per cent), bank (46 per cent) or family/friends (44 per cent) (BMG Research, 2015: 42). Dedicated or more formal sources of business advice or support were likely to have been used by only a small minority of businesses. Indeed, one in three businesses that had been trading less than five years (31 per cent) reported receiving any advice or support during start-up, 69 per cent did not (BMG Research, 2015: 43). In the area of SME support and development, there were approximately 23 local delivery services with at least 20 national schemes also available to regional businesses (SEMLEP, 2015). Fourteen of these schemes offer one to one advice, ten offering training and mentoring of some form. Eight schemes offered premises or access to premises, and finally three schemes offered grants to start-up businesses. Universities are well represented in all of these areas, although a report on the provision of start-up support in the SEMLEP region concluded that "the role of Colleges and Universities is uneven across the geography and not well understood" (SEMLEP, 2015: 39).

In summary, the South East Midlands area has a diverse range of businesses and reflects the typical LEP profile of predominately SME or micro firms with a few large employers. The larger the firm the more likely they are to work with a university, seek enterprise support, and the region is particularly well developed in terms of start-up firms and regional support. The region has a high number of innovators, based on willingness to create new products processes or services or a willingness to partner with a university to undertake innovation through knowledge exchange. The formal and informal patterns through which that knowledge exchange is embedded in university–business interaction are constructed by all partners to respond to the particular characteristics of the regional business ecosystem. The flexibility of universities in responding to the specific requirements of their region's businesses and doing so in formats that are recognised as offering value to those businesses is both a requirement and an indicator of the success of a deep and mature understanding of knowledge exchange.

The University of Bedfordshire: knowledge exchange in the South East Midlands area

As we have seen so far in this chapter, the potential for interaction between cutting-edge research and the enterprise required to generate knowledge exchange relies for its sustainability on a dual-support system, combining project funding with formula-based funding that rewards performance retrospectively based on peer review and proven impact. Universities and their research are central to the South East Midland's knowledge base, particularly in relation to start-up activity, innovation and skills development. While the skills, motivations and contexts of the various groups involved in regional business networks differ, their operation within an increasingly integrated policy and funding context intensifies and expands the links between the research base and the wider innovation ecosystem beyond the traditional pipeline and metrics, to form a more consistently reciprocal relationship between research generators and users at a regional level. In making the case for creating a new understanding of enterprise education with a combined focus on research-driven and challenge-driven knowledge exchange, it is also recognised that public investment in research and innovation both creates social and economic impact and 'crowds in' private investment in R&D (Department for Business Innovation and Skills, 2016c: 14).

Within the 2014 Research Excellence Framework (REF) on which formulaic research funding is based, UK HEIs submitted 6975 impact case studies, demonstrating the impact of their research on the economy, society, culture, public policy or services, health, the environment or quality of life.[13] In the REF submission of the University of Bedfordshire, the strength of this multifaceted integration is clear. Research users are engaged with the outputs of research, through thematic regional conferences such as "Biotechnology: Environment, Food and Health", but also in regular interactions that ensure that the research agenda is maintained within a context of well-understood regional enterprise requirements. In areas such as computing and engineering, this occurs through regional employer panels that sustain a network of technology-related companies supporting skills and training as well as understanding likely future technology.

The research that emerges from this systematic engagement is rooted in the needs of regional enterprise that may not be captured at a national level nor reflected in national funded systems of KE. The university's KE includes a strong regional focus, for example on the low levels of e-commerce adoption in regional manufacturing SMEs (Duan *et al.*, 2002). It addresses specific challenges encountered by regional SMEs, for example assessing pollution issues and monitoring methodologies to develop and apply research expertise in bio-sensors for water quality monitoring (Anyachebelu *et al.*, 2014) and may involve direct research collaboration with SMEs, for example in meeting technical challenges in the deployment of femtocells (Zhang *et al.*, 2010).

More broadly this systemic engagement ensures that the university participates through its research as a partner in meeting specific regional challenges and progressing regional strengths. Research in food tourism, for example, has informed policy and strategy in the use of food tourism to promote regional development in areas of social and economic challenge (Everett and Slocum, 2013). The university's partnership in a consortium of universities working on a £16m funded contract supporting sustainable growth in Milton Keynes, one of the fastest growing areas in the UK, without exceeding the capacity of the infrastructure, and whilst meeting key carbon reduction targets, engages major industrial partners and SMEs alike in developing innovative solutions to support economic growth through the collaborative use of big data. The university also addresses both regional and national issues for example, by understanding the role of faith in organ donation and contributing to policy (Randhawa, 2011), supporting the view that increasing organ transplantation rates by 50 per cent could achieve a further cost saving of £200 million per annum to NHS regional commissioners. While such work does attract post-hoc research funding through the periodic Research Excellence Framework, and may on occasion be successful in competitive bidding, the significant cost savings described above, for example, do not form part of the metrics set related directly to KE funding. As such, from an enterprise educator's perspective, innovative research is often overlooked or not acknowledged as having a clear financial or entrepreneurial value.

To maintain its mission focus on transforming the lives of individuals and communities, in the context of an increasingly competitive funding environment structured to sustain institutional and thereby regional hierarchies through tightly defined categories of innovation, rather than to support the full range of legitimate contributions to broadly conceived innovation, the University of Bedfordshire positions its research and innovation in a series of concentric zones of activity, recognising that while in one of these zones the immediate reward is formal research funding, its acquisition is just one of a range of valid impact types.[14]

The role of enterprise education

Securing the benefits of this broad approach to recognising institutional as well as external impact, demands consistent effort to ensure parity of esteem across

the full range of contributions made by academics to supporting regional innovation as well as demonstrating institutional and individual enterprise. Those benefits accrue directly to regional institutional profile, as well as through the
university's reputation for enterprise among its principal output – its graduates.
And the nurturing of a culture that recognises innovation as a broad set of
behavioural and dispositional attributes supports, in turn, the innovation and
enterprise orientation of those graduates. The University of Bedfordshire has a
tradition of entrepreneurial students who want to start up their own businesses
and ranks 11th of the UK HEIs for estimated turnover (£22.3 m) of graduate
start-ups measured since 2008.[15]

The university has taken part and run a variety of start-up focused funded
programmes. For example, B-innovative, funded under the Lifelong Learning
Programme of the European Commission from 2012 to 2015, constituted a
collaborative effort to transfer the entrepreneurship best practice of the
University of Bedfordshire, to the other five European partner countries.[16] It
had over 700 participants over three years and was based around a series of
seminars and workshops delivered by local entrepreneurs and ended with a
business competition. After the project closed, it was taken up and operated by
the university as a regional programme, open to students and externals residents in the area, and had approximately 40 people per year for several years
attend the workshops. In 2016–2017 the programme was reformulated as an
internally accredited course for undergraduates as an elective employability
module. Within the employability electives scheme, students are able to accu-
mulate an additional ten credits per year in skills development, in addition to
their standard 120 credits of core content per study stage. While the units are
targeted at graduate entry-level competences, their inclusion of soft skills such
as influencing and public speaking that continue to be important after graduation (Kaplan, 2014) also support student achievement within the university's
overall approach to practice-led learning and assessment. The B-innovative
syllabus, under this new arrangement, remains broadly the same, with local
entrepreneurs leading on workshops around a variety of themes informed by
our ongoing interactions with them.

This programme contributes significantly to the new business development outcomes noted above, and links closely with the 2014 Young report *Enterprise for
all*, which identified the ambition that "all university students should have access to
enterprise and entrepreneurship, including a growing ambition amongst young
people to develop their interest in social enterprise" (Young, 2014: 7). But while
the Young report takes a relatively formal view of such educational opportunities
as directly addressing the processes of business development, the guidance on
enterprise education offered by the UK's Quality Assurance Agency outlines a
broader context, defining the challenge as the development of a "mind-set and
skills to come up with original ideas in response to identified needs and shortfalls,
and the ability to act on them. In short, having an idea and making it happen"
(QAA, 2012: 2). Both components – formal enterprise opportunities in the 'practice field' of entrepreneurship, and the broader and deeper development of skills

core but not specific to enterprise, such as leadership and collaboration, problem-solving, commercial awareness and project management – are also core drivers of regional development and growth. For this reason, the University of Bedfordshire positions its work in enterprise education primarily as an aspect of staff activity (McMillan Group, 2016: 9), enabling the integration of links between this and other aspects of knowledge exchange, as outlined in Figure 10.1.

This approach supports staff active in other areas of knowledge exchange to identify enterprise education as a valid deployment of their efforts, and encourages their use of external engagement within that activity. While Rich (2015) points out the persisting divide between academic and employer perceptions of priority skills and attributes, a 2015 survey by the UK's National Centre for Universities Business found that while overall academic time spent in external engagement was low in comparison with time spent on other activities, the need to continually update both the formal curriculum and personal understanding of practice was significant in that engagement (NCUB, 2016: 2). Enterprise education and curriculum development are both and separately specified, along with student placement procurement, within the people-based category of external engagement (NCUB 2016: 4). *This bridge between the internal curriculum and external practice in the professional lives of academics is essential to enterprise education, if it* is to provide a comprehensive developmental platform in which all students acquire knowledge, skills and attributes that are valued by employers and that enhance graduates' professional lives, recognising that entrepreneurship may emerge as a later ambition and career change on the basis of a secure graduate identity (Holmes, 2013).

The University of Bedfordshire's *Cre8* curriculum framework was developed to provide support for a learner experience that is challenging and engaging in the present, while also developing the knowledge skills and attributes of value to their professional futures. A key feature of the framework (Atlay, 2010: 10) is its focus on "planned and structured opportunities" to engage in "the practices that graduates will experience outside" (Atlay, 2010: 19–21). Reviewed in 2015, the *Cre8* framework identifies learner and tutor roles in development employability as a combination of systematic knowledge, experience, and personal and practitioner skills developed in a scaffolded process integrating learning, assessment and reflection.[17] Within this curriculum framework the core curriculum supports core and co-curricular learning about enterprise development by providing a broad base of opportunities to develop broader and fundamental skillsets on which enterprise development relies and ensures that all learners explore their potential for entrepreneurship. This framework of opportunities provides experience and development in the three aspects of employability identified by Rich (2015) – knowledge, skills and social capital. It supports the context-relevant development of 'soft skills' within the context of learning and experience appropriate to a student's interests and career ambitions, rather than as a discrete curriculum component, recognising that "it is these soft skills that open doors for students and for which the employer is willing to pay a graduate premium" (Rich, 2015: 21).

CR8 — CHANGING WORLDS AND FUTURES THINKING (For Tutors)

PERSONALISED LEARNING

Personalised learning involves:

Inspiring students to enjoy learning and to have high and realistic ambitions. (P1)

Valuing and acknowledging the diversity of students' experiences and drawing on these in teaching activities. (P2)

Coaching students to improve their effectiveness as learners. (P3)

Accommodating students' personal learning styles and preferences by using a variety of teaching and assessment approaches and technologies. (P4)

Supporting students to develop **a sound value-base and to display appropriate professional attitudes.** (P5)

Enabling students to make sense of their learning in terms of the **actions, behaviours and end-goals** that are expected of them and its impact on others. (P6)

Supporting students in **identifying their strengths** (actual and potential) and understanding how these can develop and transfer to their chosen futures. (P7)

CURRICULUM

A curriculum that prepares students for a complex and changing world:

Consciously **develops students' ability to innovate** - to imagine, evaluate, implement and achieve (C1).

Is **flexible, inclusive and transparent** with clearly aligned intended outcomes, activities and assessments (C2).

Is designed to present an **integrated, developmental and increasingly challenging learning experience** which enables students to progress from guided to independent and autonomous learning (C3).

Supports key transition points and ensures that early experiences set the tone for future activities (C4).

Is informed by, and encourages **learning from and through, research, scholarship and professional practice** (C5).

Provides students with global perspectives on their subject and its application so that they are aware of environmental, social and political issues and their impact on the world (C6).

REALISTIC LEARNING

The learning experience involves activities that are:

Meaningful – students see personal, social, professional, intellectual and practical relevance in the curriculum. (R1)

Active – students are actively engaged in the learning process. (R2)

Challenging – activities challenge students' existing constructs, knowledge and assumptions and offer opportunities for creative and enjoyable learning. (R3)

Reflective – students have structured opportunities for reflection within a process of development that allows them to internalise their experiences and make connections across boundaries. (R4)

Collaborative – students learn with and through peers, tutors and others, face-to-face and online, creating and sustaining a learning community. (R5)

Co-created – students have the opportunity to influence aspects of the teaching and assessment they experience. (R6)

EMPLOYABILITY

A curriculum which supports employability involves students developing:

A systematic understanding of their subject and the associated analytical, creative and critical thinking expected of higher education. (E1)

High-level communication, interpersonal, digital and information skills that enable them to function in complex, technology rich, multi-cultural and multi-professional environments. (E2)

Practitioner and transferable skills and attributes through planned activities such as placements, internships, projects and simulations. (E3)

Personal and professional development planning abilities that combine ambitious and realistic career aspirations with the career management skills to connect the curriculum with the knowledge, skills and attributes required in workplace environments. (E4)

A portfolio of relevant experiences and the life-long learning skills required to sustain their continued development. (E5)

[Effective assessment]

Effective assessment for learning involves:

Assessment strategies which support learner development and focus on employability attributes and skills alongside academic abilities and understanding. (A1)

Assessment tasks which replicate or simulate those required by graduate employment. (A2)

Assessment briefs which clearly articulate the task, expectations and standards. (A3)

Providing **focussed, constructive and timely feedback** to support learning, improve performance, build confidence and encourage positive motivational beliefs. (A4)

Students developing self-regulatory behaviours through self- and peer- assessment against given criteria. (A5)

Students and tutors **using the outcomes of assessment to help shape future learning.** (A6)

© University of Bedfordshire (2015). For further details see www.beds.ac.uk/learning/CR8

CR8 — CHANGING WORLDS AND FUTURES THINKING (For Learners)

PERSONALISED LEARNING

Personalised learning involves:

Committing to your learning and having high and realistic ambitions.

Valuing and acknowledging your experiences and perspectives, sharing these with others and drawing on them for your learning.

Believing that you can become a more effective learner and **taking responsibility for your own learning and development** drawing on advice and support.

Exploring different learning approaches and technologies to find those that are most effective for you.

Developing a sound value-base and **displaying appropriate professional attitudes.**

Thinking about your learning in terms of the **actions, behaviours and end-goals that are expected of you and their impact on others.**

Identifying your strengths (actual and potential) and understanding how these can develop and transfer to your chosen futures.

CURRICULUM

A curriculum that prepares students for a complex and changing world:

Requires you to innovate - to imagine, evaluate, implement and achieve.

Is **flexible, inclusive and transparent** with clearly aligned intended learning outcomes, activities and assessments.

Is designed to present an integrated, developmental and challenging learning experience which **enables you to become an independent and autonomous learner.**

Supports key transition points and ensures that early experiences set the tone for future activities.

Is informed by, and encourages **learning from and through, research, scholarship and professional practice.**

Provides you with global perspectives on your subject and its application so that you are aware of environmental, social and political issues and their impact on the world.

REALISTIC LEARNING

The learning experience involves activities that are:

Meaningful – you should see the personal, social, professional, intellectual and practical relevance of your studies.

Active – you should be actively engaged in the learning process and not expect to have material simply given to you.

Challenging – activities will challenge you and offer you opportunities for creative and enjoyable learning.

Reflective – you should have structured opportunities for reflection to internalise experiences and make connections across boundaries.

Collaborative – you should be prepared to learn with and through other students, tutors and others, in classes and online, creating and sustaining a learning community.

Co-created – you should be prepared to engage with opportunities to influence aspects of the teaching and assessment you experience.

EMPLOYABILITY

A curriculum which supports employability involves students developing:

A systematic understanding of your subject and the associated **analytical, creative and critical thinking expected of higher education.**

High-level communication, interpersonal, digital and information skills that enable you to function in complex, technology rich, multi-cultural and multi-professional environments.

Practitioner and transferable skills and attributes through planned activities such as placements, internships, projects and simulations.

Personal and professional development planning abilities that combine ambitious and realistic career aspirations with the career management skills to **connect the curriculum with the knowledge, skills and attributes required in workplace environments.**

A portfolio of relevant experiences and the life-long learning skills required to sustain their continued development.

[Effective assessment]

Effective assessment for learning involves:

Recognising how assessments support your development and your employability attributes and skills alongside academic abilities and understanding.

Engaging in **assessment tasks which replicate or simulate those required by graduate employment.**

Utilising assessment briefs which clearly articulate the task, expectations and standards.

Using focussed, constructive and timely feedback to support your learning, improve your performance, build confidence and encourage positive motivational beliefs.

You developing your ability to manage your own learning through self-assessment against given criteria.

You and your tutors using the outcomes of assessment to help shape future learning.

© University of Bedfordshire (2015). For further details see www.beds.ac.uk/learning/CR8

Figure 10.1 Public space.

The QAA guidance endorses this nesting of the specifics of enterprise development within a broader conception of enterprise appropriate to a range of contexts:

> *enterprise education* is defined as the process of equipping students (or graduates) with an enhanced capacity to generate ideas and the skills to make them happen. *Entrepreneurship education* equips students with the additional knowledge, attributes and capabilities required to apply these abilities in the context of setting up a new venture or business. All of this is a prerequisite for *entrepreneurial effectiveness*, that is, the ability to function effectively as an entrepreneur or in an entrepreneurial capacity.
>
> (QAA, 2012: 2)

The University of Bedfordshire offers a comprehensive framework of activities focused on the parallel development of ambition, innovation and enterprise encompasses extra-curricular, co-curricular and core opportunities aimed at developing learner awareness, aptitude and ability at levels and paces appropriate to their varied starting points, recognising that these attributes may later be applied across a range of contexts at different career points, and that their development may be better supported outwith the constraints of the formal curriculum (Wilson, 2012: 50). Taking 'enterprise' as an example, within the practice field of enterprise development, specialist courses are available to students with immediate aspirations to start their own companies. These constitute part of the core curriculum in subject areas (such as computing and media) in which there are clearly marked regional pathways to start-up development, and are also offered at postgraduate level within the framework of a postgraduate certificate. But there are also co-curricular courses, credit-bearing outwith the core programme of study, which allow learners in other areas to gain a basic understanding of the formal and tacit requirements of successful start-up. These short courses form part of a suite of such opportunities that include employability skills (e.g. public speaking and networking) as well as the proximate area of freelancing required for those, for example, in areas of the creative industries in which freelance operation is the norm, they are accessible to students approaching the area of enterprise development only cautiously and from a range of starting points in terms of their preparedness.

At the same time, knowledge, skills and attributes including those closely aligned with enterprise activity, are defined for every course through course-level Graduate Impact Statements (GIS) designed to articulate to employers what a graduate from that course will be able to do. Regional employers are involved in programme approval events to ensure that the GIS statements associated with every course are relevant to employment in the area. Since the institution-wide curriculum review that generated these statements (2011–2015), each academic school has mapped its curriculum in detail to identify the key elements that contribute to employability and to ensure that there is a full curricular and co-curricular offering reflecting the range of opportunities available to learners as they work towards achieving their course-level GIS. Each GIS comprises three statements, identifying a graduate's immediate post-graduation capability:

- to apply subject knowledge and understanding, and use specific skills;
- to work in ways important in the field of practice;
- to demonstrate enterprise.

The guidance on generating the last of these three is deliberately broad in focus, targeting the "enhanced capacity to generate ideas and the skills to make them happen" (QAA, 2012: 2):

> This allows you to identify how your graduates will, as a characteristic of the way they work, use their initiative and resourcefulness to develop and implement ideas and practices which make a difference both to themselves and to any organisation in which they are involved.

At unit/module level, the curriculum supports the achievement of the GIS by specifying the development of generic skills in the areas of enquiry, contextual understanding, collaboration and enterprise. Here, enterprise is specified in the university guidance offered to course development teams as "a curriculum that consciously develops students' ability to innovate – to imagine, evaluate, implement and achieve".

Similarly, in the extra-curricular zone, internally funded (though not through national Knowledge Exchange funding), projects under the **Steps** programme allows student teams and staff-student teams to engage with the processes of innovation and enterprise that reflect broadly defined enterprise education activity. Steps has allocated support to more than 30 projects and more than £500,000 since the internal funding began in 2013. For example, Media Junction "enhances the Student Experience by creating opportunities for students to network with each other, across degree pathways in order to make films and create media content" and is designed to allow students to better understand how freelance work and networking is a staple of the creative industries. Similarly, Guildford Street Press is a staff research and student entrepreneurial orientated press based in the School of Art and Design at the University of Bedfordshire. It publishes printed matter for the university and wider local community, creating a platform for cross disciplinary creative thinking and the dissemination of ideas. The press provides a physical and virtual space where students, alumni and academic staff can support research activity as well as the university entrepreneurial enterprise as a whole.[18]

A final strand of the university's work is aimed at ensuring that a consistently positive message around engagement with SMEs and the potential for start-up activity is offered. This is an essential aspect of enterprise education, if students are to escape the assumption that employment in large corporates is the primary and socially preferred target for graduates, it is vital that all aspects of an institution's offering to students are consistent in expressing this. The university has been careful to scope both credit-bearing placement units and co-curricular non-credit-bearing placement opportunities, and in both to promote engagement with SMEs. It does this by, for example, specifying the minimum work threshold as an hours total (rather than in weeks), to accommodate the flexible requirements and capacity of SMEs, and providing an office environment in which students, placed in micro-businesses or start-ups with no significant office space, are allocated as an experience of flexible working. The positive impact is shared, because SMEs often lack the capacity to employ new staff that could help them generate new knowledge, and working with HEIs on placement schemes allow them to reduce the risk associated with recruitment of innovation talent more effectively.

In summary, the university's framework for enterprise education recognises the variability and complexity of learner readiness for, and graduate deployment of, enterprise skills by providing a range of opportunities to engage with "enterprise" as an attribute and a broad category of activity, as well as opportunities to experience and prepare for enterprise and entrepreneurship associated with business start-up. Opportunities in the curricular, co-curricular and extra-curricular zones are structured to facilitate engagement with enterprise at varying degrees of commitment and preparedness, recognising that in the context of lifelong learning and a work future in which portfolio careers will feature significantly, a more prescriptive approach or a more restricted definition of enterprise and enterprise-related activity is required.

As a result of these and related activities, our performance against sector-wide metrics has seen increases over the last three years, including the Destinations of Leavers from Higher Education (DLHE), within which the university's success rate has, over recent years, increased (+2.5 per cent) more than the sector (+1.9 per cent) and our competitor institutions (+2.2 per cent).[19] The recently published Longitudinal Educational Outcomes data considers the percentages in employment and/or further study one, three and five years after graduation for the 2012/2013, 2010/2011, 2008/2009, 2003/2004 cohorts.[20] This puts the university ahead of the sector in terms of graduates in the 'Sustained Employment' and 'Sustained employment with or without further study' categories in 2013/2014. (The last year for which benchmarking data is available.) In parallel, in the UK-wide National Student Survey, students have consistently rated the university in the top quartile for responses to the questions on personal development (for example "the course has helped me to present myself with confidence"; "my communication skills have improved"; and "as a result of the course, I feel confident in tackling unfamiliar problems").[21] These measures supplement the more specific metrics of graduate start-ups, within which the University of Bedfordshire has in the last nine years, generated an estimated £22m pounds worth of impact,[22] the vast majority within the SEMLEP region. And yet only a small percentage of the university's £3.9 million HEIF money received over the last ten years has gone directly to support this form of KE. If we consider this impact purely in terms of regional GVA then this would provide a financial benefit at a ratio of around £1:7. Analysis of the full impact of universities' contribution to innovation and economic growth identifies the vital role of universities in supplying graduates at various levels, able to contribute to both disruptive and incremental innovation (Dowling, 2015). In relation to the creative economy in particular, the interaction between knowledge exchange activities is recognised:

> If there is one feature that all creative clusters share, it is their reliance on creative talent often highly skilled and supplied by universities. Research at universities also creates a knowledge base that R&D-intensive creative businesses in particular draw on. Universities also undertake knowledge exchange activities which transform this knowledge into impact, through entrepreneurship, training and dissemination activities. For all of these reasons, universities are widely acknowledged as central players in the local ecosystems that drive the success of creative clusters.
>
> (Mateos-Garcia and Bakshi, 2016: 24)

More broadly, the importance of a shared experiential understanding of innovation and its implementation context is specified as an important benefit of university–business collaboration (Hughes and Kitson, 2013: 57), and the value to a region of attracting and retaining graduate skills is identified as part of the absorptive capacity on which a region's economy depends for sustainable economic advantage (Mahroum *et al.*, 2008). Yet this full economic benefit, important to a region and aligned to the university's overall corporate mission, does not count in terms of enhancing the funding allocation derived from the current formula (HEFCE, 2016), which continues to separate the activities of education and enterprise, in ways neither universities nor their many regional partners would recognise as valid or useful.

Conclusions

This chapter has sought to show the role HEIs play within national and regional economies. This includes leveraging research income through project funding and through core grants as part of the UK's national system of innovation, and embedding enterprise education within knowledge exchange. We have also seen a summary of one business region, the South East Midlands, how the regions businesses interact with universities, and an example of one modern university's KE and the often non-explicit positive impact that it has.

The dynamics of this research–enterprise interaction are multidirectional. In some cases, research is specifically local in application, as for example consultancy work, commissioned from the tourism research team at the University of Bedfordshire, contributed to the tourism development strategy in the Bedford–Milton Keynes area. Similarly, the formation of the Refugee Legal Aid Project at the University of Bedfordshire, a pro-bono legal clinic which supports refugees with their family reunion applications, is based on high-quality empirical research conducted to enhance the ability of refugee charities to provide legal support to refugees in the field of family reunion. Conversely the presence of leading research teams in a region stimulates the diffusion of research-informed innovation within that region, as, for example, the Luton-based Older People's Diabetes Network in England has stimulated regional activity in multiple areas such as care home educational strategies, hypoglycemia avoidance, enhanced medication reviews in the community, and audits of diabetes care, most with a view to better care aligned to reduced overall costs.

A third research–enterprise dynamic occurs where support for systemic national innovation or policy is based on regional research and trial. For example, NHS Luton was used as a pilot site for the 111 service by the Department of Health on the basis of the university's research in the use of telephone-based services in diverse population settings. And as we have seen, university research initially conducted locally has made significant impact upon government policy and practice in relation to public engagement and professional training in the field of organ donation (Randhawa, 2011), informing national campaigns by targeting different regional communities and providing relevant staff training leading to an increase in organ donor registrations from diverse communities.

The regional impact of a modern university's research extends beyond direct use in industry to the support for an inclusive and supportive environment on which enterprise and economic prosperity depends. Likewise, the innovative value of a university's research includes both immediately commercial applications and the development of a broadly spread capacity that applies across the economy, including public services and graduate start-ups, and enterprise education more broadly. This value is often not recognised by the metrics of national systems of innovation or KE funding nor indeed, enterprise educators who typically may focus on product or service creation and sales without drawing upon the rich KE interaction that a modern university engages with. Similarly, the benefit that enterprise educators can bring to the regions workforce by better supporting graduates to apply KE best practice, not just in terms of applying their particular degree knowledge but also their entrepreneurial zeal and enthusiasm within organisations they join needs to be better understood, and universities incentivised to support this. Supported, task specific and training-led placement schemes can help break down a traditional view of the placement student somehow being a burden to the organisations and demonstrate the benefits to innovation and enterprise that 'opening a pipeline' back to a large regionally focused knowledge base can bring. A challenge for enterprise educators is to better understand the true value of exchange, learn from it and construct better methods and frameworks of support.

The benefits to national and regional economies from university research and enterprise would be enhanced further if the focus was placed on establishing best practice for enterprise educators between true comparator universities in terms of their research and KE base and regional business profile and context in which they operate. For enterprising universities that understand the importance of developing enterprise skills for a regional workforce and accept that part of its direct role is to support organisations to grow and keep competitive, the challenge within this agenda is to develop and retain staff with the skills to develop new opportunities, apply knowledge and adjust to fast-paced change within the regional context in which the organisations are based. Better joined-up support of a university's enterprise educators and practitioners will also help build the absorptive capacity of organisations who may otherwise be unable to exploit advanced levels of research and knowledge exchange (Brown, 2016).

Funders and policy makers behind national and regional systems of innovation would do well to consider how better to reward enterprise skills activities that are co-designed with employers such as tailored CPD and elements of undergraduate and postgraduate provision, activity that the short case study of the University of Bedfordshire shows can have very tangible and positive benefits. Such bespoke provision is high-impact but can be resource-intensive and should recognised separately through the HEBCIS survey, in recognition of their contribution to regional enterprise and innovation (Taylor, 2016). More broadly, the development of graduates with the full range of skills required for them and for the UK economy to thrive in the future relies on the consistent engagement of academics with organisations in that economy, to support an educational experience, including enterprise education, that is a relevant reflection of business practice and its skills demand. With that critical and continuing contribution recognised (NCUB, 2017), both the economic contribution of universities to the economy through their development of graduate knowledge and skills, and the external engagement required to achieve that development, should be recognised in the measurement and support of this achievement.

KE activity complements research impact and can achieve much more than purely research commercialisation alone. Enterprise education must better inform potential innovators, through a wider discussion of impact, and this would clearly benefit from dedicated national and regional funds that recognise and incentivise the important role this can play on economic development. The current metrics that contribute to the evaluation of eligibility for core grant funding can be said to favour certain types of knowledge exchange and ignore others, which may hinder the governmental agenda of supporting the two-way exchange between HEIs and businesses as a regional economic driver. Innovation and knowledge exchange are broad and rich concepts too valuable to be constrained by the exigencies of funding-based definitions. Ensuring that educators work more closely with university enterprise and research practitioners would usefully extend the notion of 'enterprise' to encompass not only the traditional metrics of IP, licences, university owned spin-outs and so on, but also graduate start-ups and non-monetised knowledge exchange, and the full range of productive and impactful research-based innovation generated in UK universities.

Notes

1 https://catapult.org.uk/.
2 http://smartspecialisationhub.org/.
3 www.gov.uk/government/publications/science-and-innovation-audits-first-wave-reports.
4 www.hesa.ac.uk/data-and-analysis/performance-indicators.
5 www.unialliance.ac.uk/topics/leaders-in-cities-regions/.

6 www.sfc.ac.uk/funding/universities/Innovation/UniversityInnovationFund.aspx.
7 www.hefce.ac.uk/kess/heif/.
8 www.hefce.ac.uk/finance/fundinghe/grant/.
9 http://dera.ioe.ac.uk/27128/1/HEFCE2016_16_.pdf.
10 www.hefce.ac.uk/finance/fundinghe/grant/.
11 www.hefce.ac.uk/pubs/year/2017/CL,062017/.
12 www.hefce.ac.uk/pubs/year/2016/201616/.
13 www.ref.ac.uk.
14 www.rcuk.ac.uk/innovation/impacts/.
15 www.hesa.ac.uk/data-and-analysis/providers.
16 http://b-innovative.org/Partners/partners.html.
17 https://breo.beds.ac.uk/bbcswebdav/institution/CRe8content/CRe8overview.pdf.
18 www.beds.ac.uk/student-experience/community-at-bedfordshire/student-experience/steps.
19 www.hesa.ac.uk/news/30-06-2016/sfr237-destinations-of-leavers.
20 www.hesa.ac.uk/news/27-08-2015-graduates-in-work-or-study.
21 www.hefce.ac.uk/lt/nss/results/2016/.
22 www.hefce.ac.uk/kess/hebci/.

References

Anyachebelu, T.K., Conrad, M. and Ajmal, T. (2014), Surface water quality prediction system for Luton Hoo lake: A statistical approach. *Proc. INTECH, August 12–14 2014*.

Atlay, M., Gaitan, A. and Kumar, A. (2008). Stimulating learning – Creating CRe8. Chapter 13 In: C. Nygaard and C. Holtham, eds. *Understanding learning-centred higher education*. Copenhagen: Business School Press.

BMG Research (2015). *SEMLEP 2015 Business Survey*. Birmingham, UK: Rostock Marketing Group Ltd.

Brockway, B. (2015). *Leicester & Leicestershire Business Survey 2015*. Leicester and Leicestershire Enterprise Partnership. Available at: www.llep.org.uk/wp-content/uploads/2017/03/LLEP-Business-Survey-2015.pdf [accessed 28 May 2017).

Brown, R. (2016). Mission impossible? Entrepreneurial universities and peripheral regional innovation systems. *Industry and Innovation*, 23(2), 189–205.

Carberry, N. and Driscoll, M. (2015). Best of both worlds: Guide to business-university collaboration, CBI. Available at: www.cbi.org.uk/index.cfm/_api/render/file/?method=inline&fileID=2BCF67FC-3F8B-4262-88431CFD7E541BA0 [accessed 29 May 2017].

CBI (2016). *Innovation Survey 2016*. Available at: www.cbi.org.uk/cbi-prod/assets/File/CBI%20Innovation%20Survey%202016_%20results.pdf [accessed 28 May 2017].

Daniel, K., Sharpe, A., Driver, J., Knight, A.W., Keenan, P.O., Walmsley R.M., Robinson, A., Zhang, T. and Rawson, D. (2004). Results of a technology demonstration project to compare rapid aquatic toxicity screening tests in the analysis of industrial effluents. *Journal of Environmental Monitoring*, 11, 855–865.

Department for Business Innovation and Skills (2016a). *Success as a knowledge economy: Teaching excellence, social mobility and student choice*. London: Her Majesty's Stationery Office. Available at: www.gov.uk/government/uploads/system/uploads/attachment_data/file/523546/bis-16-265-success-as-a-knowledge-economy-web.pdf [accessed 28 May 2017].

Department for Business Innovation and Skills (2016b). *Headline findings from the UK Innovation Survey 2015*. London: Department for Business, Innovation and Skills. Available at: www.gov.uk/government/uploads/system/uploads/attachment_data/file/506953/bis-16-134-uk-innovation-survey-2015.pdf [accessed 28 May 2017].

Department for Business Innovation and Skills (2016c). *Case for the creation of UK research and innovation.* Available at: www.gov.uk/government/uploads/system/uploads/attachment_data/file/527803/bis-16-291-ukri-case-for-creation.pdf [accessed 28 May 2017].

Department for Education (2017). *Apprenticeship reform programme: Benefits realisation strategy.* London: Department for Education. Available at: www.gov.uk/government/publications/apprenticeship-reform-programme-benefits-realisation-strategy [accessed 28 May 2017].

Dowling, A. (2015). *The Dowling review of business-university research collaborations.* Available at: www.raeng.org.uk/policy/dowling-review/the-dowling-review-of-business-university-research [accessed 29 May 2017].

Duan, Y., Mullins, R., Hamblin, D., Stanek, S., Sroka, H., Machado, V. and Araujo, J. (2002). Addressing ICTs skill challenges in SMEs: Insights from three country investigations. *Journal of European Industrial Training*, 9, 430–441.

Elsevier (2013). *International comparative performance of the UK research base – 2013: A report prepared by Elsevier for the UK's Department for Business, Innovation and Skills (BIS).* Elsevier BV. Available at: www.gov.uk/government/uploads/system/uploads/attachment_data/file/263729/bis-13-1297-international-comparative-performance-of-the-UK-research-base-2013.pdf [accessed 28 May 2017].

Enterprise Research Centre (2014). *LEP growth dashboard.* Available at: www.enterpriseresearch.ac.uk/wp-content/uploads/2014/06/ERC-Conference-LEP-Growth-Dashboard-final.pdf) [accessed 28 May 2017].

Everett, S. and Slocum, S. (2013). Food and tourism: An effective partnership? A UK based review. *Journal of Sustainable Tourism*, 21(6), 789–809.

HEFCE (2016). *Higher education – Business and community interaction survey 2014–15.* Available at: www.hefce.ac.uk/media/HEFCE,2014/Content/Pubs/2016/201619/HEFCE 2016_19.pdf [accessed 29 May 2017].

HEFCE (2017). *Guide to funding: How HEFCE allocates its funds.* www.hefce.ac.uk/media/HEFCE,2014/Content/Pubs/2017/201704/HEFCE_Funding_Guide_2017-18_.pdf [accessed 29 May 2017].

HM Government (2015). *English apprenticeships: Our 2020 vision.* Available at: www.gov.uk/government/uploads/system/uploads/attachment_data/file/482754/BIS-15-604-english-apprenticeships-our-2020-vision.pdf [accessed 28 May 2017].

Holmes, L. (2013). Competing perspectives on graduate employability: Possession, position or process? *Studies in Higher Education*, 38(4), 538–554.

House of Commons (2016). T*he Government's Productivity Plan: Second Report of Session 2015–16.* London: The Stationery Office Ltd.

Hughes, A. and Kitson, M. (2013). *Connecting with the ivory tower: Business perspectives on knowledge exchange in the UK.* Cambridge. Available at: Available at: www.ncub.co.uk/index.php?option=com_docman&view=download&category_slug=publications&alias=68-connecting-with-the-ivory-tower&Itemid=2728 [accessed 28 May 2017].

IFF Research (2016). *UKCES employer skills survey 2015: UK report.* London: UK Commission for Employment and Skills.

Kaplan (2014). *Graduate recruitment report: Employer perspectives.* Available at: https://kaplan.co.uk/docs/default-source/pdfs/graduate_recruitment_report83B89056472C.pdf?sfvrsn=4 [accessed 28 May 2017)]

Kelly, U. (2016). *Economic impact on the UK of EU research funding.* London: Universities UK.

Kelly, U., McNicoll, I. and White, J. (2014). *The impact of universities on the UK economy.* London: Universities UK.

Mahroum, S., Huggins, R., Clayton, N., Pain, K. and Taylor, P. (2008). *Innovation by adoption measuring and mapping absorptive capacity in UK nations and regions.* UK: Nesta. Available at: www.nesta.org.uk/sites/default/files/innovation_by_adoption.pdf [accessed 28 May 2017].

Mateos-Garcia, J. and Bakhshi, H. (2016). *The geography of creativity in the UK: Creative clusters, creative people and creative networks,* UK: Nesta. Available at: www.nesta.org.uk/sites/default/files/the_geography_of_creativity_in_the_uk.pdf [accessed 28 May 2017].

McMillan Group (2016). *University knowledge exchange (KE) framework: Good practice in technology transfer.* UK: HEFCE.

NCUB (2016). *Fuelling the knowledge economy 1.* London: National Centre for Universities and Business.

NCUB (2017). *State of the relationship report 2017.* London: National Centre for Universities and Business.

QAA (2012). *Enterprise and entrepreneurship education: Guidance for UK higher education providers.* UK: The Quality Assurance Agency for Higher Education.

Randhawa, G. (2011). *Achieving equality in organ donation and transplantation in the UK: Challenges and solutions.* London: Race Equality Foundation.

Rhodes, C. (2016). *Business statistics* (House of Commons briefing paper number 06152, 23 November 2016). Available at: http://researchbriefings.parliament.uk/ResearchBriefing/Summary/SN06152 [accessed 28 May 2017].

Rich, J. (2015). *Employability: Degrees of value.* HEPI Occasional Paper 12, Oxford: Higher Education Policy Institute.

Russell Group (2016). *Putting Universities at the Heart of the Industrial Strategy.* Russell Group. Available at: https://ww.russellgroup.ac.uk/media/5450/putting-universities-at-the-heart-of-the-industrial-strategy-october-2016.pdf [accessed 28 May 2017].

SEMLEP (2015*). Business support mapping: Simplifying the local business support landscape, interim report to Department for Business, Innovation and Skills.* Available at: www.google.co.uk/search?client=safari&rls=en&q=Report+on+Business+Support+Offer+for+Start+Up+Businesses+in+South+East+Midlands,+SEMLEP+2015&ie=UTF-8&oe=UTF-8&gfe_rd=cr&ei=h7UNWdPFGu_GXqHnpqgF [accessed 28 May 2017]

Taylor, F. (2016). *Creating innovative regions: The role of universities in local growth and productivity.* London, UK: University Alliance.

Ulrichsen, T.C. (2015). *Assessing the economic impacts of the Higher Education Innovation Fund: A mixed-method quantitative assessment.* Available at: www.hefce.ac.uk/media/HEFCE,2014/Content/Pubs/Independentresearch/2015/Evaluations,of,HEFCE,funding,for,knowledge,exchange,the,Higher,Education,Innovation,Fund/2015_heifeval1.pdf [accessed 28 May 2017].

University Alliance (2011). *Growing the future: Universities leading, changing and creating the regional economy.* Available at: www.unialliance.ac.uk/wp-content/uploads/2011/09/UA_GROWING_THE_FUTURE_WEBVM.pdf [accessed 29 May 2017].

Wavehill (2016). *West of England Local Enterprise Partnership Skills Survey 2016.* West of England Local Enterprise Partnership. Available at: www.wavehill.com/single-post/2016/11/23/West-of-England-Local-Enterprise-Partnership-Employer-Skills-Survey [accessed 28 May 2017].

Wilson, T. (2012). *A review of business–university collaboration.* UK: Department for Business, Innovation and Skills. Available at: www.gov.uk/government/uploads/

system/uploads/attachment_data/file/32383/12-610-wilson-review-business-university-collaboration.pdf [accessed 28 May 2017].

Young, D. (2014). *Enterprise for all: The relevance of enterprise in education.* Available at: www.gov.uk/government/uploads/system/uploads/attachment_data/file/338749/EnterpriseforAll-lowres-200614.pdf [accessed 28 May 2016].

Zhang, J., De la Roche, A., Valance, A., Lopez, D., Liu, E. and Song H. (2010). *Femtocells – technologies and deployment.* UK: Wiley.

11 The changing nature of the graduate employment market

The fourth industrial revolution

Charles Beraza

Introduction

In 2015, Klaus Schwab the founder and executive chair of the World Economic Forum discussed the concept of the fourth Industrial Revolution, (Anon, 2016, 2017a; Schwab, 2016; Von Hooijdonk, 2017). The concept, sometimes referred to as industry 4.0, refers to increased connectivity and where more communication, analysis and decisions can be taken by smart machines (Marr, 2016; Rosinski, 2017), which collectively will significantly impact on business and the employment market for years to come. According to Schwab (2016: 28), the impact of the fourth industrial revolution will be "so vast and multifaceted that it makes it hard to disentangle one particular effect from the next". The importance of emerging technologies on work and the workplace and its impact on employment has much discussed since the early 2000s, but is still relatively under-researched, with no clear direction with regards to its potential impact.

> Techno-pessimists argue that the critical contributions of the digital revolution have already been made and that their impact on productivity is almost over. In the opposite camp, techno-optimists claim that technology and innovation are at an inflection point.
>
> (Schwab, 2016: 28)

Similarly, opinion is divided on how the fourth industrial revolution will change the jobs' market: "half of these experts (48 per cent) envision a future in which robots and digital agents have displaced significant numbers of both blue- and white-collar workers" while "The other half of the experts who responded to this survey (52 per cent) expect that technology will not displace more jobs than it creates by 2025" (Smith and Anderson, 2014: 5). Such discussion about tasks, reskilling and the impact of computerisation and automation would appear, at least on a superficial level, to demonstrate that economists, policy makers and businesses do not fully understand the implications of the fourth industrial revolution and how business should prepare themselves in order to stay efficient (Arntz, Gregory and Zierahn, 2016).

Although it is not yet clear what impact the fourth industrial revolution will have on the employment market, one thing we can state for certain is that it will have an impact. Similar to previous industrial revolutions, the fourth industrial revolution will create employment opportunities and skills shortages in some fields and unemployment in others (Mesnard, 2016), following the concept of 'creative destruction' developed by Schumpeter (1942). A more pessimistic view is that the fourth industrial revolution may cause mass unemployment, which would require government intervention and perhaps the introduction of a universal basic income (Cheshire, 2017). The advent of mass unemployment could further widen the current inequalities gap between highly educated and skilled workers and low educated and low skilled workers (Marr, 2016; Schwab, 2016; Vincent, 2017). To ensure the fourth industrial revolution produces less pessimistic outcomes, governments, businesses and educational establishments have to ensure that the inevitable increased application of technology is able to provide more benefits for the many and not just the few (Brynjolfsson and McAfee, 2014; Gill, 2006).

The purpose of this chapter is to shift the various interpretations of the impact of the fourth industrial revolution from a macroeconomic level to an educational and employment level, understanding that the fourth industrial revolution is going to affect all job roles, professional as well as low skilled (Susskind and Susskind, 2015), which should prove useful to academics as well as practitioners. The chapter will move the conversation beyond a superficial discussion of the general trend that the proportion of tasks related to physical and repeated work is likely to decrease (Levy, 2010), towards a more evaluative discussion on the impact of the fourth industrial revolution on the employment market facing future graduates.

The economic history of the industrial revolutions

The first industrial revolution

Four industrial revolutions categorise the last two centuries (1900s and 2000s), each of them changing the way society and the economy works and presenting new business opportunities and challenges. "Revolutions have occurred throughout history when new technologies and novel ways of perceiving the world trigger a profound change in economic systems and social structures." (Schwab, 2016: 6). This chapter does not aim to provide a detailed historical analysis; rather identify patterns and opinion that happened in the past to help us understand the future.

The first industrial revolution began in the late 1700s and ran until the 1800s, marking the transition from an economy based on food sustainability to a more monetary one (Anon, 2017b). The revolution included innovations such as the steam engine and the train, and is considered the beginning of modern industry realised initially through the development of the textile industry (Greenwood, 1999; Morgan, 2016; Van Hooijdonk, 2017). The social, economic and political consequences were significant with a large-scale reallocation of skills reflected in the employment exodus from farms to factories (Harari, 2015). During this time, one of the first known movements of resistance against the role of technology and its replacing of people took place by the *Luddites*, a group of specialised textile workers located in the north of England (Jensen, 1993; Randall, 2003; Sale, 1996). During 1811 and 1812, they attacked newly installed weaving machines, fearing the impact they would have on their jobs (Connif, 2011; Harari, 2015; Jensen, 1993; Sale, 1996). Similar situations happened in France during the 1789 revolution, and it is known that Queen Elizabeth I in Great Britain refused to grant a patent for a machine, fearing for the country's stability (Connif, 2011). The term 'luddite' now defines the fear for jobs induced by the advent of technology and might again be realised with the increasing use of technology in business and the onset of the fourth industrial revolution.

The second industrial revolution

The second industrial revolution refers to the development of mass production at the end of the 1800s and beginning of the 1900s and was accompanied by growing mass consumption (Anon, 2017b; Fujimori *et al.*, 2016; Morgan, 2016; Van Hooijdonk, 2017). This second industrial revolution put into perspective the gap between technology development and public adoption (Fujimori *et al.*, 2016) and led to massive unemployment as a result of the rural exodus (Harari, 2015). This unemployment was partially addressed by the government's launch of a reskilling initiative, which allowed people access to knowledge in order to achieve higher value to and in the economy (Fujimori *et al.*, 2016). It was in this period that knowledge became increasingly important to an individual's employability skills set.

The third industrial revolution

In contrast to the two previous industrial revolutions, the third industrial revolution in the mid-1900s was a less radical transition, and saw the introduction of computers, automation and ecological consciousness in the economy (Anon, 2017b; Elliott, 2017; Morgan, 2016; Van Hooijdonk, 2017). While the exact definition of the third industrial revolution varies (for example Rifkin (2011), defines the third industrial revolution in the context of the green economy, while Schwab (2016) considers it to be the first wave of digitalisation, with the advent of the computer and the internet), there is agreement over what the revolution produced. The third industrial revolution produced, as the others did, the reallocation of tasks and a disruption to the jobs market (Osterman, 1986), reducing the number of individuals doing, for example, administrative tasks replaced to a lesser or greater degree by technology such as Microsoft Office and subsequently by artificial intelligence (AI) (Vincent, 2017). This period signalled the importance of technology based labour to business (Ben-Ami, 2015) and the need for individuals to consider their respective levels of technological and interdisciplinary knowledge to remain competitive in the jobs market.

The fourth industrial revolution

The fourth industrial revolution refers to the present and future development of usable technologies, which will probably transform the way individuals live and work (Anon, 2017b; Elliott, 2017; Morgan, 2016; Robertson, 2000; Van Hooijdonk, 2017) but it is arguably not being embraced consistently across the globe. In some sub-Saharan countries the second industrial revolution has yet to be encountered (Harari, 2015) with people in the region of the great lake near Zambia using a steamboat to travel to certain locations (Harari, 2015). Yet at the same time some African businesses are attempting to disrupt the market by skipping the first and second industrial revolutions and to a degree, the third industrial revolution and jumping straight into the fourth industrial revolution because of the perceived economic benefits, specifically labour substitution and improved productivity (Anon, 2017c; Manyika *et al.*, 2017).

In comparison to previous revolutions, the fourth industrial revolution is evolving at an exponential pace (Elliott, 2017) and has changed the way business and individuals view the consumption of products and services, with Uber, Airbnb and Spotify examples of how technology can be used to create new value and disrupt previously accepted business models (knowledge@wharton, 2016). However, the future direction of the fourth industrial revolution is yet unknown, with legal issues surrounding hail riding services and the rules governing data protection and online privacy not yet comprehensive enough to reassure consumers on issues such as online bullying, data and identity theft and reputational damage (Brown, 2017; Dhillon, 2016; Karniel and Lavie-Dinur, 2012; Ninomiya, 2016; Steeves and Regan, 2014). This uncertainty has implications for the workplace environment (Saurin, Ratcliffe and Puybaraud, 2008) and the employment market (Morgan, 2016), which raises questions for business, future graduates, educational establishments and around the gap between education and employment. Will some sectors and governments seek to reduce the impact of technologies and not encourage its adoption in order to save jobs or perhaps even forbid a technology like China did with Facebook and WhatsApp because of the potential negative impact on society?

If we are to examine the different technologies which represent the fourth industrial revolution and their outcomes for both business and society (Schwab, 2016), we can see the technologies are particularly wide ranging and illustrate the potential both individually and collectively to impact on the future careers of graduates and the skills required to compete in the marketplace (OECD, 2016). These technologies include but are not an exhaustive list: implantable technologies, virtual reality, storage for all, the internet of and for things, the connected home, smart cities, big data for decision making, driverless vehicles, AI, robotics, bitcoin and the blockchain, the sharing economy, 3D printing and nanotechnologies (Anon, 2017b; Elliott, 2017; Morgan, 2016; Schwab, 2016; Van Hooijdonk, 2017).

AI arguably could be considered as having the most significant impact on society in general and the employment market specifically (Anon, 2017a;

Rosinski, 2017). The development of machine learning, which can replicate and imitate human behaviour to improve processes and efficiency, coupled with access to 'big data', has the ability to unlock the potential of AI development (Fujimori *et al.*, 2016). According to Fujimori *et al.*, (2016: 25) "machine[s] will be able to do pretty much anything that humans can do, and they would be better at doing that". This statement gives rise to discussion surrounding the position of a human in the economy of the future (Harari, 2015), particularly in light of the rise in automation and the increased use and usefulness of robots in business (Bostrom, 2014; Mesnard, 2016; Williams-Grut, 2016).

Automation of the economy

The O*NET list (National Center for O*NET Development for USDOL, 2017) is arguably one of the most comprehensive sets of employment related data next to the International Labour Office (International Labour Office, 2012; Slane, 2013), and is based on 702 occupations, separated in terms of non-routine and routine jobs, manual vs cognitive tasks (Handel, 2016; National Center for O*NET Development for USDOL, 2017; Slane, 2013). With the help of Oxford University's Engineering Sciences Department, the O*NET labelled each occupation as binary, either computerisable or not computerisable (Kingdollar, 2017; National Center for O*NET Development for USDOL, 2017). In other words, if a low level of skill is required, there is a higher likelihood of computerisation for the task and vice versa. The O*Net considered three 'computerisation bottlenecks' i.e. three areas where computerisation had less capacity to replace humans, which are 'perception and manipulation', 'creative intelligence' and 'social intelligence' (National Center for O*NET Development for USDOL, 2017). The initial findings confirm the results of previous studies (Anon, 2016; Anon, 2017a), that certain sectors are more vulnerable to automation than others, for example office and administrative support is more likely to be automated than education, management or healthcare, which has clear implications for graduates seeking employment in specific sectors (Fleisher and Tsacoumis, 2012; National Center for O*NET Development for USDOL, 2017; Slane, 2013; Vincent, 2017).

Bostrom (2014) also argues that by 2040 there is a 50 per cent chance that 'ultimate automation' will occur. The economic benefits of automation to business are clear: first, it permits the substitution of labour, second, it enhances performance through technology with more efficient robots (Manyika *et al.*, 2017). The five cases of automation described in Table 11.1 illustrate the potential labour substitution, performance and economic gain across sectors, which highlight implications for the labour market and graduates entering that particular labour market.

Low-skilled employees at least on a superficial level could be seen to be the group most vulnerable to automation and AI in particular, in fact, some of those individuals in the fast food sector, who provide customer service, and who are personal assistants have already experienced competition coming from technological applications like chatbots (Olson, 2016; Rosinski, 2017). Truck drivers too appear to be another group vulnerable to automation because of developments in intelligent

Table 11.1 Estimation of automation for five cases

Case	Total estimated economic gain (%)	Share of labour substitution (%)	Share of performance gain (%)
Hospital emergency department	11	70	30
Aircraft maintenance	25	66	34
Oil and gas operations	17	15	85
Grocery store	14	32	68
Mortgage application processing	–	88	12

Source: Manyika *et al.*, 2017.

and self-driving technologies (Barra, 2016; Hallett and Hutt, 2016; Kingdollar, 2017; Peterson, 2016). What these jobs have in common is the relative simplicity of the task, not necessarily the job, which is relatively easy to replicate and imitate (National Center for O*NET Development for USDOL, 2017). If the technology can be integrated into the employment role and represents a cheaper option than a staff member(s) for the business then increased automation is likely to continue, but we are some distance from this scenario (Olson, 2016). It is argued that at least in the immediate future human intervention will be required with the increased use of chatbots helping employees as much as dealing with customers (Olson, 2016).

We must also remember that the integration of technology into the employment market and the displacement of jobs is a delicate matter both in economic and political terms. If we are to recall the luddites of the 1800s, the potential of social tensions could increase (Schwab, 2016) not to mention the impact increased unemployment could have on the economy. If we were to take the three million truck drivers in the USA for example, if, through the advent of self-drive technology, those individuals were to become unemployed (Kingdollar, 2017; Petersen, 2016), their ability to contribute to the economy would be reduced. Could a government presiding over rising levels of unemployment and increased social discontent survive a term in office? What would be the social, economic and political implications if employees from a whole business sector were lost to technology? A possible solution or suggestion is on trial in Finland and soon to be piloted in Great Britain, that of universal basic income (UBI), where individuals regardless of whether they are in employment or not will receive a monthly stipend (Cheshire, 2017). The payment of this stipend and the possible scrapping of the welfare state in Finland may encourage entrepreneurial activity and creativity (Cheshire, 2017), exactly the sort of creative intelligence demanded in the fourth industrial revolution, and which is not easily replicated by computerisation and automation. The outcome of the UBI, like that of the fourth industrial revolution, is unknown but at least it does seem to be encouraging creative thinking on the part of some governments in how to deal with employment in the future.

Returning to Table 11.1 and the case of aircraft maintenance, as an illustration of how rather than replication we can have harmonisation with technology and humans able to co-exist through what is called 'predictive maintenance' (Staller, 2017). Predictive maintenance is a means of enhancing efficiency using highly skilled technicians and engineers, data and intelligent machines (Bloem *et al.*, 2014). Using automated survey drones, and maintenance robots not only reduces the overall cost to a business, it can empower the workforce (Bloem *et al.*, 2014; Manyika *et al.*, 2017) allowing them the time and space to do the added value tasks. In other words, although it is not yet clear how predictive maintenance and automation will impact the employment market (Scheffer and Girdhar, 2004), one can interpret that the increased integration of new technologies into business does not necessarily mean a reduction in employment, although there has been technological unemployment (Akst, 2013; MacCarthy, 2014; Peters, 2017), rather a displacement of the workforce which has clear implications for the future graduate.

Embracing not rejecting automation

Hospital emergency departments are an example of a business where a large workforce is performing numerous tasks of varying complexity (Manyika *et al.*, 2017). As illustrated in Table 11.1, there is high potential for labour substitution in this sector but this does not mean that a hospital will have no employees, rather, and similar to other industries, certain tasks will be performed by technology due to efficiency (Mesnard, 2016). Whether it is the application of big data, virtual reality, the use of robots or AI, technology will co-exist with humans in order to meet the increasing demands on the service. The application of course has to be appropriate, it goes without saying that robots are not (in the near future) going to operate on patients without any human supervision or input, but the usage of robots and other technology will certainly continue to expand (Graetz and Michaels, 2015; Pemberton Levy, 2015). An example of this can be observed in the task of patient diagnosis with IBM's artificial intelligence 'Watson' now able to produce diagnosis from medical imagery, with 99 per cent of diagnosis the same as those recommended by oncologists (Lohr, 2016). Given medical practitioners are becoming increasingly overwhelmed with their current workload (Byington, 2016); technology could allow doctors more time with their patients. However, it is argued that medical practitioners spend most of their time with paperwork and not necessarily diagnosing patients (Lee, 2016), and therefore 'Watson' might not assist them with paperwork but automation might. Automation will change the skill requirements of individuals, requiring them to be more flexible and adaptable (Mesnard, 2016) with medical practitioners of the future arguably becoming the intermediary between patient and automated technology (Vallancien, 2017).

Potential and current employees need to take responsibility for their employment future as they did in previous industrial revolutions, and reskill themselves in order to stay relevant to the economy (Vincent, 2017). They should take

advantage of government-led opportunities, such as the new employer apprenticeship in Great Britain for example or business-led opportunities illustrated by
Fujitsu in Ireland. In 2012, and in response to the threat of new technology and
the loss of an important contract, Fujitsu, Ireland implemented a competitive
strategy based on the development of new skills, specifically the recycling of
telecom hardware (Pollitt, 2012). This strategy not only managed to save jobs, it
also brought new business to the company, creating a new value proposition for
their customers and underlined the fact that humans can adapt to change if they
choose to do so. Change however requires a unified effort between identified
stakeholders and the willingness to retrain and reskill:

> retraining and skill-raising programmes will be important to support workers
> shifting to new roles and taking on new activities. It will also be critical for
> corporate leaders to ensure that the organisational elements of their com-
> panies are adapting to the advent of automation.
>
> (Manyika *et al.*, 2017: 17)

Reskilling for future employment

The increased use of automation is argued to be founded on financial reasoning
but also because of its potential benefits to society as a whole. It has been estimated that the implementation of industrial robots raised the annual growth of a
country's GDP by 0.37 points and labour productivity by 0.36 points (Graetz
and Michaels, 2015). Other research has found that the integration of robots into
the workforce increased overall employment by 0.18–0.34 points and wages by
0.25–0.5 per cent (Acemoglu and Restrepo, 2017ab). The work of Autor (2015)
gives an explanation about the economic patterns of automation, illustrating how
banks adapted to the third industrial revolution by reducing the number of
employees required to conduct low-level branch operations, and through technology created new value added employment positions and increased the availability of banks to consumers through 24-hour banking services. Freed from
doing low skilled activities, bank employees were able to engage in value added
activities, which command higher wages because of the associated level of skill
(Autor, 2015). Such activities involved customer sales and negotiation, with staff
delivering an increased portfolio of services as banks became more commercial.
In other words, jobs are more likely to evolve than be totally automated, with the
job market arguably moving towards being based on task and not skill (Autor,
2013, 2014), where "a task is a unit of work activity that produces output, [and]
a skill is a worker's stock of capabilities" (Autor, 2013: 5). By approaching automation in this way, we can see a clear demarcation of jobs, which assists educational establishments and graduates better prepare for the employment market.
Routine tasks which can be computerised will be performed through automation,
and more complex, non-routine tasks which are new and not possible to computerise will be performed by humans (Acemoglu and Autor, 2011; Acemoglu and
Restrepo, 2017a; Autor, 2013).

Shifting the positions-based approach used by Frey and Osborne (2013) to a task-based exercise has several practical reasons; the most obvious one is also shared by Autor (2013) in his model of task comprehension, arguing that the task is the real unit of labour rather than the skill. To illustrate the point, let us look at accountants, the probability of accountant positions being computerised is 94 per cent, which is consistent with the repetitive nature of numbers processing (Frey and Osborne, 2013). However, the reality is arguably different, accountants need social and cognitive skills to obtain the numbers and share the results with clients (Frey and Osborne, 2013; Kahn, 2017). In some cases, accountants have to engage in a wide range of tasks involving judgment, it is not simply a job of numbers processing and therefore not easily computerised (Frey and Osborne, 2013). That, however, did not stop Walmart replacing 7000 accounting and bookkeeping positions with automated cash management in 2016 (Kingdollar, 2017). Similarly on a superficial level, cooks could be said to be a vulnerable to computerisation with 75 per cent of the tasks they perform automatable (Manyika *et al.*, 2017). However, it should be noted that they are not likely to be replaced by robots for two reasons: first because many cooks engage in a range of judgement related tasks, which are not easily computerised. Second, many cooks are relatively cheap human capital, removing the incentive for a business to invest in new technologies to replace them (Chui, Manyika and Miremadi, 2016; Frey and Osborne, 2013; Manyika *et al.*, 2017). In research conducted by Manyika *et al.*, (2017) based on more than 2000 activities across 46 countries, it was estimated that there are capabilities required in order to perform specific tasks, based on the premise 'basic to execute' to 'high human', see Table 11.2, (Manyika *et al.*, 2017).

While being similar to the research of others such as Autor (2013, 2014, 2015) and Frey and Osborne (2013), the work of Manyika *et al.*, (2017) shows three useful characteristics. First, the research makes a distinction between tasks (referred to as activities), jobs and skills. Second, the research has a more practical way of assessing the technologies required to computerise each of the tasks. Third, the research has an international dimension, which is vital considering that each country has a different set of circumstances pertaining to the total amount of tasks, which are automatable (Manyika *et al.*, 2017), see Table 11.3. If we were to take Japan, for example, with 55 per cent automation potential, this can be explained by the unique set of demographic, economic and political circumstances of the country which encourages robotisation as a viable solution to falling birth rates (Acemoglu and Restrepo, 2017c; Manyika *et al.*, 2017). In Russia, there is a similar trend "where the number of employees will likely decrease by 30 per cent over the next half-century as a result of a declining birthrate" (Manyika *et al.*, 2017: 116), automation could be seen in that country as an instrument to address this decline and improve the economy and society. In other words, advanced countries may deal with automation as a solution to an ageing population, emerging countries may harness the benefits of automation to skip stages of the industrial revolution or use automation to tackle the difficulties facing their respective economies (Acemoglu and Restrepo, 2017c).

Table 11.2 Capability requirement for activity automation

Axis of capability requirement	Precise capability requirement
Sensory perception Cognitive capabilities	Sensory perception Retrieving information Recognising known patterns/categories (supervised learning) Generating novel patterns/categories Logical reasoning/problem-solving Optimising and planning Creativity Articulating/display output Coordination with multiple agents
Natural language processing	Natural language generation Natural language understanding
Social and emotional capabilities	Social and emotional sensing Social and emotional reasoning Social and emotional output
Physical capabilities	Fine motor skills/dexterity Gross motor skills Navigation Mobility

Source: Manyika *et al.*, 2017: 4.

Examining the main themes to emerge from the research into the fourth industrial revolution, we can see that predicting the exact nature of change on the employment market created by this revolution is difficult with varying perspectives on the task vs job debate (see Table 11.4). In order to discuss and understand how the fourth industrial revolution is changing the structure of skills required for graduates, we have to define which skills are already used by these graduates (OECD, 2016). Using occupational survey data and matched job categories with their requirement in term of skills, we are able to examine tasks-wise probability for computerisation (Manyika *et al.*, 2017), i.e. which skills will be required by future graduates.

Table 11.3 Country-wise automation potential

Country	Automation potential in %
Japan	55
India	52
China	51
United States	46
Europe (big 5)	46
Rest of world	50

Source: Manyika *et al.*, 2017: 9.

Table 11.4 Review of the different automation estimations

Work	Unit of Analysis	Main findings
Frey and Osborne (2013)	Jobs/occupation	47% of the US jobs are subject to automation
Arntz, Gregory and Zierahn (2016)	Tasks	9% of the OECD jobs are subject to automation
Manyika *et al.* (2017)	Tasks	Almost 50% of tasks are automatable

Job market for graduates

The automation of tasks naturally leads to a shift in the skills and knowledge required to add value in the economy, as previously described, the third industrial revolution reduced the number of secretaries and clerks, reinventing bank clerks as sales representatives (Greenwood, 1999), the fourth industrial revolution will be no different. The role of education, as has been observed through previous industrial revolutions (see Table 11.5), is central to creating a workforce capable of meeting the demands of an ever changing marketplace, with an educated society, essential to realising the full potential of the fourth industrial revolution. Educational institutions will have to adapt and redefine their purpose and role in society not only in light of the changing market dynamics but the changing needs of students in how they learn and what they learn (Lodder, 2016). A key component in this adaptation is to ensure they maintain relationships with businesses in order to understand the tasks to be carried out by graduates and the employability skills required.

According to Hutt (2016), 65 per cent of children currently in primary school will be in jobs which do not exist yet, with more than 50 per cent of the skills taught in curricula obsolete within a few years of graduation (Blivin and Wallerstein, 2016). Presented with such challenges, many further and tertiary education providers are developing a more flexible curriculum in an attempt to future proof their respective subjects and programmes and meet the changes brought about by the fourth industrial revolution. Given the future direction of the fourth industrial revolution is relatively unknown, with further disruption to the graduate skills required for employment likely, the underpinning teaching and learning themes of subjects and programmes should be moving towards developing cross-functional skills (Freeman, Field and Dyrenfurth, 2001) rather than simply to train people in single disciplines. Such a move should not be restricted to further and tertiary education, there is a need for fundamental change through the educational pipeline, from early childhood through to the retraining of young working professionals (Anon, 2017a) in order to reduce the gap between the workplace and education so that obsolete knowledge is not being taught to individuals.

The shift in emphasis from technical (more easily replicated and automatable) to more emotional, social, cognitive and manipulative intelligence (Kahn, 2017;

Table 11.5 The history of educational systems through the industrial revolutions

Industrial revolution	Period	Signature technology	Educational response
First	1700s–1800s	Steam engine (Anon, 2017b; Morgan, 2016)	Development of professional skills such as leadership and discipline-specific skills in medicine and law
Second	1800s–1900s	Electricity (Anon, 2017b; Elliott, 2017; Morgan, 2016)	Development of the public school to create a more skilled and knowledgeable workforce
Third	Mid 1900s	Electronics and information technology (Elliott, 2017; Morgan, 2016; Van Hooijdonk, 2017)	Development of technology-led programmes and integration of technology for student learning
Fourth	Early 2000s	AI and cyber-physical systems (Elliott, 2017; Morgan, 2016)	Changes to the traditional paradigms of teaching and learning, the introduction of MOOCS

National Center for O*NET Development for USDOL, 2017) is one of the expected outcomes from the fourth industrial revolution. Some universities in Great Britain have already started to embed emotional intelligence into their graduate attributes to better prepare them for the employment market (Jameson *et al.*, 2016). The specific emotional intelligences to be addressed are self-awareness, self-management and self-motivation, as well as initiative, motivation, adaptability, empathy, positivity, communication and teamwork, all identified as necessary competencies required of graduates by employers (Jameson *et al.*, 2016). These skills link to the hard and soft attributes of team working, communication, time management, autonomy, confidence, problem-solving and creativity (Jackling and Natoli, 2015; Mason, Williams and Cranmer, 2006; Rae, 2007; Turner and Mulholland, 2017; Vincent, 2017), sometimes referred to as technical and generic skills (Barrie, 2006; Fallows and Stevens, 2000); or hard skills (project management, creative thinking, problem solving and leadership); and soft skills (communication, confidence and reflection), (Draycott and Rae, 2011; Fiala, Gertler and Carney, 2014; Jones and Iredale, 2010).

Hard and soft skills are being integrated into university curricula through work based learning (WBL), engagement with real-world business problems and other activities, which prepare graduates for the current and future employment market (Galloway, Marks and Chillas, 2014; Kolb, 1984; Renganathan, Karim and Li, 2012). Skills such as project management, which involves coordination

Figure 11.1 The skills correlated the least with the computerisation of jobs.

and management abilities as well as creativity in the context of problem-solving, design thinking and the user experience (UX) (Knemeyer, 2015) are necessary for today's graduate, as these tasks are complex and more difficult to automate due to the unpredictable and complex patterns created by humans and human interaction (Chui, Manyika and Miremadi, 2016). Hard and soft skills, however, need to be combined with emotional intelligences to allow the graduate to compete against algorithms which, although able to automate customer relationships and understand customer behaviour, are unable to replicate the emotional side of relationship building (Ariely, 2017).

The fourth industrial revolution brings with it the need for a different set of graduate skills, the development of 'big data', for example, opens up new employment opportunities (Angeles, 2013) but requires a slightly different set of skills than what is currently taught in many colleges and universities (Gould, 2017). The complexity and interdisciplinary nature of 'big data' need the development of courses in 'data sciences' and 'digital management' (Ghosh, 2017), with educational establishments required to consider more synergy between disciplines so that graduates are prepared for jobs in social media management, big data analysis and as sustainability managers (Hallett and Hutt, 2016; Nikitin *et al.*, 2015). In other words, although new technologies present new challenges for the future graduate they do not necessarily mean a lack of employment opportunities, rather the skills set simply has to adapt to the changing environment. Courses on 'Design Thinking' in business schools, for example, focuses on the mindset behind the design, and it is knowledge that is seen as particularly useful for all managers (Stigliani, 2017), with the additional benefit that such thinking is not easily replicated and automated. The next few years could see the development of knowledge related to design, software development and computer programming in management disciplines, as although future graduate managers might not be asked to directly design materials or programme code, they may be required to have a understanding in order to carry out such functions as a manager and communicate with those specialists who are designing materials and programming.

It is not only in the preparation of school leavers and graduates for the employment market, where the fourth industrial revolution will have an impact on education. It will also change the way students learn with universities, such as MIT[1] and Harvard[2] already introducing MOOCs, which is knowledge readily available and free to access (Mezied, 2016; Peters, 2017). Universities have realised that it is not just the job market which the fourth industrial revolution disrupts, it is the education system itself. Traditional teaching approaches will have to mix with new technologically led provision (Mezied, 2016), with educators required to embrace this technology to improve the student experience and reduce the effort on less value added tasks (Herold, 2015; Pressey, 1932), similar to medical practitioners and engineers mentioned earlier in the chapter. Educational providers in the fourth industrial revolution will have to address some challenges, most notably their value proposition when the provision of core knowledge and learning space is arguable feely available and easily substituted.

With the advent of augmented reality and cloud technology disrupting traditional educational platforms, students are able to collaborate and co-create in a virtual learning space, albeit perhaps not as effectively as in face-to-face classroom interactions, but students now have a choice on how to best equip themselves with the skills necessary for the employment market. Education like other sectors of the economy is stepping into the unknown on how to best prepare graduates with the skills to adapt to business now and in the future, but it is a step they have to take and they should not take it alone.

Conclusion

The fourth industrial revolution is upon us, should society be concerned at the lack of certainty with regards its future? As previously indicated the future of the fourth industrial revolution is relatively unknown, on the one hand, the job market could become even more divided between the low skilled, lowly educated and low-paid individuals and the highly skilled, highly educated and highly paid individuals (Frey and Osborne, 2013; Schwab, 2016). On the other hand we could be presented with a better quality of life, with AI and automation making the lives of working humans easier rather than replacing them (Van Hooijdonk, 2017).

History has taught us that change is inevitable and will not be trouble free, so governments, businesses and educational establishments have to collectively prepare themselves and future generations for what comes next in the fourth industrial revolution. The fourth industrial revolution will require

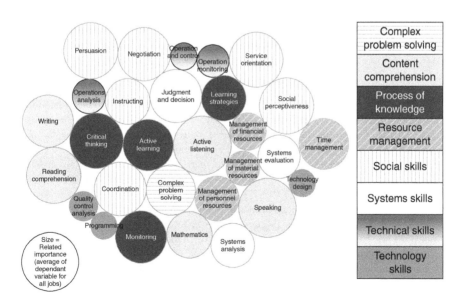

Figure 11.2 Twenty nine different skills extracted and ranked from 0**NET database.

humans to develop their creative and emotional intelligence as well as their perceptual and manipulative thinking (National Centre for O*NET Development for USDOL, 2017), otherwise the skills set of all employees and potential employees will be easily replicated and susceptible to replacement by automated platforms. Educational establishments must be a key player in preparing graduates with the necessary skills to compete in the labour market of the future, emphasising those skills which distinguish human from machine, and taking an active and not passive role. However, it is unlikely that education providers alone can address the issues of technological unemployment (Peters, 2017), they need to work with businesses to help shape the future of business, employment and the economic landscape.

Notes

1 ocw.mit.edu/
2 http://online-learning.harvard.edu/

References

Acemoglu, D. and Autor, D. (2011). Skills, tasks, and technologies: Implications for employment and earnings. In: D. Card and O. Ashenfelter, eds. *Handbook of Labor Economics*. Amsterdam: Elsevier, pp. 1043–1171.

Acemoglu, D. and Restrepo, P. (2017a). The race between machine and man: Implication of technology for growth, factor shares and employment. *NBER Working Paper No. 22252*, 1–87.

Acemoglu, D. and Restrepo, P. (2017b). Robots and jobs: Evidence from US labor markets. *NBER Working Paper No. w23285*, 1–90.

Acemoglu, D. and Restrepo, P. (2017c). Secular stagnation? The effect of aging on economic growth in the age of automation. *American Economic Review*, 107(5), 174–179.

Akst, D. (2013). What can we learn from past anxiety over automation? *The Wilson Quarterly*.

Angeles, S. (2013). Georgetown professor: Big data means big job opportunities [online]. *Business News Daily*. Available at: www.businessnewsdaily.com/5012-big-data-job-opportunities.html [accessed 7 November 2017].

Anon. (2016). *The future of jobs: Employment, skills and workforce strategy for the fourth industrial revolution.* Geneva: World Economic Forum.

Anon. (2017a). *Realizing human potential in the fourth industrial revolution: An agenda for leaders to shape the future of education, gender and work.* Geneva: World Economic Forum.

Anon. (2017b). The 4 industrial revolutions [online]. *Sentryo*. Available at: www.sentryo.net/the-4-industrial-revolutions/ [accessed 8 November 2017].

Anon. (2017c). The hardships of doing business in Africa [online]. *The Economist*. Available at:www.economist.com/news/middle-east-and-africa/21716031-what-century-old-german-ship-says-about-trade-modern-continent [accessed 1 November 2017].

Ariely, D. (2017). People don't build lasting relationships with algorithms [online]. *Huffingtonpost*. Available at: www.huffingtonpost.com/entry/dan-ariely-people-dont-build-lasting-relationships_us_595d104ee4b0326c0a8d142b [accessed 10 November 2017].

Arntz, M., Gregory, T. and Zierahn, U. (2016). The risk of automation for jobs in OECD countries: A comparative analysis. *OECD Social, Employment and Migration Working Papers* (189).

Autor, D.H. (2013). The task approach to labor markets: An overview. *Journal for Labour Market Research*, 46(3), 185–199.

Autor, D.H. (2014). Skills, education, and the rise of earnings among the "other 99 percents". *Science,* 344, 843–851.

Autor, D.H. (2015). Why are there still so many jobs? The history and future of work-place. *Automation.* 29, 3–30.

Barra, M. (2016). The next revolution in the auto industry [online]. *World Economic Forum.* Available at: www.weforum.org/agenda/2016/01/the-next-revolution-in-the-car-industry [accessed 8 November 2017].

Barrie, S.C. (2006). Understanding what we mean by the generic attributes of graduates. *Higher Education*, 51(2), 215–241.

Ben-Ami, D. (2015). Technology: The third industrial revolution [online]. *IPE.* Available at: www.ipe.com/reports/technology-sector/technology-the-third-industrial-revolution/ 10007759.fullarticle [accessed 8 November 2017].

Blivin, J. and Wallerstein, B. (2016). *Shift happens: Desperately seeking better creden-tials and hiring technologies.* Washington, DC: Innovate + Educate and Whiteboard Advisors.

Bloem, J., Van Doorn, M., Duivestein, S., Excoffier, D., Maas, R. and Van Ommeren, E. (2014). *The fourth industrial revolution: Things to tighten the link between IT and OT.* Gronigen: Sogeti.

Bostrom, N. (2014). *Superintelligence: Path, dangers, strategies.* Oxford: Oxford Univer-sity Press.

Brown, V. (2017). Cyberbullying: Words can hurt too [online]. *The Star,* Available at: www.thestar.com.my/news/nation/2017/10/19/cyberbullying-words-can-hurt-too/ [accessed 9 November 2017].

Brynjolfsson, E. and McAfee, A. (2014). *The second machine age: Work, progress, and prosperity in a time of brilliant technologies.* New York: W.W. Norton & Company.

Byington, M. (2016). Physicians are overwhelmed with their workload [online]. *Physicians Practice.* Available at: www.physicianspractice.com/blog/physicians-are-overwhelmed-their-workload [accessed 9 November 2017].

Cheshire, T. (2017). Universal basic income: Finland shows how salary for all works [online]. *SkyNews.* Available at: https://news.sky.com/story/universal-basic-income-finland-shows-how-salary-for-all-works-11119005 [accessed 10 November 2017].

Chui, M., Manyika, J. and Miremadi, M. (2016). Where machines could replace humans and where they can't (yet). *McKinsey Quarterly.*

Connif, R. (2011). What the Luddites really fought against. *Smithsonian Magazine.*

Dhillon, R. (2016). Social media monitoring an invasion of privacy, says Empower [online]. *The Rakyat Post.* Available at: www.therakyatpost.com/news/2016/01/12/ social-media-monitoring-an-invasion-of-privacy-says-empower/ [accessed 9 November 2017].

Draycott, M.C. and Rae, D. (2011). Enterprise education in schools and the role of com-petency frameworks. *International Journal of Entrepreneurial Behaviour & Research,* 17(2), 127–145.

Elliott, L. (2017). Governments have to invest in the fourth industrial revolution [online]. *Guardian.* Available at: www.theguardian.com/business/2017/jul/16/governments-have-to-invest-in-the-fourth-industrial-revolution [accessed 8 November 2017].

Fallows, S. and Stevens, C. (2000). Building employability skills into the higher education curriculum: A university-wide initiative. *Education + Training*, 42(2), 75–83.

Fiala, N., Gertler, P. and Carney, D. (November 2014). The role of hard and soft skills in entrepreneurial success: Experimental evidence from Uganda. *AEA RCT Registry*, 7.

Fleisher, M.S. and Tsacoumis, S. (2012). *O* NET analyst occupational skills ratings: Procedures update*. Raleigh, NC: National Center for O* NET Development.

Freeman, S.A., Field, D.W. and Dyrenfurth, M.J. (2001). Using contextual learning to build cross-functional skills in industrial technology curricula. *Journal of Industrial Teacher Education*, 38(3), 62–75.

Frey, C.B. and Osborne, M.A. (2013). *The future of employment: How susceptible are jobs to computerisation?* Oxford University Programme on the Impacts of Future Technology.

Fujimori, Y., Brynjolfsson, E., Pissarides, C., George, D. and Poulsen, T.L. (2016). *A world without work?* (H. Kuniya, Interviewer). World Economic Forum Meeting.

Galloway, L., Marks, A. and Chillas, S. (2014). The use of internships to foster employability, enterprise and entrepreneurship in the IT sector. *Journal of Small Business and Enterprise Development*, 21(4), 653–667.

Ghosh, P. (2017). The innovative data scientist: Overcoming the big data and data management divide [online]. *Dataversity*. Available at: www.dataversity.net/innovative-data-scientist-overcoming-big-data-data-management-divide/ [accessed 10 November 2017].

Gill, T.J. (2006). Workplace continuity: How risk and technology will affect facilities strategy. *Journal of Facilities Management*, 4(2), 110–125.

Gould, W. (2017). Data deluge [online]. *Science Journal*. Available at: http://science.psu.edu/sciencejournal/features/data-deluge [Access 7 November 2017].

Graetz, G. and Michaels, G. (2015). Robots at work. *CEP Discussion Paper No. 1335*, 1–53.

Greenwood, J. (1999). The third industrial revolution: Technology, productivity, and income inequality [online]. *Economic Review*. Available at: http://clevelandfed.org/research/review/ [accessed 9 November 2017].

Hallett, R. and Hutt, R. (2016). 10 jobs that didn't exist 10 years ago [online]. *World Economic Forum*. Available at: www.weforum.org/agenda/2016/06/10-jobs-that-didn-t-exist-10-years-ago [accessed 8 November 2017].

Handel, M.J. (2016). The O*NET content model: strengths and limitations, *Journal for Labour Market Research*, 49(2), 157–176.

Harari, Y.N. (2015). *Sapiens: A brief history of humankind*. New York: HarperCollins.

Herold, B. (2015). Technology in education: An overview [online]. *Edweek*. Available at: www.edweek.org/ew/issues/technology-in-education/index.html [accessed 9 November 2017].

Hutt, R. (2016). South-East Asia's digital jobs revolution – in 5 charts [online]. *World Economic Forum*. Available at: www.weforum.org/agenda/2016/05/south-east-asia-digital-jobs-5-charts [accessed 8 November 2017].

International Labour Office. (2012). *International Standard Classification of Occupation*. Geneva: International Labour Organization.

Jackling, B. and Natoli, R. (2015). Employability skills of international accounting graduates: Internship providers' perspectives. *Education + Training*, 57(7), 757–773.

Jameson, A., Carthy, A., McGuinness, C. and McSweeney, F. (2016). Emotional intelligence and graduates – employer's perspectives. *Procedia – Social and Behavioural Sciences*, 228, 515–522.

Jensen, M.C. (1993). The modern industrial revolution, exit, and the failure of internal control systems. *The Journal of Finance*, 48(3), 831–880.

Jones, B. and Iredale, N. (2010). Enterprise education as pedagogy. *Education + Training*, 52(1), 7–19.

Kahn, L.B. (2017). Demand for social and cognitive skills is linked to higher firm productivity [online]. *Yale Insights*. Available at: http://insights.som.yale.edu/insights/demand-for-social-and-cognitive-skills-is-linked-to-higher-firm-productivity [accessed 8 November 2017].

Karniel, Y. and Lavie-Dinur, A. (2012). Privacy in new media in Israel. How social networks are helping to shape the perception of privacy in Israeli society. *Journal of Information, Communication and Ethics in Society*, 10(4), 288–304.

Kingdollar, C. (2017). The speed of disruption and impact on business – the fourth industrial revolution has begun [online]. *General Liability*. Available at: www.genre.com/knowledge/publications/iinapc1704-en.html [accessed 6 November 2011].

Knemeyer, D. (2015). Design thinking and UX: Two sides of the same coin [online]. *Interactions*. Available at: http://interactions.acm.org/archive/view/september-october-2015/design-thinking-and-ux [accessed 9 November 2017].

Knowledge@wharton. (2016). This is the business model needed to master the fourth industrial revolution [online]. *World Economic Forum*. Available at: https://weforum.org/agenda/2016/04/this-is-the-business-model-needed-to-master-the-fourth-industrial-revolution [accessed 8 November 2017].

Kolb, D. (1984). *Experiential learning: Experience as the source of learning and development*, London: Prentice-Hall.

Lee, B.Y. (2016). Doctors wasting over two-thirds of their time doing paperwork [online]. *Forbes*. Available at: www.forbes.com/sites/brucelee/2016/09/07/doctors-wasting-over-two-thirds-of-their-time-doing-paperwork/#3aea0f2c5d7b [accessed 9 November 2017].

Levy. F. (2010). How technology changes demands for human skills. *OECD Education Working Papers*, 45, 1–18.

Lodder, J. (2016). The fourth industrial revolution and the education system, how to respond? [online]. *LinkedIn*. Available at: www.linkedin.com/pulse/fourth-industrial-revolution-education-system-how-respond-john-lodder [accessed 10 November 2017].

Lohr. S. (2016). IBM is counting on its bet on Watson, and paying big money for it [online]. *New York Times*. Available at: www.nytimes.com/2016/10/17/technology/ibm-is-counting-on-its-bet-on-watson-and-paying-big-money-for-it.html [accessed 29 October 2017].

MacCarthy, M. (2014). Time to kill the tech job-killing myth [online]. *The Hill*. Available at: http://thehill.com/blogs/congress-blog/technology/219224-time-to-kill-the-tech-job-killing-myth [accessed 7 November 2017].

Manyika, J., Chui, M., Miremadi, M., Bughin, J., George, K., Willmott, P. and Dewhurst, M. (2017). *A Future that works: Automation, Employment and Productivity*. New Jersey: McKinsey Global Institute.

Marr, B. (2016). Why everyone must get ready for the fourth industrial revolution [online]. *Forbes*. Available at: www.forbes.com/sites/bernardmarr/2016/04/05/why-everyone-must-get-ready-for-fourth-industrial-revolution/#773d78f73f90 [accessed 10 November 2017].

Mason, G., Williams, G. and Cranmer, S. (2006). *Employability skills initiatives in higher education: What effects do they have on graduate labour market outcomes?* London: National Institute of Economic and Social Research.

Mesnard, X. (2016). What happens when robots take our jobs? [online]. *World Economic Forum*. Available from: www.weform.org/agenda/2016/01/what-happens-when-rebots-take-our-jobs [accessed 8 November 2017].

Mezied, A.A. (2016). 'What role will education play in the fourth industrial revolution?' [online]. *Weforum*. Available at: www.weforum.org/agenda/2016/01/what-role-will-education-play-in-the-fourth-industrial-revolution [accessed 10 November 2017].

Morgan, J. (2016). What is the fourth industrial revolution? [online]. *Forbes*. Available at: www.forbes.com/sites/jacobmorgan/2016/02/19/what-is-the-fourth-industrial-revolution/#6ca9a599f392 [accessed 8 November 2017].

National Center for O*NET Development for USDOL. (2017). *The O*NET Content Model* [online]. *O*NET Resource Centre*. Available at www.onetcenter.org/content.html [accessed 8 November 2017].

Nikitin, A., Sharonov, A., Nikitin, G. and Repik, A. (2015). *Atlas of emerging jobs*. Moscow: Agency of Strategic Initiatives.

Ninomiya, K. (2016). Invasion of privacy on social media [online]. *LinkedIn*. Available at: www.linkedin.com/pulse/invasion-privacy-social-media-kent-ninomiya-1 [accessed 9 November 2017].

OECD. (2016). *Skills matter: Further results from the survey of adult skills*. Paris: OECD Publishing.

Olsen, P. (2016). Could chat bots replace human jobs? [online]. *Forbes*. Available at: www.forbes.com/sites/parmyolson/2016/05/09/could-chat-bots-replace-human-jobs-facebook/#2a9d3007564a [accessed 9 November 2017].

Osterman, P. (1986). The impact of computers on the employment of clerks and managers. *Industrial and Labor Relations Review*, 39(2), 175–186.

Pemberton Levy, H. (2015). Gartner predicts our digital future [online]. *Gartner*. Available at: www.gartner.com/smarterwithgartner/gartner-predicts-our-digital-future/ [accessed 29 October 2017].

Peters, M.A. (2017). Technological unemployment: Educating for the fourth industrial revolution. *Educational Philosophy and Theory*, 49(1), 1–6.

Petersen, R. (2016). The driverless truck is coming, and it's going to automate millions of jobs [online]. *TechCrunch*. Available at: https://techcrunch.com/2016/04/25/the-driverless-truck-is-coming-and-its-going-to-automate-millions-of-jobs/ [accessed 1 November 2017].

Pollitt, M. (2012). Retraining connects Fujitsu Telecom with new business opportunities: Employees' new skills set company on path to growth. *Human Resource Management International Digest*, 20(2), 29–31.

Pressey, S.L. (1932). A third and fourth contribution towards the coming "industrial revolution" in education. *School & Society*, 36, 668–672.

Rae, D. (2007). Connecting enterprise and graduate employability. *Education + Training*, 49(8/9), 605–619.

Randall, A. (2003). *Before the Luddites: Customer, community and machinery in the English woollen industry 1776–1809*. Cambridge: Cambridge University Press.

Renganathan, S., Karim, Z.A.B.A. and Li, C.S. (2012). Students' perception of industrial internship programme. *Education +Training*, 54(2/3), 180–191.

Rifkin J. (2011). *The third industrial revolution: How lateral power is transforming energy, the economy, and the world*. Basingstoke: Palgrave Macmillan.

Robertson, K. (2000). Work transformation: Integrating people, space and technology. *Facilities*, 18(10/11/12), 376–382.

Rosinski, M. (2017). Artificial intelligence and work: Preparing for the fourth industrial revolution [online]. *Astoriasoftware*. Available at: www.astoriasoftware.com/ artificial-intelligence-and-work-preparing-for-the-fourth-industrial-revolution [accessed 8 November 2017].

Sale, K. (1996). *Rebels against the future: The Luddites and their war on the industrial revolution: Lessons for the computer age*. Cambridge, Massachusetts: Perseus Publishing.

Saurin, R., Ratcliffe, J. and Puybaraud, M. (2008). Tomorrow's workplace: A futures approach using prospective through scenarios. *Journal of Corporate Real Estate*. 10(4), 243–261.

Scheffer, C. and Girdhar, P. (2004). *Practical machinery vibration analysis and predictive maintenance*. first ed. Amsterdam: Elsevier.

Schumpeter, J. (1942). *Capitalism, socialism, and democracy*. New York: Harper & Bros.

Schwab, K. (2016). *The fourth industrial revolution*. Geneva: World Economic Forum.

Slane, R. (2013). How O*NET classification helps us match jobs and skills [online]. *Emsi*. Available at: www.economicmodelling.co.uk/2013/06/11/how-onet-classification-helps-us-match-jobs-and-skills/ [accessed 8 November 2017].

Smith, A. and Anderson, J. (2014). AI, robotics, and the future of jobs [online]. *Pew Research Centre*. Available at: www.pewinternet.org/2014/08/06/future-of-jobs/ [accessed 29 October 2017].

Staller, K. (2017). Defining preventive & predictive maintenance [online]. *Daniel Penn Associates*. Available at: www.danielpenn.com/insights-resources/case-studies/preventive-predictive-maintenance/ [accessed 8 November 2017].

Steeves, V. and Regan, P. (2014). Young people online and the social value of privacy. *Journal of Information, Communication and Ethics in Society*, 12(4), 298–313.

Stigliani, I. (2017). Design thinking – the skill every MBA student needs [online]. *The Financial Times*. Available at: www.ft.com/content/cbf70424-422a-11e7-82b6-896b95f30f58 [accessed 10 November 2017].

Susskind, R. and Susskind, D. (2015). *The future of professions: How technology will transform the work of human experts*. Oxford: Oxford University Press.

Turner, J.J. and Mulholland, G. (2017). Enterprise education: Towards a framework for engaging with tomorrow's entrepreneurs. *Journal of Management Development*, 36(6), 1–18.

Vallancien, G. (2017). La chirurgie par temps de robots [online]. *Interview podcast*. Available at: www.franceculture.fr/emissions/la-conversation-scientifique/la-chirurgie-par-temps-de-robots [accessed 29 October 2017].

Van Hooijdonk, R. (2017). The fourth industrial revolution: "A fusion of our physical, digital and biological worlds" [online]. *Richard Van Hooijdonk blog*. Available at: www.richardvanhooijdonk.com/en/fourth-industrial-revolution-fusion-physical-digital-biological-worlds/ [accessed 8 November 2017].

Vincent, J. (2017). Robots and AI are going to make social inequality even worse, says new report [online]. *The Verge*. Available at: www.theverge.com/2017/7/13/15963710/robots-ai-inequality-social-mobility-study [accessed 10 November 2017].

Williams-Grut, O. (2016). Three of the world's 10 largest employers are replacing workers with robots [online]. *World Economic Forum*. Available at: http://weforum.org/agenda/2016/06/3-of-the-worlds-10-largest-employers-are-replacing-workers-with-robots [accessed 8 November 2017].

12 Leaving the comfort zone

Building an international dimension in higher education

Jessica Lichy and Bénédicte Favre

The hidden value of the international dimension for developing a graduate employability skills set

It is widely acknowledged that international experience and international awareness can offer many benefits both for individuals (new skills and competencies) and for higher education institutions (greater visibility in the international academic community). In this respect, the international dimension is a vital component of knowledge transfer and skills development by exposing new ideas and philosophies, different challenges and innovative thinking. Equally, it is fundamental for embedding a culture of relationship building, sustainable co-creation and international networking, face-to-face and virtually. The twenty-first century workplace requires individuals and organisations to be able to function internationally, digitally and sustainably. Many skills can be enhanced through the exposure to an international setting, leading to enhanced employability, enterprise and entrepreneurial engagement.

Within the scope of higher education institutions (HEI), international mobility provides an ideal opportunity for individuals seeking to broaden their experience by learning from others in a different national environment. Studying and working abroad can take the form of student and staff exchanges, degree-seeking students, 'top up' degrees, placements, research visits and other collaborative ventures beyond borders. Experiencing a different socio-cultural environment for even a short period of time can provide a transformational education experience (Clapp-Smith and Wernsing, 2014; Hunter, 2008) by putting individuals in unfamiliar situations. The variety of experience reaped from international mobility can enable individuals to acquire many new skills through living in a different cultural context, speaking a foreign language, discovering the intangible aspects of another civilization, developing new ways of communicating and adapting to the teaching and learning style of a 'host' institution – *Les voyages forment la jeunesse*! Most of all, international mobility is not merely important for students but for staff too, because staff return from abroad with different ideas and experiences to transfer to students. Students benefit immensely from the exposure to international experiences through their own mobility which is potentially reinforced and developed further by staff mobility.

On a broader scale, international mobility adds value to the key stake-holders (institutions, employers and students) by enhancing the learning experience and embellishing the brand image of a university or business school in the international marketplace, thus generating important leads for collaborative research projects and scholarly publications. Institutions are ranked on their degree of transnational co-operation, research output, inter-nationalisation, employability of graduates and volume of academic–business collaboration. These factors act as prerequisites for international accreditation bodies such as EQUIS, EPAS and AACSB. Although many such activities are enhanced by the synergy that can be developed through international mobility, there is a lack of academic research that examines the factors that drive pro-viders of higher education to develop an international dimension. In today's economic turbulence, universities and business schools are increasingly being asked to justify the tremendous investment needed to set up and maintain international partnerships and educational visits. While exchanges offer a sus-tainable mechanism for international mobility allowing a quota to study/work outside the home country, enrolments offer lucrative opportunities and com-petitive advantage for HEIs.

This chapter cites the case of a private French business school (hereafter named French HEI) and its key international partners to explore how business school managers and deans can rethink their business model to balance the costs of international mobility and thus maximise the opportunities offered by a global presence. To provide an insight into international mobility in higher education, different approaches to managing international expansion are discussed, oppor-tunities and constraints are identified, and alternative theoretical frameworks are critically analysed. The intention is to raise awareness of a tried and tested approach (or business model) and thus help practitioners, policy makers and scholars to better understand how to create value through international develop-ment (recruitment, reciprocity, exchanges and so on). The term 'business model' is used here to describe an organisation's approach to creating, delivering and capturing value, in order to cover costs and to generate revenue, to reward stake-holders and reinvest funds in order to remain competitive. Higher education today is under pressure to improve outcomes – in other words, to increase pro-ductivity – while facing increasing costs and shrinking funding. For this reason, HEIs and students should be encouraged to become more enterprising and entre-preneurial in their thinking.

Introduction

The inspiration for this chapter stems from the observations of a local business owner, reflecting on the employability of today's graduates:

> When you work abroad, you see different styles of communication, manage-ment and decision-making. This knowledge is indispensable in any busi-ness. Whether or not you want to trade with foreign markets, it's always

enriching to have an awareness of different customs, expectations and methods of work. The onus is on providers of higher education to support the international exchanges among staff and students. It's more than just learning another language. Text books and case studies are no substitute for real-life experience.

(Business owner with 23 years' commercial experience)

The views raised above by the business owner draw attention to the need for higher education (HE) providers to be more agile, think innovatively, and be more demand-responsive in order to instil a global awareness that develops employability among students. The widening gap between traditional models of pedagogy and innovative approaches raises two key questions: How can HE providers (i.e. universities and business schools) enhance the employability skills set of graduates through embedding an international dimension? How can providers facilitate the acquisition of the international skills, competencies, behaviours and mind-sets that are increasingly regarded as important employability attributes for graduates? (Pegg *et al.*, 2012).

In a rapidly changing world where the widespread use of social networking means that geographical distance is no longer a hindrance to the exchange of ideas, there is an urgent need to transmit relevant skills and knowledge for a changed (and constantly changing) job market. More than ever before, students (and staff) need to be able to communicate effectively, interact and transact with international stakeholders. The competencies required for the twenty-first century, internationally oriented workplace mean that HE providers will need to rethink the teaching policies and learning habits that run counter to this new globalised mind-set. Higher education is thus in a state of flux; existing business models are failing to meet the needs of stakeholders. As tuition fees continue to rise, enrolment in higher education has become more of an investment decision than a choice, in which the cost of study is weighed against potential future earnings. This decision in itself creates a new dynamic, influencing subject choice, the perceived value of the institution's brand, potential employability and so on. Competition between institutions is therefore rife; the marketplace is not only global but dynamic and digital too.

Responding to competitive pressure, HE providers are repositioning themselves by modifying their business model. To attract the best staff and top students, HE providers have progressively expanded beyond borders over recent decades. Numerous different approaches can be adopted to achieve international recognition including: joint curriculum building, co-operation with foreign universities for dual- and double-degree agreement, student and staff/teacher exchanges, international classes, collaborative research, cross-border agreements for shared projects, franchise programmes, joint awards, validation, articulation agreements, capacity building, progression arrangements, mobility (staff and student), research and doctoral collaboration. Although there is no standard approach for developing an international dimension, the ongoing changes in higher education underscore the need for an approach that is pragmatic, holistic and flexible – as will be illustrated in this chapter. Above all, agility is called for in order to address the emerging challenges that stem from a constantly changing environment.

Context: the changing landscape of higher education

With increasing emphasis being placed on *applied knowledge*, HEIs worldwide have adopted business jargon from the field of Total Quality Management (Murgatroyd and Morgan, 1993). Thus, in an attempt to enhance the 'student experience', students are encouraged to 'engage' in the process of education, to take responsibility for 'technology enhanced' learning and to contribute to the 'outcomes' of the institution. In many private institutions, students are considered as 'customers' or 'key stakeholders' (King, 2012), irrespective of the fact that students may be unable to act as bona fide consumers because they have no prior knowledge of participating in higher education. Students today have rising expectations of what they should be 'given' in return for their fees, including a certain level and quality of support, facilities and resources. Marshall (2011: 105) points to the importance of reciprocal relationships and trust; "universities should be partnerships between staff and students, with the student voice promoted and listened to". In addition to the physical infrastructure, students also pay attention to brand (the school's name and logo), supported by the school's international reputation and visibility. Thus, the school's 'trademark' or *market position* is used as a benchmark by prospective students and other stakeholders. Hawawini (2005: 778) suggests that "a strong brand is more likely the outcome of a successful business model than the other way around".

Higher education is a fast growing service industry. As institutions expand beyond borders, they need to multiply efforts to collaborate with diverse stakeholders worldwide such as accreditation agencies, students and parents, and international partners (including exchange students in their role as 'trading currency'). Jacobs and van der Ploeg (2006: 553) believe that "educational quality, teaching performance and career opportunities are what matters to students and graduates" and that "research quality, quality and motivation of students, the status of the institution, and tenure possibilities are crucial to professors and researchers". Student numbers, market share and the reputation of the institution are the issues at stake for school managers. As higher education institutions expand into new markets, it is becoming increasingly difficult to satisfy stakeholder requirements, the intricacies of which are discussed below.

Miles, Hazeldine and Munila (2004: 30) describe accreditation as "a hallmark of quality and [it] provides students and other business-school stakeholders with an objective, third-party assurance that the business school is conforming to sound academic management practices and a somewhat accepted curriculum". Global accreditation bodies require institutions to demonstrate an international presence, in order to claim excellence and argue 'world class' status (EPAS 2015; Thomas *et al.* 2014). The greater the international dimension of an institution, the more it will meet the accreditation criteria; special attention is paid to the number of exchange partners and also the ratio of international students who graduate. Levels of international mobility within higher education are a reasonable gauge of the strategic priorities of an institution to support the international dimension (Leask 2007). International mobility and international enrolments reflects the openness and ability of both an institution and an individual to work with different cultures and linguistic communities (Ministère des Affaires étrangères et du Développement international 2013). For EPAS accreditation, the most straightforward international accreditation delivered by the European Foundation for Management Development, an institution has to emphasise achievements in the areas of academic rigour, practical relevance and internationalisation. The EPAS evaluation report includes the provision of strategic advice on how a programme may be improved so as to compete more effectively in international markets. The purpose of accreditation is to ensure a high level of educational quality; naturally, schools publicise their accreditation certificates to attract applicants (students and staff), to enhance reputation and ranking. Institutions must conform to the multiple criteria (for example, the extent to which the programme has an international focus and a balance between academic and managerial dimensions) set by accreditation bodies and strive for validation in order to survive. As a result, accreditation agencies have become a key stakeholder group.

In addition to accreditation, 'student satisfaction' is often used as a benchmark of quality, although Harvey (2003: 4) points out that "it is not always clear how views collected from students fit into institutional quality improvement policies and processes". Yet, marketing literature uses student satisfaction data to publicise and illustrate the quality of the institution itself. The more satisfied the students (and fee-payers), the greater the opportunities for recruitment – a process known as *prescription*. As reputation depends heavily on prescription, institutions will broadcast positive student feedback (testimonies, photos and videos) in their marketing efforts (e.g. web content, prospectus, student fairs, etc.) as a means of promoting the institution and encouraging prospective students (local and international) to apply.

Great attention is paid to creating a positive 'student experience' in every domain of higher education: admission, induction, courses and teaching methods, international visiting professors, assessments, internship possibilities, international student exchange programmes and destinations offered, graduation, the campus itself, student associations and alumni. Thus, prospective students from India or China, for example, will expect to see Indian or Chinese student testimonials in the marketing literature. As stakeholders, the international partners play a crucial role. They can be considered as the *goodwill ambassadors* of a school. In other words, they act as intangible assets that can enhance brand image. In the same way that an institution displays its accreditation certificates, the international partners reflect the scope of international mobility for studying abroad and academic collaboration. Thus, the wider the choice of international destinations on offer (particularly English-speaking destinations), the more attractive the school appears to prospective students – many of whom acknowledge that, in today's global marketplace, recruiters require graduates to demonstrate employability skills: fluency in English *and* other languages, in addition to business acumen and entrepreneurial skills.

To a certain extent, an institution pampers its relations with partner institutions and will dedicate resources to guaranteeing student satisfaction and enhancing the learning experience of incoming students. There is an unwritten understanding among managers of international services that similar efforts will be reciprocated by the partner institution towards visiting students. This investment yields rich student feedback that is used by both the home and host institution to promote academic mobility to international destinations. Above all, the experience of international mobility can be used not only to enhance the reputation of an institution per se, but also to broaden the skills and knowledge of the individual by providing valuable insights into the wider world. These insights can be integrated into teaching and learning as a source of inspiration for developing skills that can enhance employability and entrepreneurial thinking.

Stepping out of the comfort zone

In today's dynamic marketplace, "the rise in the knowledge economy and the global competition for skills and competencies have provided a new driver for the internationalization of education systems in many OECD countries" (OECD 2010: 310). To be sustainable, HE providers need to develop a *realistic* approach to expanding beyond borders. Therefore, a case-by-case approach (rather than a standardised approach) is called for when building international networks and nurturing cross-cultural relationships. Attention needs to be paid to local needs, problems and opportunities. In time, standard procedures will emerge, for example customised offers to attract certain cultural markets, which can then be incorporated and reiterated when expanding into other similar cultural markets.

Traditionally, higher education has always been "more internationally open than most sectors because of its immersion in knowledge, which never showed much respect for juridical boundaries" (Marginson and van der Wende, 2007: 5). However, Doh (2010: 135) points out that "despite the rapid globalization of the organizations that serve as the employers of business school students and the subject of business school research, business schools themselves are shockingly national – even regional – in their organizational scope and footprint". At the time of writing, many institutions lack the resources to face up to the challenges of global competition, new legal frameworks, and costly accreditation procedures. Some institutions are still getting to grips with how to provide education services to a digital-savvy student intake with increasingly high expectations. Employers, however, need business schools to deliver management education that is global in outlook and context; often calling into question the relevance of certain long-standing programmes and outdated teaching methods that can be found in higher education today. It is totally unrealistic to assume that the international dimension can be created by sending a small cohort of students (or staff) to partner institutions overseas. The international dimension needs to be integrated in the corporate culture, reflecting commitment at every level of the organisation whilst also engaging top-down and bottom-up thinking. This view is supported by Jones (2012: 9), "we cannot simply rely on the mobile minority of students to respond to employers' needs". To ignore the changing landscape of higher education would be marketing myopia: "global growth in international education continues to be strong and for many institutions international students make an important cultural and economic contribution" (Ross and Grace, 2012: 536). In other words, while focusing on enterprising and employability activities is fundamental, international mobility is equally important for complementing the employability skills set of graduates. Resources need to be apportioned to international mobility; communication efforts need to frame the expense as an investment in the future of the student (and fee-payers) as well as that of the institution.

Acknowledging that cultural competence and critical thinking are enhanced by international travel (Finley, Taylor and Warren, 2007), many institutions are seeking ways to expand the education offer to develop the employability skill set of graduates. Some HEIs have responded to competition in the home market by extending the delivery of programmes to students in different continents; either physically or digitally. This process of international collaboration exists at many levels, the most common being exchange students, visiting professors, summer schools, dual awards, programmes taught in English and international recruitment. Few HEIs are 'born global'. The process of internationalising education services tends to resemble the Uppsala model whereby an organisation goes through a series of incremental steps (exporting, licensing production, affiliations, joint ventures and sole ventures) towards an international presence whilst overcoming the challenge of psychic distance (Hallén and Wiedersheim-Paul, 1984). Psychic Distance refers to "the distance between the home market and a foreign market, resulting from the perception of both cultural and business differences" (Evans and Mavondo, 2002: 517). It is based on the barriers to effective information flow between a country market and a firm; thus the greater these barriers, the greater the Psychic Distance. In many cases, the distance comes about as a result of perceived social and cultural 'differences' between countries (Hallén and Wiedersheim-Paul, 1984). Note that the concept concerns the *perceived* distance and consequences (Child, Rodrigues and Frynas, 2009; Prime, Obadia and Vida, 2009) and that perception is interpretive and highly subjective (Swift, 1999). Expansion into overseas markets is often hindered by various intangible barriers, particularly culture and language, serving as a reminder of the iceberg analogy (Rocher, 1969) where only 10 per cent of cultural differences are visible (such as dress code and body language) and the rest are hidden (such as work ethic and humour). The iceberg model underscores the need for highly developed skills in cross-cultural understanding and cross-cultural awareness for networking and conducting business beyond borders. There is a growing awareness of the importance of international mobility as an integral element of the employability skill set.

Insights into theoretical perspectives

A key implication of the current shift to privatisation, commodification and mar-ketisation of higher education has been the additional opening up and reinforce-ment of mind-sets and perspectives in relation to all manner of transformation and innovation (Rae, 2014). In the changing relationship between provider and user, the modus operandi of HE providers has been redefined with greater focus on learner (or customer) satisfaction (Eagle and Brennan, 2007; Pitman, 2000;). The emphasis is also on building sustainable alliances between different stake-holders internationally, based on open collaboration and partnerships between higher education and employers, with other HE providers, and with a range of funding bodies and key partners worldwide. Ongoing changes in modern society require higher education providers to respond with innovative adaptation. It is becoming increasingly apparent that there is a need to rethink higher education as an international 'eco-system' – which is not without organisational risk, but it is more likely to stimulate and sustain economic growth than if higher education continues to operate as a 'silo'. Globalisation and digitisation provide further challenges for higher education providers. In preparation for this changed environment, it would be beneficial for individuals (staff and students) to have first-hand experience of the international business environment. This knowledge would be extremely valuable for enriching innovative thinking and identifying business opportunities. It begs the question, however, of *how* HE providers can create a cost-effective infrastructure that enables international mobility and inter-national expansion of education services?

The literature on internationalising higher education reveals the scope and complexity of spanning boundaries. The work of Knight and de Wit (1995) suggests that the main reason for internationalising is to increase the inter-national and intercultural knowledge and skills of students, and to promote research which addresses interdependence (cultural, economic, environmental and political) among nations. Several approaches have been explored by HE providers to build an international dimension that produces an open, tolerant and cosmopolitan learning environment. Taylor (2004: 150) states that "although this outburst of activity is clearly visible in many universities throughout the world, it is much less clear to what extent conventional plan-ning theory and methodologies have been applied to the process of inter-nationalization". The extent to which an HEI can create an international dimension will depend on the size of the institution and market position or *ranking* – "rankings bring insight into the academic experience and offer an opportunity for productive change and innovation" (Jain and Golosinski, 2009: 104). Usually, the emphasis is on designing interdisciplinary programmes that blend foreign languages and international studies into marketing, finance and management, in addition to collaborative activities particularly transnational research involving other institutions, as a means to strengthening links with the international business world. This approach provides a robust foundation onto which greater collaboration can be anchored.

Embarking upon the process of creating an international dimension will invariably necessitate change within the institution in terms of developing new competences, new activities (academic and extracurricular), a new culture (resulting from bringing together different nationalities) and instilling transversal international values throughout the *entire* institution. The transformation "requires a commitment and involvement at all levels: leadership, faculty, students and administrative staff" (de Wit, 2010: 16). It has to be a truly inclusive process. Paradoxically, to onlookers it may resemble a set of isolated activities loosely based on an intercultural theme. In practice, it involves building a sustainable infrastructure for sending and receiving individuals between the home and host institutions, overcoming geographic constraints and spanning social, cultural and linguistic boundaries. There is no single approach to balancing the sustainability argument versus the ideal approach to furnish students with the necessary employability skills. What works for one institution (or person) may not work as effectively for another, owing to differences in accreditation, strategy, corporate culture, politics and so on.

Various frameworks are discussed in the literature for integrating an international dimension into higher education. Frameworks include: the 'benefits-driven model' (Wu and Yu, 2006: 213) focusing on specific benefits of internationalisation (i.e. student demand, globalisation and collaborative programmes that can reduce tuition fees); the 'infusion approach', which involves introducing international knowledge and perspectives in such a way that students perceive these as relevant to their pre-existing or evolving educational and career interests (Skidmore *et al.*, 2005); and 'network power' (King, 2010: 588) that describes the alliances formed through person-to-person projects on the basis of shared interests, rather than by trans-ministerial agreement. Other motives for expanding education beyond borders can be broadly described as political, economic, academic or socio-cultural (Jiang, 2008). De Meyer, Harker and Hawawini (2004: 108) put forward four approaches to internationalising: import (establishing formal and informal projects to attract foreign degree students); export (knowledge is disseminated via research and teaching); partnership (exchange of students and faculty) and network (merger of geographically separate institutions or establishing new campuses in other countries). Knight and de Wit (1999) present a typology of approaches: activity (international students, development assistance and academic mobility), competency (impact of internationalised curricula on the skills developed by students, faculty and staff), ethos (developing a culture with an explicit international dimension) and process (integration of an international dimension into the corporate culture, guiding policies and procedures of an institution). The decision to embark upon a process of creating an international dimension will also depend on leadership vision, willingness to take risks and academic metrics such as size and scope of the HEI, programmes delivered, mission statement and goals, resources available and location. There is no formal approach for expanding beyond borders; institutions may choose to use a single model, adapt a model or even create a hybrid model based on combining elements of several different approaches.

Hawawini (2005: 773) points out that:

> obviously, not every school should aim to become a truly global knowledge and learning network. Many will continue to serve their local market. Others will adopt a more regional scope. And a few will be truly global. But the local and regional schools will to some degree, have to internationalise.

This view is supported by Babb, Womble and De'Armond (2013) and ongoing research at the IAU (International Association of Universities), confirming that the creation of an international dimension is seen as central to an institution's future planning, and is of greater and growing importance to HEI leaders, than ever before (IAU, 2010).

In the light of unprecedented challenges, the broadening of the education offer to provide international experience and skills (for both staff and students) can be interpreted as a priority. However, the literature offers only a partial and somewhat outdated explanation of how to accomplish the daunting task of preparing the student with the necessary employability skills for a changed and increasingly changing employment environment. Within the context of higher education, the literature takes a rather silo approach in documenting and explaining efforts to develop an international experience and its importance to the graduate, complementing other enterprise and entrepreneurial skills developed through the curriculum.

Higher education in Continental Europe: an *aperçu* of France

Notwithstanding Brexit, the European context illustrates the synergies that facilitate international outreach, networking and boundary-spanning. The 1999 Bologna Process resulted in harmonising higher education qualifications across Europe – with the result that France now follows the path, long-recognised in the UK: degree (in three years or 180 *European Credit Transfer System* or ECTS credits), Masters (in five years or 300 ECTS) and PhD (in six years). France operates a two-tier system, with the academic elite seeking entrance to one of the elite *grandes écoles* (*écoles supérieures*) and the rest enrolling at a state university. After the *baccalauréat* (equivalent of the British 'A' level), state universities recruit students through an open system. The fee-paying *grandes écoles* and smaller business schools recruit a limited number of students through an entrance exam. Student selection is nationwide for the *grande école*, but more regional for private institutions and for universities. Annual tuition fees for a university can cost in the region of €160–€320, a *grande école* will charge from €12,000, and a business school will charge from €7000. Fee-paying parents therefore pay attention to detail: the tangible return on investment (employability, ranking, academic reputation) plus the extent to which the international dimension is embedded in the curriculum (dual awards, classes taught in English, visiting professors, partner institutions) – before enrolling their son/daughter.

One of the knock-on effects of twenty-first century globalisation has been the significant growth in academic mobility across countries for the purpose of studying, working or research (Rodríguez, Martínez-Roget and Pawlowska, 2012). Programmes that support international academic mobility include Erasmus Plus, 'Study Abroad', Nordplus, Fulbright and Banco Santander (Directorate-General for Internal Policies, 2015). Although each programme varies in structure, they have roughly the same objective: to enable individuals to study or work "in a foreign country for an extended period of time with a goal of enhancing levels of international understanding and concern" (Liping *et al.*, 2015: 50). These programmes have evolved considerably over past years: "what has changed … is the increased modes of delivery which now encompass dual and joint degrees, accreditation, validation and, in its most developed format, branch campuses" (Fielden and Gillard, 2011: 7). Cross-border activities reflect the readiness of an institution to engage with the rest of the world. Expanding education beyond borders is now a lucrative source of income for some institutions: "compared to domestic students, foreign students generate additional income for institutions which are encouraged to become entrepreneurial in the international education market" (OECD, 2004: 4). Consequently, HE providers compete fiercely to expand education services beyond borders and to offer international mobility.

Outside the English-speaking world, the international dimension poses certain socio-linguistic difficulties. English and French have, for centuries, both been used as dominant languages in international communications, but nowadays French speakers have been fighting a losing battle against English speakers to maintain French as a global lingua franca (Oakes, 2002). Marking the end of an era: "The supremacy of French as a diplomatic language lasted from the fifteenth to the twentieth century" (Darby, 2009: 210). English is the recognised international language of trade and commerce. French universities and business schools have therefore had to internationalise the in-coming cohort and to develop 'Study Abroad' programmes *delivered in English* to compete internationally with the attractive image of Anglo-Saxon destinations (Britain, Ireland, Canada, the USA and Australia). "Instruction in English has made [a] broader range of sites available, especially in countries whose languages are less commonly studied" (Zachrisson, 2009: 29). Although cultural awareness and language skills are no guarantee of employment, they "seem increasingly required as international trade barriers fall and a more global economy grows" (Baker, 2006: 115). Students worldwide are aware that they must master English if they want an international career.

Critics of Study Abroad programmes believe that students may be constrained by the capacity to function in a foreign language and within a different academic culture. Allen (2010) claims that students often do not take full advantage of learning opportunities during their Study Abroad. Hughes (2008) condemns the dominance of Anglophone countries in student exchange programmes, raising the question of equity and quality at national, institutional and individual levels. Rogerson-Revell (2007: 103) holds that English "can also present challenges both linguistically and culturally, particularly as more and more interactions are between speakers whose first language is not English". Despite these criticisms of Study Abroad programmes, what can be claimed from information available in the public domain is the following: first, an increasing number of students opt for destinations where courses are delivered in English (in order to improve their employability); and second, the total number of students studying abroad is continually increasing (UKCISA, 2016; UNESCO, 2016), lured by the prospects of broadening their employability skills set through socio-cultural discovery. These trends reflect both the global expansion of education and the attractiveness of internationalising the student experience (Varela and Gatlin-Watts, 2014). In view of the increases in student mobility, it seems that students have realised the importance of exploring different horizons – which may lead to new opportunities that could germinate into income-generating projects.

Developing a business model for sustainable internationalisation: the case of French *HEI*

Endorsing the notion that international mobility adds to the student experience, the French government has long viewed higher education as an important industry, with international students categorised as an 'invisible export', and international education represented as an 'export industry' (Raffarin, 2003). In the case of *French HEI*, two popular mobility programmes are offered: Erasmus and 'Study Abroad'. On average, over a third of students and 5 per cent of staff participate annually in these international mobility programmes. Two-thirds of the student exchanges take place with Anglo-Saxon partner institutions (the UK, Canada, the USA, Australia and South Africa) – and the rest in Latino or Asian institutions. Linguistic ability therefore plays a significant role in the selection of the Study Abroad destination. Nearly three-quarters of outgoing students opt for courses delivered in English and approximately only a quarter are attracted by other languages.

French HEI is a private institution of higher education with campus locations across France and offshore, established in 1983 to provide business education to Baccalauréat holders. The curriculum is based on extensive collaboration with the corporate world in order to produce graduates who will be fully operational in the world of work, either as an employee or self-employed. At the end of the five-year *Programme Grande Ecole*, students will have accomplished at least 18 months' work or study in an international context; the international experience is a mandatory component of the curriculum aimed at boosting employability. The development of an international dimension at French HEI is innovative in terms of the market-oriented approach that has been developed to meet two key challenges: the stiff competition from Anglo-Saxon institutions, and the constraints imposed by regulatory bodies at national and European level.

In non-English speaking countries, the necessity for an international dimension is especially important; in the case of France, students (and their fee-paying parents) increasingly choose a business school according to internationalisation metrics such as the number of mandatory foreign languages, the number of foreign partners and the number of dual degrees on offer (Nourry *et al.*, 2012). A working knowledge of several languages and cultural awareness is nowadays considered essential in the employability skills set – i.e. the skills needed to make the student cohort more 'employment-ready', able to work for themselves and/or for others. Responding to demand, French HEI redefined its business model to reflect a new market position that embeds a culture of international expansion and international mobility. The intention was to put in place a new philosophy and redefined market position, by employing the business model concept as a system for creating value. Refocusing attention on building an international dimension required rethinking the current system in place, particularly the financial aspects, social and ethical issues, managing human resources, sustainability and so on.

Transforming students into engaged stakeholders in the internationalisation process, Erasmus and Study Abroad were made obligatory at French HEI, in the belief that such courses can introduce students to the global perspective of business discipline and provide valuable international experience (Moghaddam, Peyvandi and Wang, 2009). For participants, the experience of international mobility creates a buzz that resonates beyond borders; social media, word-of-mouth and peer pressure play an important role in attracting prospective students (and spontaneous job applicants) to French HEI from both France and overseas. As a result of mandating international mobility, French HEI accommodates over 300 exchange students and summer school students into undergraduate and postgraduate programmes. Academics are required to ensure that intercultural exchange takes place during class activities so that students with similar education backgrounds can learn to interact with students from different cultural backgrounds and linguistic communities. French HEI adheres to the belief that these exchanges can only be beneficial to students if a balance can be maintained among nationalities; if one nationality were to become too dominant, a community may develop within it and eventually hinder intercultural exchange.

French HEI remains opens to international collaboration with smaller and/or lesser known business schools, as these schools often allow participating institutions more flexibility. Whereas larger and/or public institutions tend to prefer 'one for one' student/staff exchange agreements, smaller schools are often ready to explore more innovative ways to collaborate with partner schools abroad. Innovative practice may include, for example, developing new programmes tailored to the needs of students from a partner university. With a predominantly flexible approach, French HEI has experienced high levels of student and staff satisfaction with partner institutions whose business models are sufficiently flexible to accommodate fluctuations in enrolment, student programmes interest and the financial constraints of institutions from year to year. Ongoing collaboration can be attributed to the adoption of a hybrid approach; a pragmatic mix of different options that fit within the constraints of the institutional structure. Using this approach, French HEI has built a network of over 100 partner intuitions, spanning 40 different countries.

Furthermore, French HEI uses reciprocity to balance the number of in-coming foreign students accommodated by the host institution with the number of out-going French students sent to a host institution. The *bilateral exchange agreement* defines the number of students to be exchanged per year, the duration of the exchange and the validation of the agreement. In this type of agreement, tuition fees are always waivered. Students thus do not pay additional tuition fees for adding an international dimension to their curricula. This approach is not always feasible, though. French HEI strives to balance in-coming and out-going students; there are far more French students wishing to study in the UK than British-enrolled students wishing to study in France, especially as the Study Abroad course is now compulsory within the international programmes at French HEI.

Reciprocity goes beyond the strict academic dimension of an international exchange. To build a good rapport with partner institutions, the International Office at French HEI provides ancillary services for incoming students including a 'welcome committee' of student volunteers, transport upon arrival at the airport, accommodation, travel passes and extra-curricular social activities to encourage networking with home students. According to staff and student feed-back, these services are fundamental to ensure the satisfaction of incoming students and have considerable impact on how they perceive the quality of the French HEI experience. They play a key role in reputation building within the student community both at the home institution and the host institution. Such services (however costly to offer) are essential for maintaining the success and sustainability of the partnership. The net result is enhanced employability skills for those engaged in exchanges – through both the cultural experience and the numerous softer skills acquired through participating in international mobility. These skills can transform a participant from 'unenterprising' to 'enterprising'. Note, however, that students vary in their response to the stimuli of international mobility; some are instantly motivated to use their new skills and others have a more latent/reflective approach.

In some situations where the number of incoming students and outgoing students is unbalanced (more *out* than *in*) and where popular Anglo-Saxon destinations are oversubscribed, French HEI will invest in the relationship by offering scholarships and summer schools. Since 2009, French HEI has given a scholarship to each of the five American partner universities to cover the accommodation costs for one student. Many French students are attracted to the USA to discover the 'American dream'. The return on investment was mutually beneficial in terms of brand recognition and immediate. The American partners have been sending four students for Study Abroad and eight students for the summer school at French HEI annually, primarily to give their students exposure to business and teaching practices beyond the parameters of their own institution, but specifically to this French HEI because of reputation and their tradition of engagement with employment related practices. The scholarship system has had the net effect of increasing the number of incoming students by making the Study Abroad trip free-of-charge, except the air fare. The 12-week summer school programme (May to July) was launched in 2010 to respond to demand from British and American students for short-stay international experience. The summer school serves two key purposes; first, as is credited it allows students to fast-track their education; second, it enables French HEI to send extra students to the much sought-after Anglo-Saxon destinations. Flexible reciprocity is fundamental for the success and sustainability of international collaboration and underpins the French HEI's approach to mobility.

The business model for internationalising French HEI is *multidimensional*, based on developing sustainable partnerships extensively and intensively. Above all, the aim is to embed an international dimension into the culture of the institution. The extensive approach focuses on quantity and variety of destinations, to respond to the increasing number of outgoing students. The intensive approach reinforces existing partnerships, by capitalising on good working relationships with established partners. Long-standing co-operation and dynamic mobility between institutions reflects the synergy that has been created. With certain 'high profile' partners, French HEI has intensified the relationship beyond mobility agreements by, for example, drawing up articulation agreements (students transfer their local credits to the host institution); double degrees (students transfer their credits to the host institution and graduate from both institutions); dual awards (a programme is developed and delivered by two educational institutions); joint research projects (co-publication with overseas researchers); and franchising programmes in foreign countries. Intensity has also been created through customisation; for example, in 1991 French HEI initiated a student exchange with a business school in the north-east of England. Initially, the co-operation allowed final-year bachelor students to spend one semester at the partner university and graduate with an International Business Diploma delivered by the host institution. In 1995, both partner institutions extended the scope of the exchange agreement by allowing students to spend the complete year with the partner. In 2000, the partners signed an Erasmus agreement, thus making exchange students eligible for an Erasmus study grant. In 2005, the partners agreed for the exchange programme to be at BA Honours level, thus replacing the International Business diploma. This particular partnership represents an eloquent example of the importance of embedding reciprocity and mutually beneficial relationships for all invested stakeholders to ensure an international dimension in the curriculum is both sustainable and capable of growth.

While the combination of intensive and extensive efforts can be used to generate sustainable internationalisation, caution needs to be exercised when standardising this approach for different markets. Negotiating, communicating and decision-making differ considerably from one cultural context to another. This approach relies heavily on personal relationships. Mutual co-operation, consistency and understanding between the host and home institution is fundamental for exchange to take place and then be developed. Consequently, the departure of a key member of the partnership in one institution can seriously challenge the quality and durability of a bilateral agreement, and may create problems. Although a signed agreement may be in place, an institution cannot be forced to accommodate a student if it decides not to. For example in 2010, a Chinese partner university chose not to enrol a French HEI student because the signatory of the agreement had left, and the new member of staff in that position saw no point in continuing the co-operation. Conversely, a good working relationship and strong interpersonal links between the host and home institution can increase commitment and unity amongst the people managing the partnership. For example in 2011, an Indian partner university failed to confirm French HEI outgoing student applications despite numerous phone calls and emails. It later materialised that owing to a new accreditation (and a new manager of international relations), the Indian partner no longer accepted 'under accredited' students, overruling the bilateral agreement with French HEI. Having built an excellent relationship with a different partner institution (same country, same city), the other partner accepted enrolling the French HEI students, regardless of the number of applicants already registered and the tardiness of the request. This illustration endorses the work of Mehta and Mehta (2010), who found that relational investments are required for improving the longevity of partnerships, and further underscores the difficulties of navigating through partnerships with regard to student and staff mobility.

Although the literature tends to focus on the business aspects of developing an international dimension and encouraging pragmatic thinking, very few studies have been undertaken to further our understanding of the students' perspectives and their interpretations of the international aspects of higher education as far as employability and enterprise are concerned. The following sections provide a snapshot of how the international experience is internalised by students. Acknowledging the richness of the transversal skills that can be acquired during a semester or a year abroad, it is clear that the breadth and depth of an international experience can lead to the development of not only employability skills, but this 'experiential learning' can also lead to innovative business activity. The learning curve is beneficial and relevant for both students and staff who participate in international mobility.

Learning from the international journey: to what extent does the experience of international mobility shape employability?

Over recent years, faced with an increasingly competitive job market and lethargic economy, many graduates of French HEI opt to become self-employed, both in France and abroad. The role of international mobility in the employability skills set is alluded to in the literature but not dealt with explicitly. It seems that international mobility and employability are still very much regarded as two separate silos, both in the literature and in current management thinking. The authors each have over ten years' experience of observing and participating in international mobility and employability activities at French HEI. Based on this experience and in the light of the existing literature discussed hitherto, the authors wanted to capture a snapshot of student views about their international experience and the extent to which this experience can play a determining role in developing employability skills and entrepreneurial thinking. The belief is that by coaching students to develop employability skills and by making international mobility an obligatory component of the curriculum, this experience has brought about a desire to pursue an entrepreneurial activity.

Exploring the wider motivations for this choice, the authors organised informal focus groups with 36 alumni of French HEI to ascertain the impact of the experience gained during their semester or year abroad. The underlying purpose of the focus groups was to prompt discussion by posing general questions concerning the ways in which international mobility can enhance the development of employability skills – and, in some cases, trigger entrepreneurship. Six focus groups were formed; each composed of six former students aged 25–39, 13 female and 23 male participants, who have set up their own business since graduating – thus 36 participants in total.

The participants shared their general experience gained from international mobility, as well as the experience gained in the context of enterprise, employability and entrepreneurial skills. To focus the discussion, the authors used question prompts such as: "What general experience did you gain from your international mobility?", "To what extent did your international experience relate to enterprise and employability?" and "How far did your degree and institution facilitate your entrepreneurial skills?"

For each focus group, the authors transcribed and analysed the responses. Transcripts were colour coded based on their varying themes. Themes arising from the data were examined to explore true experiences of participants, avoiding relying on the interpretation of the researcher. The emergence of these themes throughout the process of coding and analysing the transcripts generated a list of master themes alluding to the merits of mobility on being enterprising and employable: the genesis of the project (international mobility acting as a catalyst); intrinsic motivations (personal context); underpinning knowledge (the link between enterprise education and institution); and inspiration (role of international mobility in developing the graduates' employability skill set).

The comments raised by the participants in the focus groups reveal some interesting points, in particular the subjectivity and diversity in entrepreneurial thinking within the context of international mobility. The selection of representative comments illustrates the extent to which students internalise their international experience and draw from it (consciously and subconsciously) for enterprising behaviour and employability skills.

With regard to the first theme, which is more contextual in nature and concerns general experiences of international mobility, although there was no commonality of responses there were some sub-themes which were mentioned by the majority of respondents and centred on the acquiring of subject related knowledge, focusing career aspirations and the development of employability skills which would benefit their future career. Typical responses were: "I did several international placements as part of my degree programme; this experience helped me gain knowledge of business"; "The year aboard was a wake-up call; I realised it was time to think about the future ahead. I started looking around at different career options then when I got back home I knew what I wanted to do"; and "include a quote which mentions development of employ-ability skills". A minority of respondents explicitly mentioned that the inter-national mobility assisted in their formulation of a business idea with a typical response being "My year abroad was like a sabbatical, I dedicated time to learn and develop an idea for creating my own business". These collective responses underline the importance of international mobility to the enhancement of a stu-dent's employability skills set, strengthening subject knowledge and preparing them to work for themselves or as an employee and is supported by the literature (UNESCO, 2016; Pegg *et al.*, 2012; Ross and Pegg, 2012; OECD, 2010; Finley, Taylor and Warren 2007). The relationship between international mobility and a student's employability skills set will be explored in a little more depth in sub-sequent themes. However with regards to the first theme and given the context, perhaps unsurprisingly, there was a lack of commonality in the responses, with the majority of respondents having different experiences of participating in inter-national mobility. In setting up a business, the participants evoked the notion of exploiting opportunities (for example, chance meetings) and the effectiveness of letting ideas mature over time. Gathering knowledge, direction and feedback seems to be a fundamental part of preparing a project to set up a business. Equally significant was the acquisition of cross-cultural skills that enhanced the existing skill set by crossing the boundaries of knowledge on enterprise, employ-ability and entrepreneurial skills.

With regards the second theme which is more focused on the role inter-national experience plays in cultivating enterprise and employability skills, although there was also no commonality of responses there were three key sub-themes to emerge which cover all responses. They centre around develop-ing generic skills and knowledge, business skills and focusing the student on which career they wanted to pursue. With regards to the latter theme, students indicated a range of careers they were now focused on pursuing, covering the spectrum of opportunities from starting up their own business, to becoming a freelance consultant, pursuing a career in events management and establishing a career in a community based business. The fact there was no commonality is perhaps unsurprisingly given the fact that every participant will gain and develop different skills depending on their previous experiences and the experiences they have on their respective international opportunities. Typical responses were: "While I was abroad on my work placement – I saw the types of skills and knowledge I would need to stand out from the crowd. It's all about managing the risks, and reaping the benefits, of international mobility". "Some of the modules I chose during my Erasmus year were related to devel-oping a business ... I talked with my tutors then looked for potential business partners [during my time abroad]" and "I learned [the skills] how to turn my ideas into sustainable [business] opportunities"; and "The study abroad helped me focus on the type of work I wanted to do". A minority of respondents were more specific about the skills this international mobility gave them, with a typical response being:

> if you're a student at home, you can think that a burst pipe is inconvenient … but when it happens while you're abroad, you have to find out *HOW* and *WHO* to sort it out, in a foreign language. For me, the international experience taught me a lot about socio-cultural discovery and crisis management.

The tangible benefits of international mobility are not always immediately apparent. For some students, an understanding of the business world is 'awakened' by a combination of the various skills acquired during the academic cursus *and* the international discovery. As argued in the literature, international engagement can provide a transformational education experience (Clapp-Smith and Wernsing, 2014; Hunter, 2008), and it would appear that the majority of participants found the international mobility both useful in terms of developing social and business skills but it also assisted them in confirming career choices and making first steps towards realising those choice through networking and developing partnerships. The majority of respondents used this experience not simply to understand a different culture, they used the opportunity to develop their business skills to make themselves more employable. On a superficial level one may have expected students to simply want the outcomes of fun, learning a language and more broadly experience a different culture. However it would appear that participants were more sophisticated and forward planning in their thinking when enrolling in the international mobility initiative, using the opportunity to gain the skills necessary to enhance their current skills set and to differentiate themselves in the employment market. A further interesting aside is the fact that many students, not quite the majority, following their time abroad, expressed an interest in developing their own business, rather than seeking a position with an employer. This implies that the international engagement in particular may indeed 'awaken' the entrepreneurial spirit among participants, the next theme will investigate this further.

When discussing the relationship between career, entrepreneurship and institutional degree programme, participants recognised the indirect influence of the academic programme underpinning a student's enterprise and employability skills. Once again, the compulsory international experience of the programme seems to have been instrumental in generating the necessary competences – *life skills, social skills and employability skills* – for setting up a business. Similar to previous themes, there was no commonality in the responses but the main sub-themes were the importance of practical engagement, the time allocation which permitted entrepreneurial freedom and the ability to network. Typical responses were:

> the formal classroom side of things helped me focus on how to go about structuring and project-managing my business idea but it wasn't until I went off to do my work placement in Spain that I saw in reality what I had to do: take the risk in order to achieve success.

By engaging on international mobility "I was given a lighter timetable so I could start setting it [a business] up"; "I actively networked throughout my studies and while working abroad; I used these contacts to help me get the project launched, especially the contacts from my work placement". A minority of respondents mentioned the influence of the academic structure on a subconscious level towards entrepreneurial activity, with a typical response being "At the time, I couldn't see how the class content would help me set up a business ... but now I'm up and running, maybe it did help subconsciously to sow the seed".

For some students, the international experience seems to act as a catalyst in triggering (or formulating) the genesis of a business idea. The international work placement and the Erasmus placement are often cited as key defining moments when learning took place (actively and passively), influencing the career choices made in later years. All participants agreed that the institution and the international mobility programme assisted them in getting the necessary employability skills, but it would appear the international mobility programme in particular allowed the entrepreneurial skills to develop. It is fundamental that students develop their skills to be able to generate a new business idea, venture, product or service. It seems, however, that formal academic structures could be improved to allow students more opportunities to explore and develop their applied employability and entrepreneurial skills, this improvement, according to research, should consider a studying/working abroad component whether that is through informal channels or as a spin-off from degree requirements. The popularity of international mobility programme has continued to grow (UKCISA, 2016; UNESCO, 2016; Varela and Gatlin-Watts, 2014), able to nurture innovative thinking when the business ideas are identified and shared within a safe academic supported environment. However they require to be integrated into the curriculum and not merely 'bolted on', so their benefits can be truly realised. To enhance the employability skills set of graduates, institutions need to move away from 'silo' thinking in order to construct an appropriate framework that supports students in developing their business, enterprise and entrepreneurial skills (Rae, 2014; Varela and Gatlin-Watts, 2014).

Taken as a whole, the international academic journey can be said to enhance employability, enterprise and entrepreneurship. It brings about new skills and can inspire or trigger (rather than enable) innovative activity such as setting up in business, as a result of the skills acquired during this journey. Therefore, it is worth institutions overcoming the identified barriers and obstacles to develop partnerships and opportunities for students to experience international mobility. Students reap immense benefit and knowledge from the international experience. The time taken for a business idea to germinate seems to vary from one individual to another. The role played by mandatory study abroad and work abroad is non-negligible, however, suggesting that the experience of a different socio-cultural context can widen the skill set to include the knowledge and competences needed for *not only* setting up a business but also for greater employability, enterprise and entrepreneurship. Indeed, an unfamiliar environment can be a challenging experience by forcing an individual to develop coping strategies to deal with an unusual situation or adverse risk. It follows that the ability to remain agile and to be able to adapt to unaccustomed situations will contribute to both the employability skill set and to an awakening of entrepreneurial flair.

Discussion and concluding comments

The business model at French HEI has proved successful in providing a viable solution to the annual problem of placing a large number of French outgoing students into foreign partner institutions. Ongoing measurements of satisfaction (student survey data, feedback from visiting professors and partner institutions, business engagement activities etc.) indicate that French HEI is perceived as a competent provider of international knowledge transfer within established markets. Success can be gauged in terms of: ongoing developments to widen academic collaboration with foreign partner institutions, invitations to participate in international events organised by partners (research symposia, guest lectures, book chapter collaboration etc.), requests to 'connect' via social media with former exchange students, intense networking for sharing recruitment opportunities – marking the 30th anniversary of Erasmus, an estimated five million students have taken part and one million babies were conceived (Laurent, 2017).

Sustainability will be ensured through maintaining flexible reciprocity and agile response to changes in the education landscape, increasingly oriented towards employability, enterprise and entrepreneurship. For the individual learner, the benefits are tangible; international experience of mandatory work placement and studying abroad have improved the employability prospects of graduates and in some cases raised the awareness of entrepreneurial thinking. The learning process is sufficiently adaptable to accommodate students (and staff) who wish to develop innovative activities during their time at the international institution.

In the context of lessons learned and moving forward, as the international dimension become more recognised, alternative revenue is needed to fund international marketing outreach, and also to finance the non-exchange students. Ongoing expenses need to be covered, for example, to maintain brand building through promotional events, accreditation procedures and campus services. For many institutions, the current focus is on attracting international fee-paying students from emerging markets, particularly during the current economic austerity, which is having a negative effect on the number of French applicants.

Whichever approach is chosen for integrating an international dimension into an institution, the experience of work and study abroad at a host institution and the presence of foreign students (and staff) at the home institution provide an overall positive influence which benefits the school, the student body, faculty and indirectly the reputation of the institution. These synergies consistently lead to better graduates: more resourceful and innovative – and above all better equipped for the twenty-first century job market with skills in employability, enterprise and entrepreneurship.

Simply, the more international a student cohort, the more attractive the school appears to prospective students looking for a multicultural campus of 'global citizens', and the more attractive a student is to prospective employers, given their enhanced employability skills set. In today's global market place, it is irrational to ignore the need to tailor an offer to international stakeholders. Since the early 2000s, French HEI has repositioned itself, transforming the provincial

French business school with a mostly local (French) market into a competent provider of the 'international student experience' recognised by the French government. Working closely with partner institutions worldwide, the emphasis at French HEI is firmly placed on maintaining competitive advantage through reciprocal exchange as the cornerstone of a sustainable and increasingly rich international dimension.

Caution needs to be exercised when integrating an international dimension; various approaches can be taken, standing as a reminder that there is no single strategy, no '*one size fits all*'. The choice of strategy reflects the different levels of development and commitment of the institution. Furthermore, given the changing landscape (technological, economic, demographic) in the current education sector, the strategy chosen for internationalizing needs to be reviewed periodically and adapted accordingly in response to emerging demand. The challenge for each institution is to develop best practice for reciprocity and recruitment (bearing in mind the dependency on interpersonal relationships), to foster employability skills and entrepreneurial initiatives, as well as to raise awareness in the international academic community. Top-down and bottom up commitment is needed across the institution for establishing and maintaining the international dimension. However, frameworks are comparatively limited for engaging faculty and researchers in international mobility – see 'benefits-driven model' (Wu and Yu, 2006), 'infusion approach' (Skidmore *et al.*, 2005), 'network power' (King, 2010: 588). More research is needed (cross disciplinary, not silo) to understand the intricacies and idiosyncrasies of taking students, in particular, and academics outside their comfort zone. There needs to be an integrated institutional approach to enhancing the employability, enterprise and entrepreneurship skills of students, in order to prepare them for their career choices, whether that be working for an employer or being self-employed.

End-of-chapter questions for reflection

Many issues stem from the discussion of the role played by international mobility in developing employability, enterprise and entrepreneurship skills. Perhaps the most crucial element is the necessity to embed a transversal international dimension in higher education as a conduit for evoking skills development. Consider the two initial questions outlined in the chapter:

1   How can HE providers (i.e. universities and business schools) enhance employability, enterprise and entrepreneurship for graduates through embedding an international dimension?
2   How can providers facilitate the acquisition of the international skills, competencies, behaviours and mind-sets that are increasingly regarded as important employability attributes for graduates?

These two broad questions can be used for reflective thinking; engaging the stakeholder at the centre of this discussion, the student, into considering how the international dimension can enhance the student experience and broader employability, enterprise and entrepreneurial skills and the more holistic perspective of the academic institution in the whole employment, entrepreneurship debate. For example, students could be asked to prepare a report on:

> To what degree would there be a difference of opinion between the four key stakeholders (students, teachers, academic managers and policy makers) regarding the redesign of teaching and learning for a greater focus on employability? Answers will vary but need to take into consideration the financial, political, technological and social factors.

> How might the cultural context influence the importance of employability skills and innovative thinking?

> Answers will differ according to ethnography, demographics and country of origin but need to address observed similarities and differences between national approaches.

References

Allen, H. (2010). Interactive contact as linguistic affordance during short-term study abroad: Myth or reality? *Frontiers: The Interdisciplinary Journal of Study Abroad*, 19, 1–26.

Babb, J., Womble, L. and De'Armond, D. (2013). Embedding international experiences in business curriculum design: Cultivating a study abroad programme. *Research in Higher Education Journal*, 20, 1–15.

Baker, C. (2006). *A parents' and teachers' guide to bilingualism*. 2nd ed. Wales: Multilingual Matters.

Child, J., Rodrigues, S.B. and Frynas, G.J. (2009). Psychic distance, Its impact and coping modes, *Management International Review*, 49(2), 199–224.

Clapp-Smith, R. and Wernsing, T. (2014). The transformational triggers of international experiences. *Journal of Management Development*, 33(7), 662–679.

Darby, J. (2009). French antipathy to Turkey's EU candidacy: The language dimension. *Journal of Multilingual and Multicultural Development*, 30(3), 205–217.

De Meyer, A., Harker, P.T. and Hawawini, G. (2004). The globalization of business education. In: R.E. Gunther, H. Gatignon and J.R. Kimberly, eds. *The Insead-Wharton alliance on globalizing: strategies for building successful global businesses*. Cambridge: Cambridge University Press, p. 108.

De Wit, H. (2010). Internationalization of higher education in Europe and its assessment, trends and issues [online] The Netherlands. Available at: www.nvao.net/page/downloads/Internationalization_of_Higher_Education_in_Europe_DEF_december_2010.pdf [accessed: 29 October 2016].

Directorate-General for Internal Policies (July 2015). Policy Department B: Structural and cohesion policies, Culture and education, internationalization of higher education [online]. Brussels. Available at: www.europarl.europa.eu/RegData/etudes/STUD/2015/540370/IPOL_STU(2015)540370_EN.pdf [accessed: 29 October 2016].

Doh, J.P. (2010). From the editors: Why aren't business schools more global and what can management educators do about it? *Academy of Management Learning & Education*, 9(2), 165–168.

Eagle, L. and Brennan, R. (2007). Are students customers? TQM and marketing perspectives. *Quality Assurance in Education*, 15(1), 44–60.

EPAS (2015). EFMD programme accreditation system: The EFMD accreditation for international degree programmes in business and management [online]. Brussels. Available at: www.efmd.org/epas [accessed 13 August 2016].

Evans, J. and Mavondo, F. (2002.) Psychic distance and organizational performance: An empirical examination of international retailing operations, *Journal of International Business Studies*, 33(3), 515–532.

Fielden, J. and Gillard, E. (2011). *A guide to offshore staffing strategies for UK universities*. Research Series 7. London: UK Higher Education International and Europe Unit.

Finley, J.B., Taylor, S.L. and Warren, D.L. (2007). Investigating graduate business students' perceptions of the educational value provided by an international travel course experience. *Journal of Teaching in International Business,* 19(1), 57–82.

Hallén, L. and Wiedersheim-Paul, F. (1984). The evolution of psychic distance in international business relationships. In: I. Hagg and F. Wiedersheim-Paul, eds. *Between market and hierarchy*. University of Uppsala, Department of Business Administration, Uppsala, pp. 15–27.

Harvey, L. (2003). Student feedback, April, *Quality in Higher Education*, 9(1), 3–20.

Hawawini, G. (2005). The future of business schools, *Journal of Management Development*, 24(9), 770–782.

Hughes, R. (2008). Internationalization of higher education and language policy: Questions of quality and equity, *Higher Education Management and Policy*, 20(1), 102–119.

Hunter, A. (2008). Transformative learning in international education. In: V. Savicki, ed. *Developing intercultural competence and transformation: Theory, research, and application in international education.* Sterling, VA: Stylus Publishers. www.sciencedirect.com/science/article/pii/S0261517713002227 – vt1www.sciencedirect.com/science/article/pii/S0261517713002227 – vt1.

IAU (2010). Internationalization of higher education: Global trends. Regional perspectives – Rapport sur la 3e Enquête mondiale de l'AIU [online] Paris. Available at: http://test.www.iau-aiu.net/fr/content/enqu%C3%AAtes-mondiales [accessed: 29 October 2016].

Jacobs, B and van der Ploeg, F. (July 2006). How to reform higher education in Europe: Summary, *Economic Policy*, 536–592.

Jain, D.C. and Golosinski, M. (2009). Sizing up the tyranny of the ruler, *Academy of Management Learning & Education*, 8(1), 99–105.

Jiang, X. (2008). Towards the internationalization of higher education from a critical perspective. *Journal of Further and Higher Education*, 32(4), 347–358.

Jones, E. (2012). Internationalization and employability: Are we missing a trick? *EAIE Forum*, winter, 6–9.

King, R. (2010). Policy internationalization, National variety and governance: Global models and network power in higher education states, *The International Journal of Higher Education and Educational Planning*, 60(6), 583–594.

King, R. (5 January 2012). Freedom to succeed. *Times Higher Education* [online] England. Available at: www.timeshighereducation.co.uk/story.asp?storycode=418605 [accessed: 29 October 2016].

Knight, J. and de Wit, H. (1995). Strategies for internationalization of higher education: Historical and conceptual perspectives. In: H. de Wit, ed. *Strategies for internationalization of higher education: A comparative study of Australia, Canada, Europe and the United States of America.* Amsterdam: European Association for International Education.

Knight, J. and de Wit, H. (1999). *Quality and internationalisation in higher education.* Paris: OECD.

Laurent, S. (8 January 2017). Erasmus – vrai ou faux. France. Available at: www.lci.fr/societe/erasmus-vrai-ou-faux-million-de-bebes-faillite-brexit-retour-sur-quelques-idees-recues-sur-le-programme-europeen-2020727.html [accessed: 10 March 2017].

Leask, B. (2007). International teachers and international learning. In: E. Jones and S. Brown, eds. *Internationalizing higher education.* London: Routledge, 86–94. www.sciencedirect.com/science/article/pii/S0261517713002227–vt1.

Liping, A.C., Wei, W., Lu, Y. and Day, J. (2015). College students' decision-making for study abroad – Anecdotes from a U.S. hospitality and tourism internship program in China, *Journal of Teaching in Travel & Tourism*, 15(1), 48–73.

Marginson, S. and van der Wende, M. (2007). *Globalisation and higher education*, 7(7), 1–85. OECD Education Working Papers Series).

Marshall, P. (2011). *Blue skies: New thinking about the future of higher education – A collection of short articles by leading commentators.* Louis Coiffait, ed. London: Pearson.

Mehta, N. and Anju, M. (2010). It takes two to tango: How relational investments improve IT outsourcing partnerships, *Communications of the ACM*, 53(2), 160–164.

Miles, M.P., Hazeldine, M.F. and Munila, L.S. (2004). The 2003 AACSB accreditation standards and implications for business faculty: A short note, *Journal of Education for Business*, 80(1), 29–34.

Ministère des Affaires étrangères et du Développement international (2013). La mobilité internationale est une chance pour notre jeunesse, pas une menace pour la France [online]. Available at: www.diplomatie.gouv.fr/fr/services-aux-citoyens/actualites/article/la-mobilite-internationale-est-une [accessed: 7 November 2016].

Moghaddam J.M, Peyvandi, Ali and Wang, Jia (2009). The effect of personality traits on the perceived effectiveness of summer study abroad programs: An empirical study in the United States, *International Journal of Management*, 26(3), 426–435.

Murgatroyd, Stephen J. and Morgan, Colin (1993). *Total quality management and the school.* Philadelphia: Open University Press.

Nourry, M-A., Taquet, M., Villemagne, A. and Dhumerelle, V. (December 2012). Classement 2012–2013: comment choisir son école de commerce postbac? *l'Etudiant* [online] Paris. Available at: www.letudiant.fr/etudes/ecole-de-commerce/ecoles-de-commerce-postbac-en-4-ou-5-ans-le-banc-d-essai-12046.html [accessed: 18 November 2016].

Oakes, L. (2002). Multilingualism in Europe: An effective French identity strategy? *Journal of Multilingual & Multicultural Development*, 23(5), 371–388.

OECD (2004). Policy brief: Internationalization of higher education [online] Paris. Available at: www.oecd.org/education/innovation-education/33734276.pdf [accessed 13 November 2016].

OECD (2010). Education at a glance [online] Paris. Available at: www.oecd.org/edu/highereducationandadultlearning/45926093.pdf [accessed 7 November 2016].

Pegg, A., Waldock, J., Hendy-Isaac, S. and Lawton, R. (2012). *Pedagogy for employability.* Heslington, York: Higher Education Academy.

Pitman, T. (2000). Perceptions of academics and students as customers: A survey of administrative staff in higher education, *Journal of Higher Education Policy and Management*, 22, 165–175.

Prime, N., Obadia, C. and Vida, I. (2009). Psychic distance in exporter-importer relationships: A Grounded theory approach. *International Business Review*, 18(2), 184–198.

Raffarin, J.-P. (27 February 2003). *Speech to First World Investment Conference.*

Rae, D. (2014). Graduate entrepreneurship and career initiation in the 'New Era' economy. *Journal of General Management*, 40(1), 79–95.

Rocher, G. (1969). Introduction à la sociologie générale, Tome 1 [online] Canada. Available at: www.international.gc.ca/cfsi-icse/cil-cai/magazine/v02n01/doc3-eng.pdf [accessed: 23 November 2016].

Rodríguez, X.A., Martínez-Roget, F. and Pawlowska, E. (2012). Academic tourism demand in Galicia, Spain. *Tourism Management*, 33(6), 1583–1590.

Rogerson-Revell, P. (2007). Using English for international business: A European case study. *English for Specific Purposes*, 26, 103–120.

Ross, M. and Grace, D. (2012). Exploring the international student recruitment industry through the Strategic Orientation Performance Model. *Journal of Marketing Management*, 28(5–6), 522–545.

Skidmore, D., Marston, J; and Olson, G. (2005). An ifusion approach to internationalization: Drake University as a case study, *Frontiers: The Interdisciplinary Journal of Study Abroad*, 11, 187–203.

Swift, J.S. (1999). Cultural closeness as a facet of cultural affinity. A contribution to the theory of psychic distance. *International Marketing Review*, 16(3), 182–201.

Taylor, J. (2004). Toward a strategy for internationalization: Lessons and practice from four universities. *Journal of Studies in International Education*, 8(2), 149–171.

Thomas, L., Billsberry, J., Ambrosini, V. and Barton, H. (2014). Convergence and divergence dynamics in British and French business schools: How will the pressure for accreditation influence these dynamics? *British Journal of Management*, 25(2), 305–319.

UKCISA (30 March 2016). International student statistics: UK higher education. Available from: http://institutions.ukcisa.org.uk//info-for-universities-colleges-schools/policy-research-statistics/research-statistics/international-students-in-uk-he/ [accessed: 13 November 2016].

UNESCO (2016). Global flow of tertiary-level students. Available from: www.uis.unesco.org/EDUCATION/Pages/international-student-flow-viz.aspx [accessed 9 November 2016].

Varela, O.E. and Gatlin-Watts, R. (2014). The development of the global manager: An empirical study on the role of academic international sojourns, *Academy of Management Learning & Education*, 13(2), 187–207. http://dx.doi.org/10.5465/amle.2012.0289.

Wu, M. and Yu, P. (2006). Challenges and opportunities facing Australian universities caused by the internationalization of Chinese higher education, *International Education Journal*, 7(3), 211–221.

Zachrisson, C.U. (2001). *New study abroad destinations: Trends and emerging opportunities.* In: M. Tillman, ed. *Study abroad: A 21st century perspective, Volume II, the changing landscape.* Stamford, CT: American Institute for Foreign Study Foundation, pp. 28–30.

Index

Page numbers in *italics* denote tables, those in **bold** denote figures.